What we've seen with the development of this pandemic is not just an exposure of the falseness of capitalism, but the fundamental truths of living: That to care and to be cared for is to be human. That the values of capital are nakedly hollow next to the values of community.

WHAT IF WE BUILT A WORLD AROUND

COMMUNITY CARE?

We are in the gap between before and after. No future is guaranteed. What can we build on the other side of this crisis?

Colleen Tighe   1

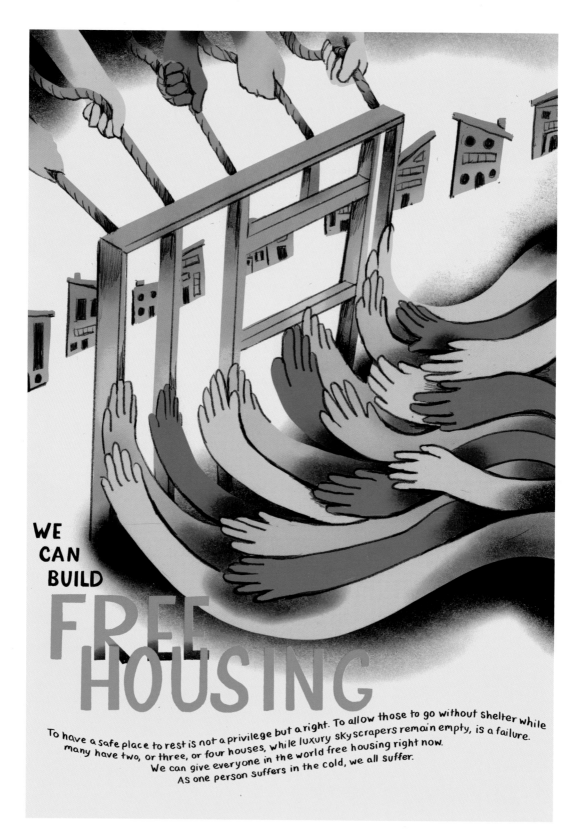

WE
CAN
BUILD
FREE
HOUSING

To have a safe place to rest is not a privilege but a right. To allow those to go without shelter while luxury skyscrapers remain empty, is a failure. many have two, or three, or four houses, while luxury skyscrapers remain empty, is a failure.
We can give everyone in the world free housing right now.
As one person suffers in the cold, we all suffer.

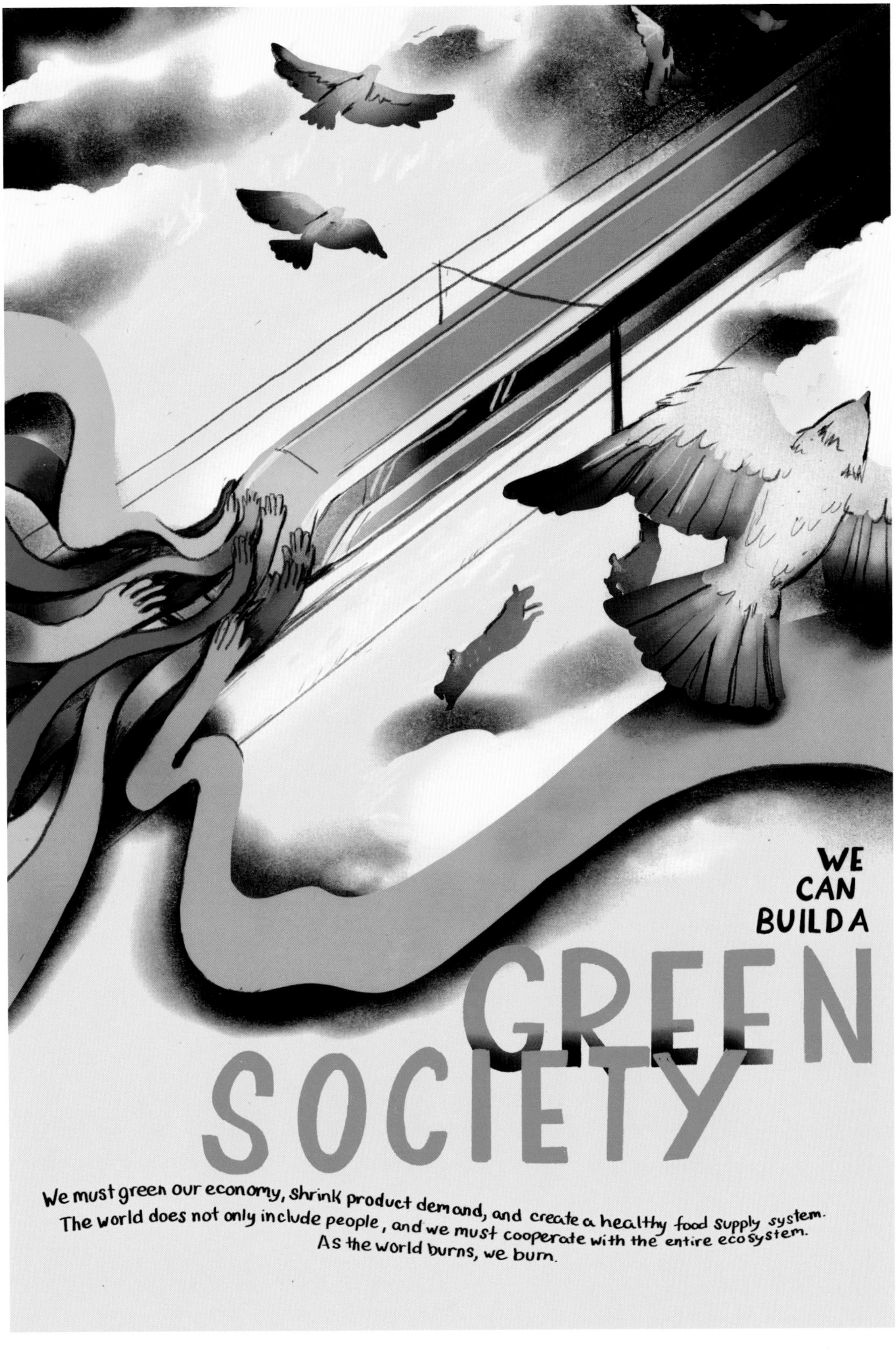
WE
CAN
BUILD A
GREEN
SOCIETY
We must green our economy, shrink product demand, and create a healthy food supply system.
The world does not only include people, and we must cooperate with the entire ecosystem.
As the world burns, we burn.

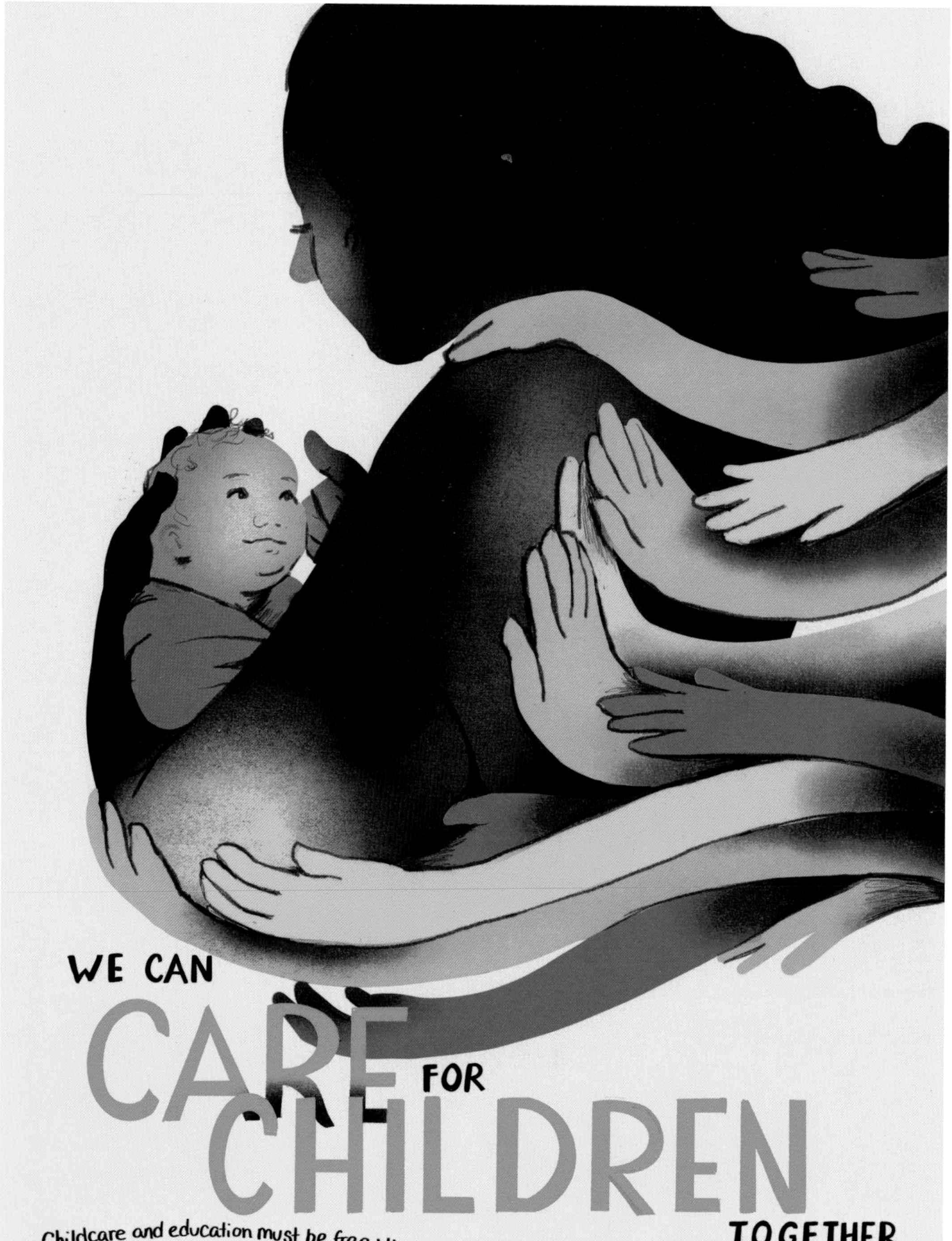
WE CAN
CARE FOR
CHILDREN
TOGETHER
Childcare and education must be free. When one person learns, laughs, and plays, we grow together.
Childcare workers and teachers must be paid reflective of the massive duty they perform to society,
We must support children outside of the nuclear family.
A child is no one's property, but everyone's responsibility.

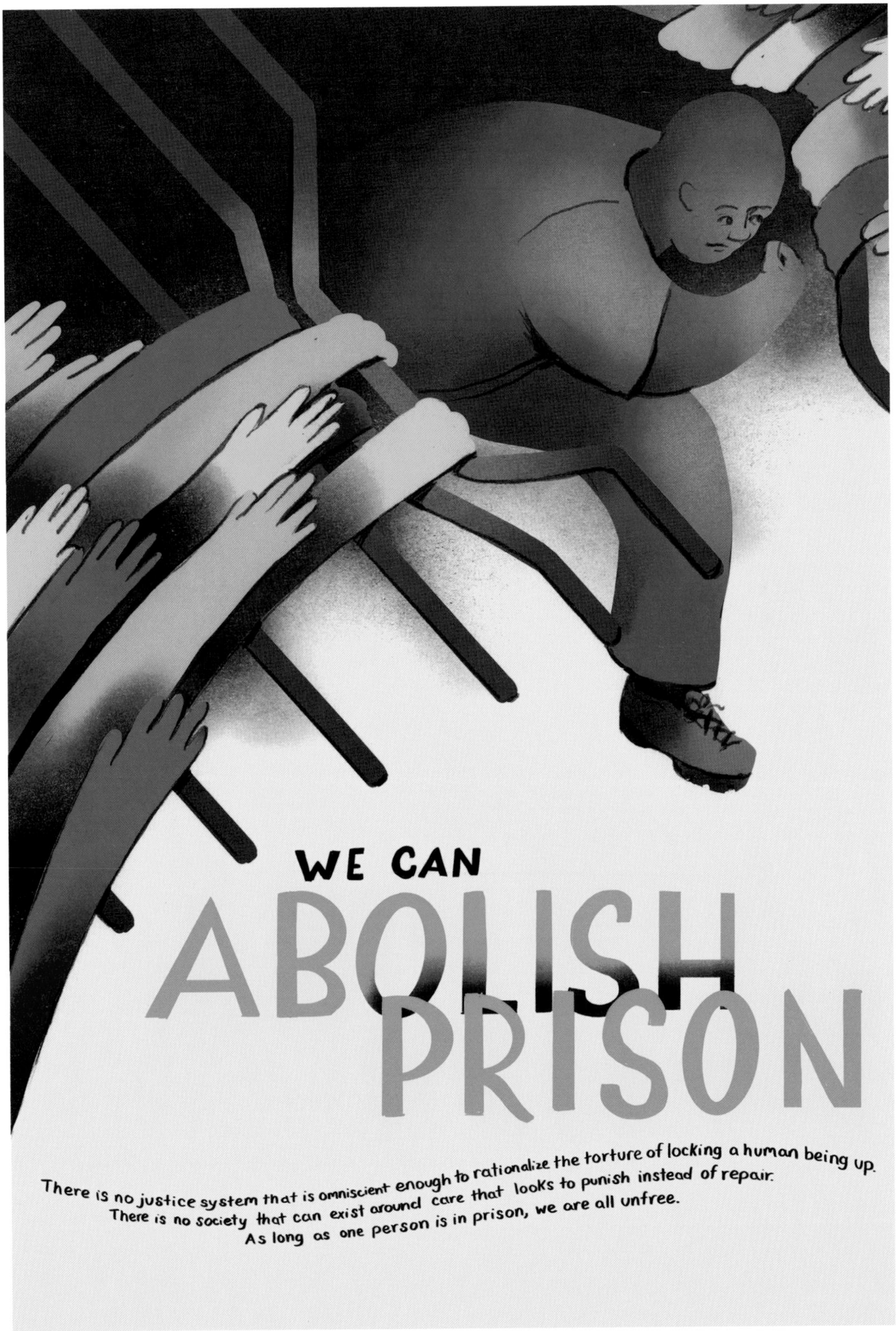
WE CAN
ABOLISH
PRISON
There is no justice system that is omniscient enough to rationalize the torture of locking a human being up.
There is no society that can exist around care that looks to punish instead of repair.
As long as one person is in prison, we are all unfree.

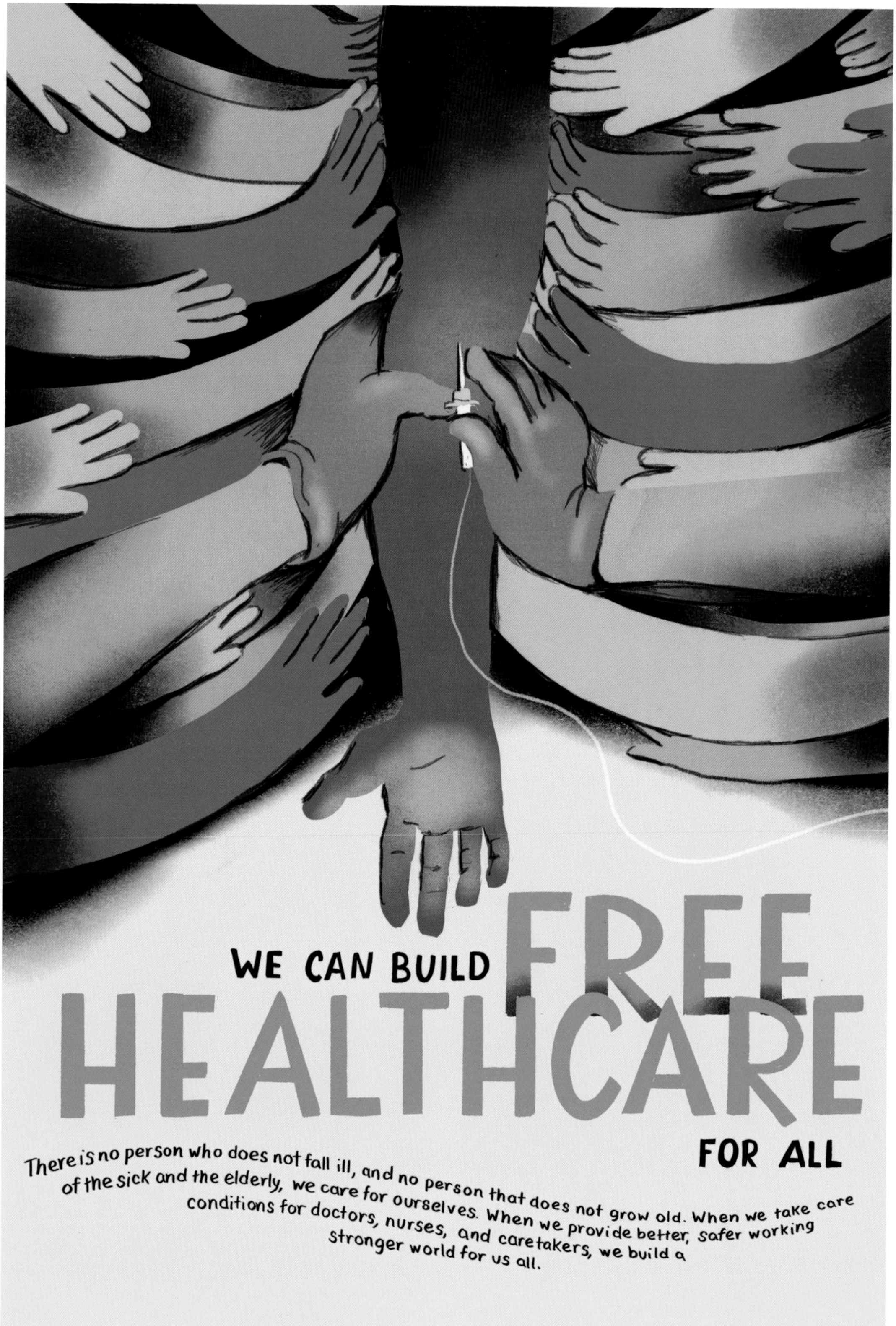
WE CAN BUILD FREE
HEALTHCARE
FOR ALL
There is no person who does not fall ill, and no person that does not grow old. When we take care of the sick and the elderly, we care for ourselves. When we provide better, safer working conditions for doctors, nurses, and caretakers, we build a stronger world for us all.

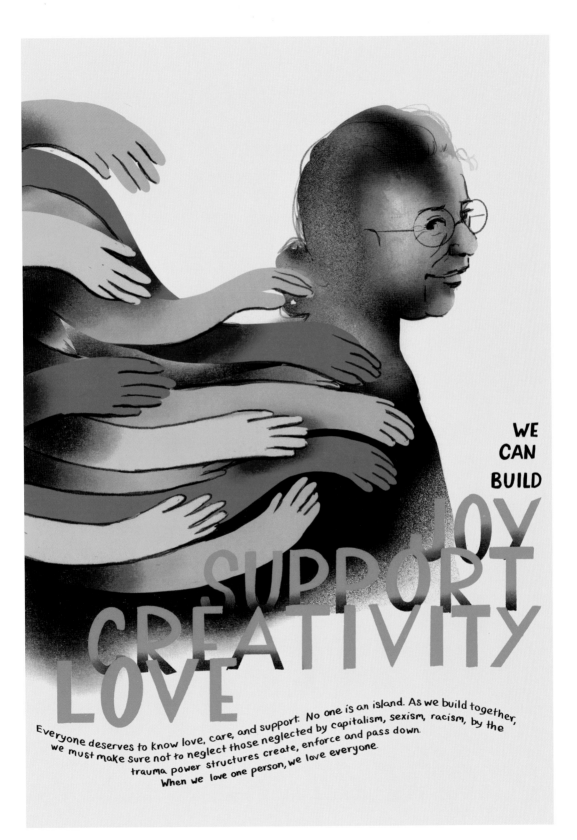

WE CAN BUILD

JOY
SUPPORT
CREATIVITY
LOVE

Everyone deserves to know love, care, and support. No one is an island. As we build together, we must make sure not to neglect those neglected by capitalism, sexism, racism, by the trauma power structures create, enforce and pass down. When we love one person, we love everyone.

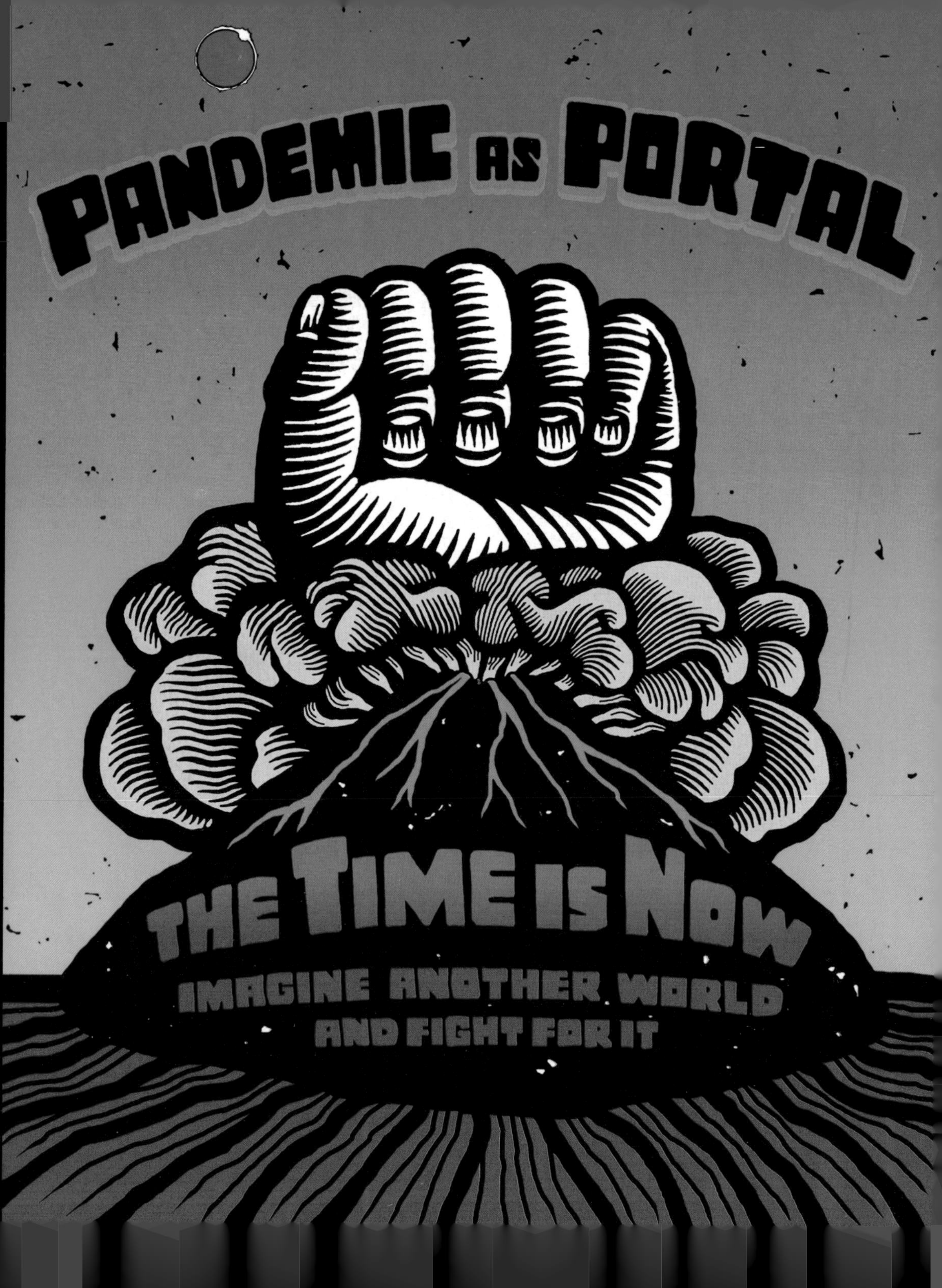
PANDEMIC AS PORTAL
THE TIME IS NOW
IMAGINE ANOTHER WORLD
AND FIGHT FOR IT

WORLD WAR 3 ILLUSTRATED #51

It takes us about a year to produce an issue of **World War 3 Illustrated.**
We started work on this one in the fall of 2019, which seems like a lifetime ago.
We decided that the theme would be "The World We Are Fighting For" because we
imagined the 2020 election to be a titanic battle between two alternate realities,
the fascist future offered by Donald Trump, and the humane socialist vision of
Bernie Sanders. We invited artists to share their hopes and fears.
Who would have imagined that we were thinking small?
While a lot of us were working on comics about climate change, we did not
anticipate that another ecological disaster, COVID-19, would transform society.
Suddenly we are all characters in a dystopian science fiction novel.
World War 3 Illustrated has covered police brutality since our 4th issue, in 1984.
It has been horrifying to watch the list of names of people killed by cops grow
longer and longer, with no solution in sight. Today thousands are marching,
statues are falling, police stations are burning, cops are being fired,
and there are calls to defund the police. Abolition is in the air.
In the 1980s squatters demanded a moratorium on evictions.
In the last three months, many cities have actually had such a
moratorium to deal with the economic effects of the pandemic.
Ideas that seemed utopian six months ago now appear practical.
Another world ACTUALLY **IS** possible. That world is up for grabs.
More than ever, actions we take now will define the future of our political
systems, our planet, our very survival. At this critical juncture we have to ask:
What do we really care about? What are we fighting for?
In this issue artists young and old, famous, infamous, or obscure, some of whom
we've known all our lives and some who we've just met, bring heart and vision, fire
and beauty, passion and humor to these questions. Some bring a roadmap for change.
Others simply tell us what their values are, who their loved ones are, what they are
holding on to in the struggle to exist. Some lean into the mysterious, the poetic, the
unfinished and unknowable. Artists tell us 'how' as well as 'why'. They tell us about
their experience of activism, whether it's direct action, voting, or just talking with people.
Across these pages, we are moving forward together, with our eyes on the horizon-
pens, pencils, brushes and paper at the ready.

CONTENTS

Cover *Deep Pampas* **José Muñoz**
Inside cover **Courtney Menard**

Edited by **Ethan Heitner, Peter Kuper and Seth Tobocman**

World War 3 Illustrated #51
© 2020 World War 3 Incorporated
**All art and text © 2020
to the individual artists**
Cover design by Jordan Worley
Special thanks to Betty Russell,
Tamara Tornado and Antonia House
Website: www.ww3.nyc
Printed in Canada

"SUIT YOURSELVES. I'M BREAKING OUT OF HERE."

Hilary Allison

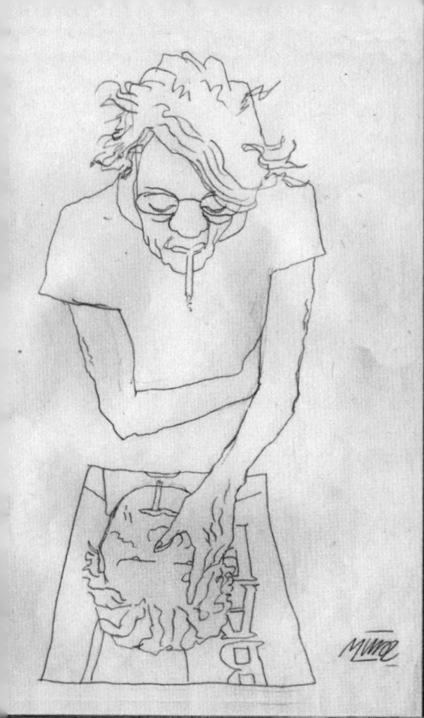

ABOUT OUR COVER ARTIST:

José Muñoz was born in Argentina in 1942 and moved to Europe in 1972, at a time when death squads were massacring Argentine socialists.

In Italy he would collaborate with writer Carlos Sampayo, also an Argentine expatriate. They produced crime comics, usually set in New York, but the turbulence of Latin America was always in the background. There were pieces focused on the Vietnam War, racism, police brutality, the CIA and Nicaragua.

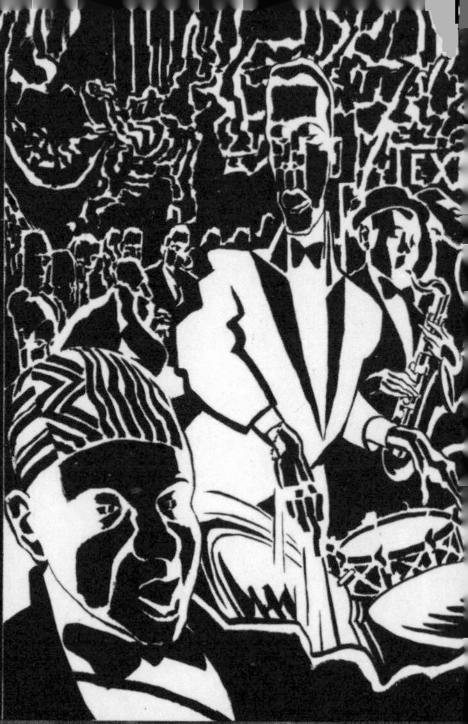

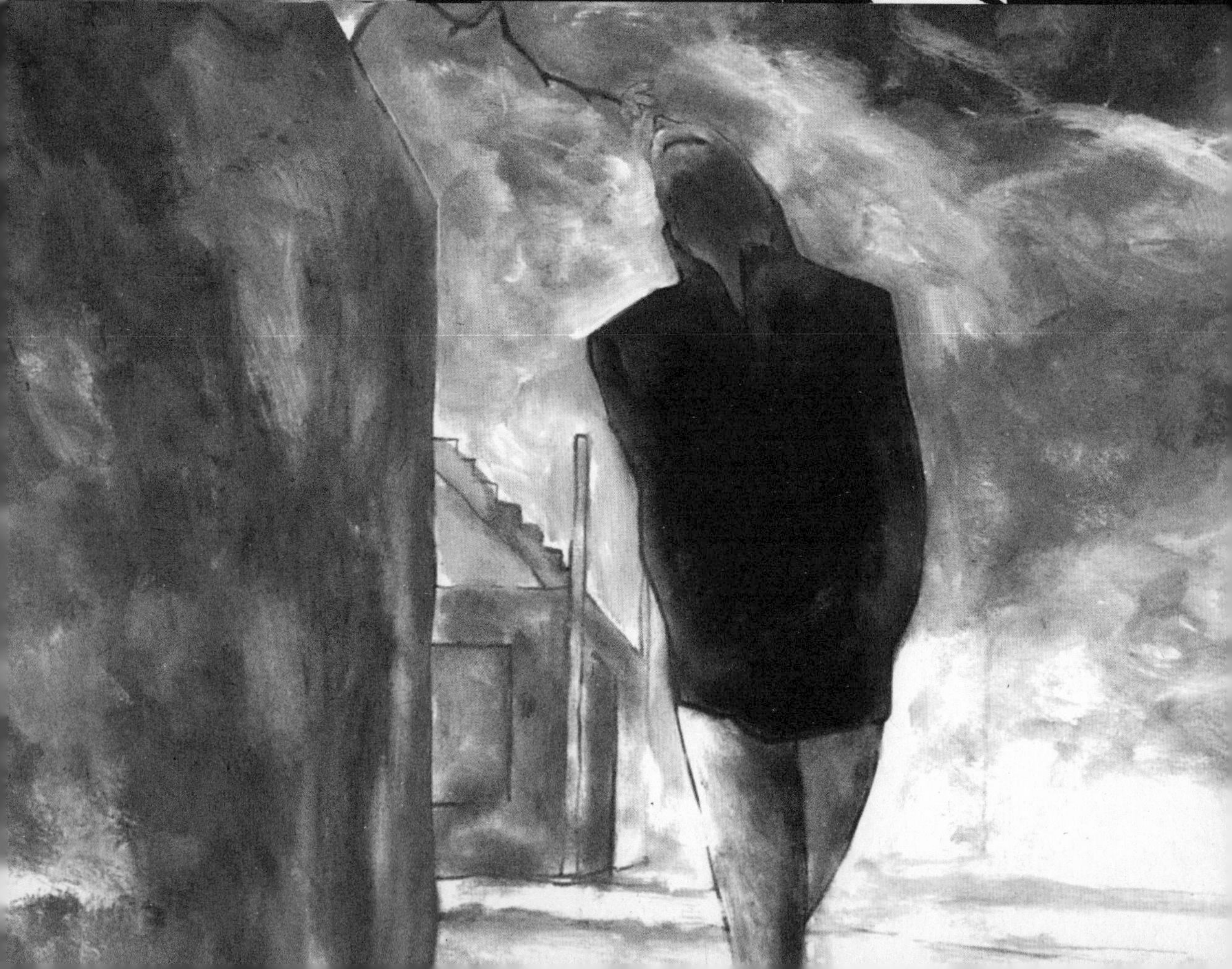

Muñoz's unique drawing style is often emulated but never replicated. The artist plays a game of hide and seek with the audience. To absorb all the details requires scrutiny that comes with great rewards.

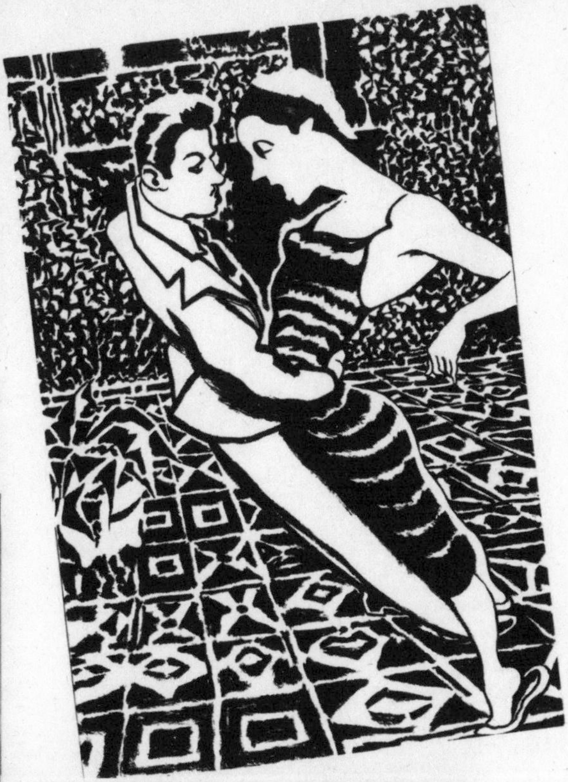

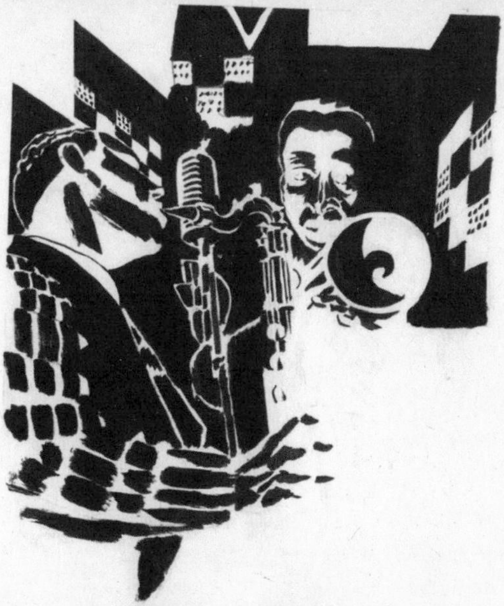

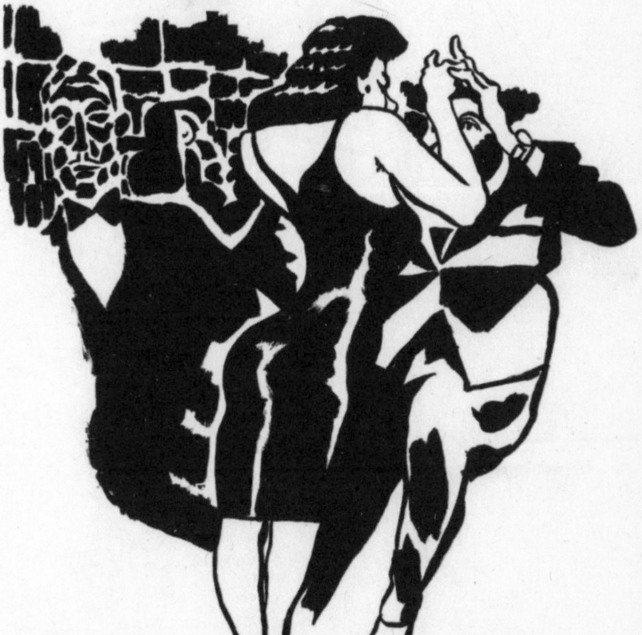

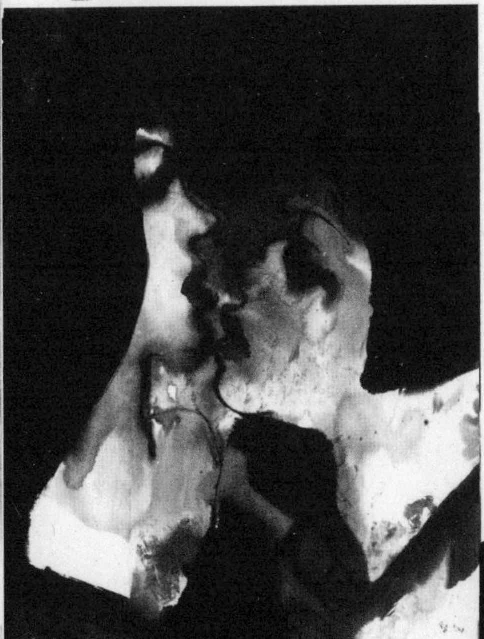

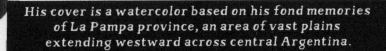

His cover is a watercolor based on his fond memories of La Pampa province, an area of vast plains extending westward across central Argentina.

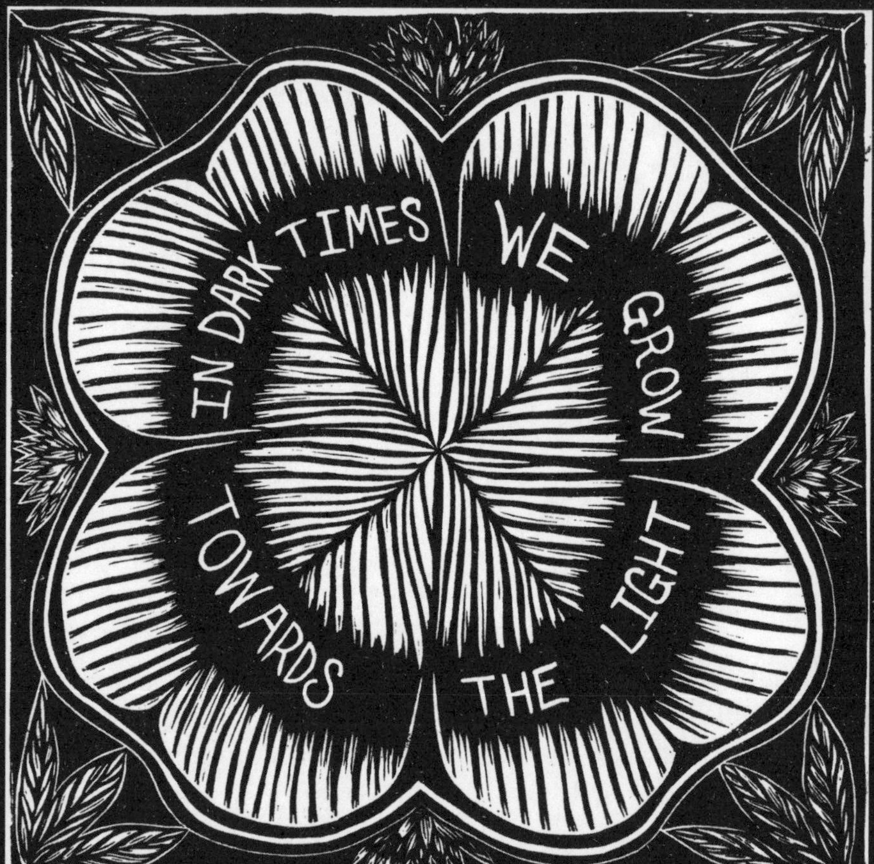
IN DARK TIMES
WE GROW
TOWARDS
THE LIGHT

Standing on the Shoulders of Young Giants

by Elizabeth Haidle

Greta Thunberg began her personal protest against climate change by skipping school on Fridays to sit outside the Swedish parliament with a homemade sign.

Children and teens around the world have witnessed her example and taken inspired, collective action of their own accord.

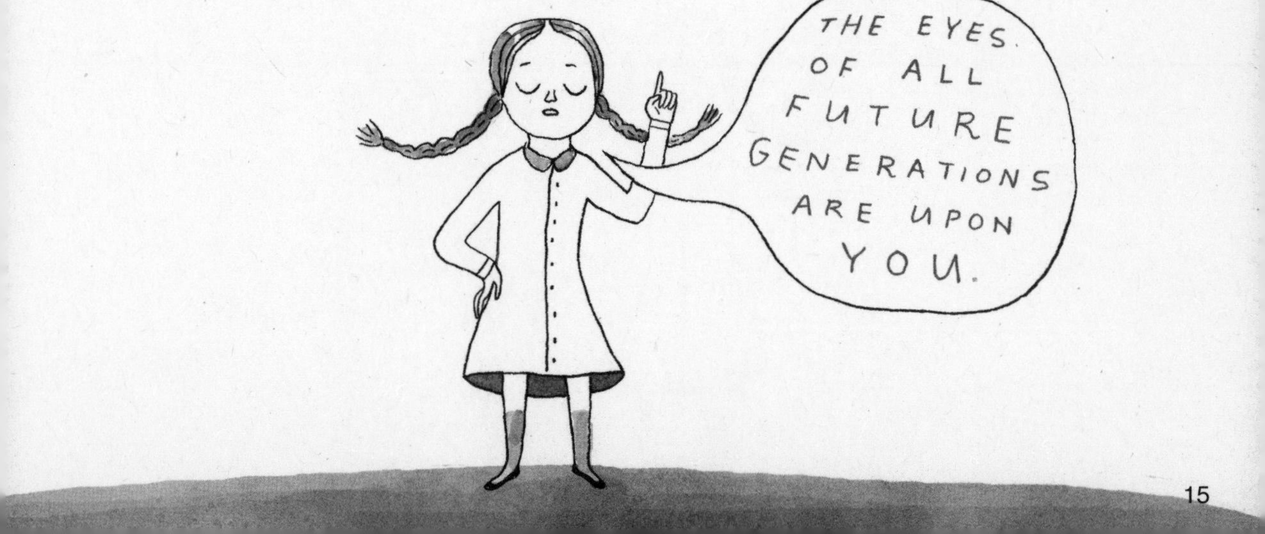
THE EYES OF ALL FUTURE GENERATIONS ARE UPON YOU.

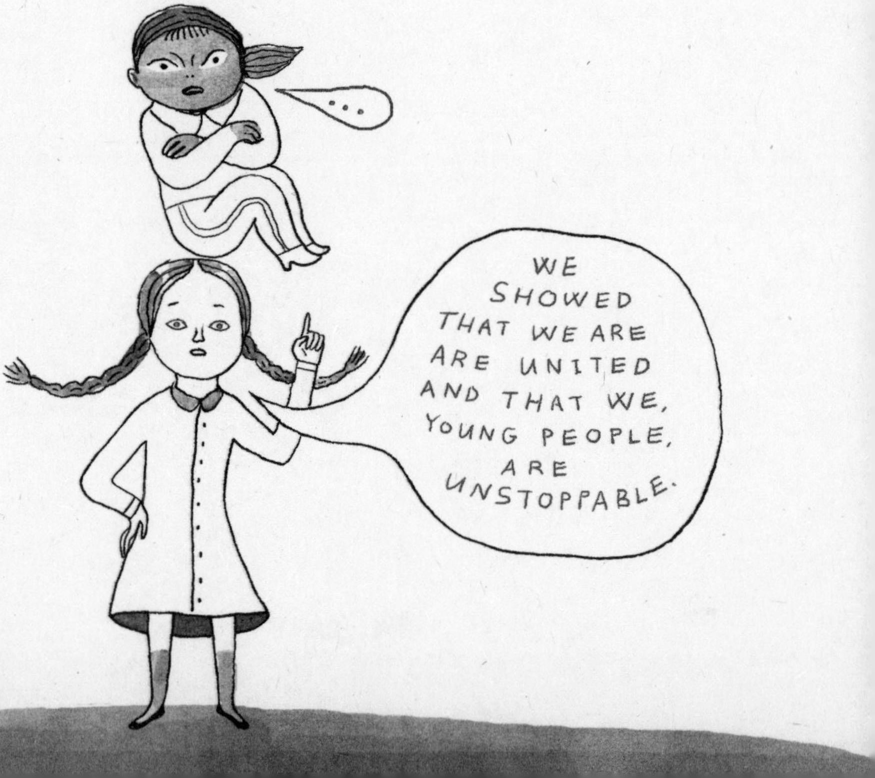
...
WE SHOWED THAT WE ARE ARE UNITED AND THAT WE, YOUNG PEOPLE, ARE UNSTOPPABLE.

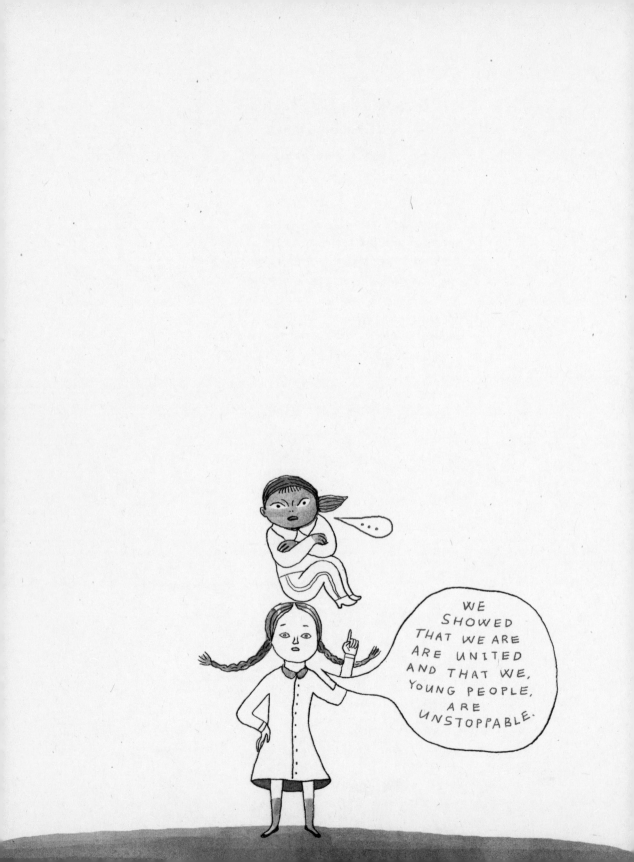

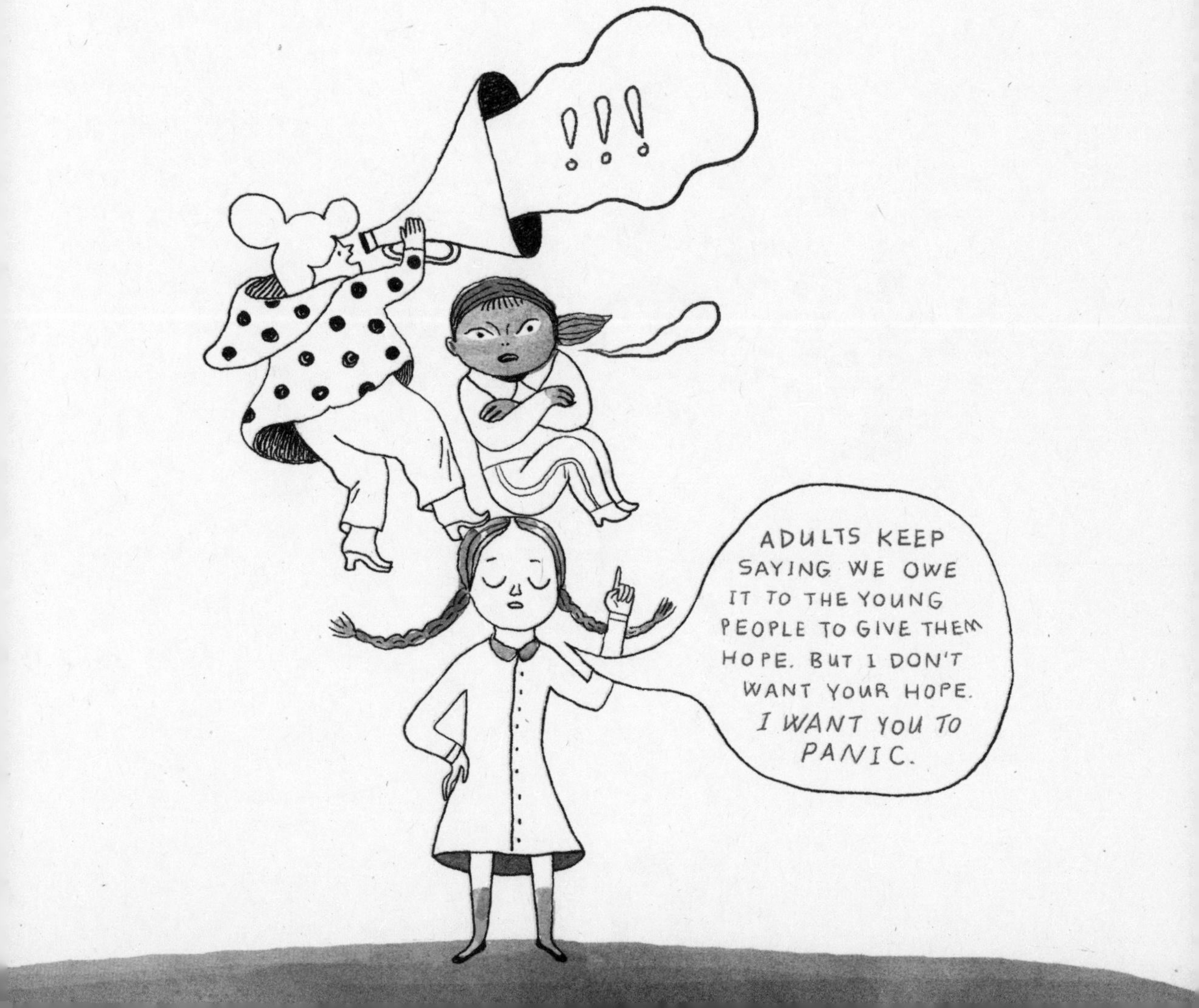
!!!
ADULTS KEEP SAYING WE OWE IT TO THE YOUNG PEOPLE TO GIVE THEM HOPE. BUT I DON'T WANT YOUR HOPE. I WANT YOU TO PANIC.

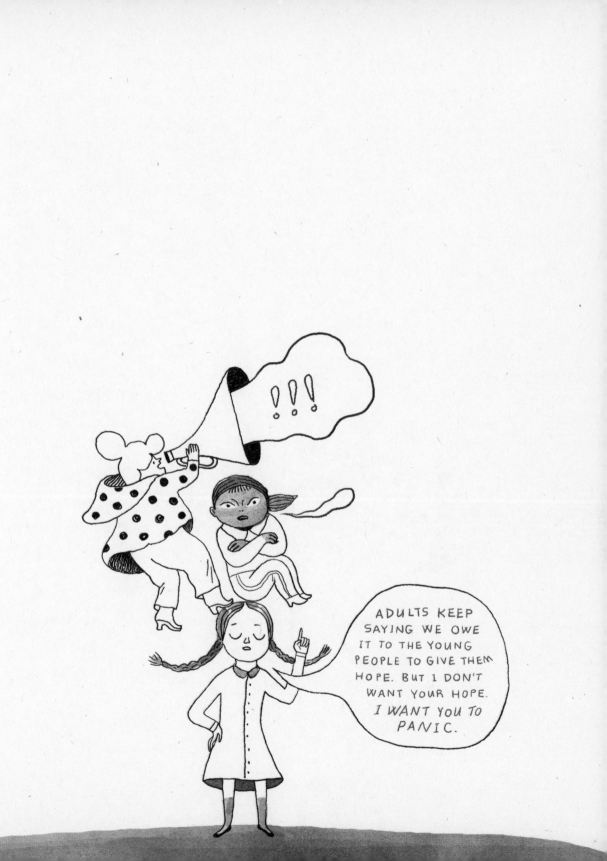

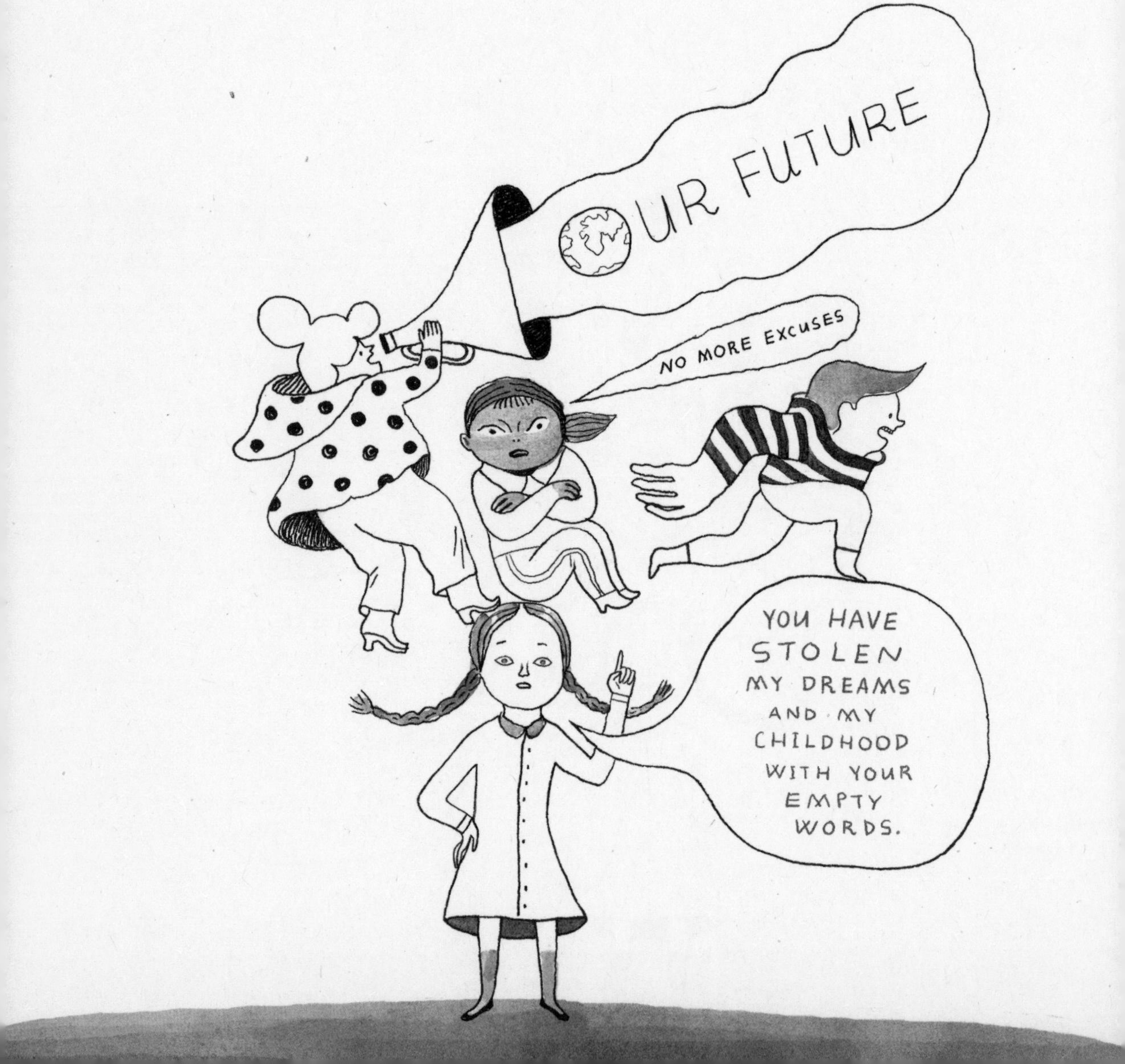
OUR FUTURE
NO MORE EXCUSES
YOU HAVE STOLEN MY DREAMS AND MY CHILDHOOD WITH YOUR EMPTY WORDS.

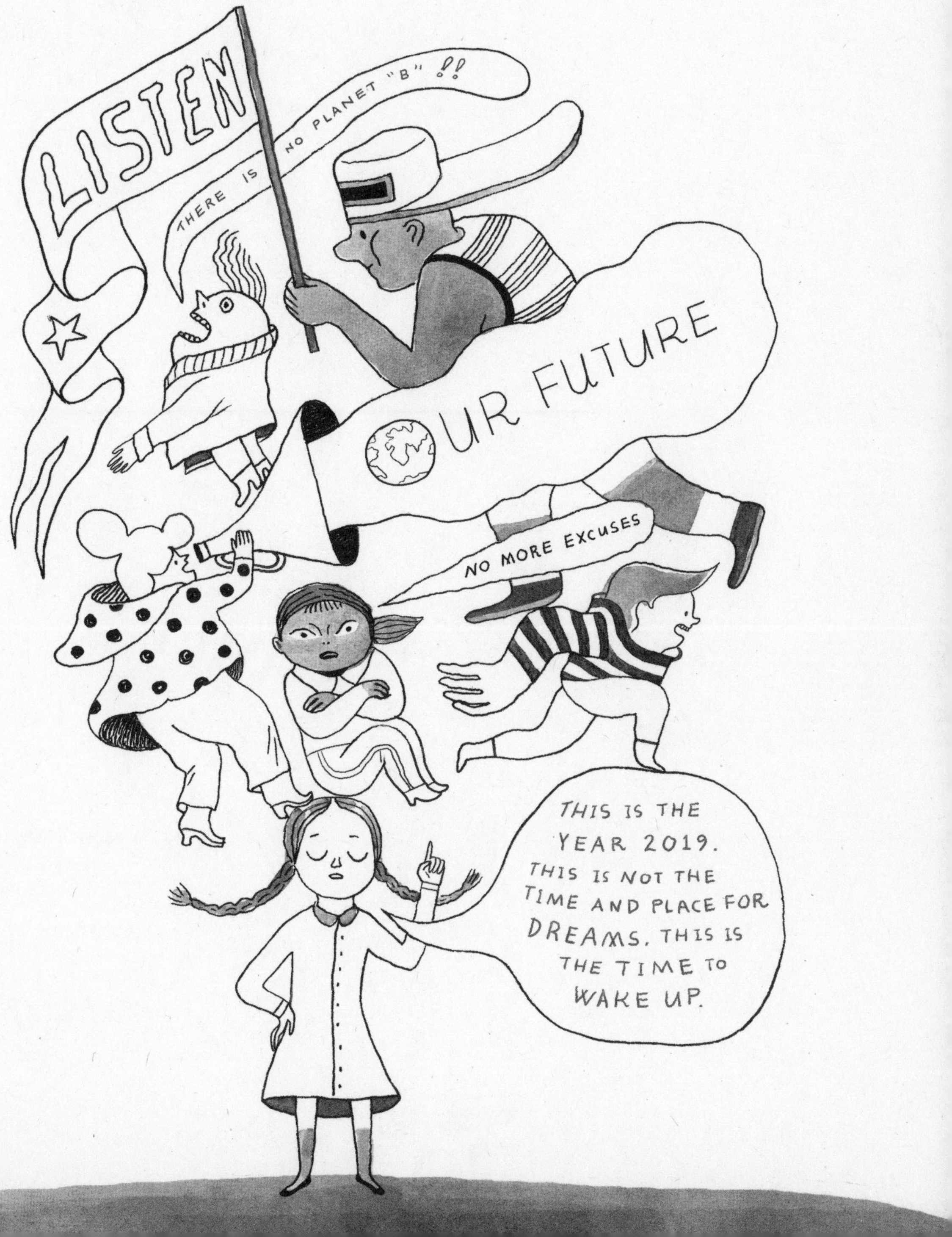
LISTEN
THERE IS NO PLANET "B" !!
OUR FUTURE
NO MORE EXCUSES
THIS IS THE YEAR 2019. THIS IS NOT THE TIME AND PLACE FOR DREAMS. THIS IS THE TIME TO WAKE UP.

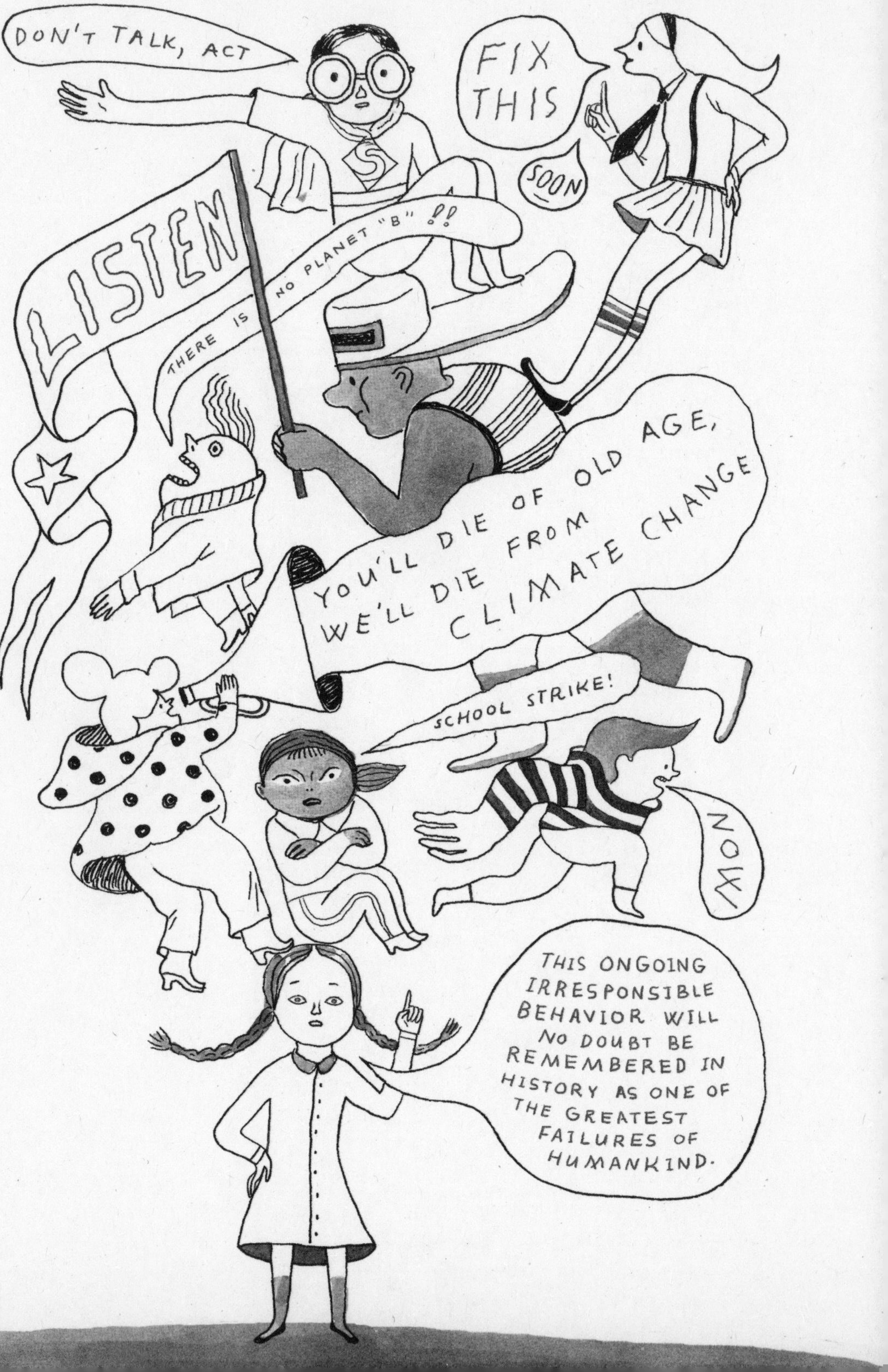
DON'T TALK, ACT
FIX THIS
SOON
LISTEN
THERE IS NO PLANET "B" !!
YOU'LL DIE OF OLD AGE, WE'LL DIE FROM CLIMATE CHANGE
SCHOOL STRIKE!
NOW
THIS ONGOING IRRESPONSIBLE BEHAVIOR WILL NO DOUBT BE REMEMBERED IN HISTORY AS ONE OF THE GREATEST FAILURES OF HUMANKIND.

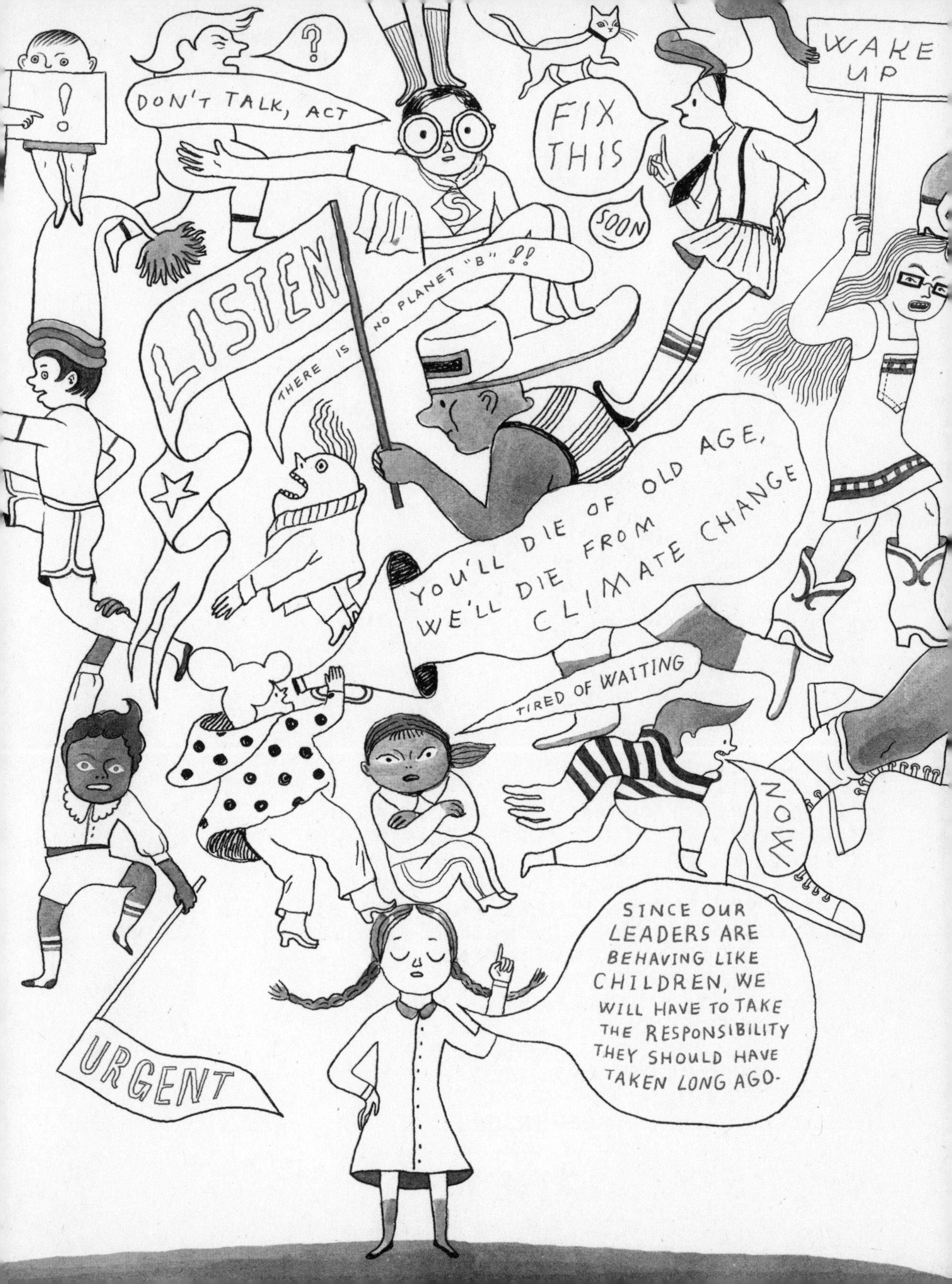
!
?
DON'T TALK, ACT
FIX THIS
SOON
WAKE UP
LISTEN
THERE IS NO PLANET "B" !!
YOU'LL DIE OF OLD AGE, WE'LL DIE FROM CLIMATE CHANGE
TIRED OF WAITING
NOW
URGENT
SINCE OUR LEADERS ARE BEHAVING LIKE CHILDREN, WE WILL HAVE TO TAKE THE RESPONSIBILITY THEY SHOULD HAVE TAKEN LONG AGO.

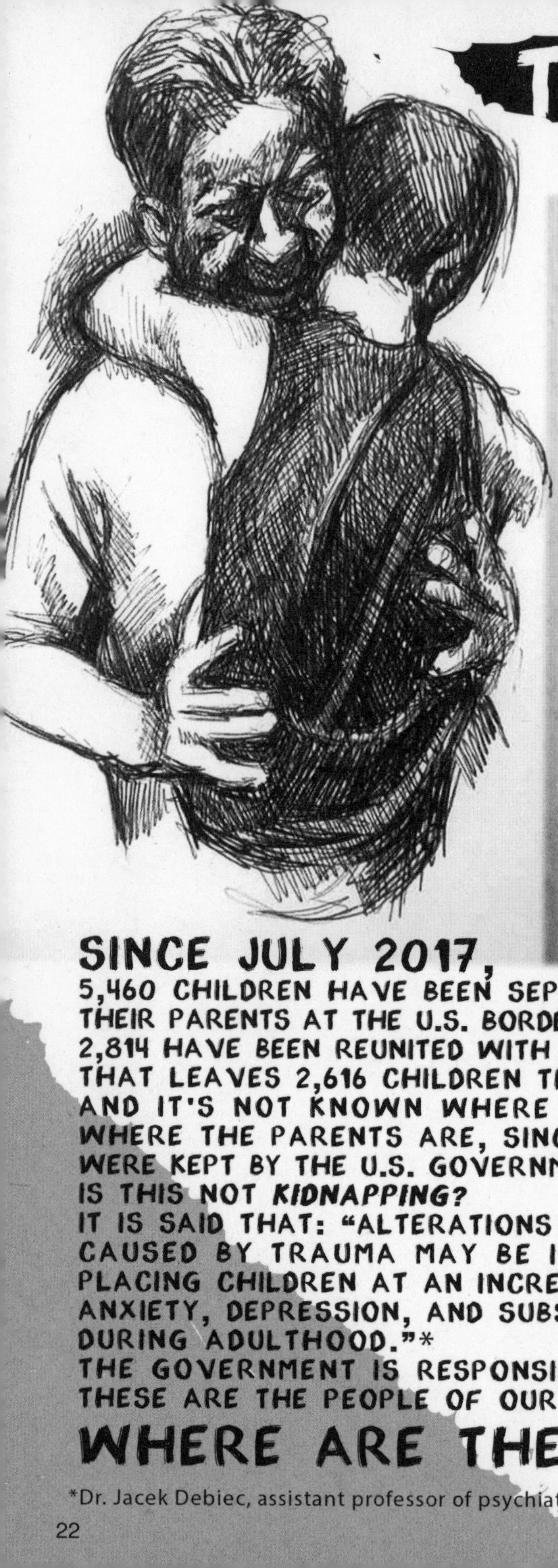

TRAGIC JOY

BY JACKIE LIMA

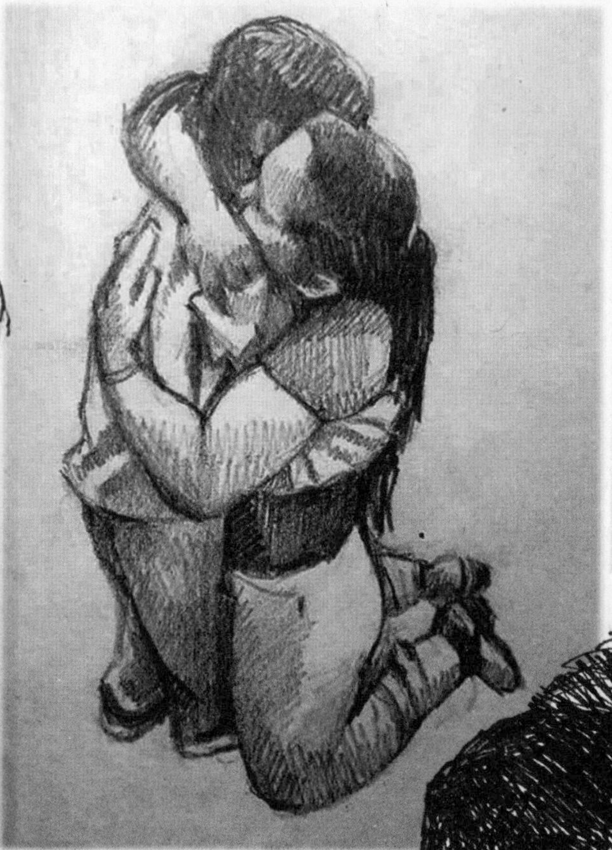

SINCE JULY 2017,

5,460 CHILDREN HAVE BEEN SEPARATED FROM THEIR PARENTS AT THE U.S. BORDER WITH MEXICO. 2,814 HAVE BEEN REUNITED WITH THEIR FAMILIES. THAT LEAVES 2,616 CHILDREN THAT HAVE NOT AND IT'S NOT KNOWN WHERE THEY ARE OR WHERE THE PARENTS ARE, SINCE NO RECORDS WERE KEPT BY THE U.S. GOVERNMENT.
IS THIS NOT *KIDNAPPING?*
IT IS SAID THAT: "ALTERATIONS IN THE BRAIN CAUSED BY TRAUMA MAY BE IRREPARABLE, PLACING CHILDREN AT AN INCREASED RISK FOR ANXIETY, DEPRESSION, AND SUBSTANCE ABUSE DURING ADULTHOOD."*
THE GOVERNMENT IS RESPONSIBLE.
THESE ARE THE PEOPLE OF OUR FUTURE.

WHERE ARE THEY?

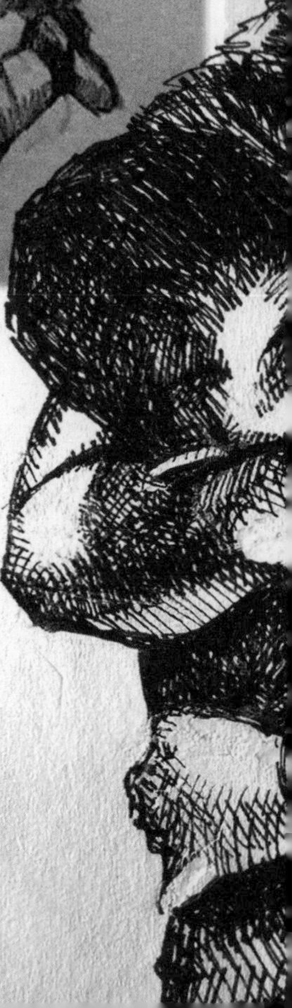

*Dr. Jacek Debiec, assistant professor of psychiatry at Michigan Medicine

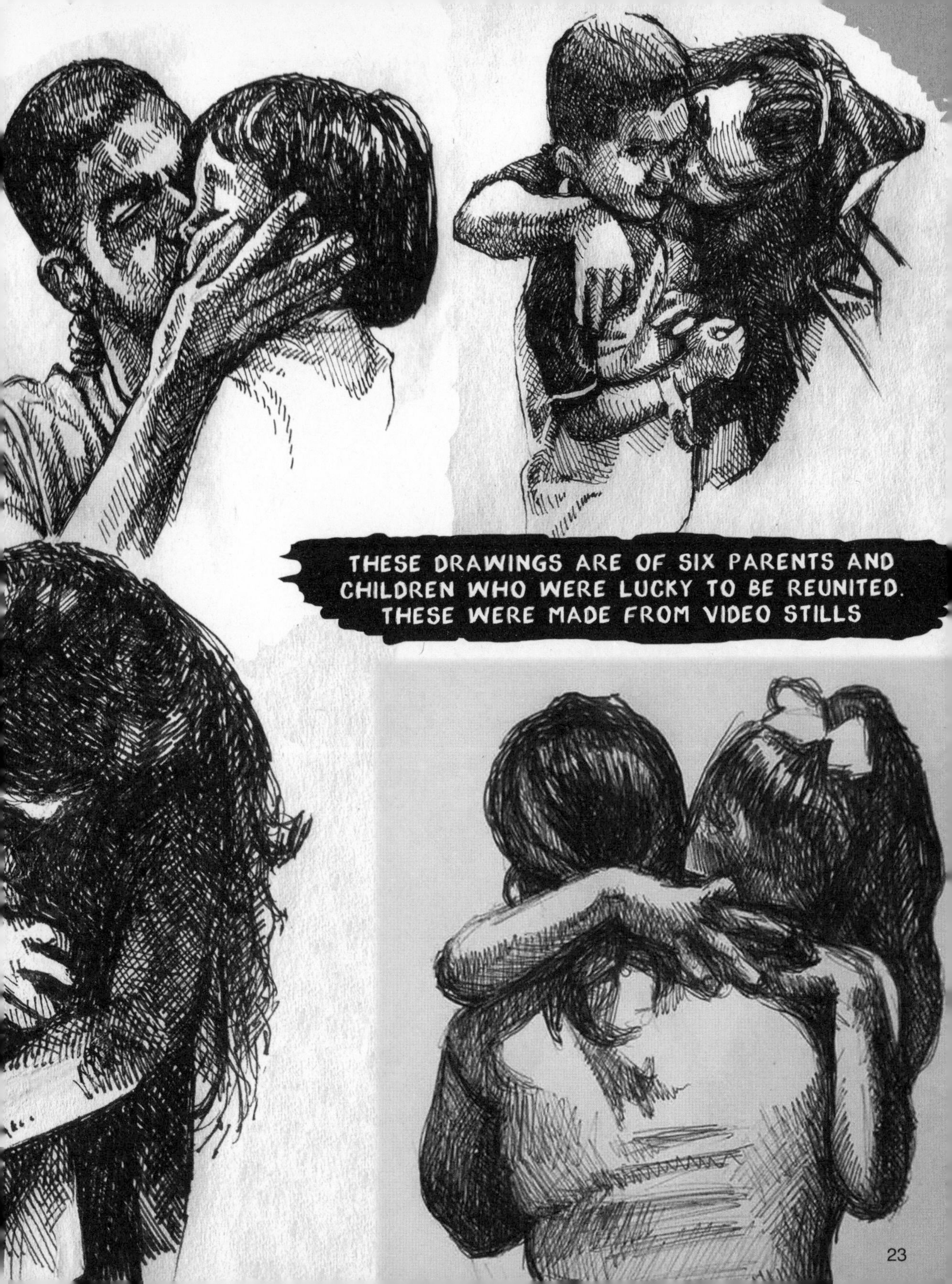
THESE DRAWINGS ARE OF SIX PARENTS AND CHILDREN WHO WERE LUCKY TO BE REUNITED. THESE WERE MADE FROM VIDEO STILLS

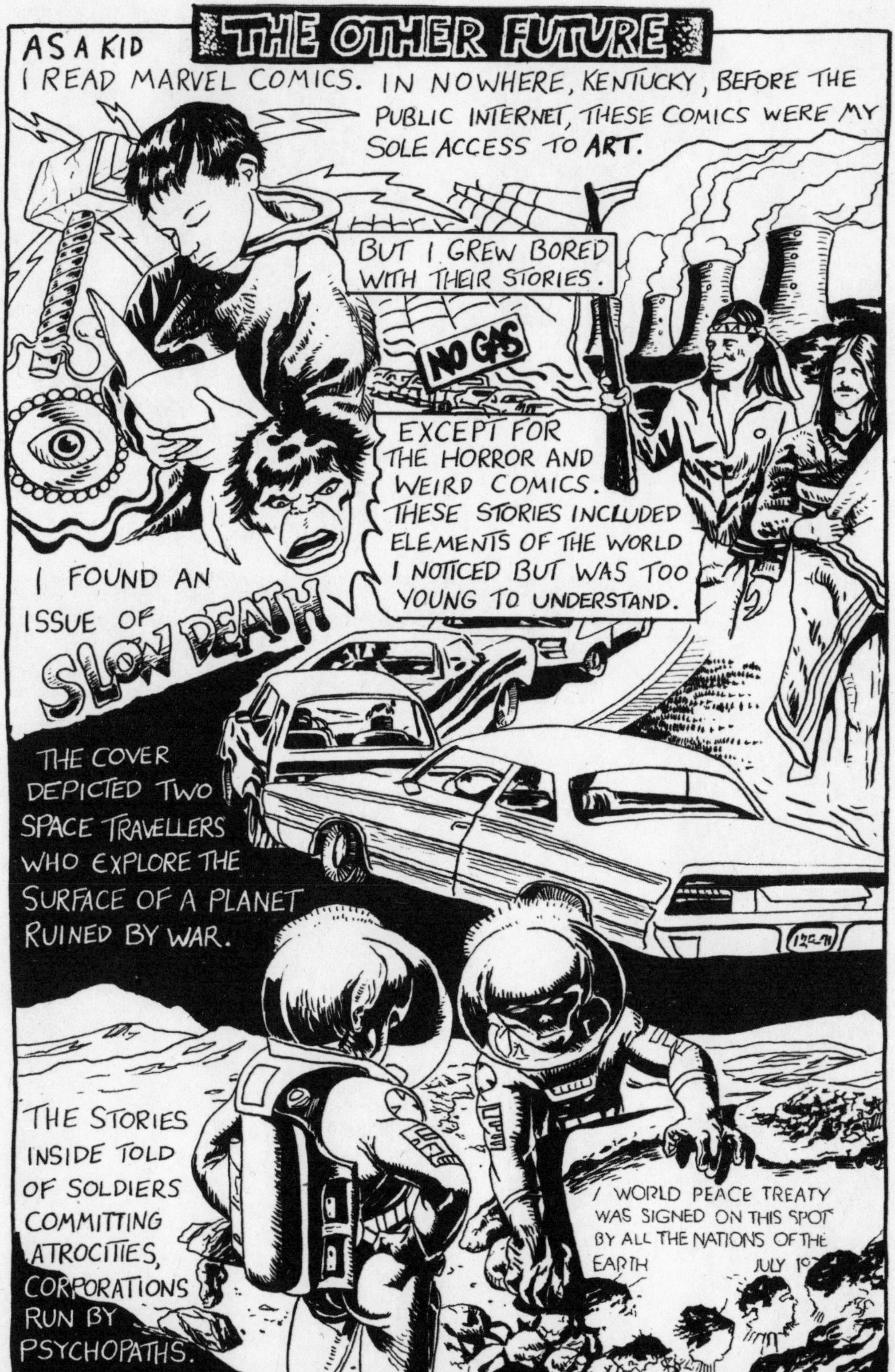
THE OTHER FUTURE
AS A KID
I READ MARVEL COMICS. IN NOWHERE, KENTUCKY, BEFORE THE PUBLIC INTERNET, THESE COMICS WERE MY SOLE ACCESS TO ART.
BUT I GREW BORED WITH THEIR STORIES.
NO GAS
EXCEPT FOR THE HORROR AND WEIRD COMICS. THESE STORIES INCLUDED ELEMENTS OF THE WORLD I NOTICED BUT WAS TOO YOUNG TO UNDERSTAND.
I FOUND AN ISSUE OF
SLOW DEATH
THE COVER DEPICTED TWO SPACE TRAVELLERS WHO EXPLORE THE SURFACE OF A PLANET RUINED BY WAR.
THE STORIES INSIDE TOLD OF SOLDIERS COMMITTING ATROCITIES, CORPORATIONS RUN BY PSYCHOPATHS.
/ WORLD PEACE TREATY WAS SIGNED ON THIS SPOT BY ALL THE NATIONS OF THE EARTH
JULY 19

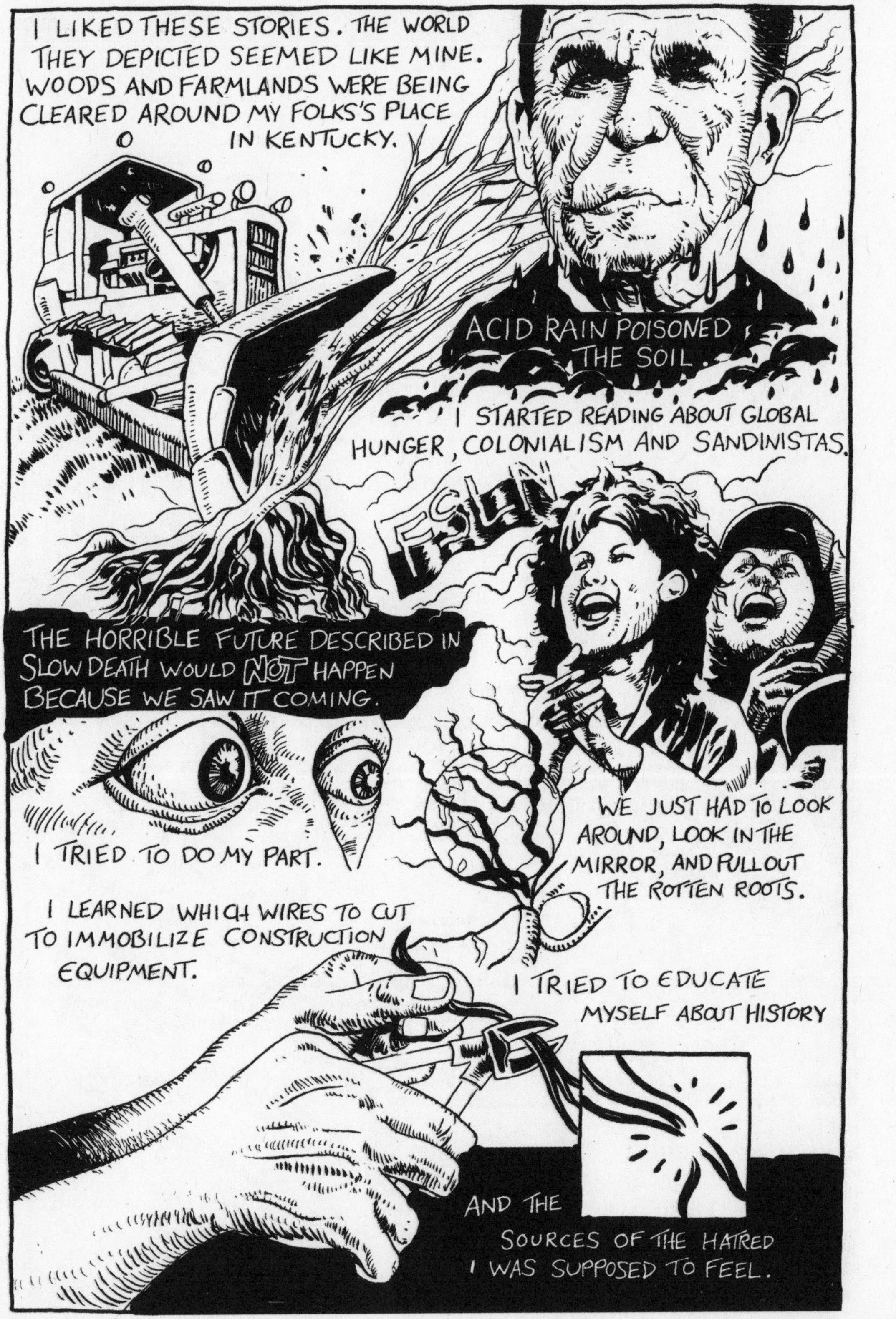
I LIKED THESE STORIES. THE WORLD THEY DEPICTED SEEMED LIKE MINE. WOODS AND FARMLANDS WERE BEING CLEARED AROUND MY FOLKS'S PLACE IN KENTUCKY.
ACID RAIN POISONED THE SOIL.
I STARTED READING ABOUT GLOBAL HUNGER, COLONIALISM AND SANDINISTAS.
FSLN
THE HORRIBLE FUTURE DESCRIBED IN SLOW DEATH WOULD NOT HAPPEN BECAUSE WE SAW IT COMING.
WE JUST HAD TO LOOK AROUND, LOOK IN THE MIRROR, AND PULL OUT THE ROTTEN ROOTS.
I TRIED TO DO MY PART.
I LEARNED WHICH WIRES TO CUT TO IMMOBILIZE CONSTRUCTION EQUIPMENT.
I TRIED TO EDUCATE MYSELF ABOUT HISTORY
AND THE SOURCES OF THE HATRED I WAS SUPPOSED TO FEEL.

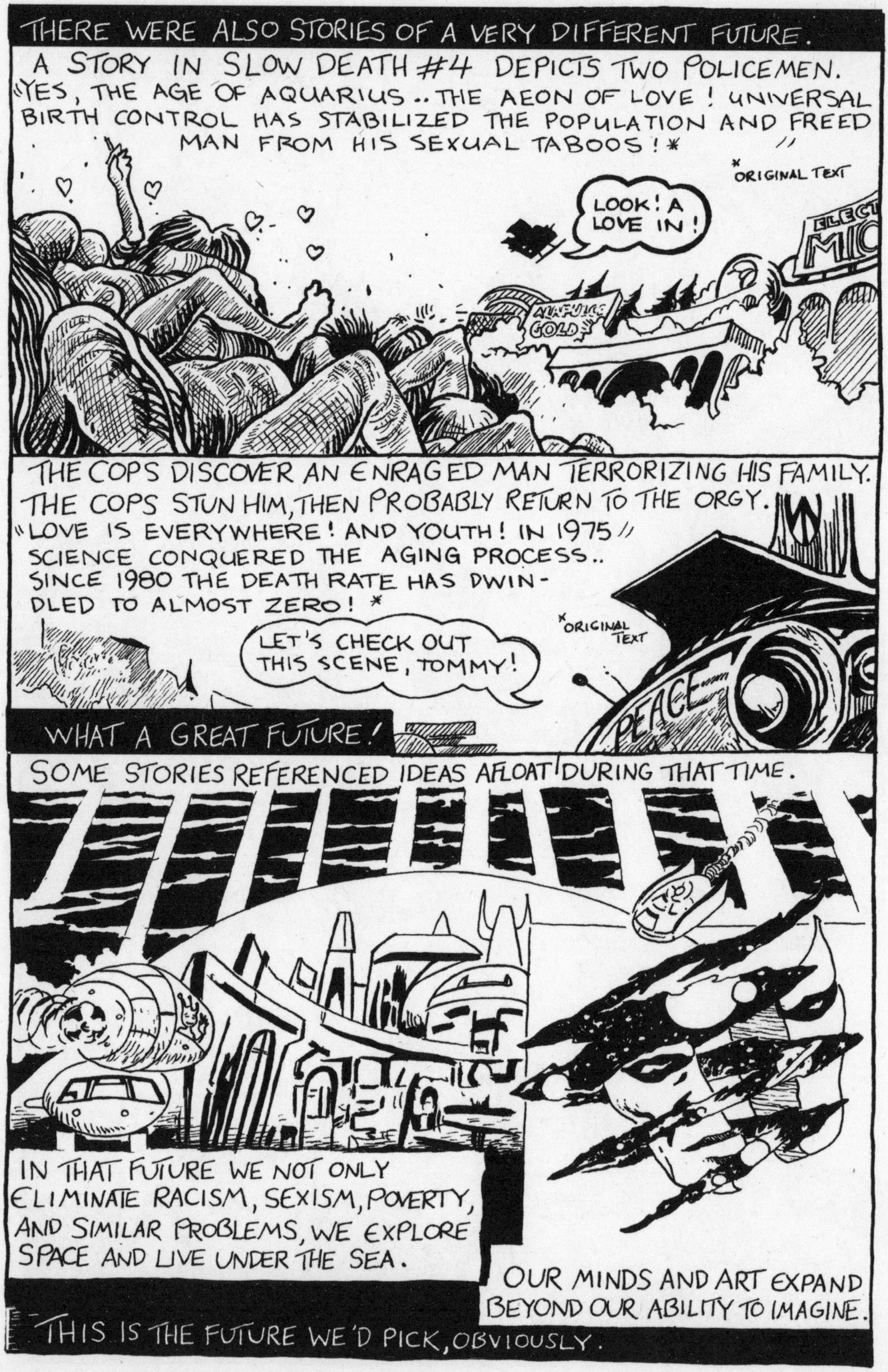
THERE WERE ALSO STORIES OF A VERY DIFFERENT FUTURE.
A STORY IN SLOW DEATH #4 DEPICTS TWO POLICEMEN.
"YES, THE AGE OF AQUARIUS.. THE AEON OF LOVE! UNIVERSAL BIRTH CONTROL HAS STABILIZED THE POPULATION AND FREED MAN FROM HIS SEXUAL TABOOS!*"
*ORIGINAL TEXT
LOOK! A LOVE IN!
GOLD
THE COPS DISCOVER AN ENRAGED MAN TERRORIZING HIS FAMILY. THE COPS STUN HIM, THEN PROBABLY RETURN TO THE ORGY.
"LOVE IS EVERYWHERE! AND YOUTH! IN 1975 SCIENCE CONQUERED THE AGING PROCESS.. SINCE 1980 THE DEATH RATE HAS DWINDLED TO ALMOST ZERO! *"
*ORIGINAL TEXT
LET'S CHECK OUT THIS SCENE, TOMMY!
PEACE
WHAT A GREAT FUTURE!
SOME STORIES REFERENCED IDEAS AFLOAT DURING THAT TIME.
IN THAT FUTURE WE NOT ONLY ELIMINATE RACISM, SEXISM, POVERTY, AND SIMILAR PROBLEMS, WE EXPLORE SPACE AND LIVE UNDER THE SEA.
OUR MINDS AND ART EXPAND BEYOND OUR ABILITY TO IMAGINE.
THIS IS THE FUTURE WE'D PICK, OBVIOUSLY.

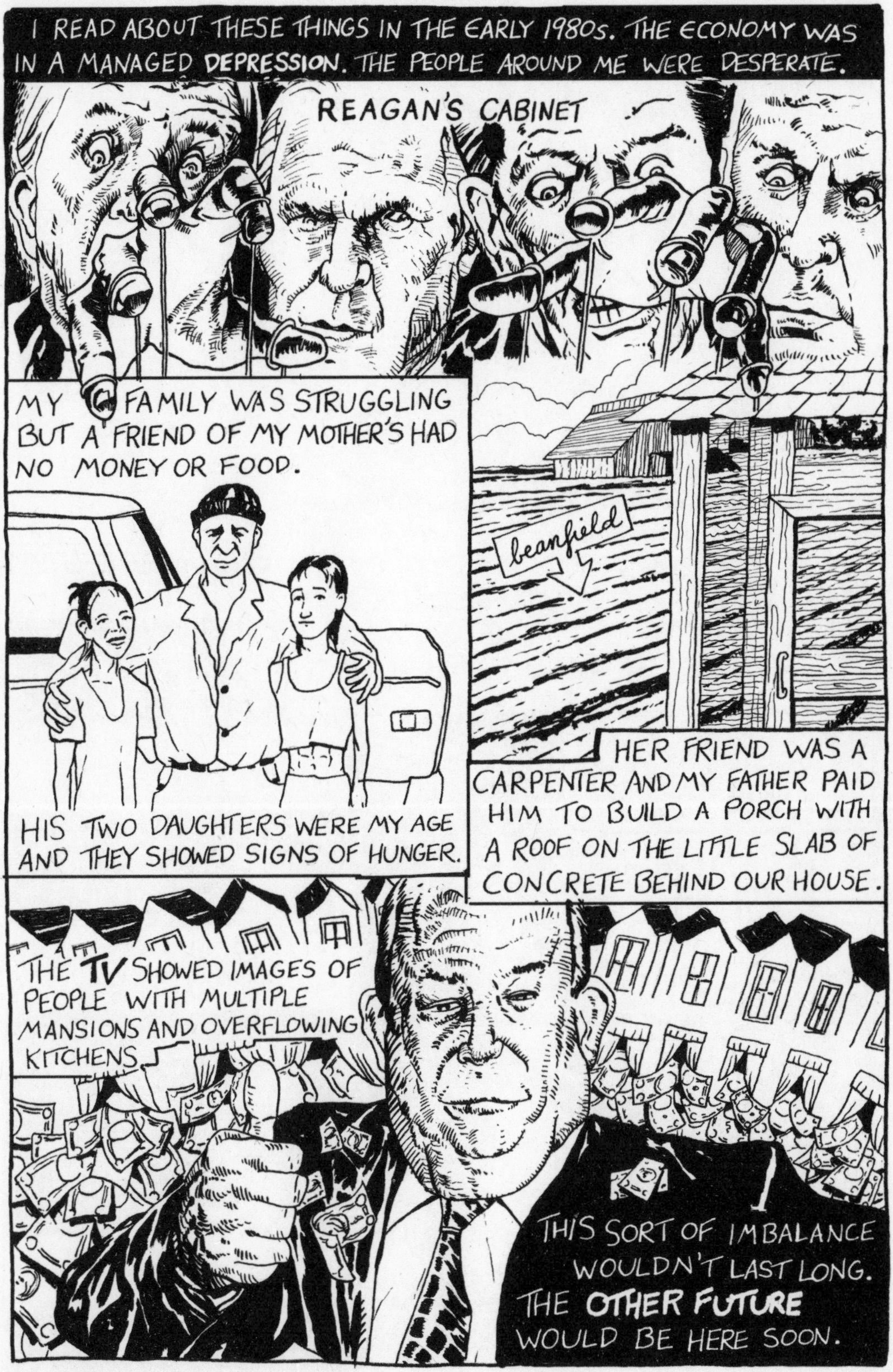
I READ ABOUT THESE THINGS IN THE EARLY 1980s. THE ECONOMY WAS IN A MANAGED DEPRESSION. THE PEOPLE AROUND ME WERE DESPERATE.
REAGAN'S CABINET
MY FAMILY WAS STRUGGLING BUT A FRIEND OF MY MOTHER'S HAD NO MONEY OR FOOD.
HIS TWO DAUGHTERS WERE MY AGE AND THEY SHOWED SIGNS OF HUNGER.
beanfield
HER FRIEND WAS A CARPENTER AND MY FATHER PAID HIM TO BUILD A PORCH WITH A ROOF ON THE LITTLE SLAB OF CONCRETE BEHIND OUR HOUSE.
THE TV SHOWED IMAGES OF PEOPLE WITH MULTIPLE MANSIONS AND OVERFLOWING KITCHENS.
THIS SORT OF IMBALANCE WOULDN'T LAST LONG. THE OTHER FUTURE WOULD BE HERE SOON.

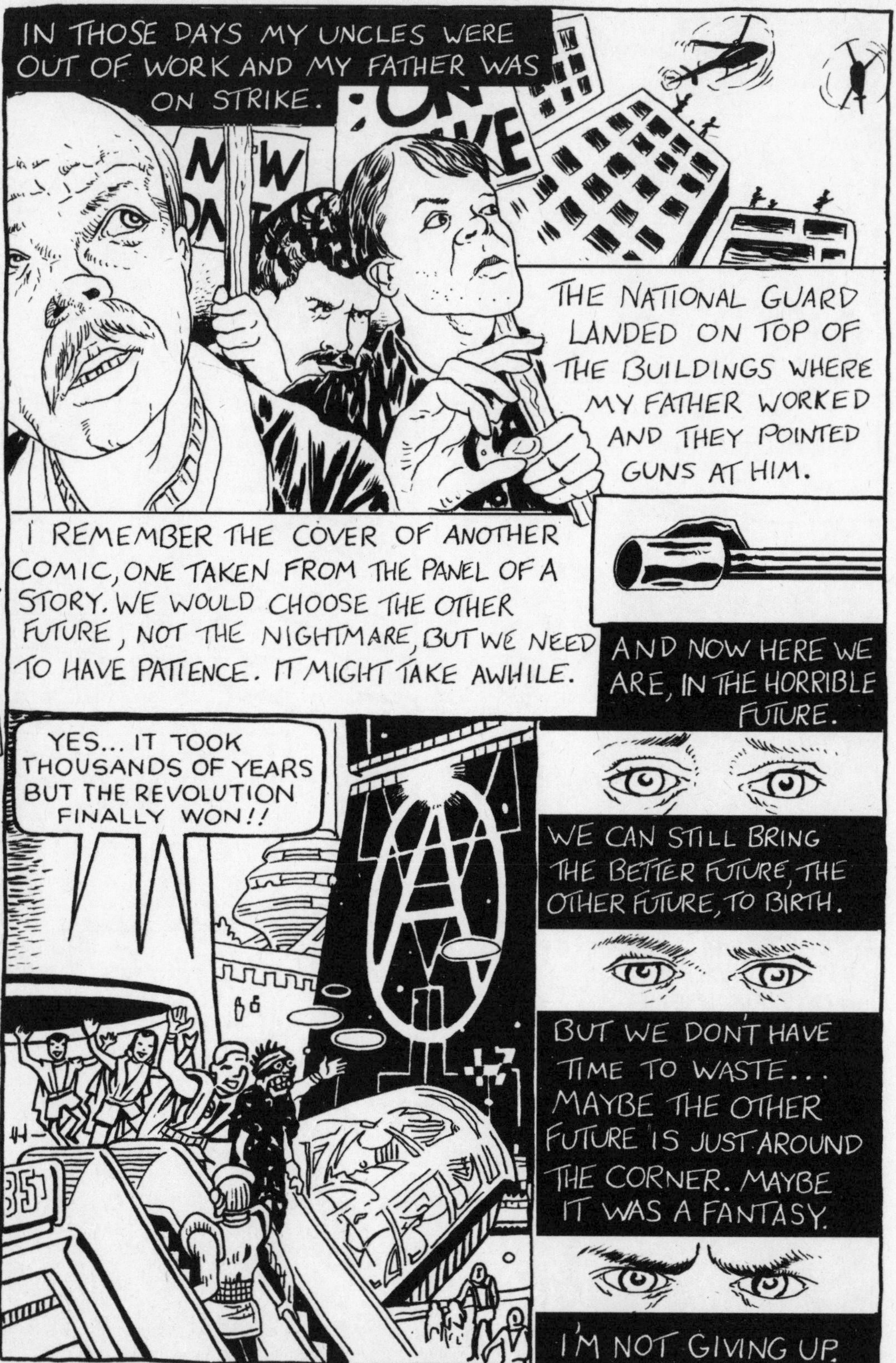
IN THOSE DAYS MY UNCLES WERE OUT OF WORK AND MY FATHER WAS ON STRIKE.
THE NATIONAL GUARD LANDED ON TOP OF THE BUILDINGS WHERE MY FATHER WORKED AND THEY POINTED GUNS AT HIM.
I REMEMBER THE COVER OF ANOTHER COMIC, ONE TAKEN FROM THE PANEL OF A STORY. WE WOULD CHOOSE THE OTHER FUTURE, NOT THE NIGHTMARE, BUT WE NEED TO HAVE PATIENCE. IT MIGHT TAKE AWHILE.
AND NOW HERE WE ARE, IN THE HORRIBLE FUTURE.
YES... IT TOOK THOUSANDS OF YEARS BUT THE REVOLUTION FINALLY WON!!
WE CAN STILL BRING THE BETTER FUTURE, THE OTHER FUTURE, TO BIRTH.
BUT WE DON'T HAVE TIME TO WASTE... MAYBE THE OTHER FUTURE IS JUST AROUND THE CORNER. MAYBE IT WAS A FANTASY.
I'M NOT GIVING UP.

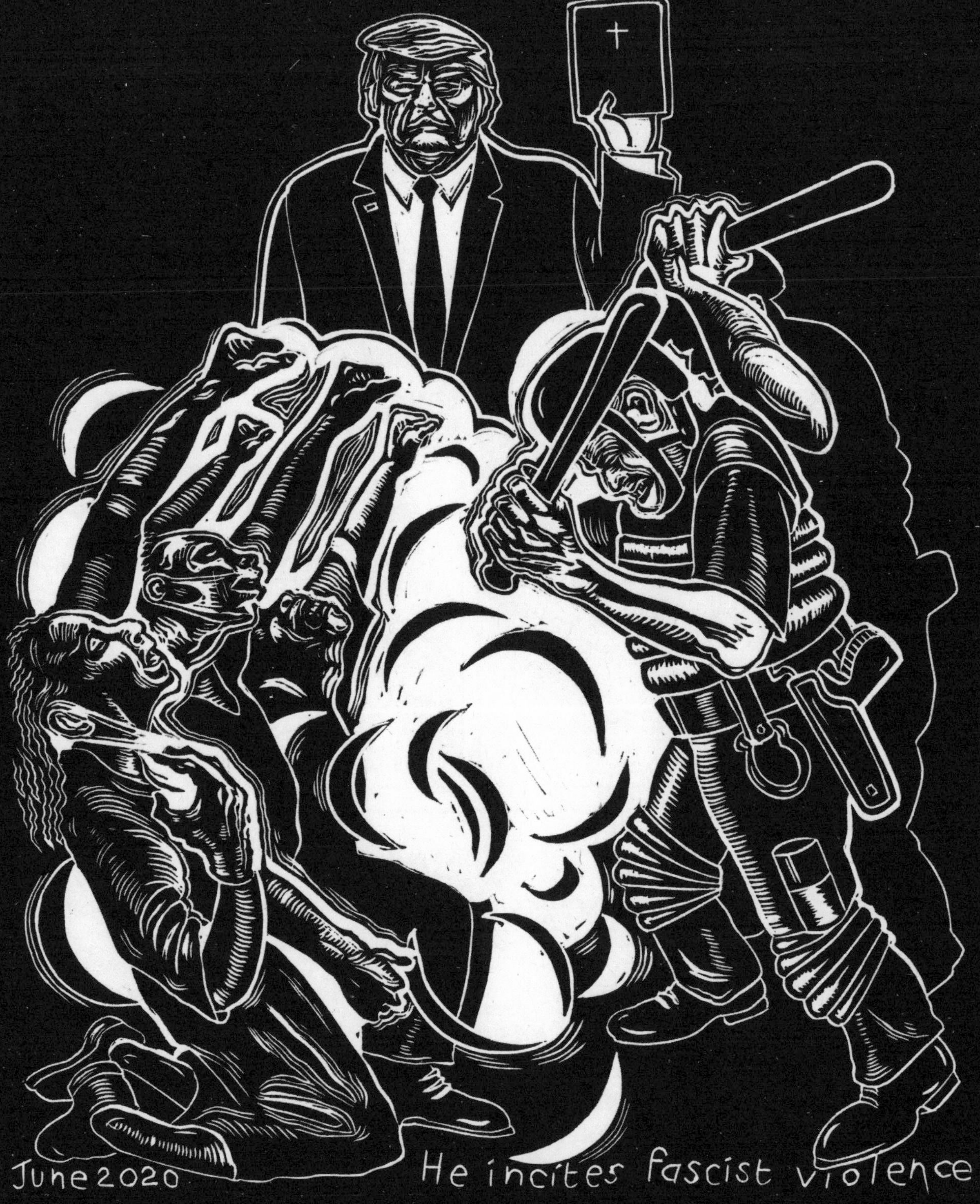
June 2020
He incites fascist violence

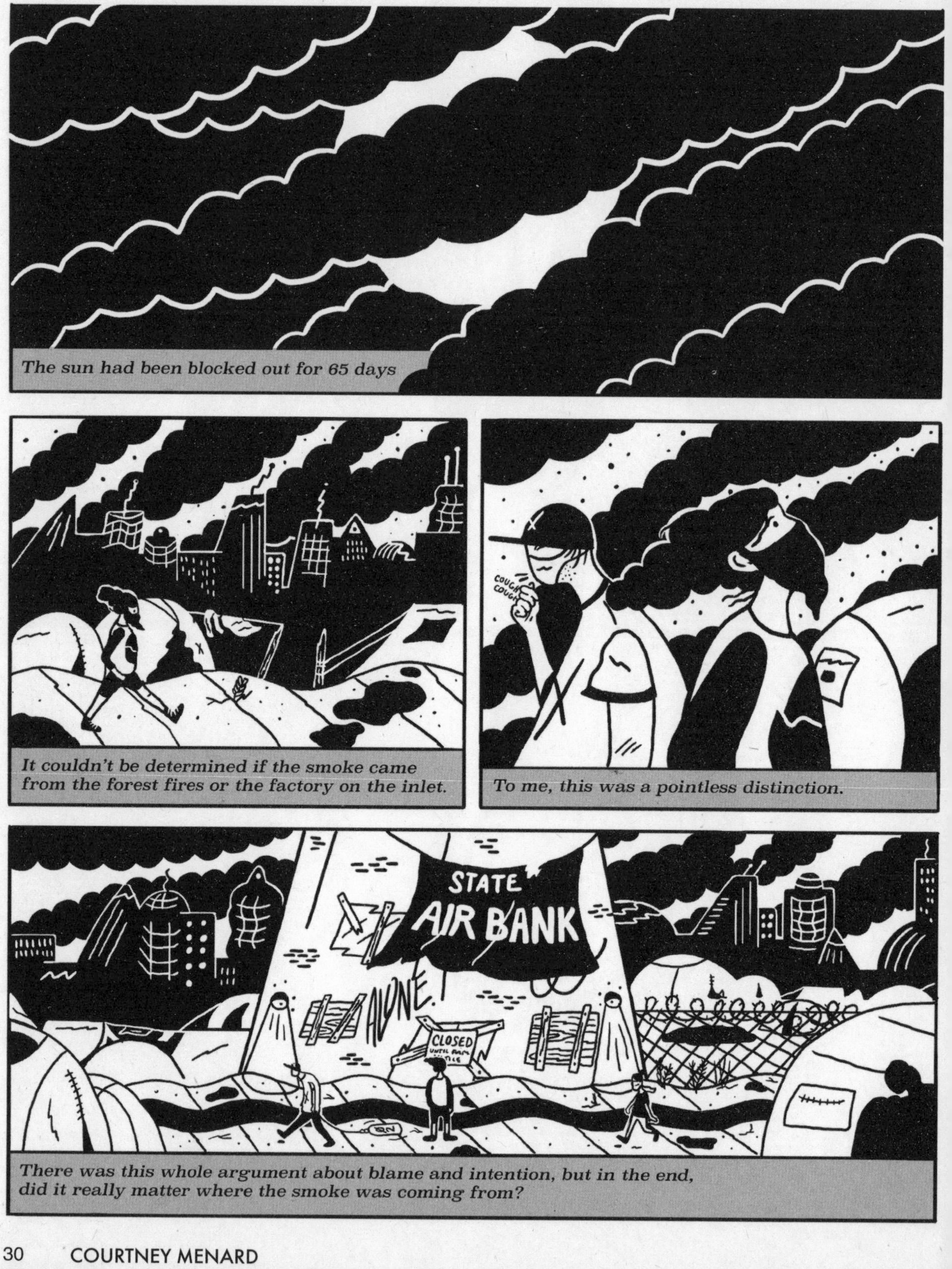
The sun had been blocked out for 65 days
It couldn't be determined if the smoke came from the forest fires or the factory on the inlet.
COUGH COUGH
To me, this was a pointless distinction.
STATE AIR BANK
ALONE!
CLOSED
There was this whole argument about blame and intention, but in the end, did it really matter where the smoke was coming from?

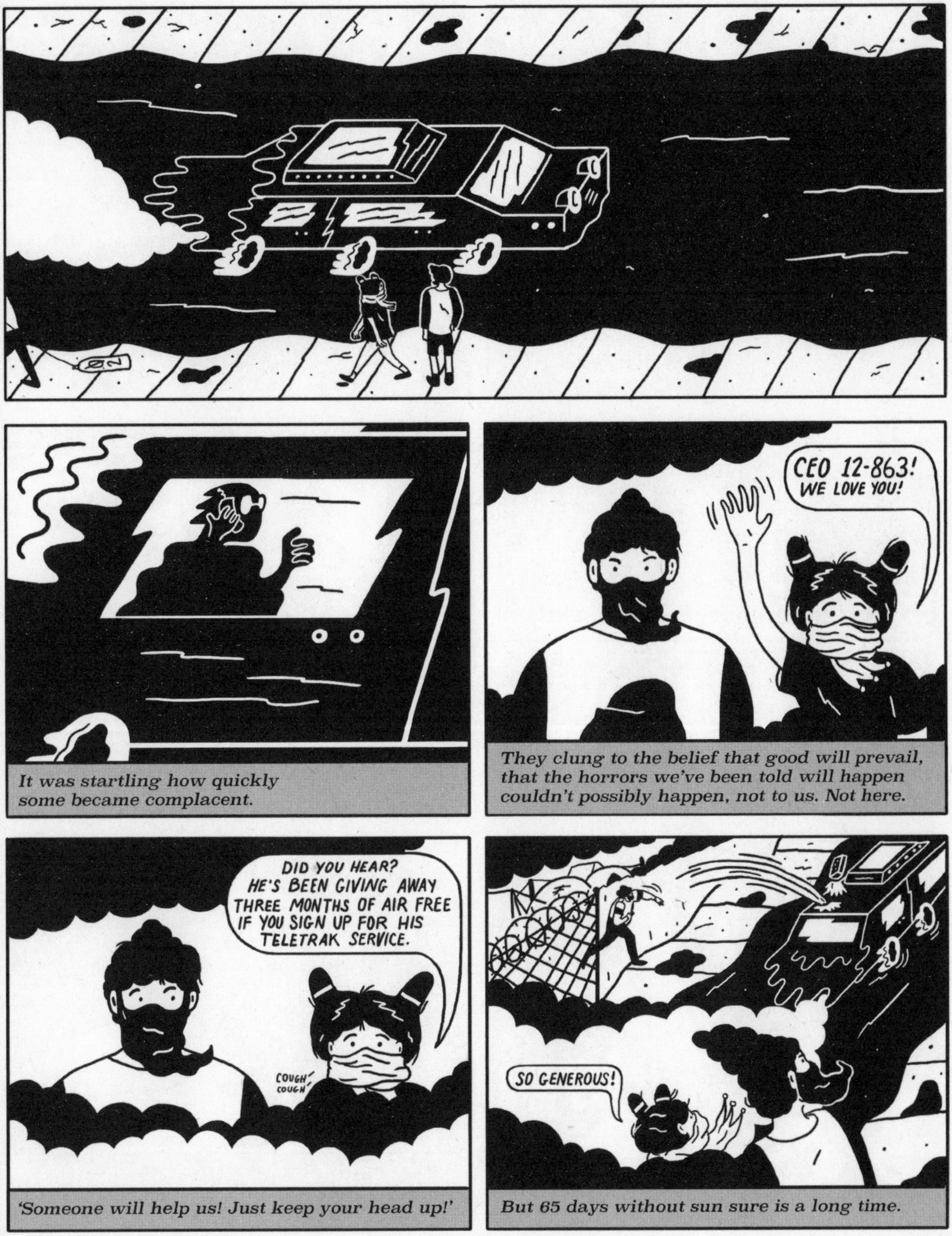
CEO 12-863! WE LOVE YOU!
It was startling how quickly some became complacent.
They clung to the belief that good will prevail, that the horrors we've been told will happen couldn't possibly happen, not to us. Not here.
DID YOU HEAR? HE'S BEEN GIVING AWAY THREE MONTHS OF AIR FREE IF YOU SIGN UP FOR HIS TELETRAK SERVICE.
COUGH! COUGH!
'Someone will help us! Just keep your head up!'
SO GENEROUS!
But 65 days without sun sure is a long time.

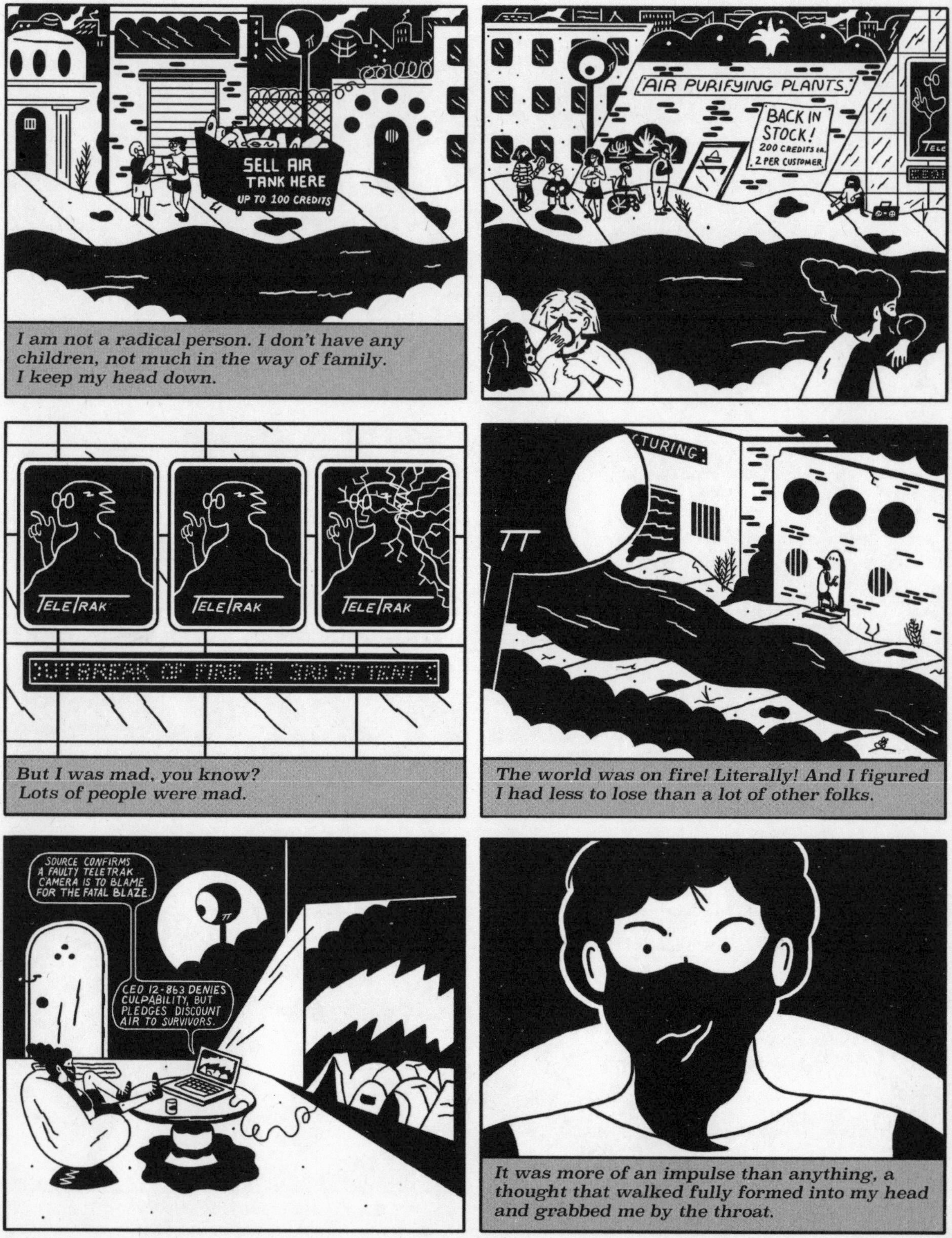
SELL AIR
TANK HERE
UP TO 100 CREDITS
I am not a radical person. I don't have any children, not much in the way of family. I keep my head down.
AIR PURIFYING PLANTS
BACK IN STOCK!
200 CREDITS EA.
2 PER CUSTOMER
TELETRAK
TELETRAK
TELETRAK
But I was mad, you know? Lots of people were mad.
The world was on fire! Literally! And I figured I had less to lose than a lot of other folks.
SOURCE CONFIRMS A FAULTY TELETRAK CAMERA IS TO BLAME FOR THE FATAL BLAZE.
CEO 12-863 DENIES CULPABILITY, BUT PLEDGES DISCOUNT AIR TO SURVIVORS.
It was more of an impulse than anything, a thought that walked fully formed into my head and grabbed me by the throat.

Figuring out where the CEO lived wasn't hard.

We lived in the same neighborhood.

My father used to say it's not how many days you have left, it's how many **good** days you have left.

But the way things were going, it was hard to tell what even counted as a 'good day'.

The goal post kept moving.

We could all be dead tomorrow.

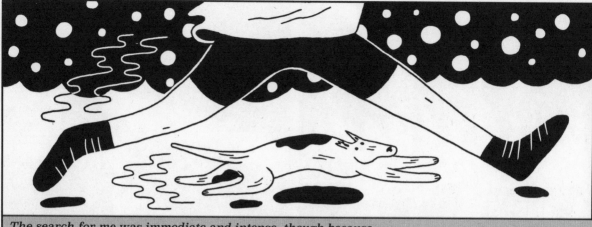

The search for me was immediate and intense, though because face masks had become ubiquitous there wasn't much to go on.
WANTED
REWARD
KILL UR LOCAL CEO
CLEAN AIR NOW
MEMORIAL
SERVICE
Still, I fled to the outskirts of the city, moved frequently, gathered news where I could.
The media was quick to drum up sympathy for the CEO, but it was short lived.
UNDER NEW MANAGEMENT
Workers walked out, tenants kept their rent. Other CEOs began to disappear or suddenly step down, handing the reins over to their former employees. In response, the government shut down the internet.
People found other ways. I met a group who set up their own networks. Strangers protected strangers. New communities were built as others were burned.

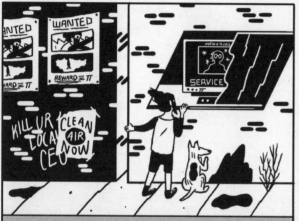

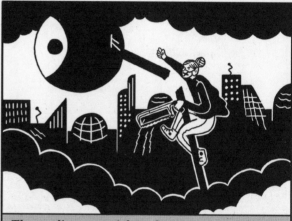

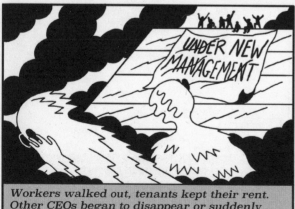

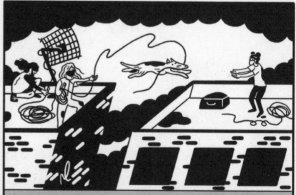

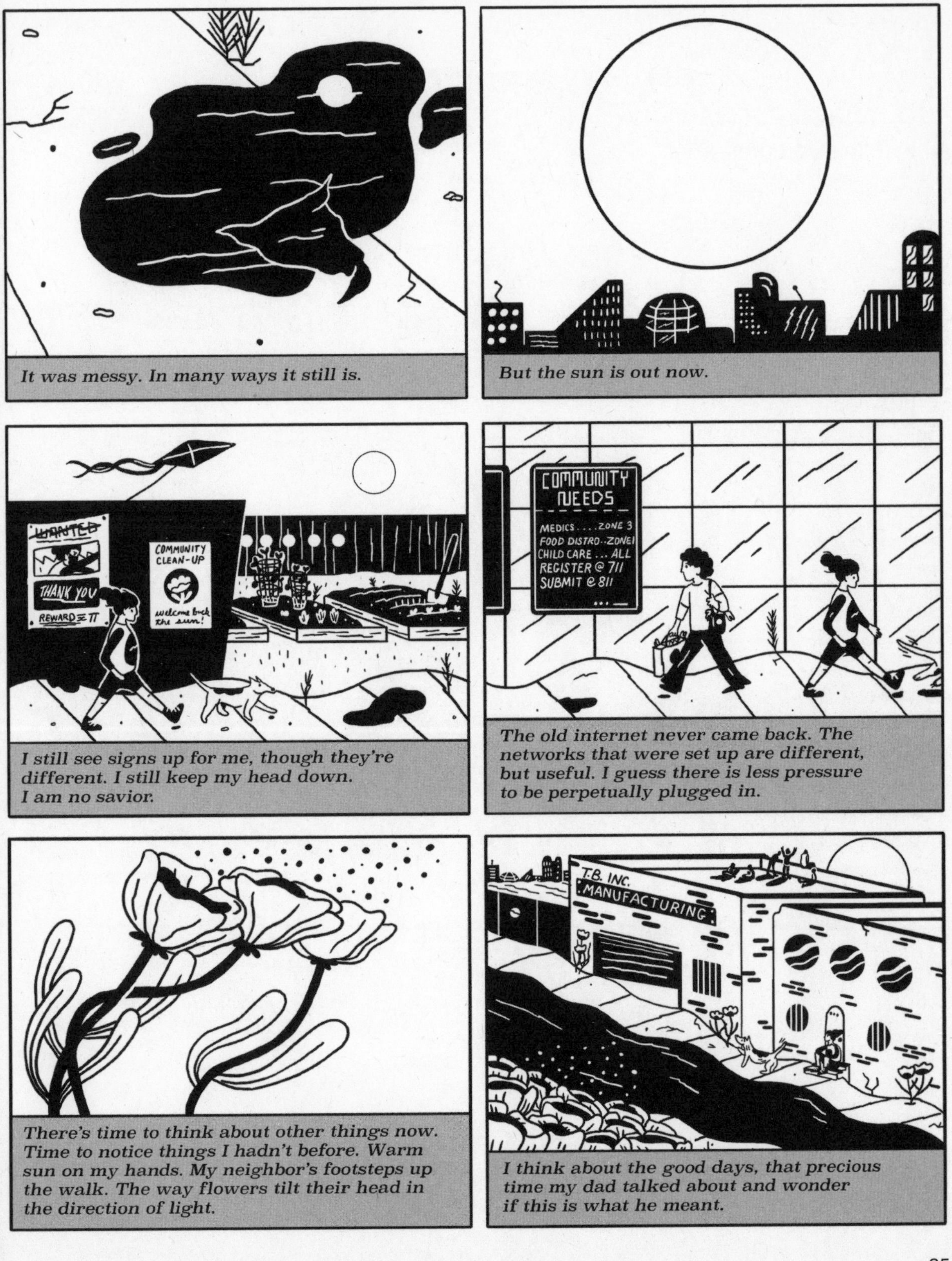

It was messy. In many ways it still is.
But the sun is out now.
WANTED
THANK YOU
REWARD
COMMUNITY CLEAN-UP
welcome back the sun!
I still see signs up for me, though they're different. I still keep my head down. I am no savior.
COMMUNITY NEEDS
MEDICS . . . . ZONE 3
FOOD DISTRO . . ZONE 1
CHILD CARE . . . ALL
REGISTER @ 711
SUBMIT @ 811
The old internet never came back. The networks that were set up are different, but useful. I guess there is less pressure to be perpetually plugged in.
There's time to think about other things now. Time to notice things I hadn't before. Warm sun on my hands. My neighbor's footsteps up the walk. The way flowers tilt their head in the direction of light.
T.B. INC.
MANUFACTURING
I think about the good days, that precious time my dad talked about and wonder if this is what he meant.

An Evening Demonstration.

A SMALL CROWD GATHERS OUTSIDE OF A EXCLUSIVE DOWNTOWN CONDOMINIUM.
DON'T DO IT!
DON'T DO IT!
NOT TONIGHT PLEASE!
IN A WIDELY PUBLICIZED REAL-ESTATE DEAL, MORGAN CHILIAC AND HIS WIFE, EUROPA,
SON OF THE CEO OF KHILIOI FOODS CORPORATION.
DAUGHTER OF THE AMBASSADOR TO KARELIA.
JUST PURCHASED A 10.5 MILLON DOLLAR APARTMENT IN THIS BUILDING.
WE LIKE THE NEIGHBORHOOD'S MIX OF DOWNTRODDEN AND MONEYED FAMILIES...
AND THE TUBERCULAR STREET PEOPLE.
AS THE NEWLYWEDS PREPARE FOR BED, THE CROWD GROWS IN SIZE.
DON'T DO IT!
THE LIKLIHOOD OF THEIR HAVING MORE THAN ONE CHILD WHO WILL PERPETUATE THEIR LIFESTYLE IS VERY HIGH.
SHE'S SEEING A FERTILITY SPECIALIST.
REVOLUTIONARY LEADERS SOMETIMES COME FROM THE UPPER CLASSES.
DON'T HOLD YOUR BREATH.
THE YET TO BE CONCEIVED CHILD HAS ALREADY BEEN ENROLLED IN A NEIGHBORHOOD NURSERY SCHOOL.
THEIR REPRODUCTIVE RIGHTS ARE SCREWING 7.4 BILLION PEOPLE.
AND, UNDER AN EARLY ADMISSIONS POLICY, THE SAME CHILD HAS BEEN ACCEPTED BY THE PALZEE PRIVATE MILITARY ACADEMY.
HAVEN'T YOU GUYS HEARD OF BIRTH CONTROL?
THE ICE-CAPS ARE MELTING!
NOT TONIGHT
THE CHANTING OF THE ANGRY CROWD PENETRATES THEIR SOUNDPROOF WINDOWS.
THEY'RE OUT THERE AGAIN TONIGHT.
DON'T DO IT!
PLEASE, EUROPA, DON'T WORRY. THEY'D HAVE TO GET PAST THE POLICE AND THE DOORMAN.
BUT HE'S NOT ARMED.
THE THREAT OF THE MOB, WITH ITS CRUDELY LETTERED PLACARDS, TITILATES THE YOUNG WOMAN.
COME, MORGAN, LET'S GO TO BED.
DON'T DO IT!
NOT TONIGHT!
OH, MORGAN!
OH, EUROPA!

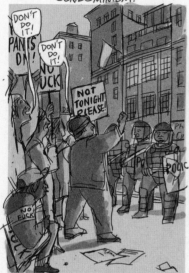

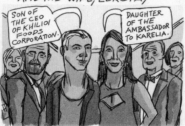

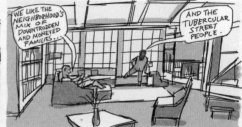

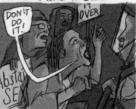

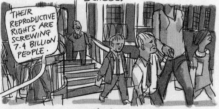

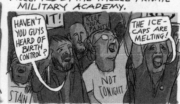

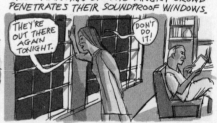

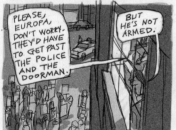

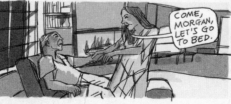

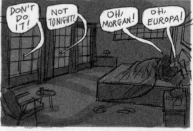

DETROIT ROOTS

Bec Young

I moved to Detroit at 22 after I read Detroit: I Do Mind Dying.

I got involved with a community bike shop, developing programs for kids and teens.

We drew "life wheels" while we waited for patch glue to dry.
Mechanics mend spokes
So they run "true"
Wobbly spokes are areas of difficulty.
Kids tend to be honest.

Detroit activism:

sovereignty
food
water
housing
safety
transportation

(the basics)

school
dad
BIKES
Neighbor hood
brother
school
Garden
sister
bike life

The wobbly neighborhood spoke
made me think of the damaged and
abandoned houses on every block.

My perceptions of them
changed over time.

Or, really, I was changed by them.

There is beauty in the ruins you have to know how to look.

Open space equals possibilities.

But these houses belonged to people.

Who were forced out by racist housing policies...

redlining, zoning, overassessment of property taxes, defacto segregation, destruction of neighborhoods for highways, forclosure...

The anarchists like to quote Durruti:

"We are not in the least afraid of ruins, we carry a new world here in our hearts"

I am afraid, though, afraid of the despair waiting for me

around every corner

I grasp at dignity like the single porch post

I feel empathy for the broken, wounded places.

Then only numbness

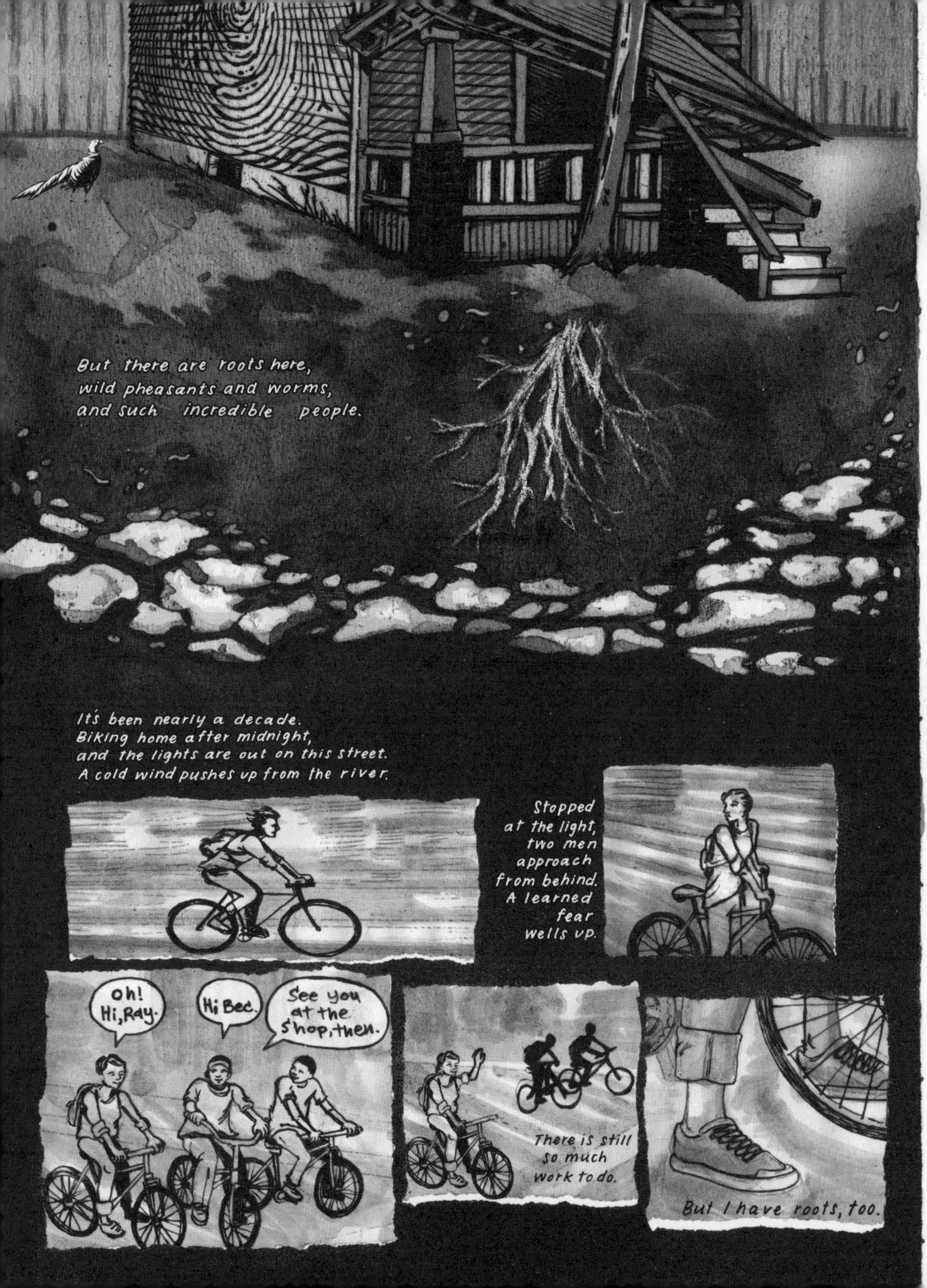
But there are roots here,
wild pheasants and worms,
and such incredible people.
It's been nearly a decade.
Biking home after midnight,
and the lights are out on this street.
A cold wind pushes up from the river.
Stopped at the light, two men approach from behind. A learned fear wells up.
Oh! Hi, Ray.
Hi Bec.
See you at the shop, then.
There is still so much work to do.
But I have roots, too.

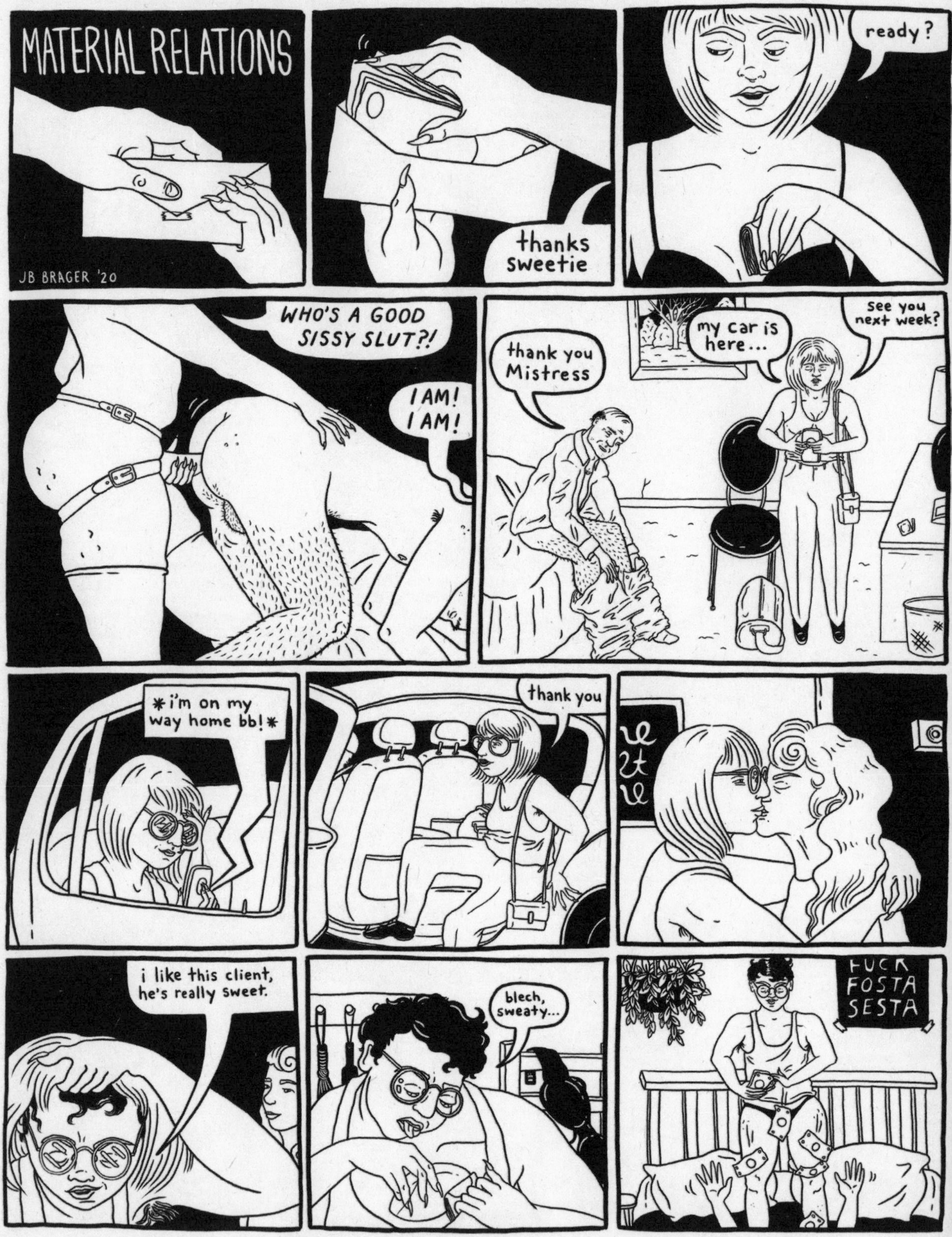
MATERIAL RELATIONS
JB BRAGER '20
thanks sweetie
ready?
WHO'S A GOOD SISSY SLUT?!
I AM! I AM!
thank you Mistress
my car is here...
see you next week?
i'm on my way home bb!
thank you
i like this client, he's really sweet.
blech, sweaty...
FUCK FOSTA SESTA

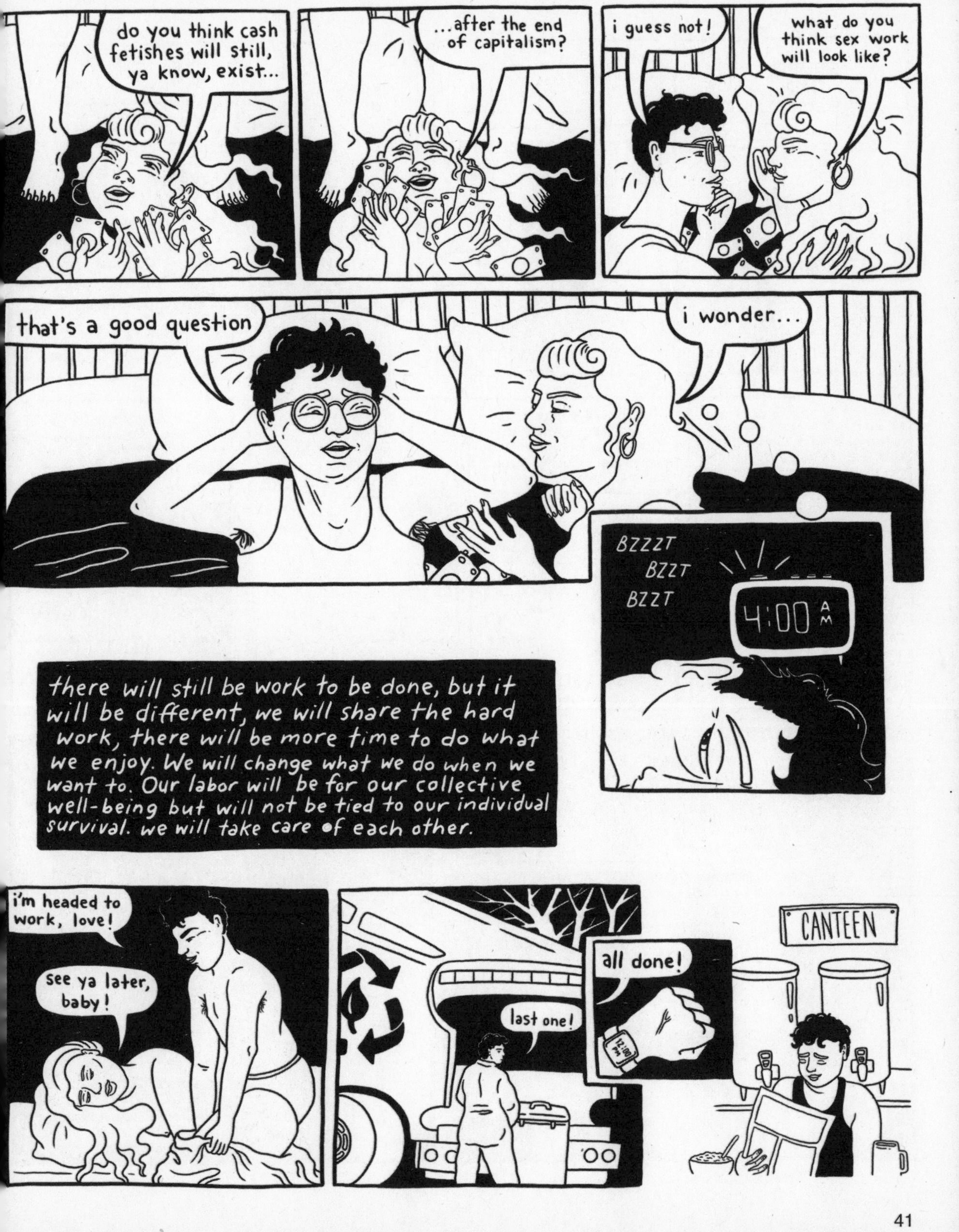

do you think cash fetishes will still, ya know, exist...
...after the end of capitalism?
i guess not!
what do you think sex work will look like?
that's a good question
i wonder...
BZZZT
BZZT
BZZT
4:00 AM
there will still be work to be done, but it will be different, we will share the hard work, there will be more time to do what we enjoy. We will change what we do when we want to. Our labor will be for our collective well-being but will not be tied to our individual survival. we will take care of each other.
i'm headed to work, love!
see ya later, baby!
last one!
all done!
12:00 PM
CANTEEN

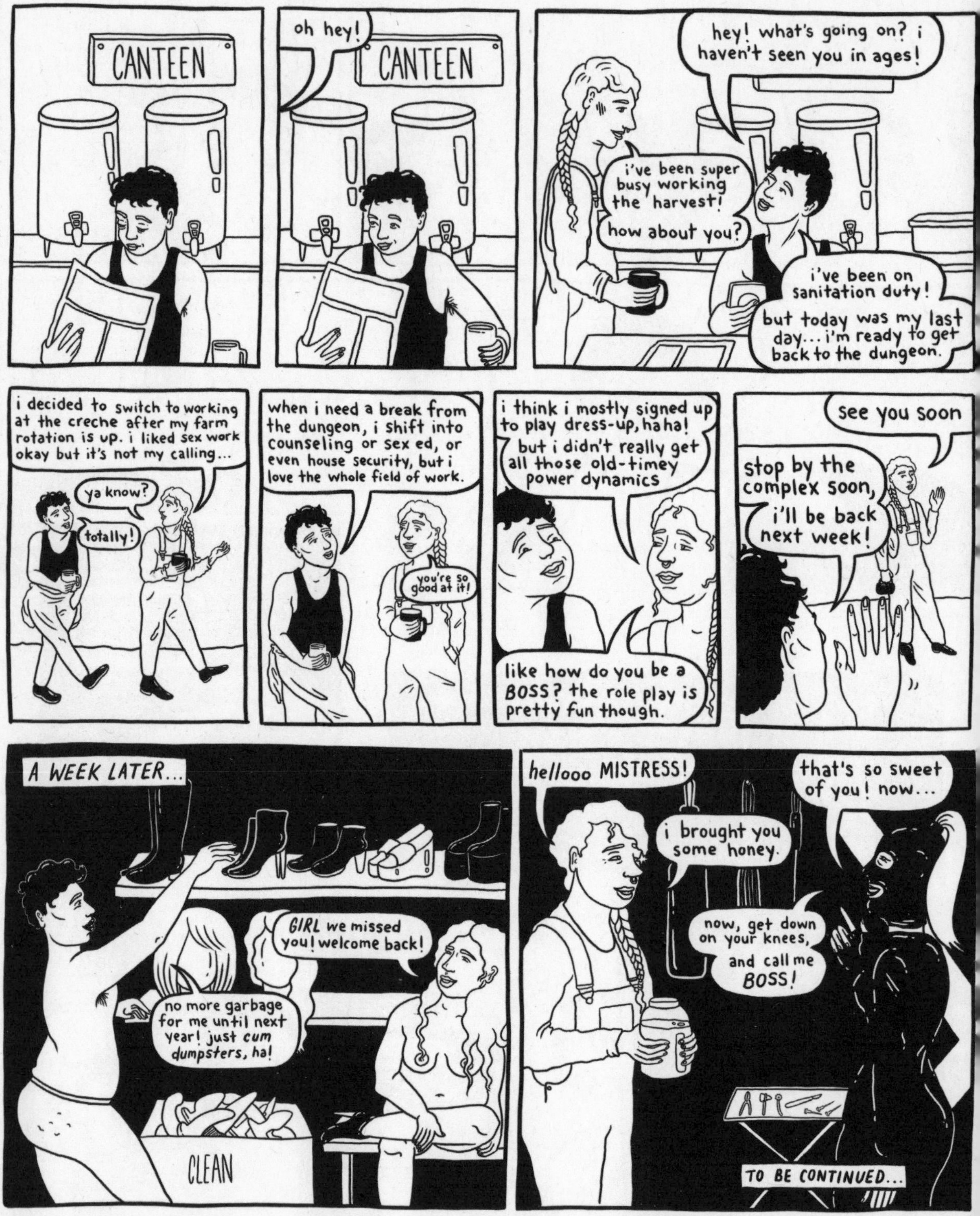
CANTEEN
oh hey!
CANTEEN
hey! what's going on? i haven't seen you in ages!
i've been super busy working the harvest!
how about you?
i've been on sanitation duty!
but today was my last day... i'm ready to get back to the dungeon.
i decided to switch to working at the creche after my farm rotation is up. i liked sex work okay but it's not my calling...
ya know?
totally!
when i need a break from the dungeon, i shift into counseling or sex ed, or even house security, but i love the whole field of work.
you're so good at it!
i think i mostly signed up to play dress-up, haha!
but i didn't really get all those old-timey power dynamics
like how do you be a BOSS? the role play is pretty fun though.
see you soon
stop by the complex soon,
i'll be back next week!
A WEEK LATER...
GIRL we missed you! welcome back!
no more garbage for me until next year! just cum dumpsters, ha!
CLEAN
hellooo MISTRESS!
i brought you some honey.
that's so sweet of you! now...
now, get down on your knees, and call me BOSS!
TO BE CONTINUED...

THE CITY IS OURS!

text by Eric Laursen
art by Ethan Heitner

As the COVID-19 pandemic rages, tenants in New York City and around the country are getting mad, getting organized—and many are going on strike.

By early May, more than 640,000 tenants had stopped paying rent and were demanding rent cancellation, a rent freeze, and a moratorium on evictions, among other actions. By early June, almost 100,000 people had signed a petition to Governor Andrew Cuomo calling for a rent suspension.

The coronavirus turned a crisis into a catastrophe. More than a 26 million people filed for unemployment, and one study found that 16.5 million renter households had lost income because of the pandemic—more than 7 million of whom were struggling to pay rent even before the pandemic.

NEW YORK CITY TENANTS SHOCK THE REAL ESTATE BARONS!

Working households, many of them out of work, were having trouble meeting basic living costs, let alone pay the rent.

"Can't pay? Won't pay!"

But tenants, organizers, and their supporters in Congress and in Albany were ready. COVID-19 arrived at a moment when tenants are more organized and powerful than at any time in decades, and had just won a major victory against landlords.

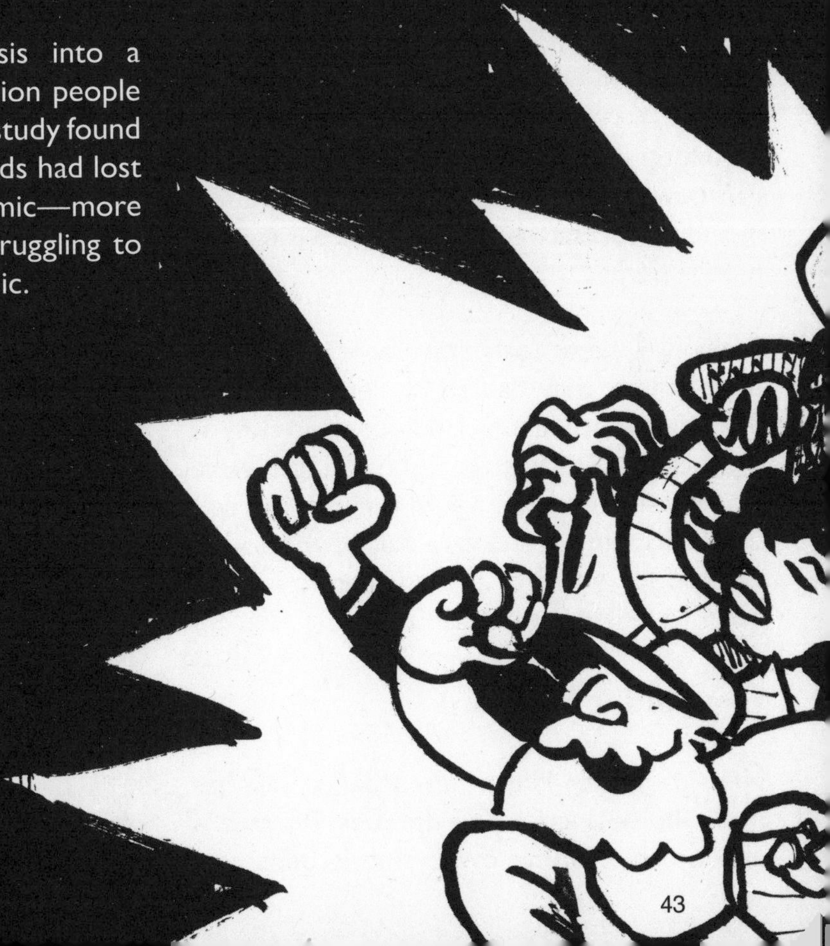

A coalition of housing activists shocked the political establishment when they pushed the Housing Stability and Tenant Protection Act of 2019 through the New York State Senate. The first pro-tenant reform to pass in the state in more than a half-century, it blindsided New York's powerful real estate interests. It was also the biggest in a series of successes for housing activists in other cities like Cleveland, San Francisco, Philadelphia, Newark, and Santa Monica.

The new law includes:
- Limits on security deposits!
- New protections against evictions!
- Prohibition of tenant blacklists!
- Elimination of vacancy decontrol and high-income deregulation!
- Limiting the amount that landlords can jack up rents to pay for major capital improvements!

Counties outside the New York City area can now choose to adopt rent stabilization, including for newer forms of housing like mobile homes.

Previously, New York State rent laws were time-limited; they had to be renewed every five years, which helped landlords chip away at protections. But this time, the changes were made permanent. Passage of the new law was the fulfillment of a dream for activists who worked for years to bring it about. It gives hope to tenants and organizers.

How did it happen?

New York City, like other urban areas, has had a housing crisis for decades. Rents are unaffordable. Home ownership is becoming unaffordable, too. Public housing is being privatized or allowed to deteriorate. People are being forced into homelessness, or forced to move out.

Even if you have a place to live, it costs most of your income to keep it: money you could have spent on education, transportation, or child care. That would have made you—and your community—more secure, more prosperous, and able to look forward to a better future for your children.

All this as the city grows richer and richer—for the 1%.

Landlord interests buy politicians, who bend the laws and regulations to serve property barons, not people. More high-end housing and fancy commercial space is being created than the city can absorb.

Public common spaces are being eliminated. Gentrification destroys low-income communities. Services for the homeless are being curtailed.

It's like the city is sending a message to the non-rich: "GET OUT!" But this time, people fought back effectively!

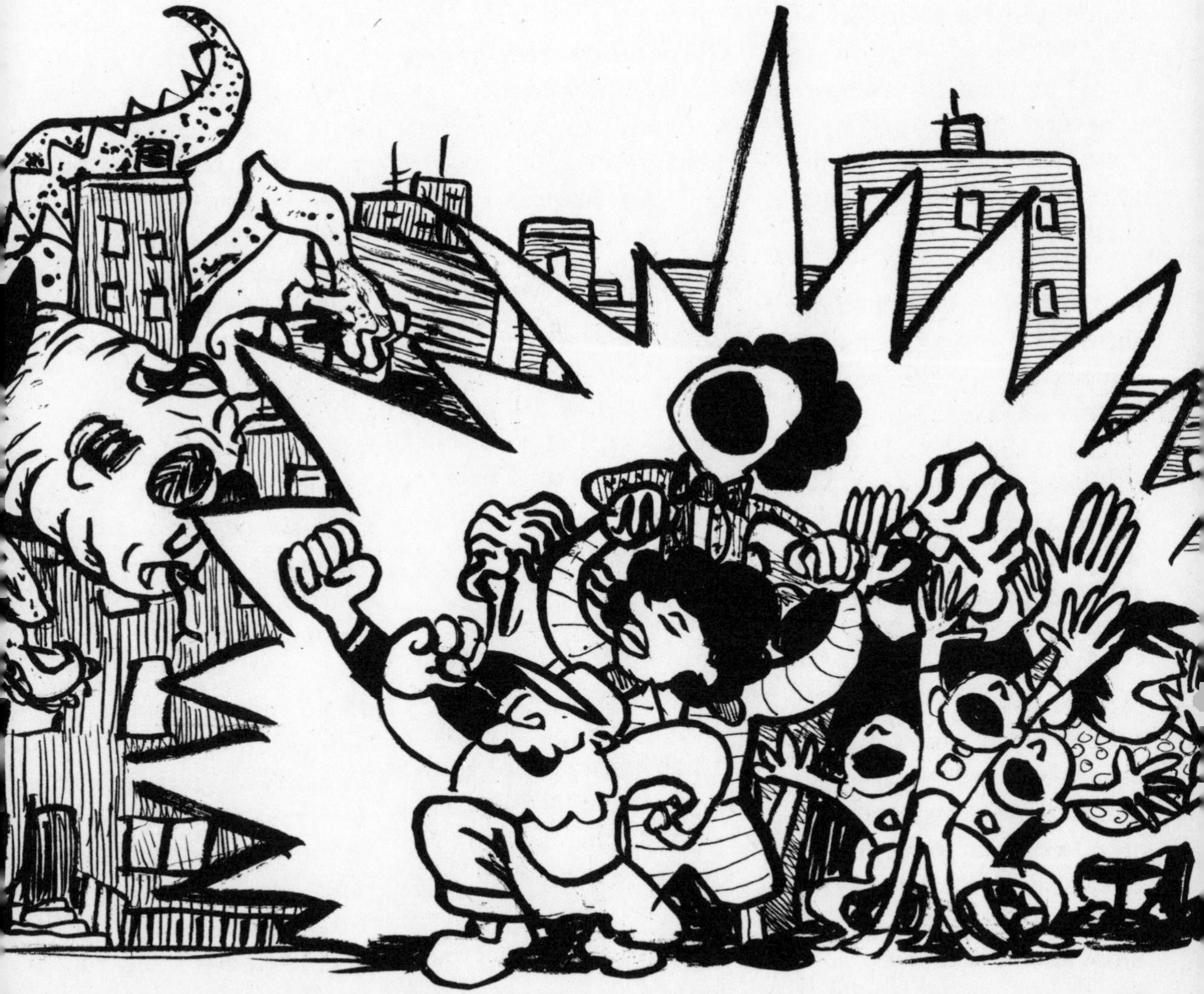

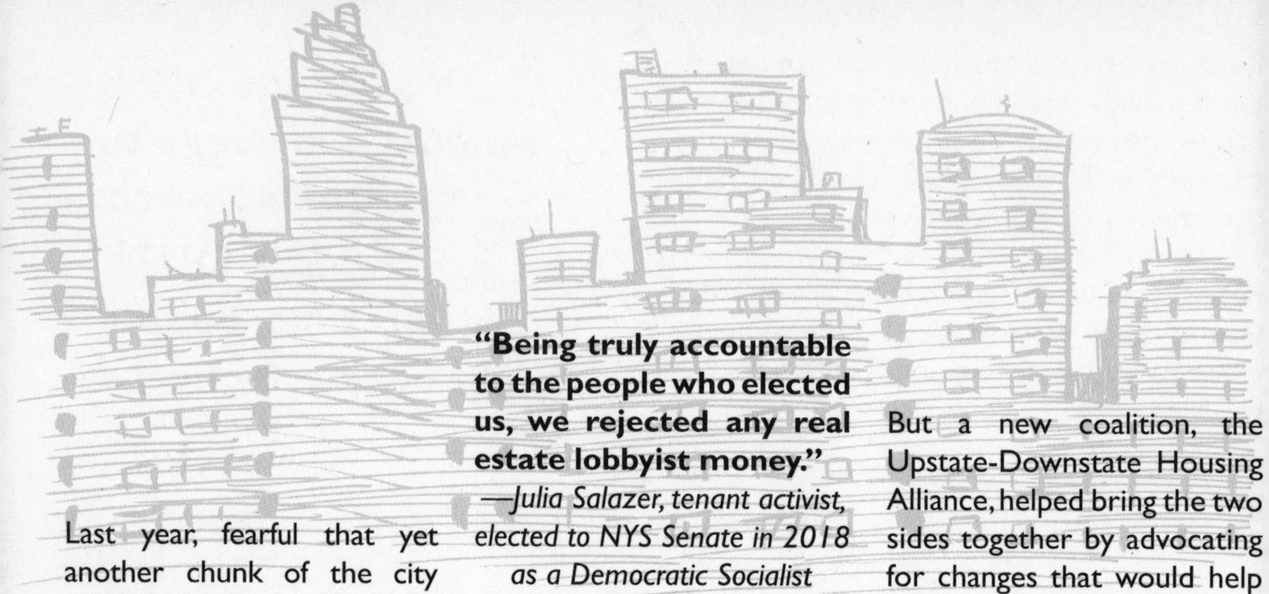

Last year, fearful that yet another chunk of the city would be lost to gentrification, activists forced Amazon to cancel its plans to take over a section of Queens for a new headquarters, despite strong establishment political support.

In 2017, New York became the first U.S. city to guarantee tenants the right to counsel in eviction cases. Other cities followed suit. A study found that evictions declined five times as fast in zip codes where tenants had a right to counsel, compared to those where they did not.

In 2018, outrage at gentrification helped elect a slew of new, pro-tenant lawmakers to the State Assembly and Senate. Democrats got control of the Senate for the first time in decades, laying the groundwork for the new law.

"Being truly accountable to the people who elected us, we rejected any real estate lobbyist money."
—Julia Salazer, tenant activist, elected to NYS Senate in 2018 as a Democratic Socialist

"The pendulum is swinging [against landlords]."
—Andrea Stewart-Cousins, Democratic majority leader, NYS Senate

It's always about organizing!

Tenants' rights groups and housing activists had been trying for years to reform the laws, without much success. What changed?

In New York State, the landlords had always benefited from an upstate/downstate-split; rent control and stabilization were always seen as issues in New York City and the surrounding counties—but nowhere else.

But a new coalition, the Upstate-Downstate Housing Alliance, helped bring the two sides together by advocating for changes that would help renters upstate.

"For the first time, tenants were coming to Albany and testifying about their experiences—and refusing to let legislators and real estate lobbyists push the myth that it's just a New York City issue."
—Julia Salazar

Meanwhile, those activists worked harder to get tenants directly involved in the campaign and they put forward candidates committed to housing reform.

More radical groups of tenants in places like Crown Heights changed the direction of the old coalitions, which at times had included groups that worked closely with real estate interests. They also started working to elect more progressive city and state lawmakers.

Landlords didn't see it coming. They thought they would have to make limited concessions that they could control. Then they thought Gov. Cuomo, who had always sided with them, would veto the bill.

But Cuomo, seeing the way the political wind was blowing, signed it anyway.

Tenants and organizers are learning tried-and-true lessons.

The struggle to get affordable housing has always been central to the fight for social justice.

People who grew up in public housing: Sonia Sotomayor Lloyd Blankfein Jimmy Carter Elvis Presley Jay-Z

On-the-ground-organizing, usually by people dismissed as radical, has always been vital.

In Vienna in 1927, the socialists would demand and then build, massive public housing, which would provide top quality homes for the working-class—and still does. In the U.S. during the New Deal era, the activists battled successfully for rent control and public housing became a reality.

But when grassroots organizing doesn't happen, real estate interests dominate. Powerful real estate developers, landlords, and property managers buy politicians, flout all the rules, and hide behind corporate structures.

What the landlords say:

Some of the most effective tools in the landlords arsenal are the think-tanks that publish "research" attempting to "prove" that rent control doesn't work and public housing is always substandard.

These think-tanks claim that rent control means landlords "can't make a profit."

Which, they say, leads to housing shortages, and makes it harder for landlords to maintain buildings.

Which, they theorize, leads to deteriorating and unhealthy housing for tenants.

They insist that this, is the reason, that landlords concentrate on the "uncontrolled" sector—that is, luxury apartments—leading to exactly the opposite of the result that affordable-housing advocates want.

"In many cases rent control appears to be the most efficient technique presently known to destroy a city—except for bombing."
—Swedish economist Assar Lindbeck, 1972

But none of this is true!

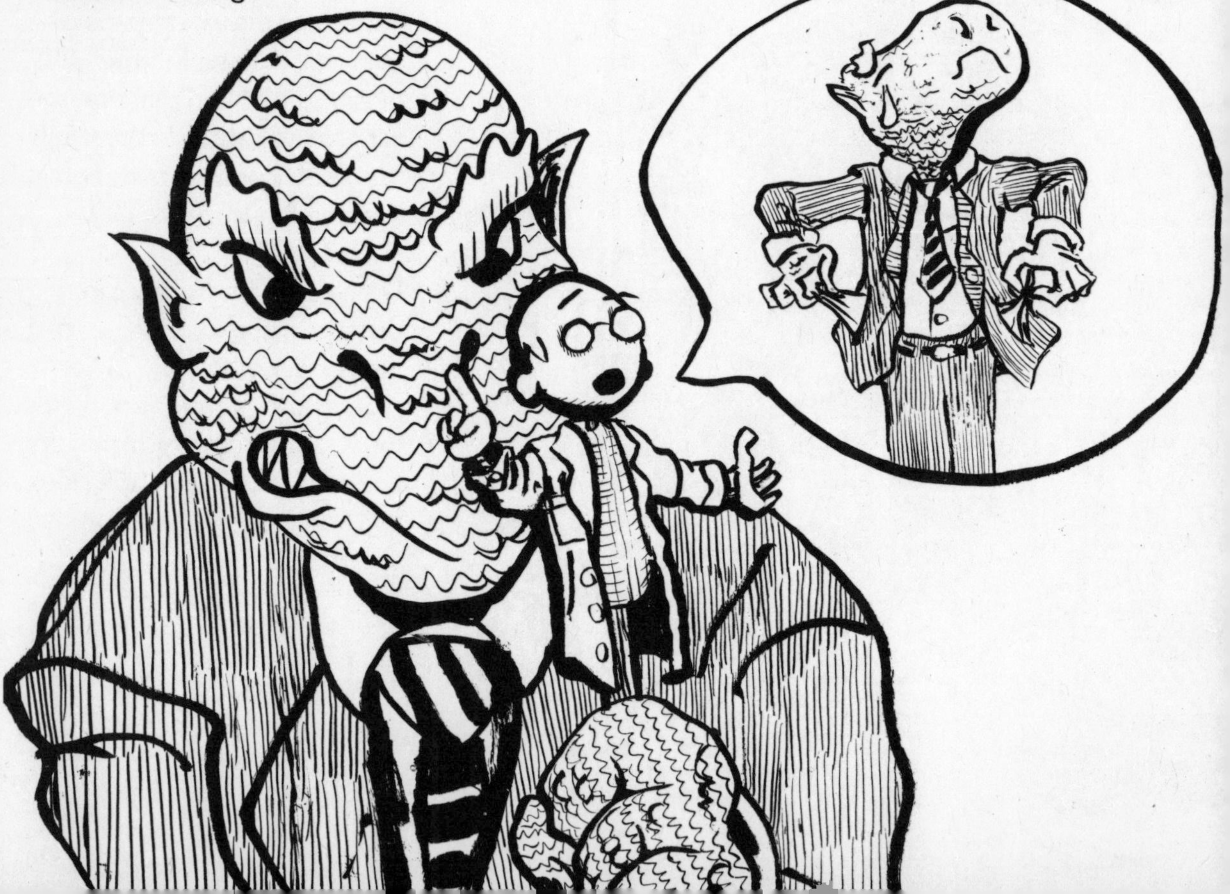

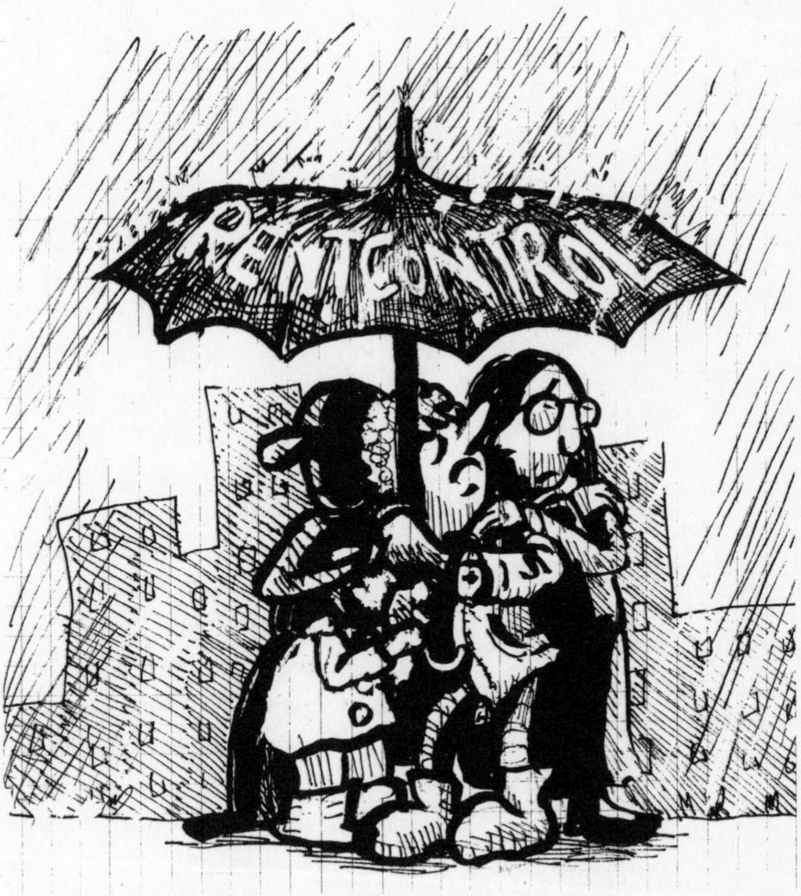
RENT CONTROL

Rent control helps maintain existing stocks of affordable housing.

Which increases residential stability andprotects tenants from eviction.

Which limits gentrification and encourages mixed income and mixed-age neighborhoods.

Even in New York, our stabilized rents are high enough that landlords can make needed repairs. If they don't, it is because they don't want to—and nobody is forcing them to.

Above all, it decreases racial disparities in income and wealth, by letting low-income people keep more of their earnings for education, transit, and child care, which helps them rise in the world.

It helps keep supportive, low-income communities together, and that helps them to rise together.

It enables the elderly to age in place, with their families and friends.

So what do we do next?

COVID-19 has made housing reform more urgent than ever. Tenants are using credit cards to cover their rent bills. Many small landlords face foreclosure if they can't pay their mortgages: losing what is often their only asset.

Salazar proposed a bill in the State Senate that would reduce or cancel rent for both residential tenants and small-business renters, many of whom have also been hit hard.

Congresswoman Ilhan Omar (D-Minn.) introduced the Rent and Mortgage Cancellation Act, which transfers landlords' mortgages to the federal government and recoups rent losses—if they agreed to a rent freeze and give up on collecting back rents from the lockdown period.

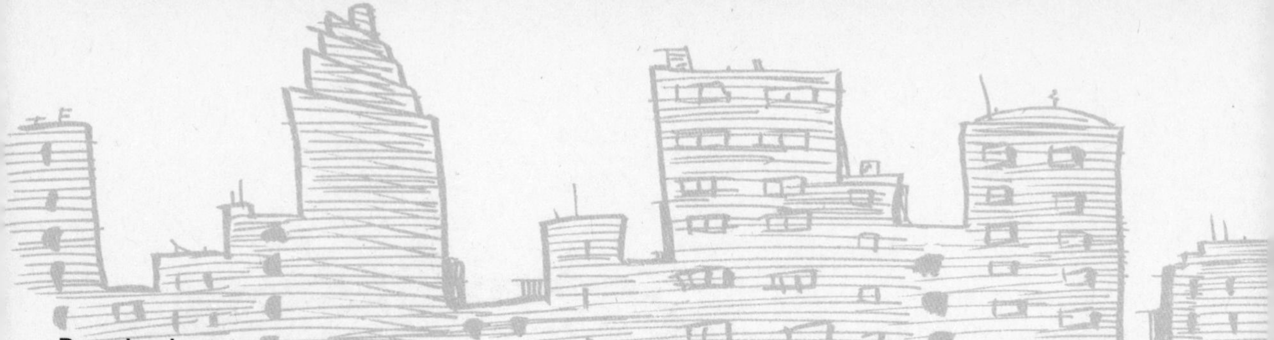

But the housing crisis will continue after the virus is tamed. More grassroots-organizing, and more direct action, will be needed.

"We're demanding that we not return to the world we lived in pre-COVID—a world with 92,000 homeless New Yorkers and millions of people living just one paycheck away from an eviction."

—Cea Weaver, campaign coordinator, Housing Justice for All

The new housing law must be enforced. Officials have got to be appointed who have the people's welfare, not real estate profits, at heart, and the state's Tenant Protection Unit needs the funding and resources to do its job.

Tenants have to educate themselves about the new law, their new rights, and how to make sure they're honored.

"Tenants need to be included in the process. They need to be prepared to enforce their own rights."

—Emily Goldstein, director of organizing and advocacy for the Association for Neighborhood and Housing Development

We still need a "good cause" eviction law, which would have made it more difficult for landlords to remove tenants except for misdeeds. It was supposed to be in the new law last year, but supporters in the State Senate couldn't get enough of their colleagues support it. They're trying again this year.

"It's not just about eliminating vacancy bonuses. Nobody should live in fear of losing their place to live. Everybody has to have the right to renew a lease."

—Cea Weaver

Brokers dominate the rental market, and charge exorbitant fees. When the state barred them from charging broker fees on rentals earlier this year, they pushed new tenants to pay anyway, then got a judge to block the rule. Lawmakers must find a way to stop this abusive practice.

Ever since a landmark court case in 1979, New York City has been required to provide shelter and board for the homeless. The city has violated the consent decree it signed and has attacked the "right to shelter" over and over. Lawmakers need to make it part of the law.

Property tax laws need to be reformed, closing loopholes that enable real estate developers and managers to hide much of their profits.

Even with all this, the need for more affordable housing is far more than the commercial market can handle. We need

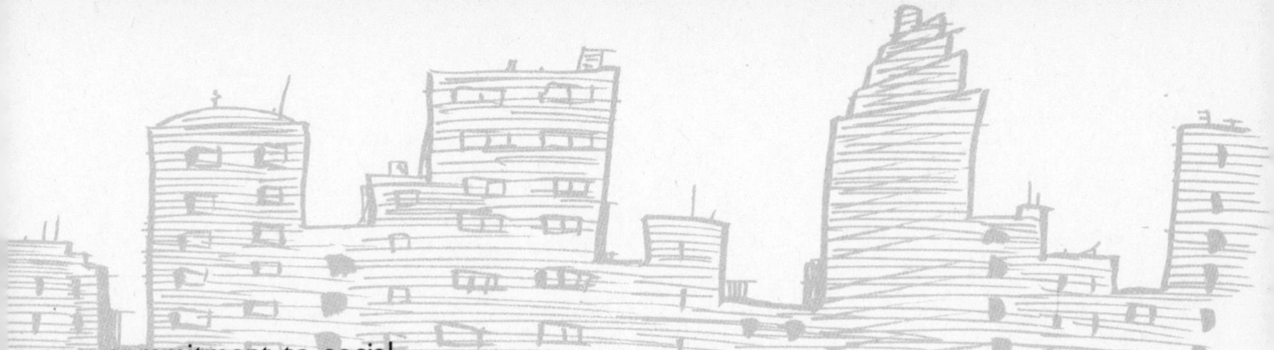

a new commitment to social housing, throwing out the failed policy of relying on tax incentives to coax private interests to build more affordable units, like Section 8 housing. Real money needs to committed to fixing existing facilities and building new ones—and much of it will have to come from Washington.

"And there has to be some form of accountability. Social housing should be controlled democratically by the residents."

—Cea Weaver

We need a new commitment to subsidized housing to combat homelessness.

"We need to fundamentally shift from temporary fixes, like homeless shelters, to permanent ones."

—Julia Salazar

To get all of this done, tenants and activists also need to take a wider look at how policy is made—not just tenant and housing law.

"If you have good tenant protections, but land use policy still encourages speculation, it doesn't add up for people who need affordable housing."

—Emily Goldstein

The Housing Stability and Tenant Protection Act is a great start for all of this, especially the vacancy control and rent-increase provisions. That's because they make it harder for a landlord to "buy low and sell high" and therefore help get the speculative money out of housing that results in escalating property values—and rents.

"Getting the speculative money out is a precondition to considering much more creative things."

—Sam Stein, former tenant activist and author,
Capital City: Gentrification and the Real Estate State.

Of course, landlords are not taking this lying down. They're going to court with lawsuits aimed at overturning the new law. Tenant activists must be ready to fight the backlash and to preserve their gains.

Housing is a human right!

The best thing about New York rent law reform is that does recognize this basic principle. But it's also good economics. Communities do not prosper in the long run when housing is being commodified and treated as a luxury; too many people are too busy paying rent to pursue education, good jobs, and proper care for their children.

"Our purpose is to bring stability and to empower people who've had to live precariously, without security, which affects every aspect of your life."

—*Julia Salazar*

Democracy suffers when real estate interests are more powerful than people's interests.

Passage of the Housing Stability and Tenant Protection Act shows us that good housing policy doesn't happen from the top down. It is crafted from the bottom up, starting with grassroots organizing. The COVID rent strike keeps us on that road.

Groups that are making this happen:

Association for Neighborhood and Housing Development
VOCAL-NY
Community Service Society of New York
Housing Justice for All Coalition
Legal Aid Society of New York
New York Communities for Change
Tenants Political Action Committee
Upstate-Downstate Housing Alliance
Community Voices Heard
Housing Rights Initiative
Make the Road New York
Right to the City Alliance
The Action Network
Metropolitan Council on Housing

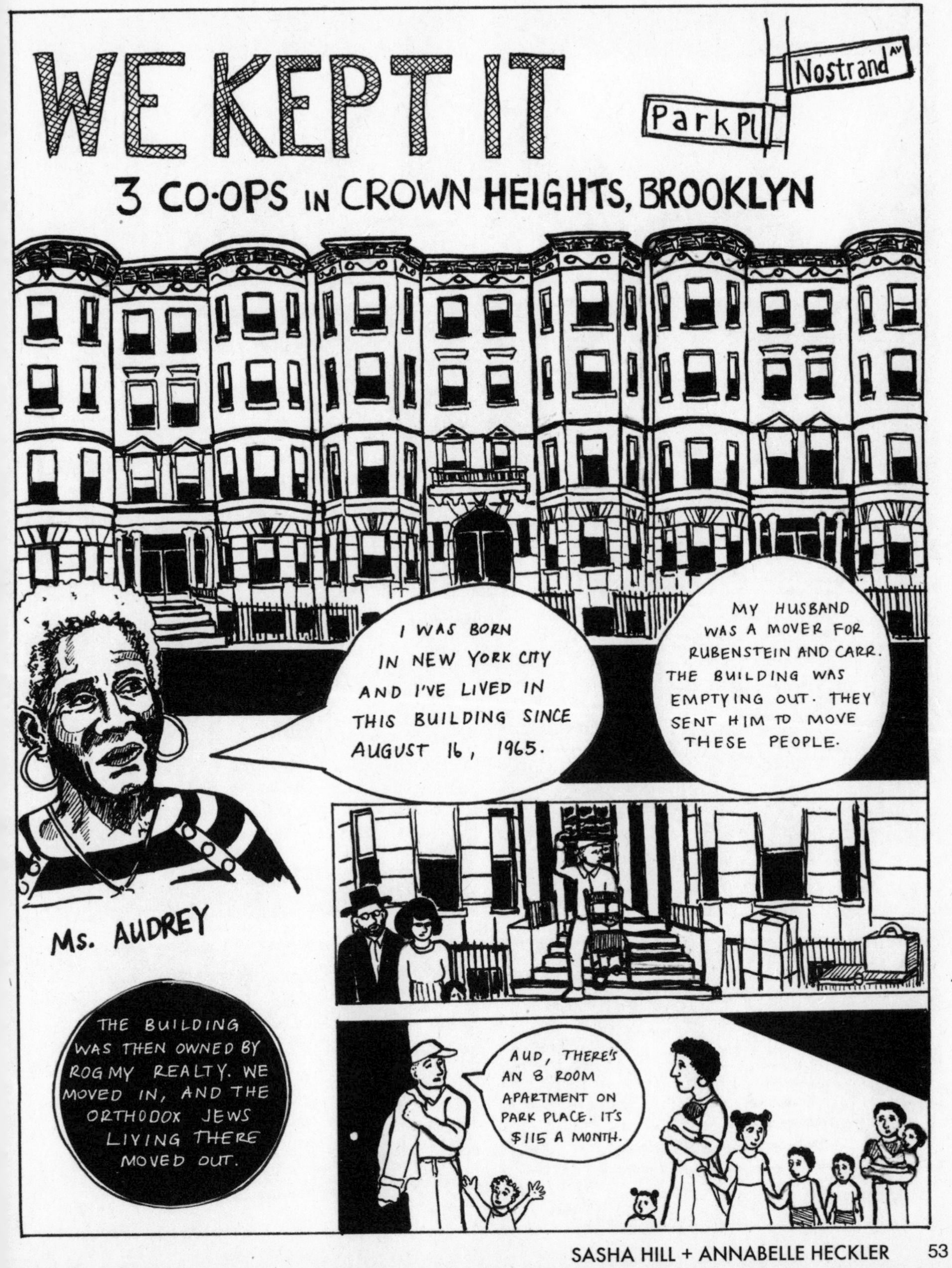
WE KEPT IT
Nostrand AV
Park Pl
3 CO-OPS IN CROWN HEIGHTS, BROOKLYN
Ms. AUDREY
I WAS BORN IN NEW YORK CITY AND I'VE LIVED IN THIS BUILDING SINCE AUGUST 16, 1965.
MY HUSBAND WAS A MOVER FOR RUBENSTEIN AND CARR. THE BUILDING WAS EMPTYING OUT. THEY SENT HIM TO MOVE THESE PEOPLE.
THE BUILDING WAS THEN OWNED BY ROGMY REALTY. WE MOVED IN, AND THE ORTHODOX JEWS LIVING THERE MOVED OUT.
AUD, THERE'S AN 8 ROOM APARTMENT ON PARK PLACE. IT'S $115 A MONTH.

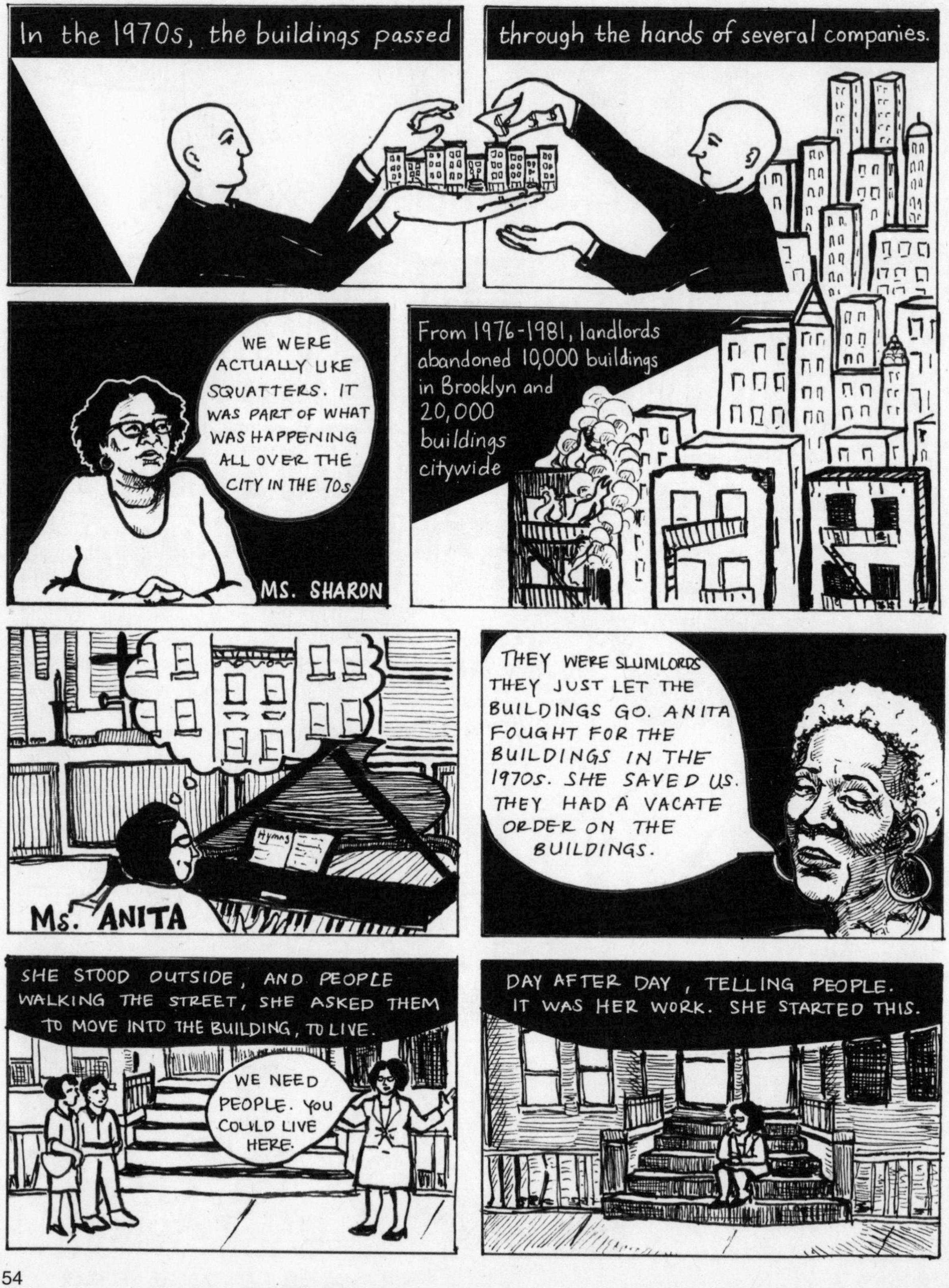
In the 1970s, the buildings passed
through the hands of several companies.
WE WERE ACTUALLY LIKE SQUATTERS. IT WAS PART OF WHAT WAS HAPPENING ALL OVER THE CITY IN THE 70s
MS. SHARON
From 1976-1981, landlords abandoned 10,000 buildings in Brooklyn and 20,000 buildings citywide
Hymns
Ms. ANITA
THEY WERE SLUMLORDS THEY JUST LET THE BUILDINGS GO. ANITA FOUGHT FOR THE BUILDINGS IN THE 1970s. SHE SAVED US. THEY HAD A VACATE ORDER ON THE BUILDINGS.
SHE STOOD OUTSIDE, AND PEOPLE WALKING THE STREET, SHE ASKED THEM TO MOVE INTO THE BUILDING, TO LIVE.
WE NEED PEOPLE. YOU COULD LIVE HERE.
DAY AFTER DAY, TELLING PEOPLE. IT WAS HER WORK. SHE STARTED THIS.

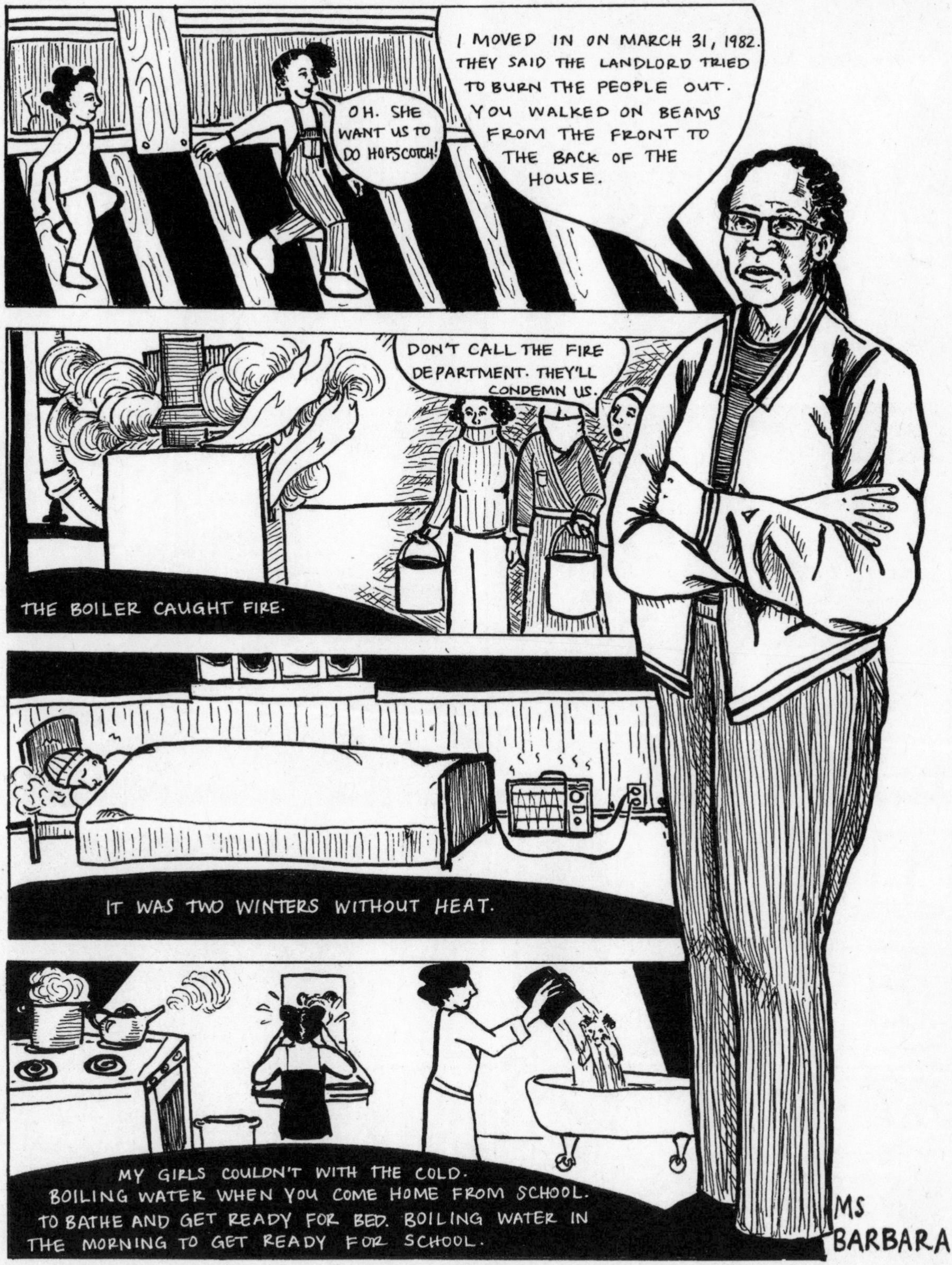
I MOVED IN ON MARCH 31, 1982. THEY SAID THE LANDLORD TRIED TO BURN THE PEOPLE OUT. YOU WALKED ON BEAMS FROM THE FRONT TO THE BACK OF THE HOUSE.
OH. SHE WANT US TO DO HOPSCOTCH!
THE BOILER CAUGHT FIRE.
DON'T CALL THE FIRE DEPARTMENT. THEY'LL CONDEMN US.
IT WAS TWO WINTERS WITHOUT HEAT.
MY GIRLS COULDN'T WITH THE COLD. BOILING WATER WHEN YOU COME HOME FROM SCHOOL. TO BATHE AND GET READY FOR BED. BOILING WATER IN THE MORNING TO GET READY FOR SCHOOL.
MS BARBARA

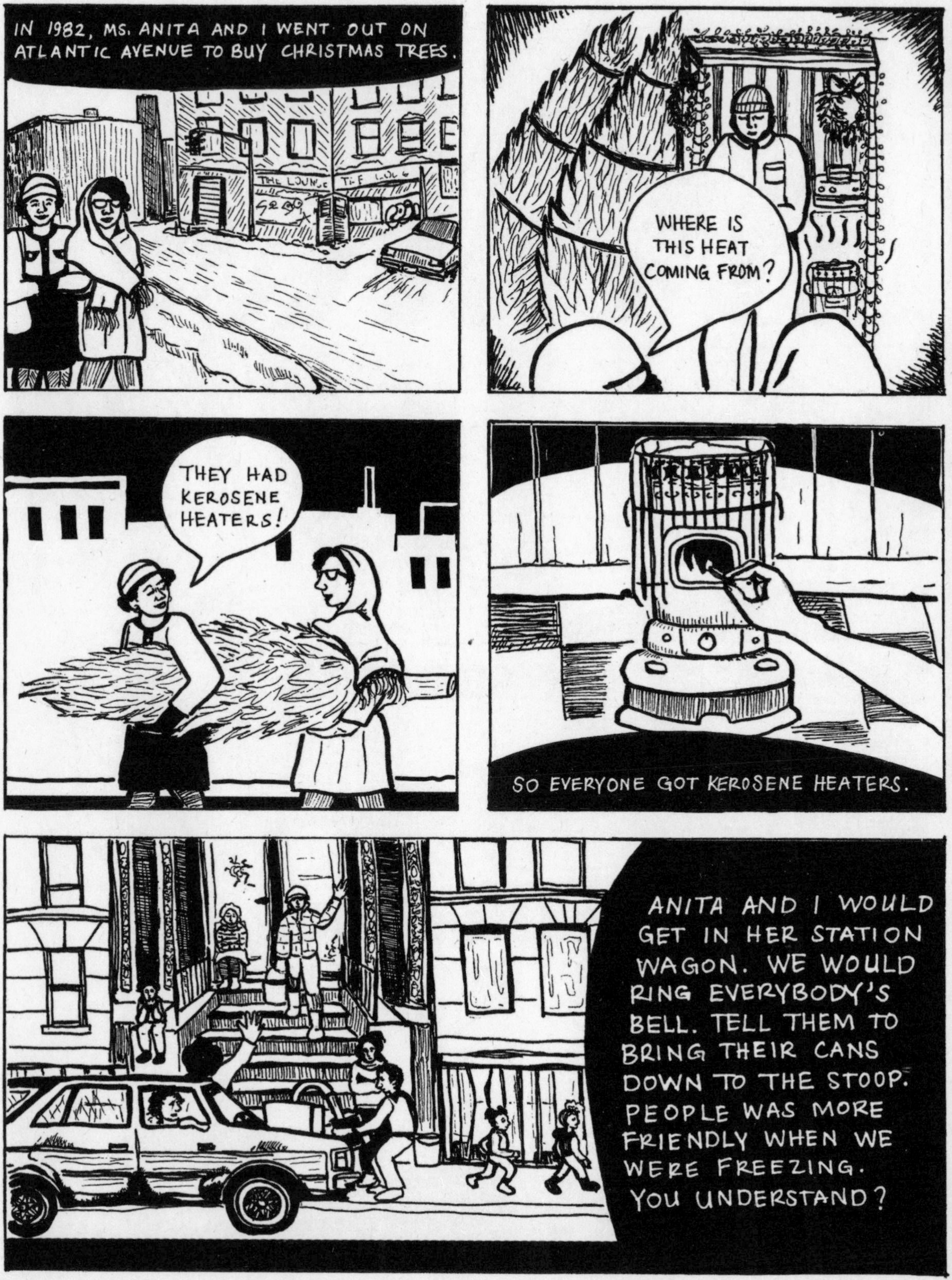
IN 1982, MS. ANITA AND I WENT OUT ON ATLANTIC AVENUE TO BUY CHRISTMAS TREES.
WHERE IS THIS HEAT COMING FROM?
THEY HAD KEROSENE HEATERS!
SO EVERYONE GOT KEROSENE HEATERS.
ANITA AND I WOULD GET IN HER STATION WAGON. WE WOULD RING EVERYBODY'S BELL. TELL THEM TO BRING THEIR CANS DOWN TO THE STOOP. PEOPLE WAS MORE FRIENDLY WHEN WE WERE FREEZING. YOU UNDERSTAND?

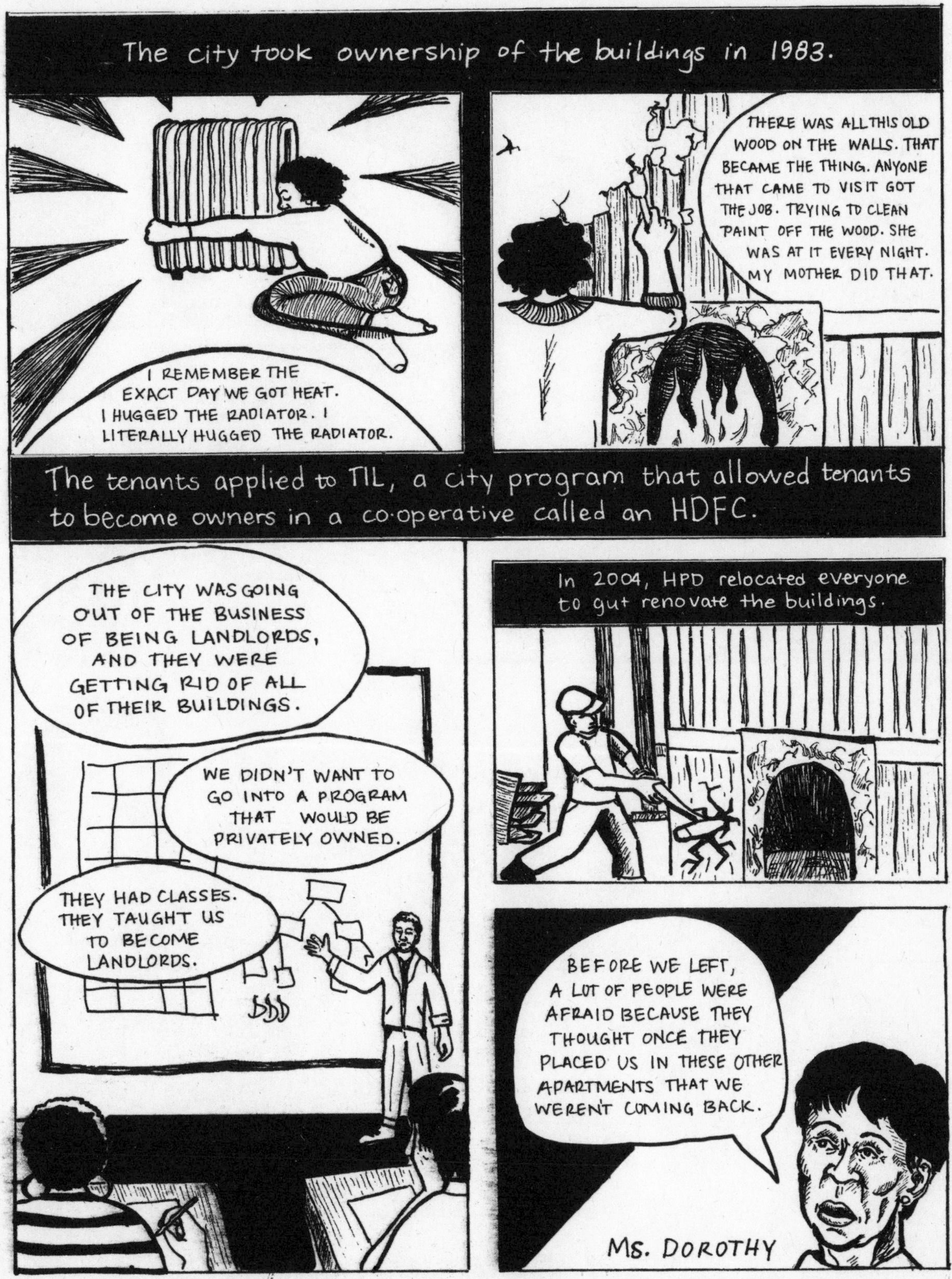
The city took ownership of the buildings in 1983.
I REMEMBER THE EXACT DAY WE GOT HEAT. I HUGGED THE RADIATOR. I LITERALLY HUGGED THE RADIATOR.
THERE WAS ALL THIS OLD WOOD ON THE WALLS. THAT BECAME THE THING. ANYONE THAT CAME TO VISIT GOT THE JOB. TRYING TO CLEAN PAINT OFF THE WOOD. SHE WAS AT IT EVERY NIGHT. MY MOTHER DID THAT.
The tenants applied to TIL, a city program that allowed tenants to become owners in a co-operative called an HDFC.
THE CITY WAS GOING OUT OF THE BUSINESS OF BEING LANDLORDS, AND THEY WERE GETTING RID OF ALL OF THEIR BUILDINGS.
WE DIDN'T WANT TO GO INTO A PROGRAM THAT WOULD BE PRIVATELY OWNED.
THEY HAD CLASSES. THEY TAUGHT US TO BECOME LANDLORDS.
In 2004, HPD relocated everyone to gut renovate the buildings.
BEFORE WE LEFT, A LOT OF PEOPLE WERE AFRAID BECAUSE THEY THOUGHT ONCE THEY PLACED US IN THESE OTHER APARTMENTS THAT WE WERENT COMING BACK.
MS. DOROTHY

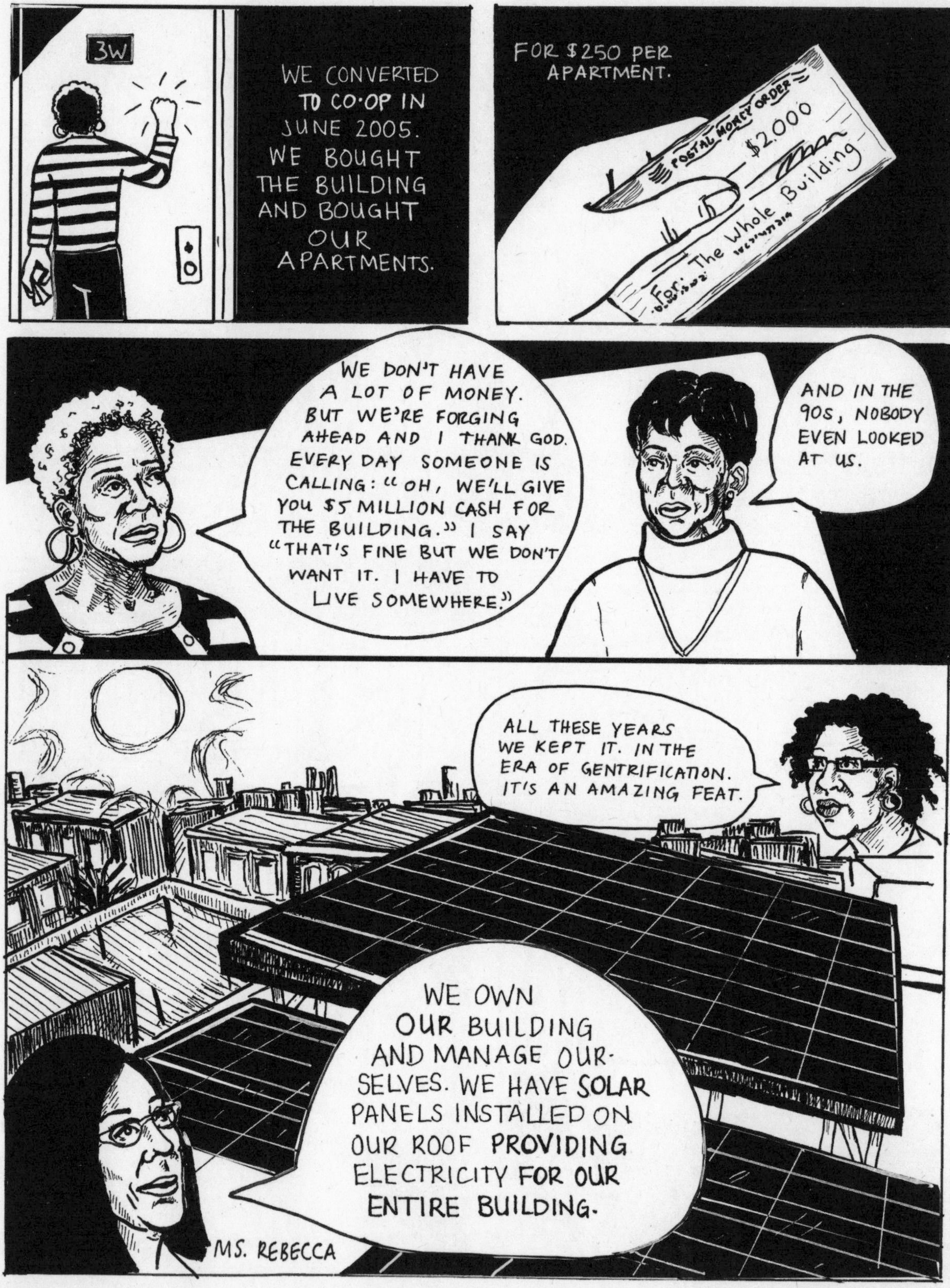
3W
WE CONVERTED TO CO·OP IN JUNE 2005. WE BOUGHT THE BUILDING AND BOUGHT OUR APARTMENTS.
FOR $250 PER APARTMENT.
POSTAL MONEY ORDER
$2,000
For: The Whole Building
WE DON'T HAVE A LOT OF MONEY. BUT WE'RE FORGING AHEAD AND I THANK GOD. EVERY DAY SOMEONE IS CALLING: "OH, WE'LL GIVE YOU $5 MILLION CASH FOR THE BUILDING." I SAY "THAT'S FINE BUT WE DON'T WANT IT. I HAVE TO LIVE SOMEWHERE."
AND IN THE 90S, NOBODY EVEN LOOKED AT US.
ALL THESE YEARS WE KEPT IT. IN THE ERA OF GENTRIFICATION. IT'S AN AMAZING FEAT.
WE OWN OUR BUILDING AND MANAGE OURSELVES. WE HAVE SOLAR PANELS INSTALLED ON OUR ROOF PROVIDING ELECTRICITY FOR OUR ENTIRE BUILDING.
MS. REBECCA

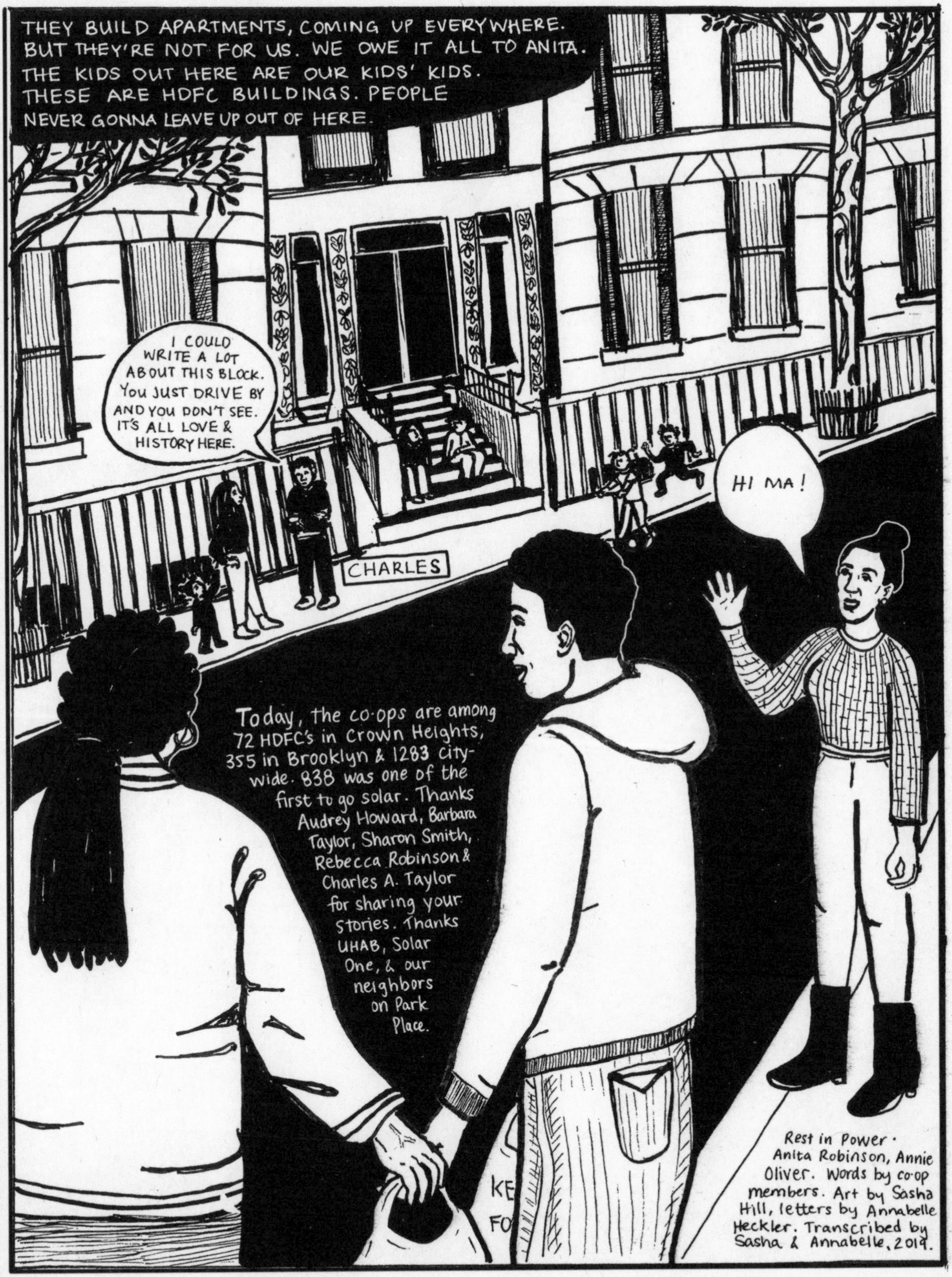
THEY BUILD APARTMENTS, COMING UP EVERYWHERE. BUT THEY'RE NOT FOR US. WE OWE IT ALL TO ANITA. THE KIDS OUT HERE ARE OUR KIDS' KIDS. THESE ARE HDFC BUILDINGS. PEOPLE NEVER GONNA LEAVE UP OUT OF HERE.
I COULD WRITE A LOT ABOUT THIS BLOCK. YOU JUST DRIVE BY AND YOU DON'T SEE. IT'S ALL LOVE & HISTORY HERE.
CHARLES
HI MA!
Today, the co-ops are among 72 HDFC's in Crown Heights, 355 in Brooklyn & 1283 city-wide. 838 was one of the first to go solar. Thanks Audrey Howard, Barbara Taylor, Sharon Smith, Rebecca Robinson & Charles A. Taylor for sharing your stories. Thanks UHAB, Solar One, & our neighbors on Park Place.
Rest in Power · Anita Robinson, Annie Oliver. Words by co-op members. Art by Sasha Hill, letters by Annabelle Heckler. Transcribed by Sasha & Annabelle, 2019.

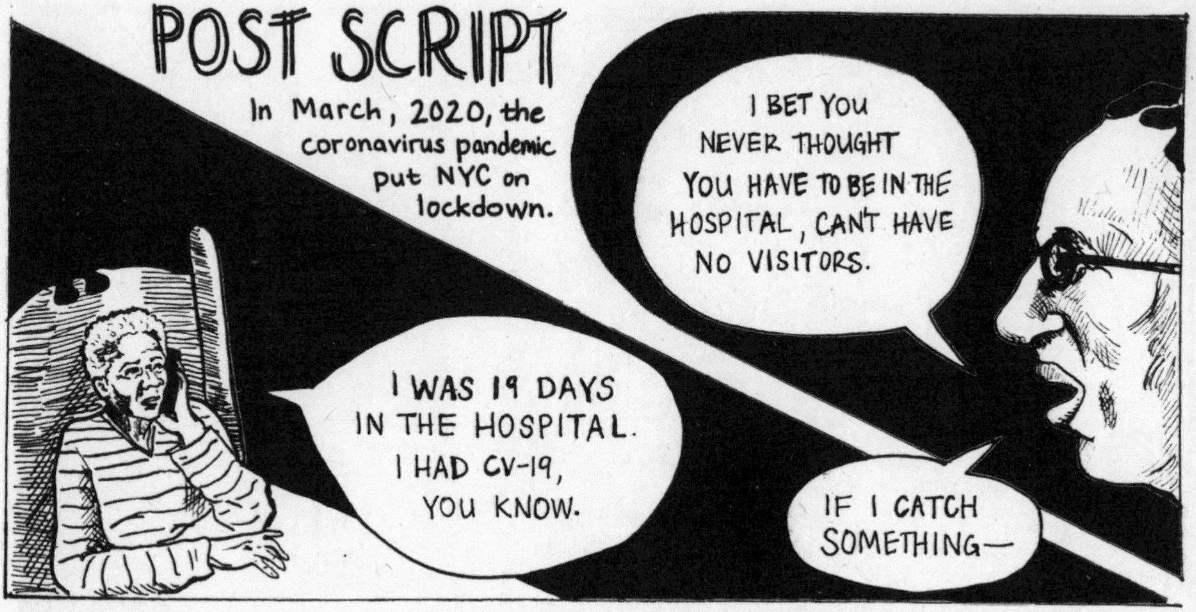
POST SCRIPT
In March, 2020, the coronavirus pandemic put NYC on lockdown.
I BET YOU NEVER THOUGHT YOU HAVE TO BE IN THE HOSPITAL, CAN'T HAVE NO VISITORS.
I WAS 19 DAYS IN THE HOSPITAL. I HAD CV-19, YOU KNOW.
IF I CATCH SOMETHING—

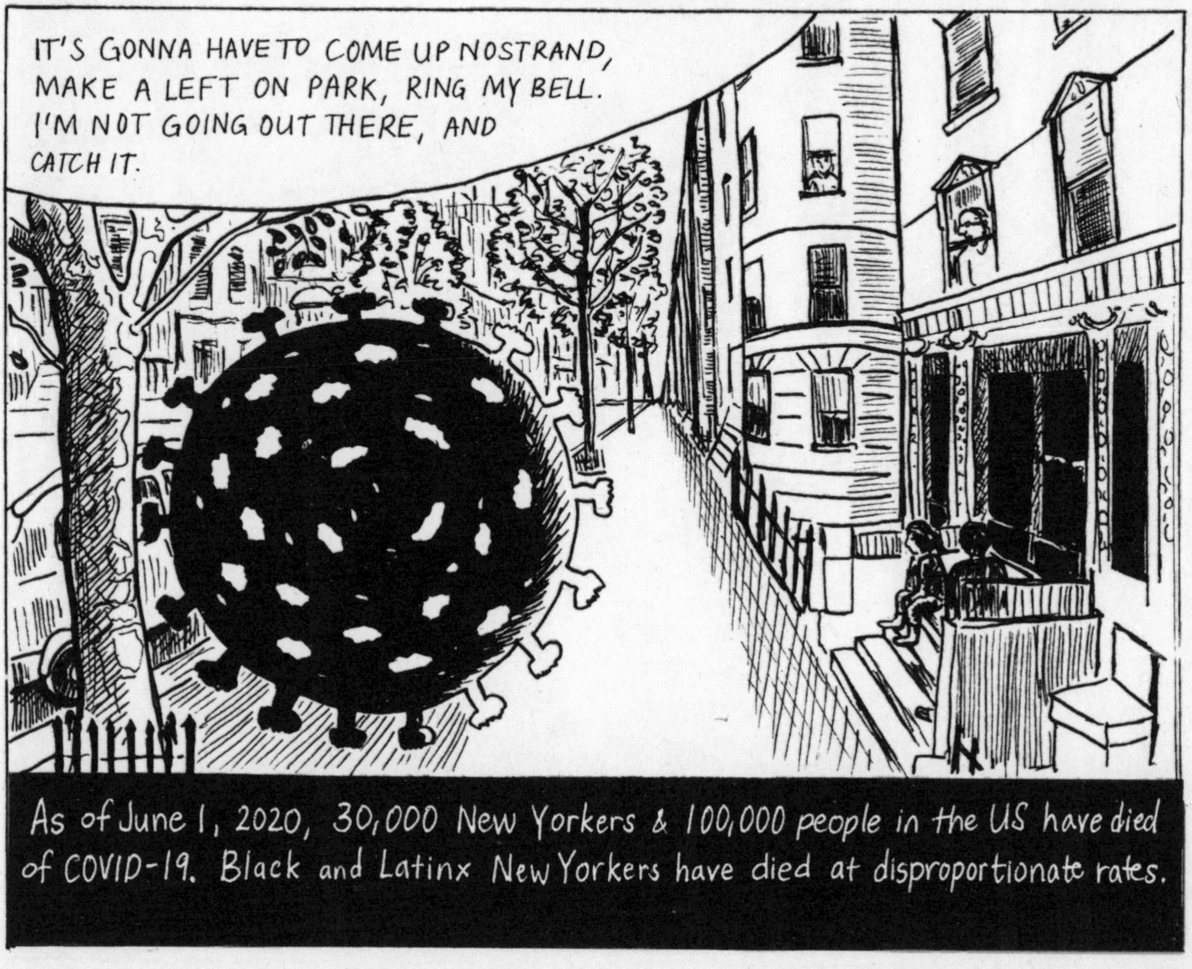
IT'S GONNA HAVE TO COME UP NOSTRAND, MAKE A LEFT ON PARK, RING MY BELL. I'M NOT GOING OUT THERE, AND CATCH IT.
As of June 1, 2020, 30,000 New Yorkers & 100,000 people in the US have died of COVID-19. Black and Latinx New Yorkers have died at disproportionate rates.

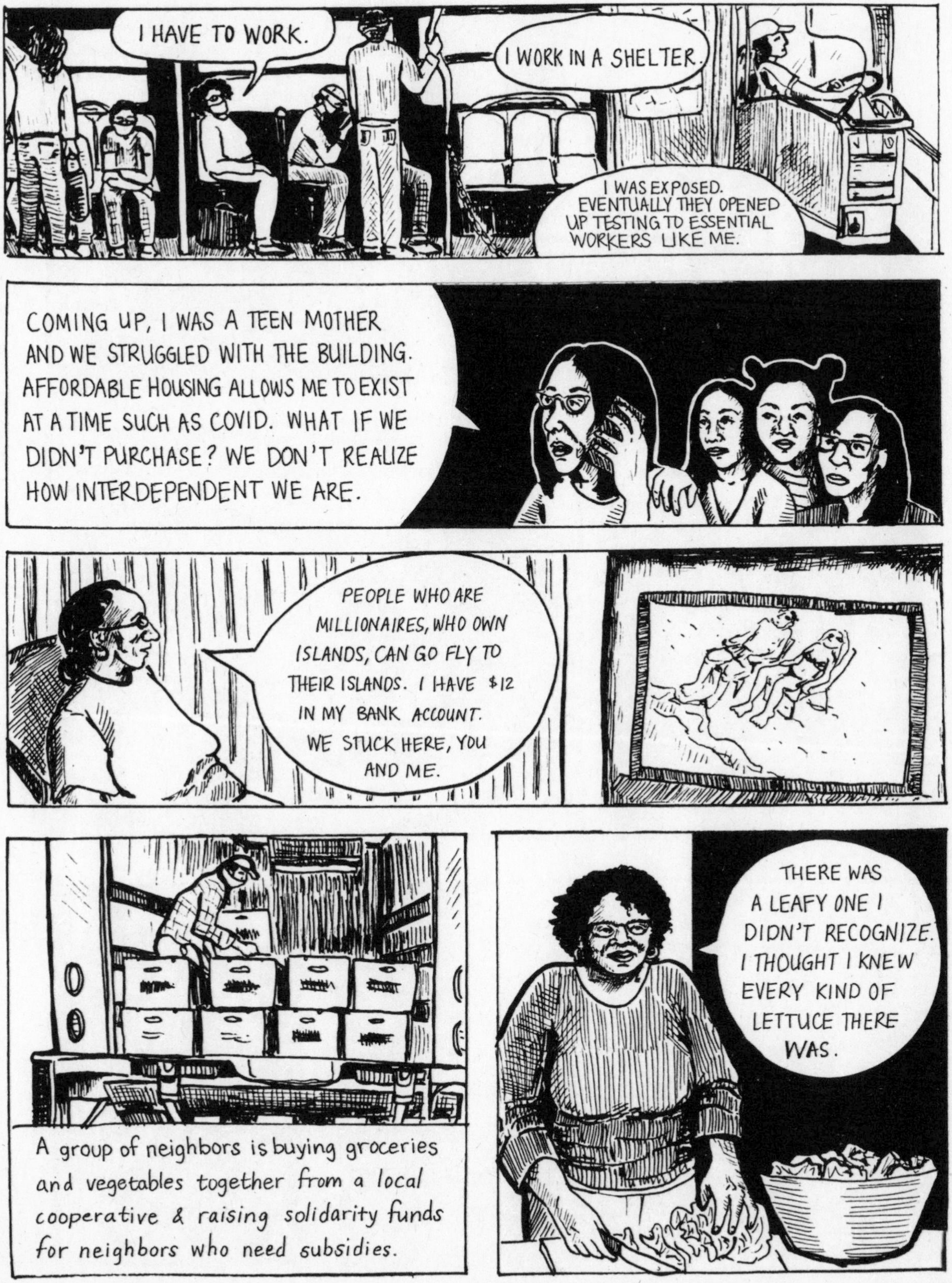
I HAVE TO WORK.
I WORK IN A SHELTER.
I WAS EXPOSED. EVENTUALLY THEY OPENED UP TESTING TO ESSENTIAL WORKERS LIKE ME.
COMING UP, I WAS A TEEN MOTHER AND WE STRUGGLED WITH THE BUILDING. AFFORDABLE HOUSING ALLOWS ME TO EXIST AT A TIME SUCH AS COVID. WHAT IF WE DIDN'T PURCHASE? WE DON'T REALIZE HOW INTERDEPENDENT WE ARE.
PEOPLE WHO ARE MILLIONAIRES, WHO OWN ISLANDS, CAN GO FLY TO THEIR ISLANDS. I HAVE $12 IN MY BANK ACCOUNT. WE STUCK HERE, YOU AND ME.
A group of neighbors is buying groceries and vegetables together from a local cooperative & raising solidarity funds for neighbors who need subsidies.
THERE WAS A LEAFY ONE I DIDN'T RECOGNIZE. I THOUGHT I KNEW EVERY KIND OF LETTUCE THERE WAS.

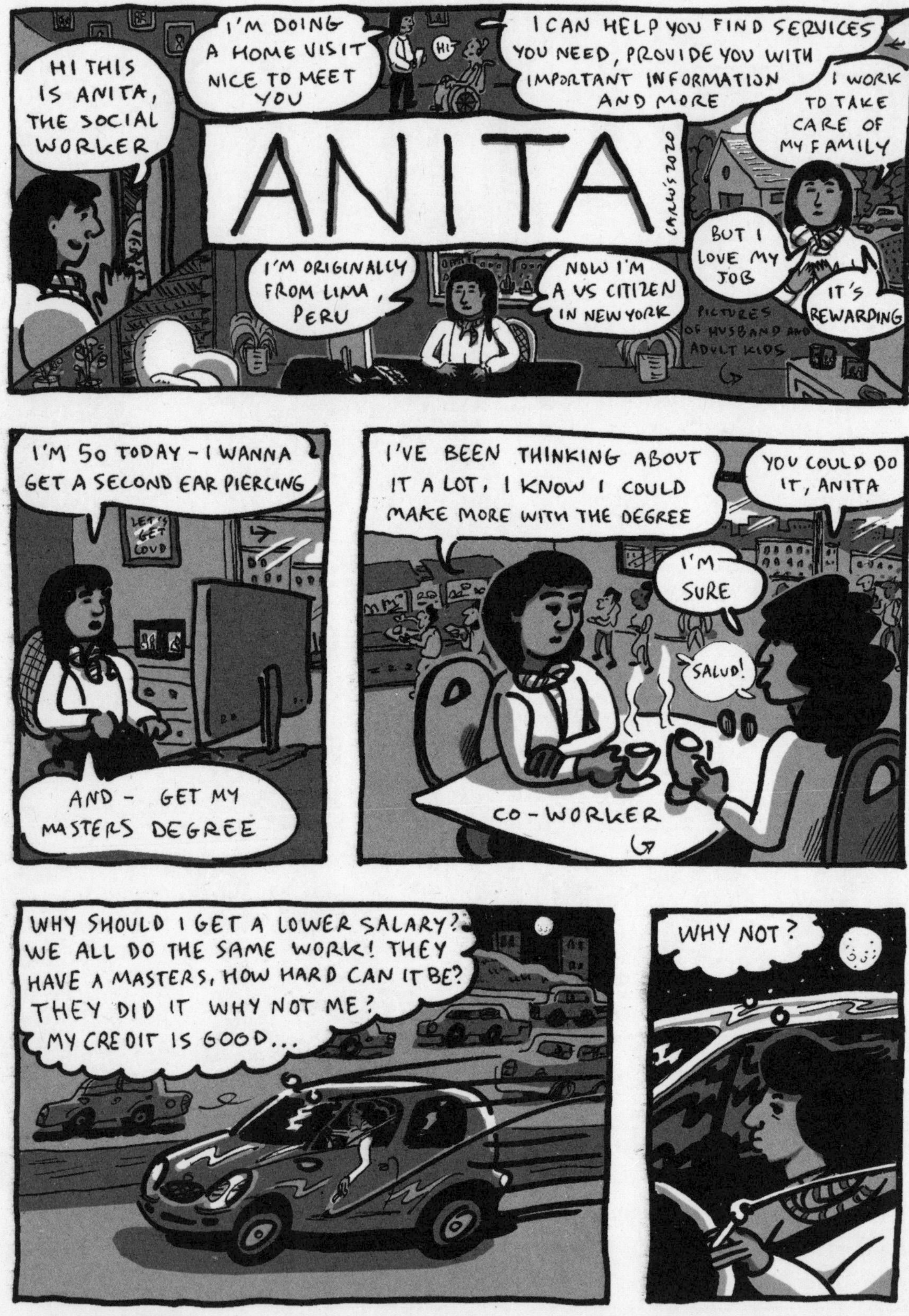
ANITA
CARLO'S 2020
HI THIS IS ANITA, THE SOCIAL WORKER
I'M DOING A HOME VISIT NICE TO MEET YOU
HI
I CAN HELP YOU FIND SERVICES YOU NEED, PROVIDE YOU WITH IMPORTANT INFORMATION AND MORE
I WORK TO TAKE CARE OF MY FAMILY
BUT I LOVE MY JOB
IT'S REWARDING
I'M ORIGINALLY FROM LIMA, PERU
NOW I'M A US CITIZEN IN NEW YORK
PICTURES OF HUSBAND AND ADULT KIDS
I'M 50 TODAY - I WANNA GET A SECOND EAR PIERCING
LET'S GET LOUD
AND - GET MY MASTERS DEGREE
I'VE BEEN THINKING ABOUT IT A LOT, I KNOW I COULD MAKE MORE WITH THE DEGREE
YOU COULD DO IT, ANITA
I'M SURE
SALUD!
CO-WORKER
WHY SHOULD I GET A LOWER SALARY? WE ALL DO THE SAME WORK! THEY HAVE A MASTERS, HOW HARD CAN IT BE? THEY DID IT WHY NOT ME? MY CREDIT IS GOOD...
WHY NOT?

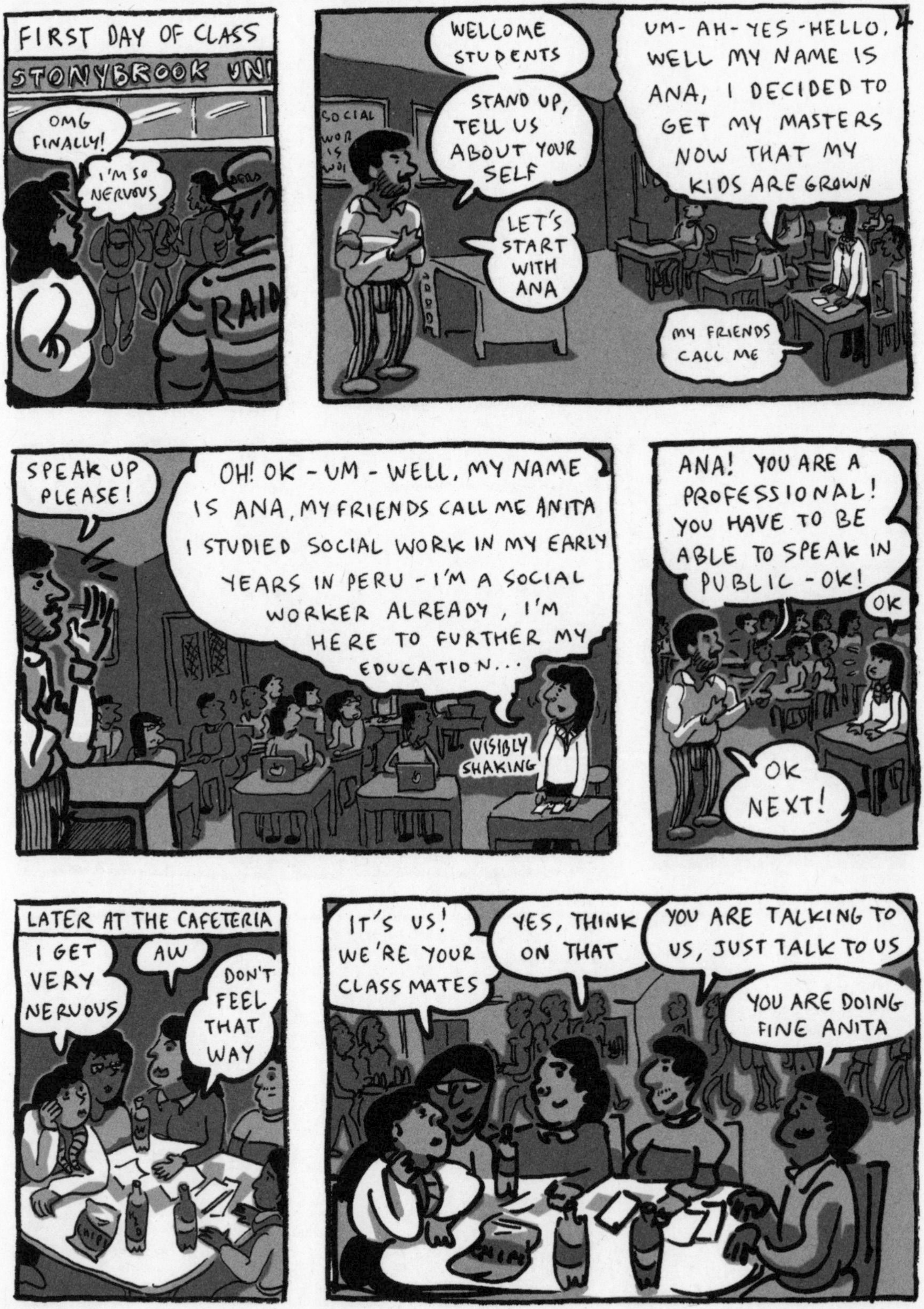
FIRST DAY OF CLASS
STONYBROOK UNI
OMG FINALLY!
I'M SO NERVOUS
WELLCOME STUDENTS
STAND UP, TELL US ABOUT YOUR SELF
LET'S START WITH ANA
UM- AH- YES -HELLO, WELL MY NAME IS ANA, I DECIDED TO GET MY MASTERS NOW THAT MY KIDS ARE GROWN
MY FRIENDS CALL ME
SPEAK UP PLEASE!
OH! OK - UM - WELL, MY NAME IS ANA, MY FRIENDS CALL ME ANITA I STUDIED SOCIAL WORK IN MY EARLY YEARS IN PERU - I'M A SOCIAL WORKER ALREADY, I'M HERE TO FURTHER MY EDUCATION...
VISIBLY SHAKING
ANA! YOU ARE A PROFESSIONAL! YOU HAVE TO BE ABLE TO SPEAK IN PUBLIC - OK!
OK
OK NEXT!
LATER AT THE CAFETERIA
I GET VERY NERVOUS
AW
DON'T FEEL THAT WAY
IT'S US! WE'RE YOUR CLASSMATES
YES, THINK ON THAT
YOU ARE TALKING TO US, JUST TALK TO US
YOU ARE DOING FINE ANITA

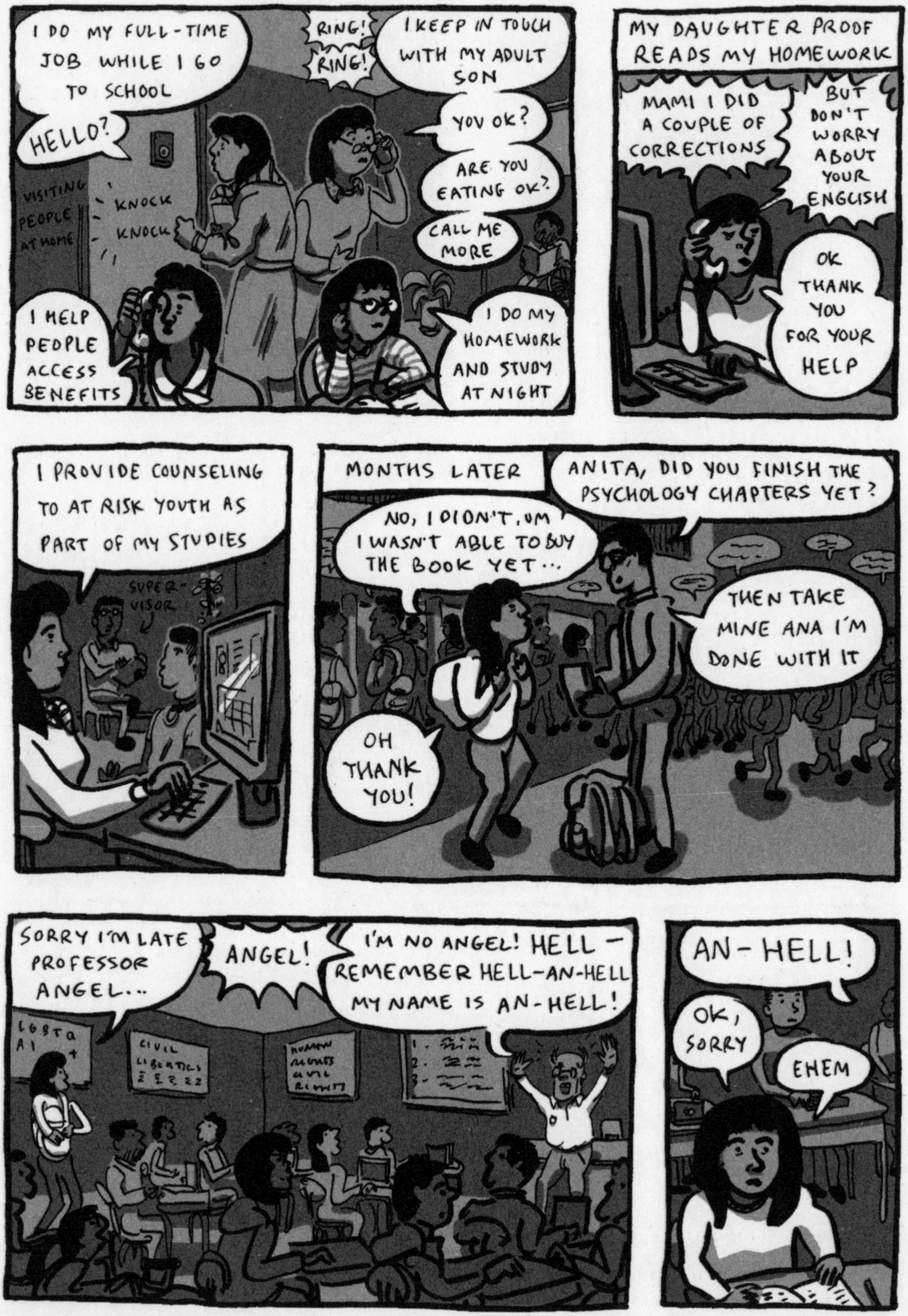
I DO MY FULL-TIME JOB WHILE I GO TO SCHOOL
HELLO?
VISITING PEOPLE AT HOME
KNOCK KNOCK
I HELP PEOPLE ACCESS BENEFITS
RING! RING!
I KEEP IN TOUCH WITH MY ADULT SON
YOU OK?
ARE YOU EATING OK?
CALL ME MORE
I DO MY HOMEWORK AND STUDY AT NIGHT
MY DAUGHTER PROOF READS MY HOMEWORK
MAMI I DID A COUPLE OF CORRECTIONS
BUT DON'T WORRY ABOUT YOUR ENGLISH
OK THANK YOU FOR YOUR HELP
I PROVIDE COUNSELING TO AT RISK YOUTH AS PART OF MY STUDIES
SUPER-VISOR
MONTHS LATER
ANITA, DID YOU FINISH THE PSYCHOLOGY CHAPTERS YET?
NO, I DIDN'T, UM I WASN'T ABLE TO BUY THE BOOK YET...
THEN TAKE MINE ANA I'M DONE WITH IT
OH THANK YOU!
SORRY I'M LATE PROFESSOR ANGEL...
ANGEL!
I'M NO ANGEL! HELL - REMEMBER HELL-AN-HELL MY NAME IS AN-HELL!
CIVIL LIBERTIES
AN-HELL!
OK, SORRY
EHEM

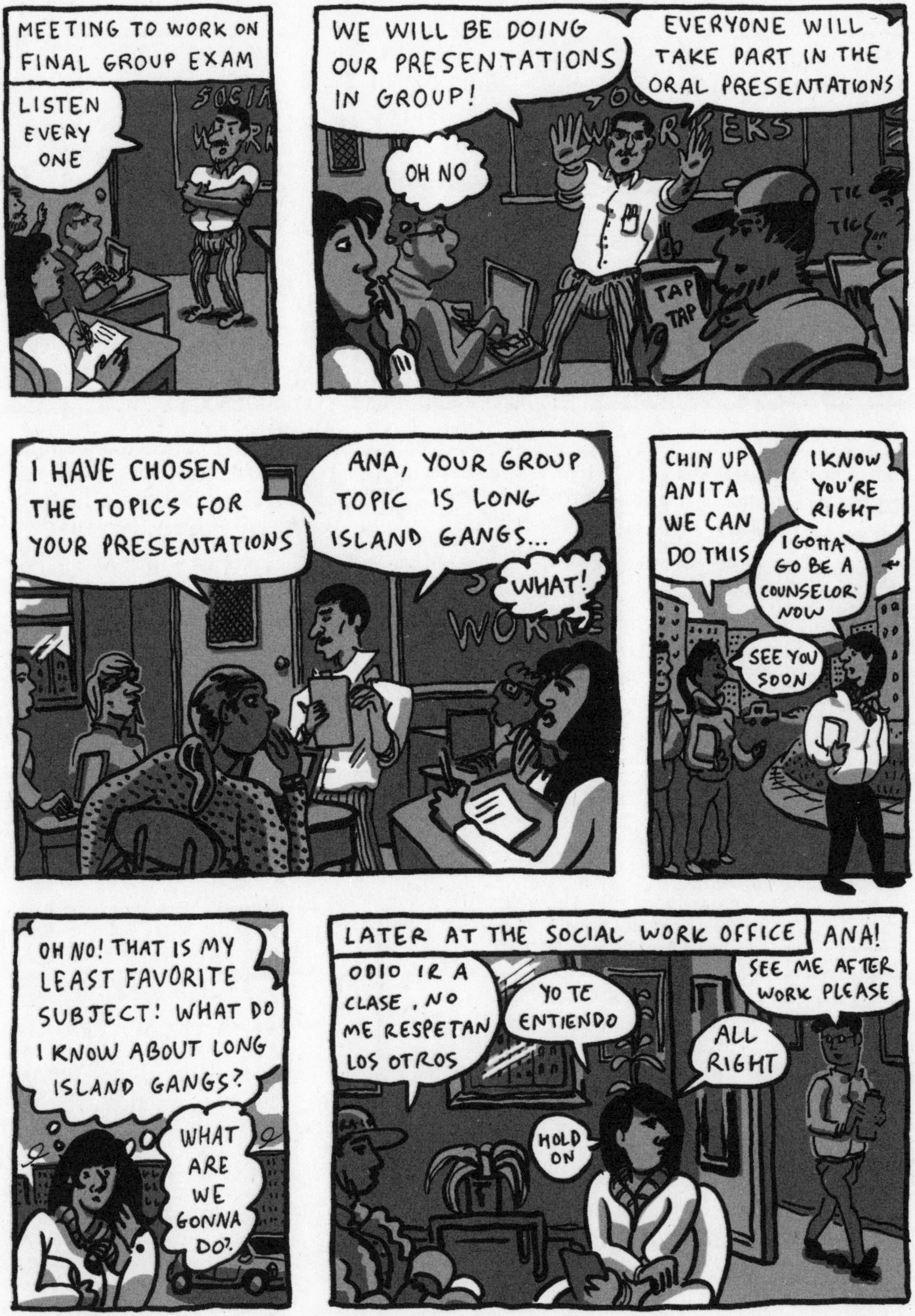
MEETING TO WORK ON FINAL GROUP EXAM
LISTEN EVERY ONE
WE WILL BE DOING OUR PRESENTATIONS IN GROUP!
EVERYONE WILL TAKE PART IN THE ORAL PRESENTATIONS
OH NO
TIC TIC
TAP TAP
I HAVE CHOSEN THE TOPICS FOR YOUR PRESENTATIONS
ANA, YOUR GROUP TOPIC IS LONG ISLAND GANGS...
WHAT!
CHIN UP ANITA WE CAN DO THIS
I KNOW YOU'RE RIGHT
I GOTTA GO BE A COUNSELOR NOW
SEE YOU SOON
OH NO! THAT IS MY LEAST FAVORITE SUBJECT! WHAT DO I KNOW ABOUT LONG ISLAND GANGS?
WHAT ARE WE GONNA DO?
LATER AT THE SOCIAL WORK OFFICE
ODIO IR A CLASE, NO ME RESPETAN LOS OTROS
YO TE ENTIENDO
ANA! SEE ME AFTER WORK PLEASE
ALL RIGHT
HOLD ON

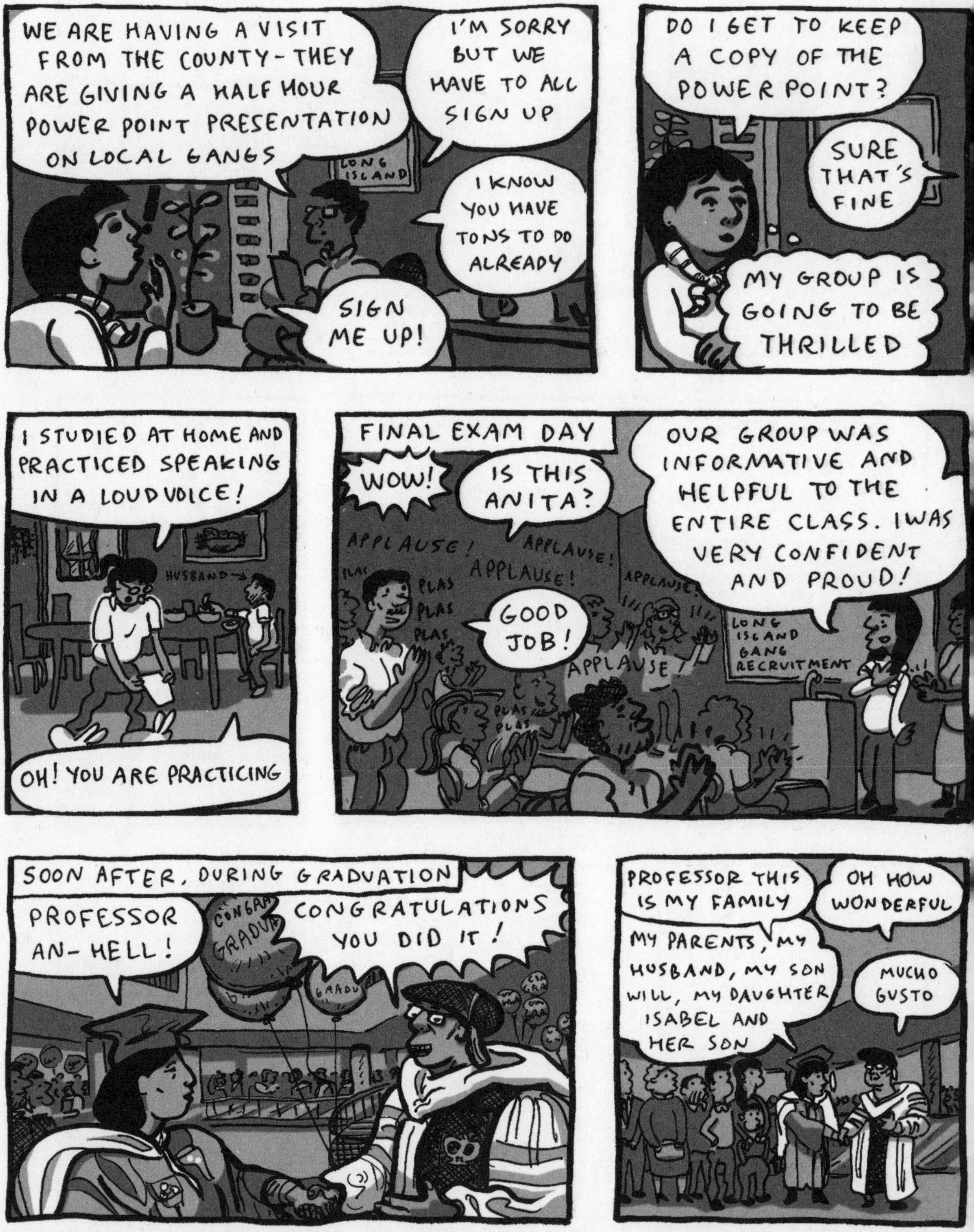
WE ARE HAVING A VISIT FROM THE COUNTY - THEY ARE GIVING A HALF HOUR POWER POINT PRESENTATION ON LOCAL GANGS
I'M SORRY BUT WE HAVE TO ALL SIGN UP
LONG ISLAND
I KNOW YOU HAVE TONS TO DO ALREADY
SIGN ME UP!
DO I GET TO KEEP A COPY OF THE POWER POINT?
SURE THAT'S FINE
MY GROUP IS GOING TO BE THRILLED
I STUDIED AT HOME AND PRACTICED SPEAKING IN A LOUD VOICE!
HUSBAND →
OH! YOU ARE PRACTICING
FINAL EXAM DAY
WOW!
IS THIS ANITA?
OUR GROUP WAS INFORMATIVE AND HELPFUL TO THE ENTIRE CLASS. I WAS VERY CONFIDENT AND PROUD!
APPLAUSE! APPLAUSE! APPLAUSE! APPLAUSE!
PLAS PLAS PLAS
GOOD JOB!
LONG ISLAND GANG RECRUITMENT
APPLAUSE!
PLAS PLAS
SOON AFTER, DURING GRADUATION
PROFESSOR AN-HELL!
CONGRATULATIONS YOU DID IT!
PROFESSOR THIS IS MY FAMILY
OH HOW WONDERFUL
MY PARENTS, MY HUSBAND, MY SON WILL, MY DAUGHTER ISABEL AND HER SON
MUCHO GUSTO

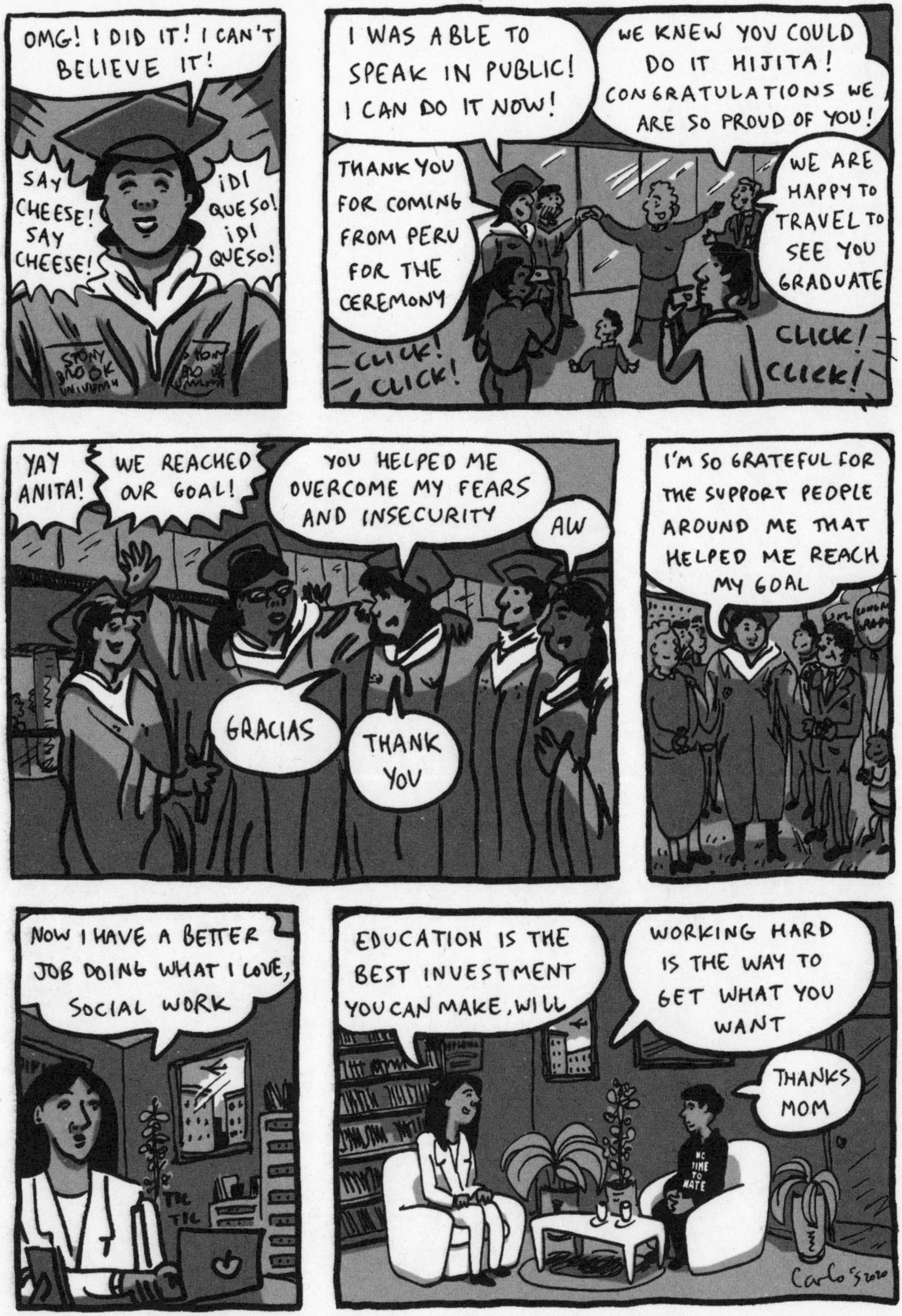
OMG! I DID IT! I CAN'T BELIEVE IT!
SAY CHEESE! SAY CHEESE!
¡DI QUESO! ¡DI QUESO!
STONY BROOK UNIVERSITY
I WAS ABLE TO SPEAK IN PUBLIC! I CAN DO IT NOW!
WE KNEW YOU COULD DO IT HIJITA! CONGRATULATIONS WE ARE SO PROUD OF YOU!
THANK YOU FOR COMING FROM PERU FOR THE CEREMONY
WE ARE HAPPY TO TRAVEL TO SEE YOU GRADUATE
CLICK! CLICK!
CLICK! CLICK!
YAY ANITA!
WE REACHED OUR GOAL!
YOU HELPED ME OVERCOME MY FEARS AND INSECURITY
AW
GRACIAS
THANK YOU
I'M SO GRATEFUL FOR THE SUPPORT PEOPLE AROUND ME THAT HELPED ME REACH MY GOAL
NOW I HAVE A BETTER JOB DOING WHAT I LOVE, SOCIAL WORK
TIC TIC
EDUCATION IS THE BEST INVESTMENT YOU CAN MAKE, WILL
WORKING HARD IS THE WAY TO GET WHAT YOU WANT
THANKS MOM
NO TIME TO HATE
Carlos 2020

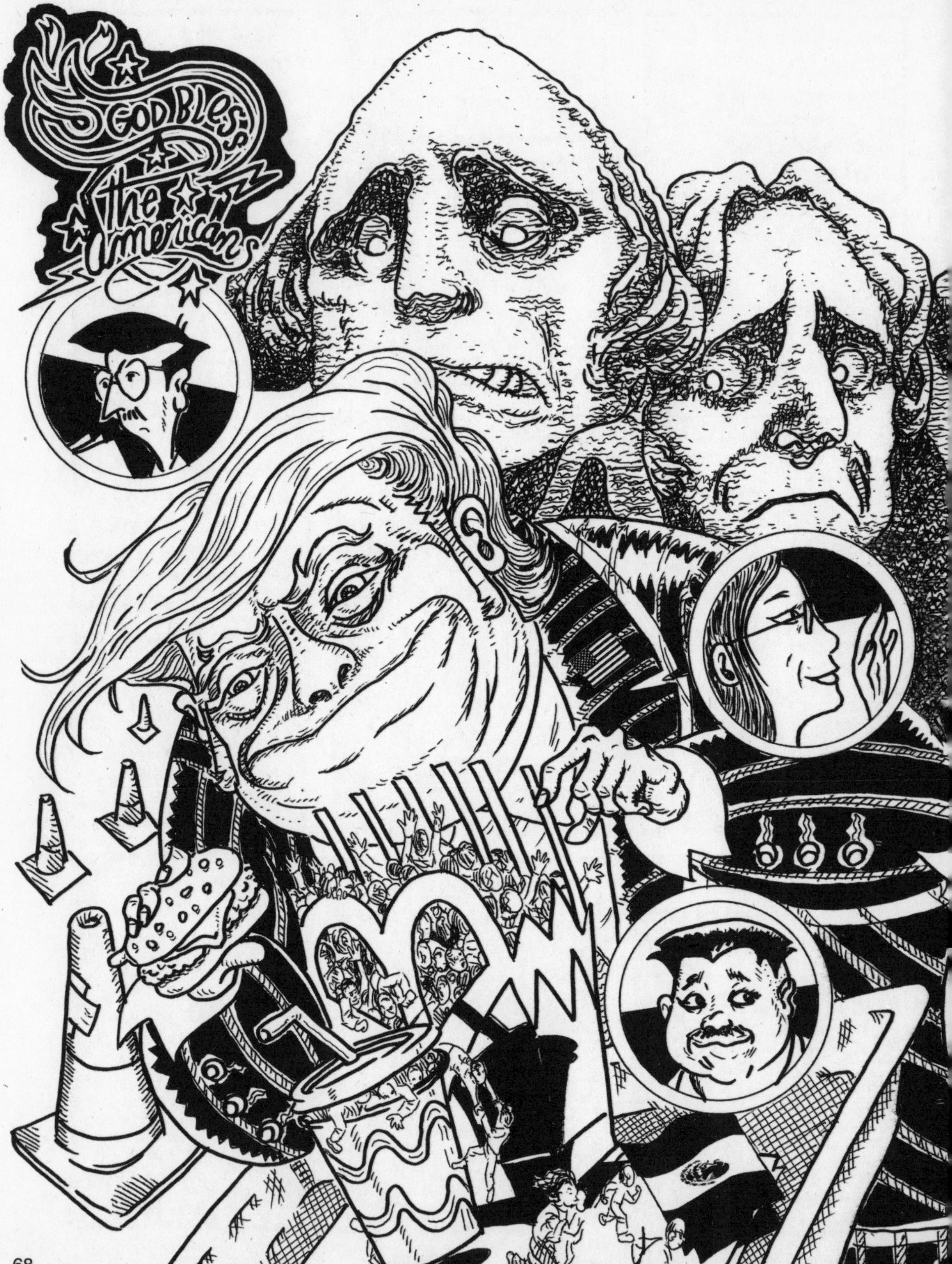
God Bless the Americans

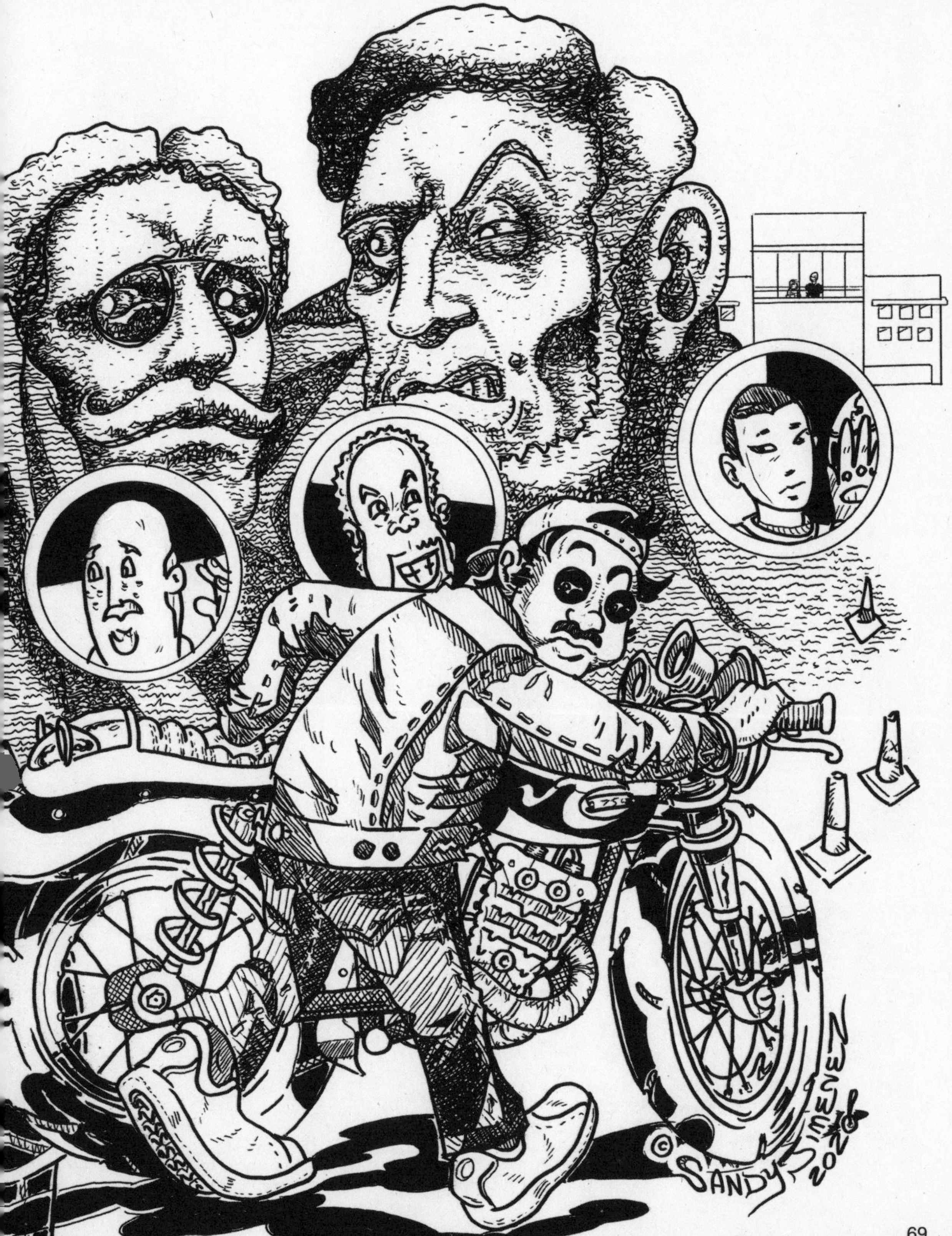
©SANDY JIMENEZ 2020

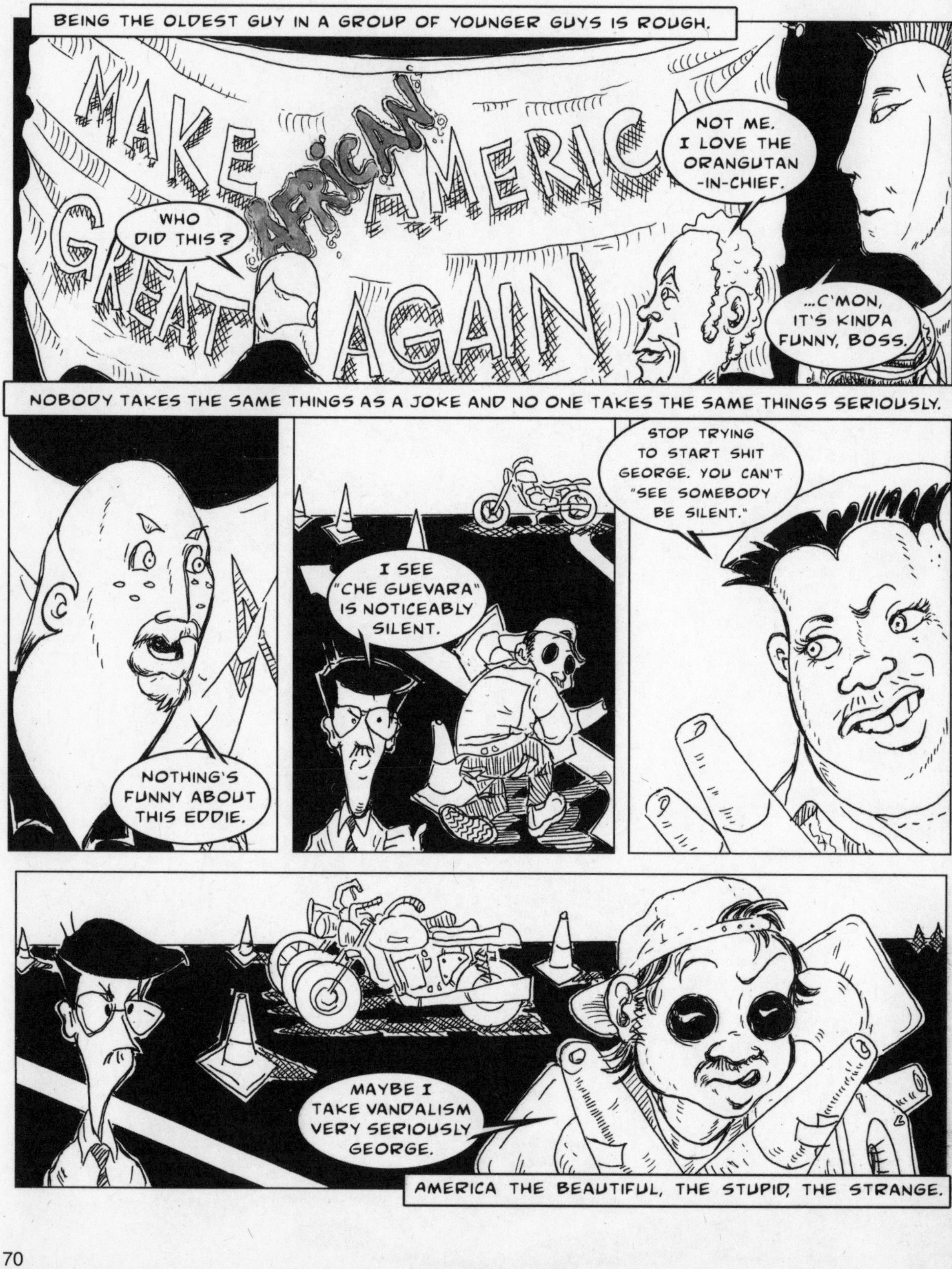
BEING THE OLDEST GUY IN A GROUP OF YOUNGER GUYS IS ROUGH.
MAKE AFRICAN AMERIC
GREAT AGAIN
WHO DID THIS?
NOT ME. I LOVE THE ORANGUTAN -IN-CHIEF.
...C'MON, IT'S KINDA FUNNY, BOSS.
NOBODY TAKES THE SAME THINGS AS A JOKE AND NO ONE TAKES THE SAME THINGS SERIOUSLY.
NOTHING'S FUNNY ABOUT THIS EDDIE.
I SEE "CHE GUEVARA" IS NOTICEABLY SILENT.
STOP TRYING TO START SHIT GEORGE. YOU CAN'T "SEE SOMEBODY BE SILENT."
MAYBE I TAKE VANDALISM VERY SERIOUSLY GEORGE.
AMERICA THE BEAUTIFUL, THE STUPID, THE STRANGE.

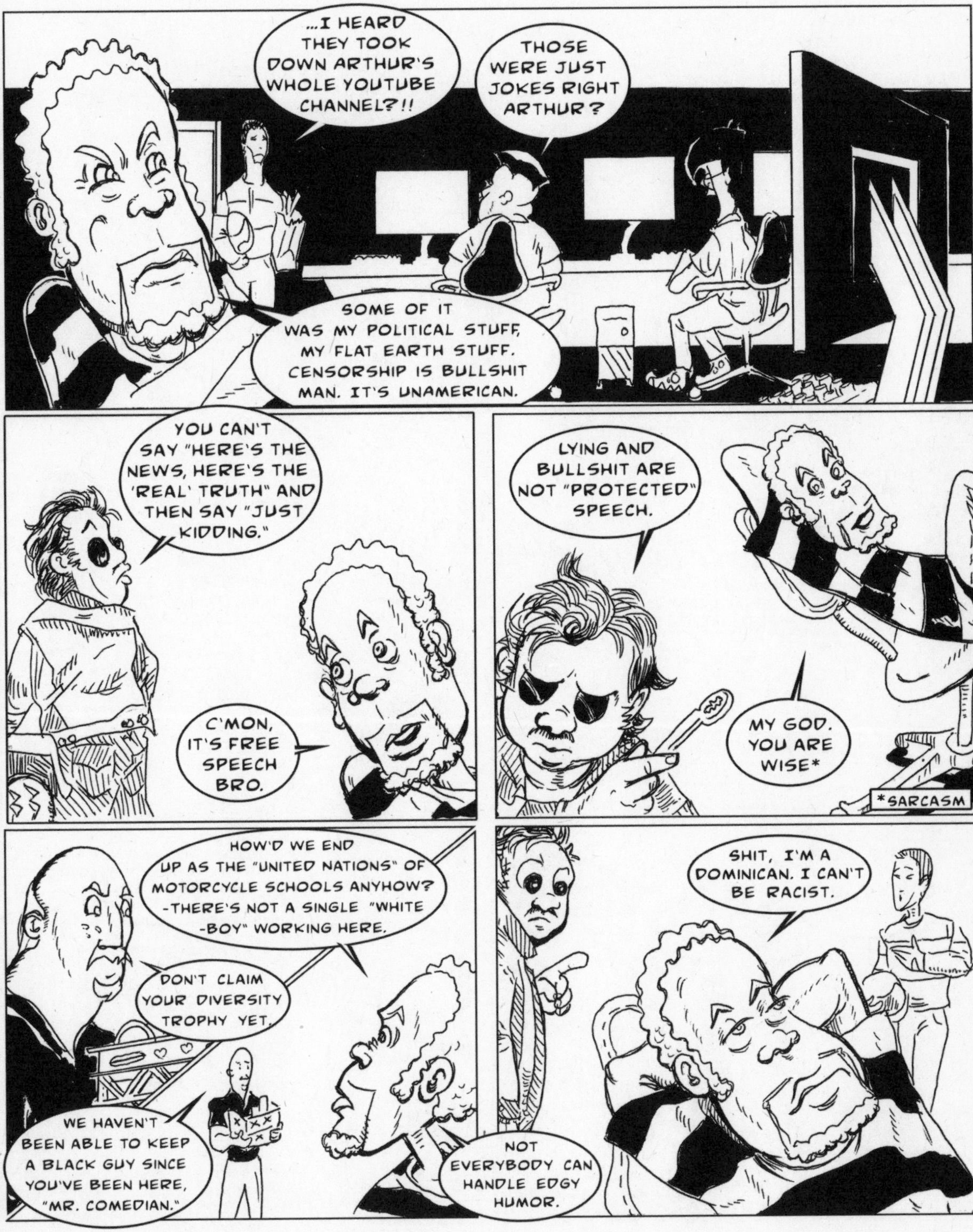
...I HEARD THEY TOOK DOWN ARTHUR'S WHOLE YOUTUBE CHANNEL?!!
THOSE WERE JUST JOKES RIGHT ARTHUR?
SOME OF IT WAS MY POLITICAL STUFF, MY FLAT EARTH STUFF. CENSORSHIP IS BULLSHIT MAN. IT'S UNAMERICAN.
YOU CAN'T SAY "HERE'S THE NEWS, HERE'S THE 'REAL' TRUTH" AND THEN SAY "JUST KIDDING."
C'MON, IT'S FREE SPEECH BRO.
LYING AND BULLSHIT ARE NOT "PROTECTED" SPEECH.
MY GOD. YOU ARE WISE*
*SARCASM
HOW'D WE END UP AS THE "UNITED NATIONS" OF MOTORCYCLE SCHOOLS ANYHOW? -THERE'S NOT A SINGLE "WHITE -BOY" WORKING HERE.
DON'T CLAIM YOUR DIVERSITY TROPHY YET.
WE HAVEN'T BEEN ABLE TO KEEP A BLACK GUY SINCE YOU'VE BEEN HERE, "MR. COMEDIAN."
NOT EVERYBODY CAN HANDLE EDGY HUMOR.
SHIT, I'M A DOMINICAN. I CAN'T BE RACIST.

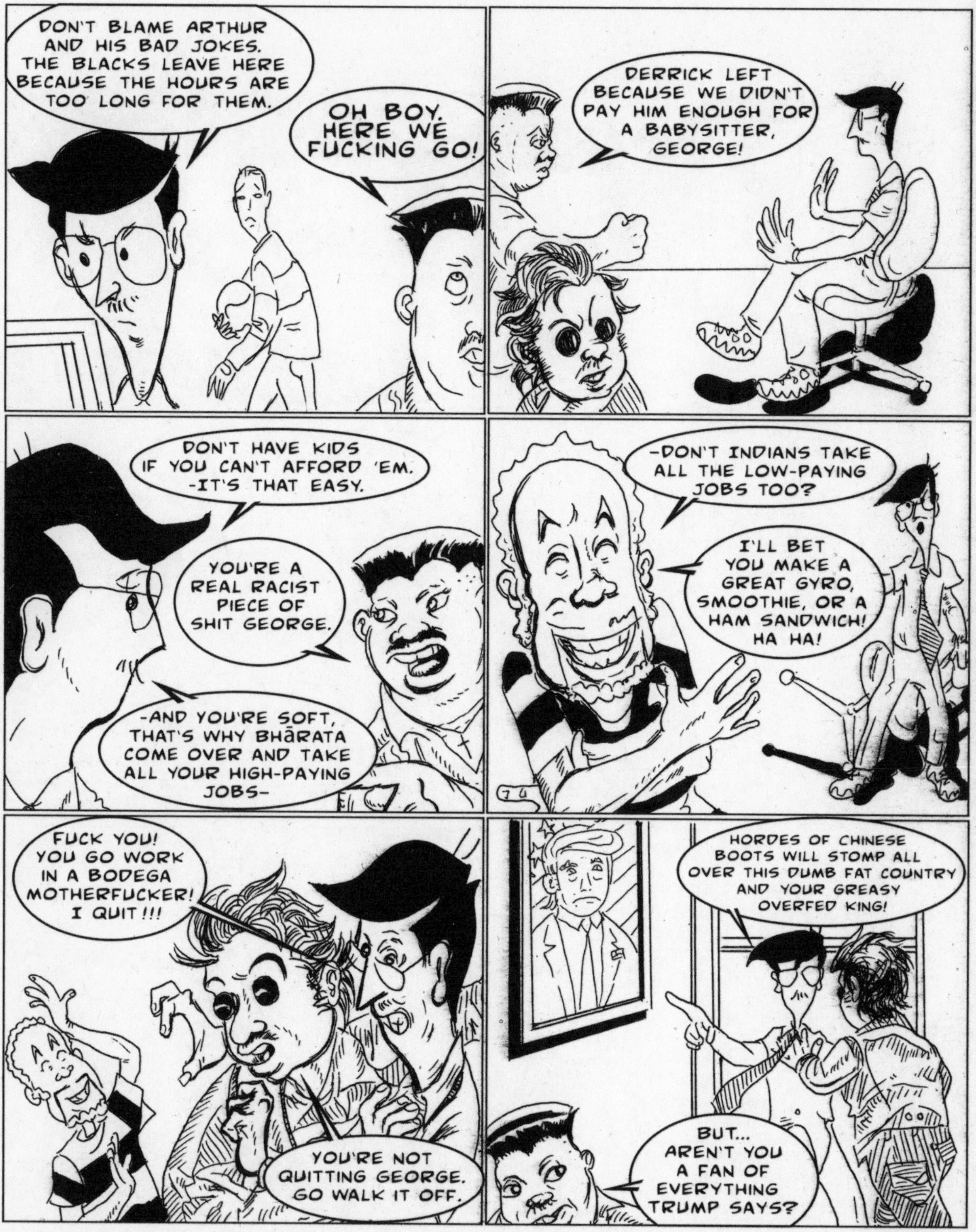
DON'T BLAME ARTHUR AND HIS BAD JOKES. THE BLACKS LEAVE HERE BECAUSE THE HOURS ARE TOO LONG FOR THEM.
OH BOY. HERE WE FUCKING GO!
DERRICK LEFT BECAUSE WE DIDN'T PAY HIM ENOUGH FOR A BABYSITTER, GEORGE!
DON'T HAVE KIDS IF YOU CAN'T AFFORD 'EM. -IT'S THAT EASY.
YOU'RE A REAL RACIST PIECE OF SHIT GEORGE.
-AND YOU'RE SOFT, THAT'S WHY BHĀRATA COME OVER AND TAKE ALL YOUR HIGH-PAYING JOBS-
-DON'T INDIANS TAKE ALL THE LOW-PAYING JOBS TOO?
I'LL BET YOU MAKE A GREAT GYRO, SMOOTHIE, OR A HAM SANDWICH! HA HA!
FUCK YOU! YOU GO WORK IN A BODEGA MOTHERFUCKER! I QUIT!!!
YOU'RE NOT QUITTING GEORGE. GO WALK IT OFF.
HORDES OF CHINESE BOOTS WILL STOMP ALL OVER THIS DUMB FAT COUNTRY AND YOUR GREASY OVERFED KING!
BUT... AREN'T YOU A FAN OF EVERYTHING TRUMP SAYS?

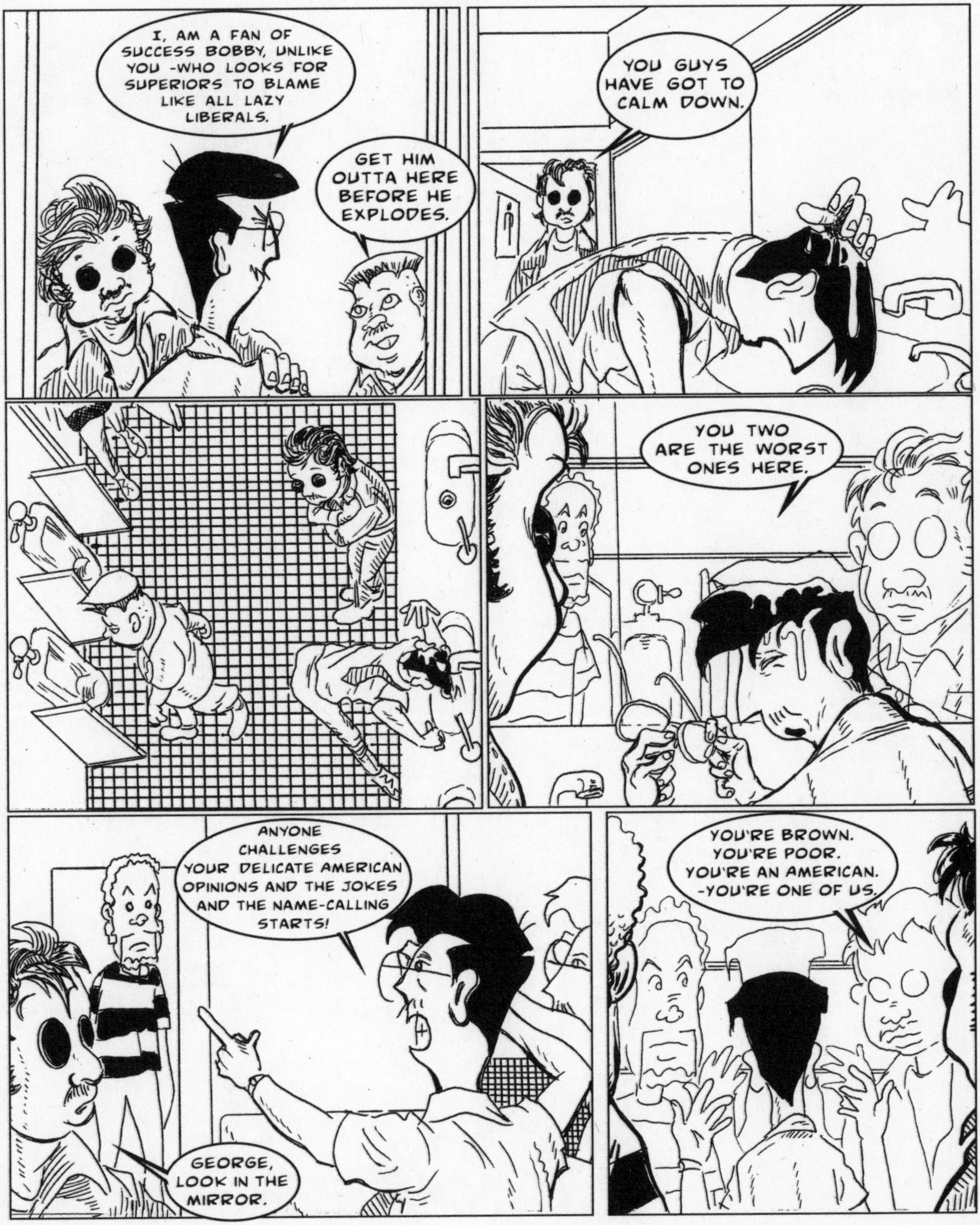
I, AM A FAN OF SUCCESS BOBBY, UNLIKE YOU -WHO LOOKS FOR SUPERIORS TO BLAME LIKE ALL LAZY LIBERALS.
GET HIM OUTTA HERE BEFORE HE EXPLODES.
YOU GUYS HAVE GOT TO CALM DOWN.
YOU TWO ARE THE WORST ONES HERE.
ANYONE CHALLENGES YOUR DELICATE AMERICAN OPINIONS AND THE JOKES AND THE NAME-CALLING STARTS!
GEORGE, LOOK IN THE MIRROR.
YOU'RE BROWN. YOU'RE POOR. YOU'RE AN AMERICAN. -YOU'RE ONE OF US.

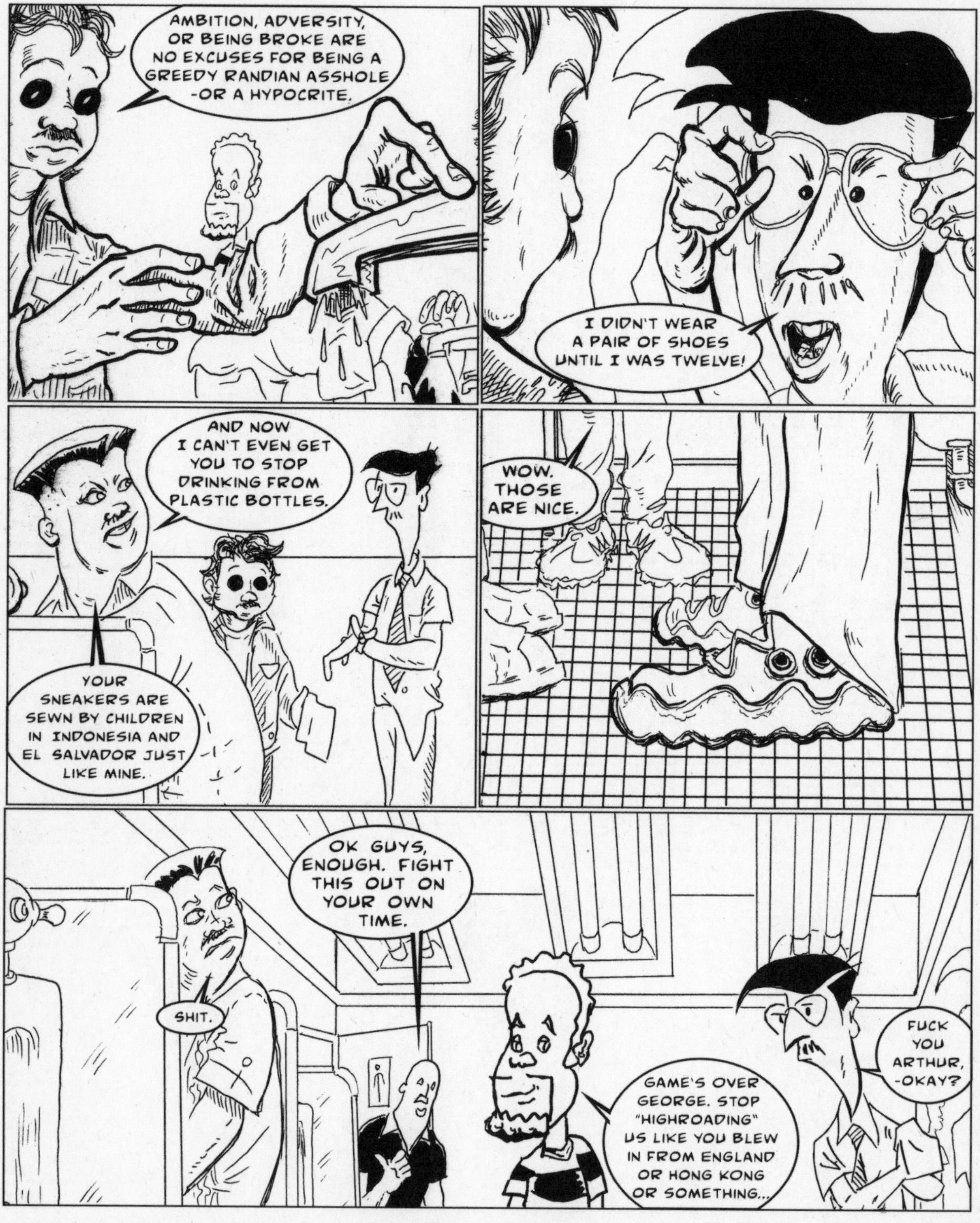
AMBITION, ADVERSITY, OR BEING BROKE ARE NO EXCUSES FOR BEING A GREEDY RANDIAN ASSHOLE -OR A HYPOCRITE.
I DIDN'T WEAR A PAIR OF SHOES UNTIL I WAS TWELVE!
AND NOW I CAN'T EVEN GET YOU TO STOP DRINKING FROM PLASTIC BOTTLES.
YOUR SNEAKERS ARE SEWN BY CHILDREN IN INDONESIA AND EL SALVADOR JUST LIKE MINE.
WOW. THOSE ARE NICE.
OK GUYS, ENOUGH. FIGHT THIS OUT ON YOUR OWN TIME.
SHIT.
GAME'S OVER GEORGE. STOP "HIGHROADING" US LIKE YOU BLEW IN FROM ENGLAND OR HONG KONG OR SOMETHING...
FUCK YOU ARTHUR, -OKAY?

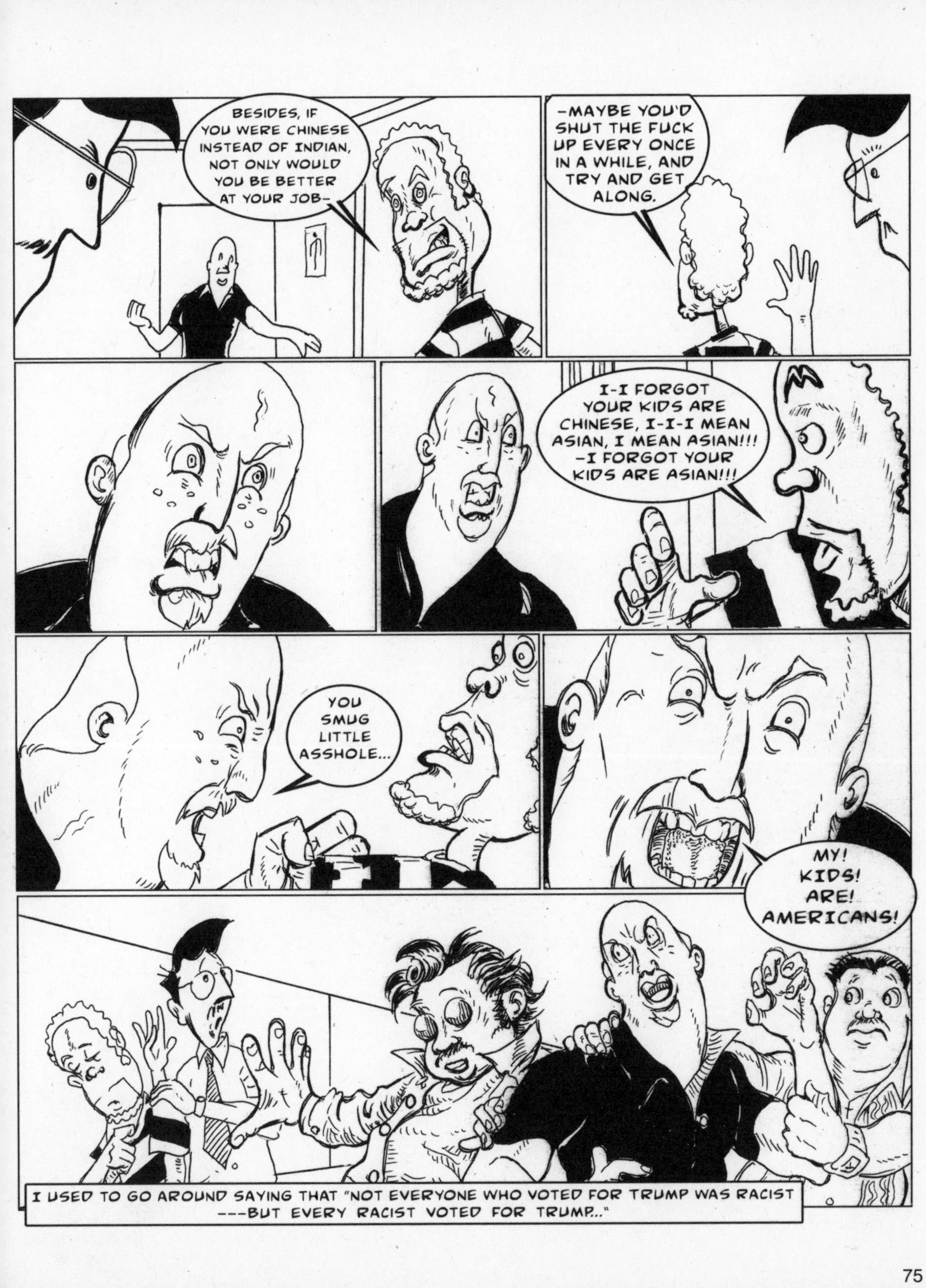
BESIDES, IF YOU WERE CHINESE INSTEAD OF INDIAN, NOT ONLY WOULD YOU BE BETTER AT YOUR JOB-
-MAYBE YOU'D SHUT THE FUCK UP EVERY ONCE IN A WHILE, AND TRY AND GET ALONG.
I-I FORGOT YOUR KIDS ARE CHINESE, I-I-I MEAN ASIAN, I MEAN ASIAN!!! -I FORGOT YOUR KIDS ARE ASIAN!!!
YOU SMUG LITTLE ASSHOLE...
MY! KIDS! ARE! AMERICANS!
I USED TO GO AROUND SAYING THAT "NOT EVERYONE WHO VOTED FOR TRUMP WAS RACIST ---BUT EVERY RACIST VOTED FOR TRUMP..."

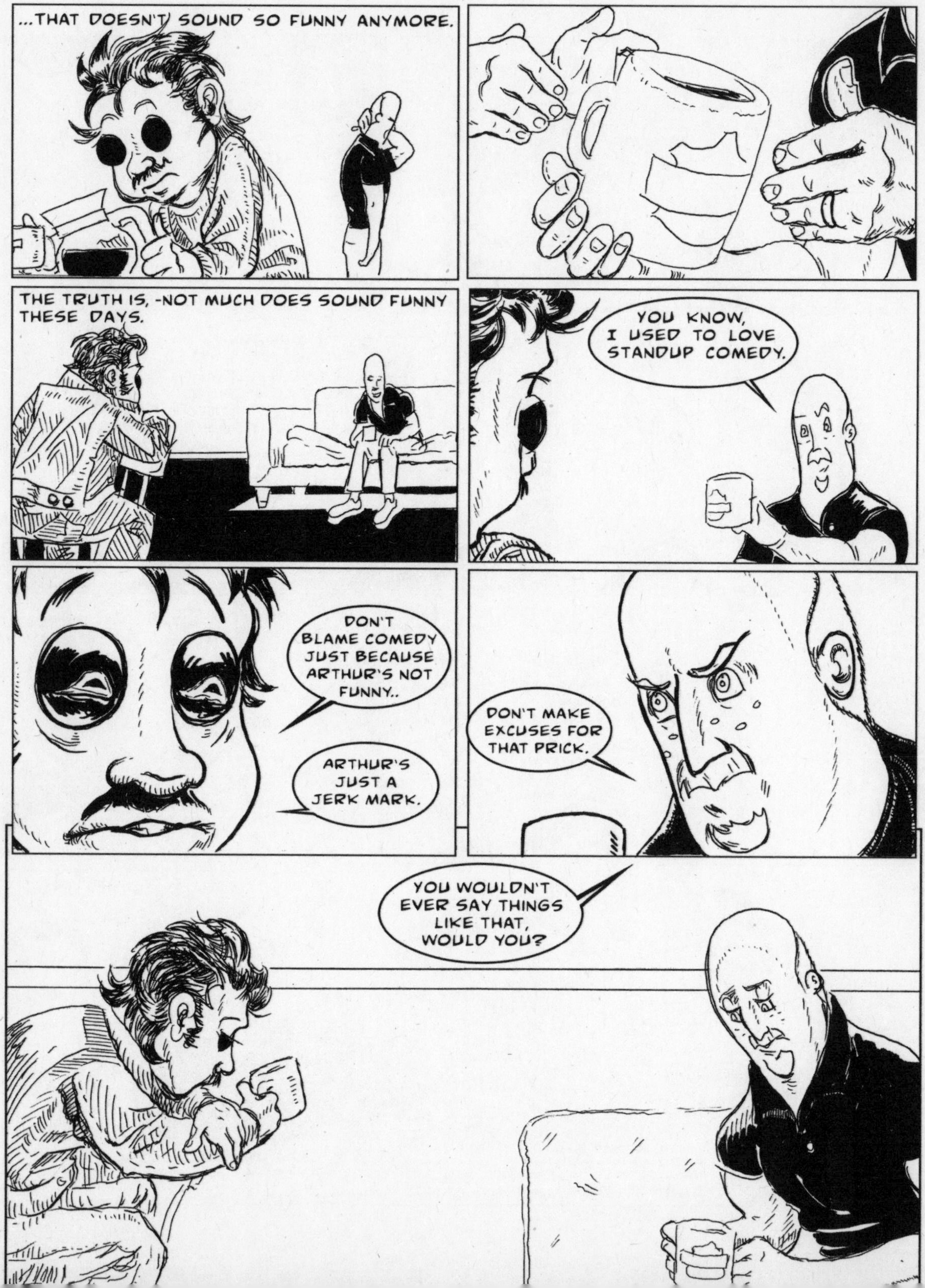
...THAT DOESN'T SOUND SO FUNNY ANYMORE.
THE TRUTH IS, -NOT MUCH DOES SOUND FUNNY THESE DAYS.
YOU KNOW, I USED TO LOVE STANDUP COMEDY.
DON'T BLAME COMEDY JUST BECAUSE ARTHUR'S NOT FUNNY..
ARTHUR'S JUST A JERK MARK.
DON'T MAKE EXCUSES FOR THAT PRICK.
YOU WOULDN'T EVER SAY THINGS LIKE THAT, WOULD YOU?

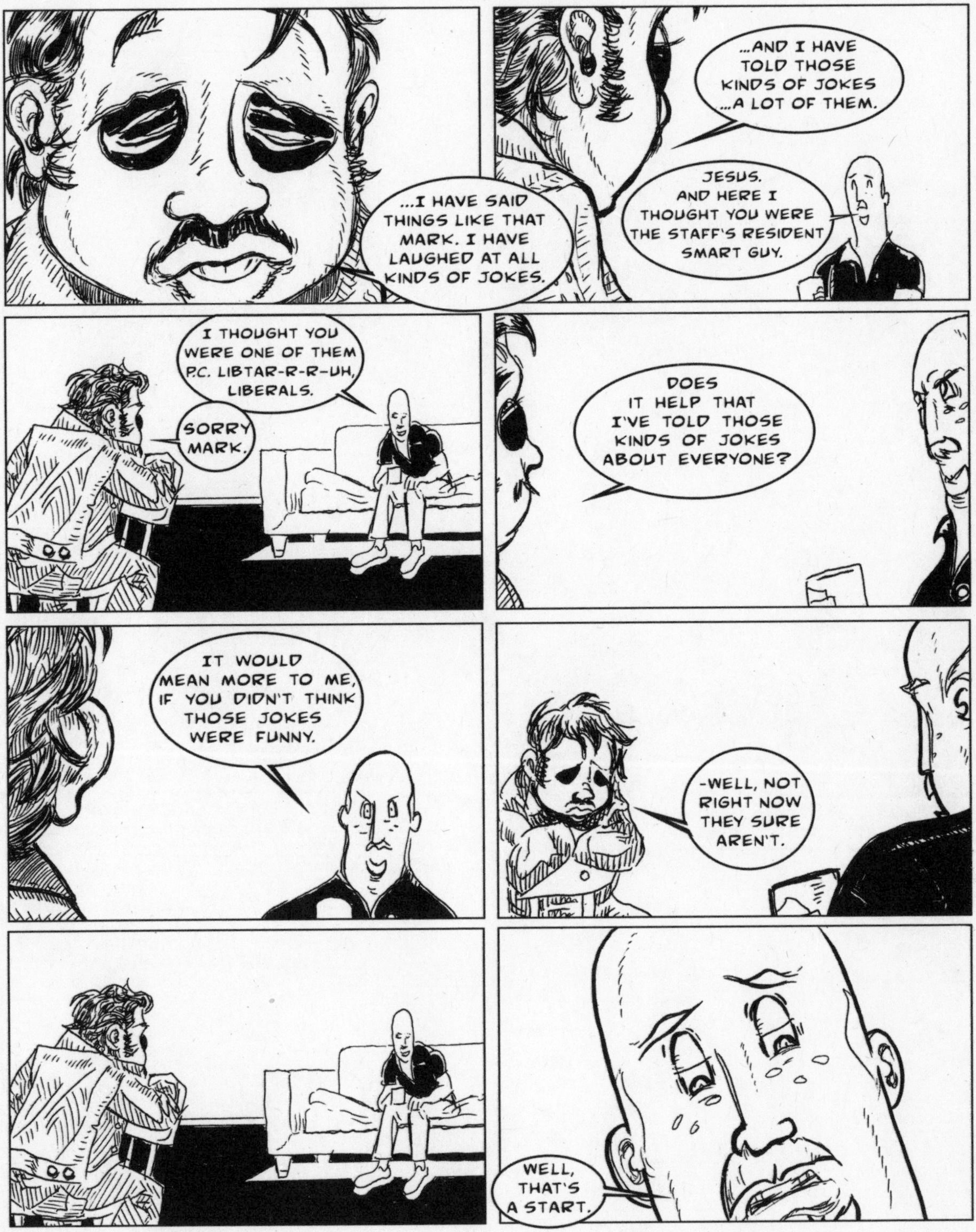
...I HAVE SAID THINGS LIKE THAT MARK. I HAVE LAUGHED AT ALL KINDS OF JOKES.
...AND I HAVE TOLD THOSE KINDS OF JOKES ...A LOT OF THEM.
JESUS. AND HERE I THOUGHT YOU WERE THE STAFF'S RESIDENT SMART GUY.
I THOUGHT YOU WERE ONE OF THEM P.C. LIBTAR-R-R-UH, LIBERALS.
SORRY MARK.
DOES IT HELP THAT I'VE TOLD THOSE KINDS OF JOKES ABOUT EVERYONE?
IT WOULD MEAN MORE TO ME, IF YOU DIDN'T THINK THOSE JOKES WERE FUNNY.
-WELL, NOT RIGHT NOW THEY SURE AREN'T.
WELL, THAT'S A START.

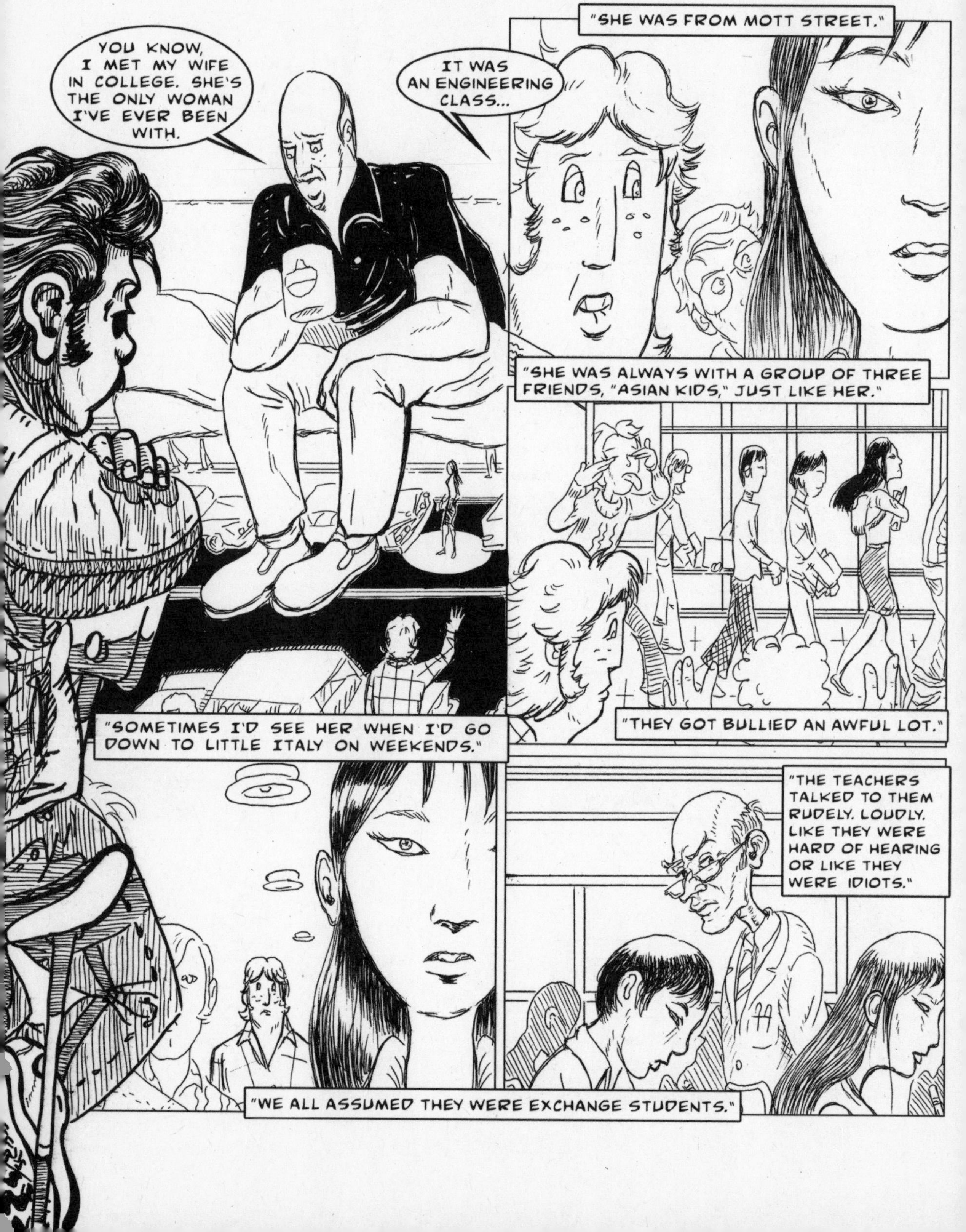
YOU KNOW, I MET MY WIFE IN COLLEGE. SHE'S THE ONLY WOMAN I'VE EVER BEEN WITH.
IT WAS AN ENGINEERING CLASS...
"SHE WAS FROM MOTT STREET."
"SHE WAS ALWAYS WITH A GROUP OF THREE FRIENDS, "ASIAN KIDS," JUST LIKE HER."
"THEY GOT BULLIED AN AWFUL LOT."
"SOMETIMES I'D SEE HER WHEN I'D GO DOWN TO LITTLE ITALY ON WEEKENDS."
"THE TEACHERS TALKED TO THEM RUDELY. LOUDLY. LIKE THEY WERE HARD OF HEARING OR LIKE THEY WERE IDIOTS."
"WE ALL ASSUMED THEY WERE EXCHANGE STUDENTS."

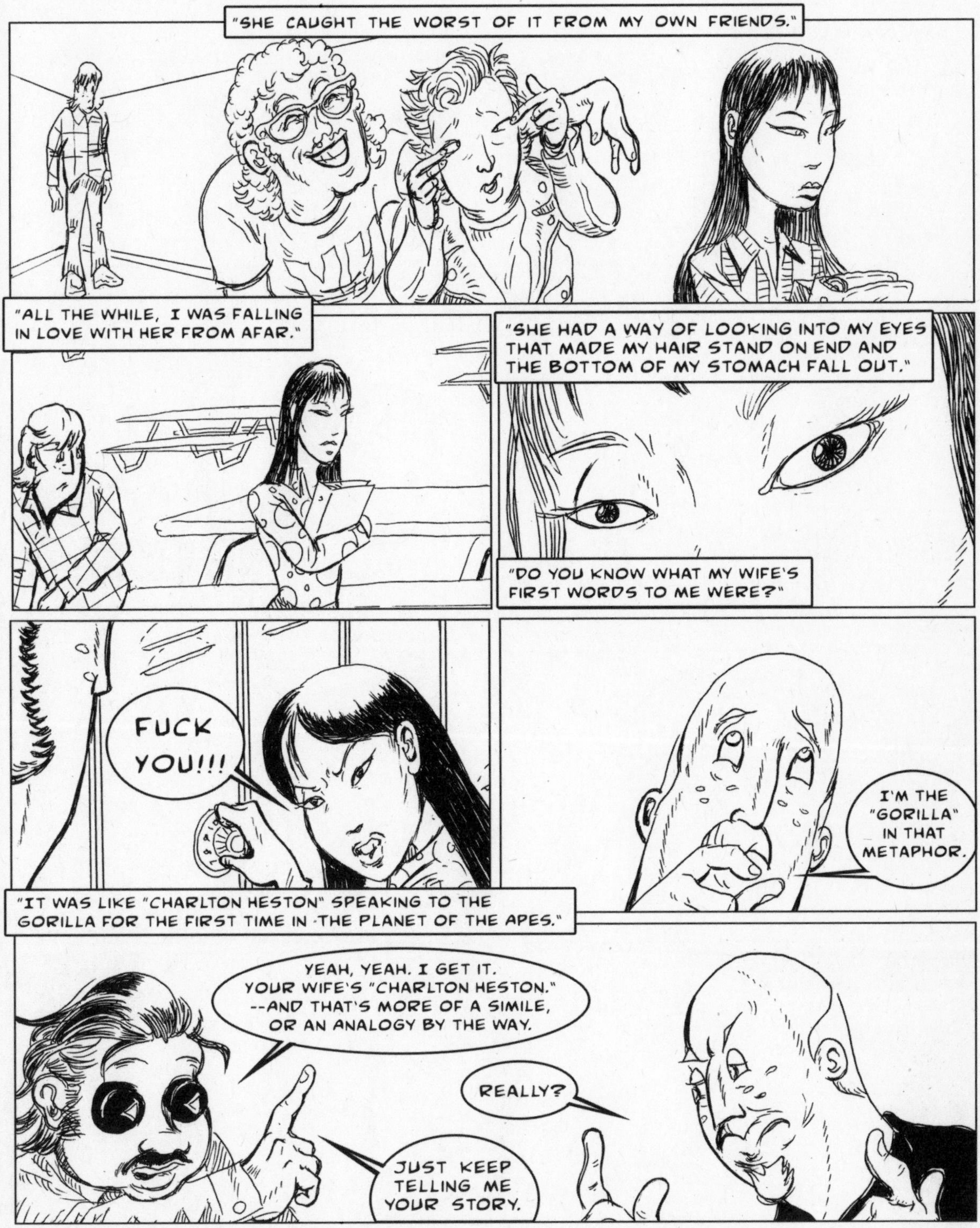
"SHE CAUGHT THE WORST OF IT FROM MY OWN FRIENDS."
"ALL THE WHILE, I WAS FALLING IN LOVE WITH HER FROM AFAR."
"SHE HAD A WAY OF LOOKING INTO MY EYES THAT MADE MY HAIR STAND ON END AND THE BOTTOM OF MY STOMACH FALL OUT."
"DO YOU KNOW WHAT MY WIFE'S FIRST WORDS TO ME WERE?"
FUCK YOU!!!
"IT WAS LIKE "CHARLTON HESTON" SPEAKING TO THE GORILLA FOR THE FIRST TIME IN -THE PLANET OF THE APES."
I'M THE "GORILLA" IN THAT METAPHOR.
YEAH, YEAH. I GET IT. YOUR WIFE'S "CHARLTON HESTON." --AND THAT'S MORE OF A SIMILE, OR AN ANALOGY BY THE WAY.
REALLY?
JUST KEEP TELLING ME YOUR STORY.

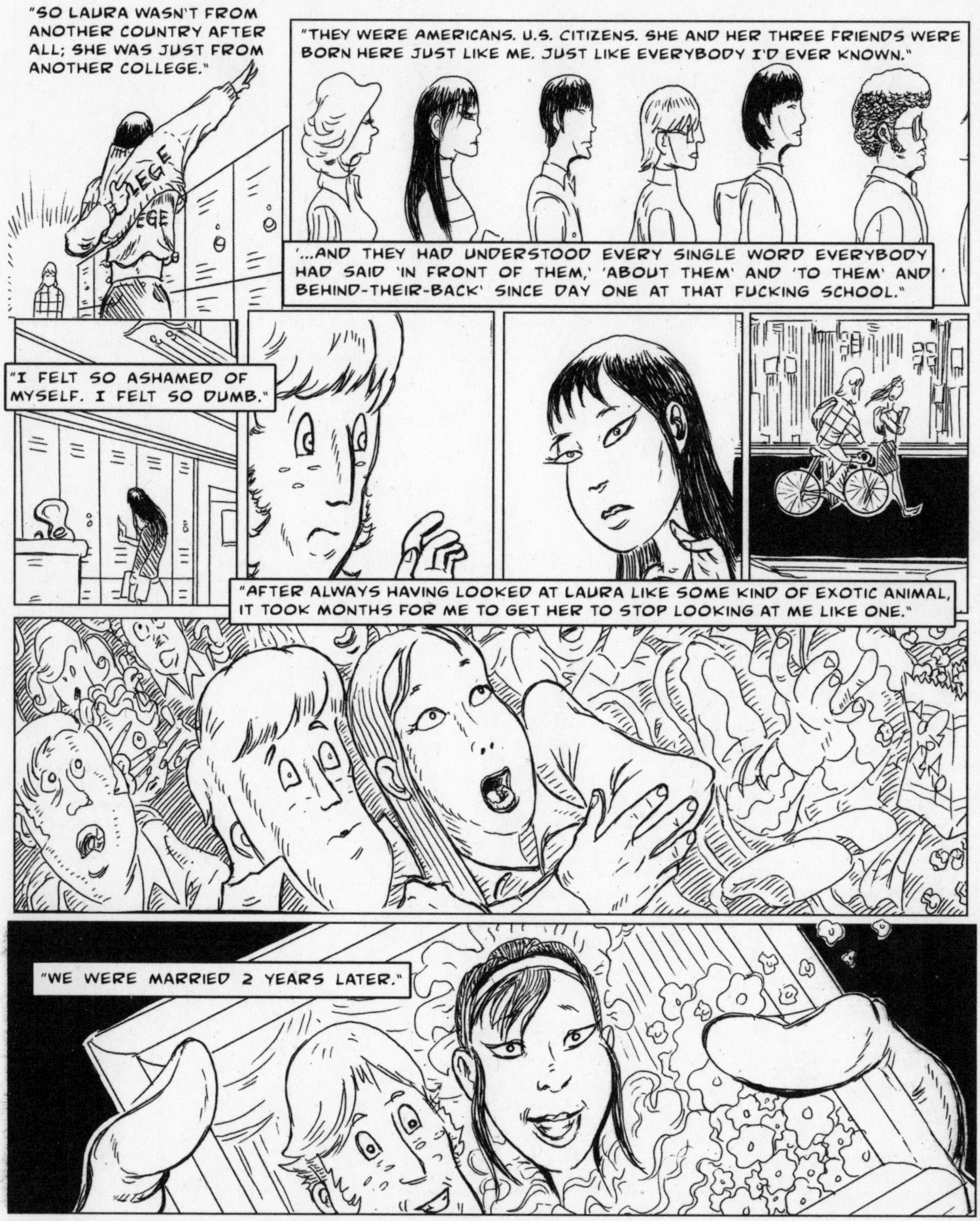
"SO LAURA WASN'T FROM ANOTHER COUNTRY AFTER ALL; SHE WAS JUST FROM ANOTHER COLLEGE."
LEGE
EGE
"THEY WERE AMERICANS. U.S. CITIZENS. SHE AND HER THREE FRIENDS WERE BORN HERE JUST LIKE ME. JUST LIKE EVERYBODY I'D EVER KNOWN."
'...AND THEY HAD UNDERSTOOD EVERY SINGLE WORD EVERYBODY HAD SAID 'IN FRONT OF THEM,' 'ABOUT THEM' AND 'TO THEM' AND 'BEHIND-THEIR-BACK' SINCE DAY ONE AT THAT FUCKING SCHOOL."
"I FELT SO ASHAMED OF MYSELF. I FELT SO DUMB."
"AFTER ALWAYS HAVING LOOKED AT LAURA LIKE SOME KIND OF EXOTIC ANIMAL, IT TOOK MONTHS FOR ME TO GET HER TO STOP LOOKING AT ME LIKE ONE."
"WE WERE MARRIED 2 YEARS LATER."

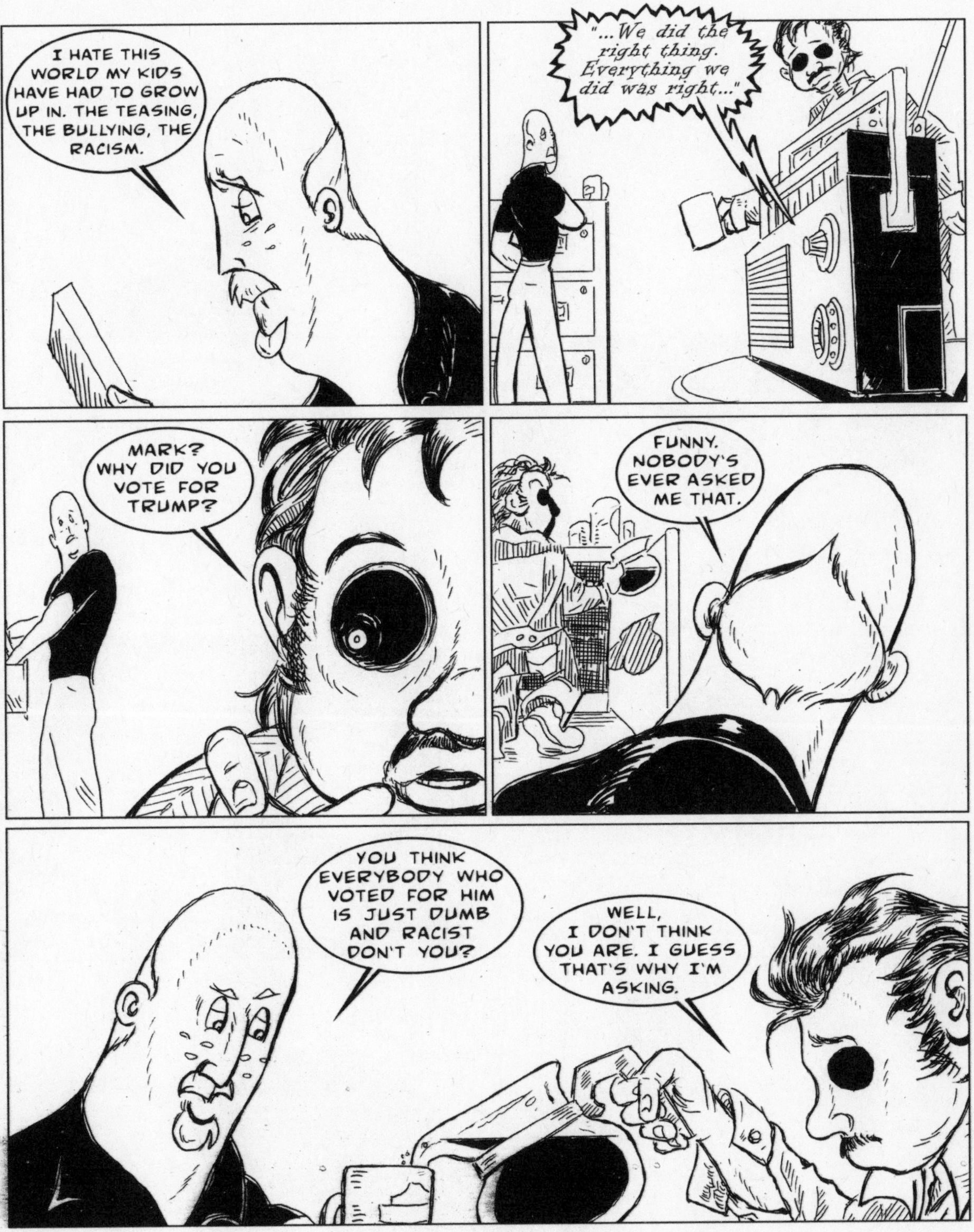
I HATE THIS WORLD MY KIDS HAVE HAD TO GROW UP IN. THE TEASING, THE BULLYING, THE RACISM.
"...We did the right thing. Everything we did was right..."
MARK? WHY DID YOU VOTE FOR TRUMP?
FUNNY. NOBODY'S EVER ASKED ME THAT.
YOU THINK EVERYBODY WHO VOTED FOR HIM IS JUST DUMB AND RACIST DON'T YOU?
WELL, I DON'T THINK YOU ARE. I GUESS THAT'S WHY I'M ASKING.

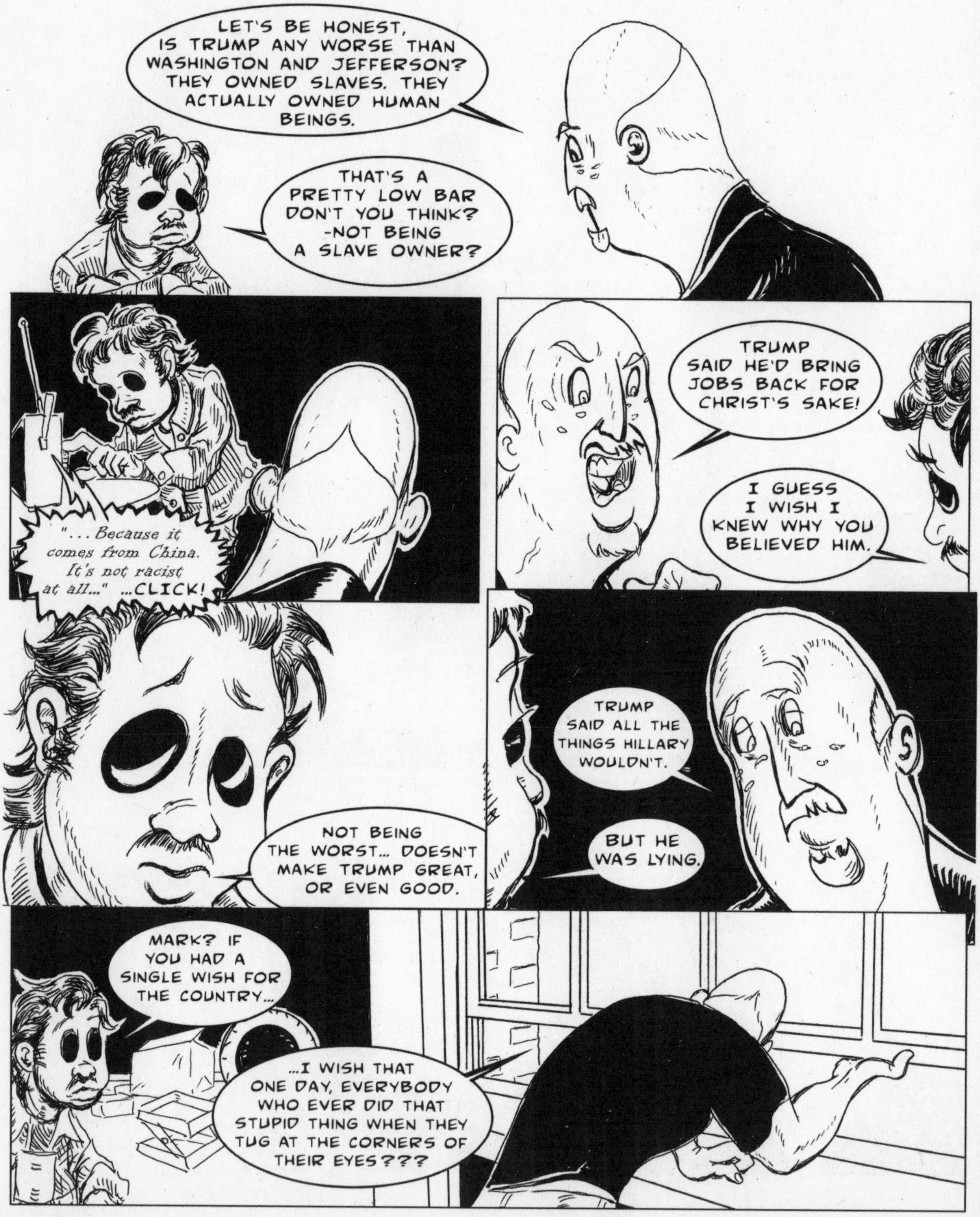
LET'S BE HONEST, IS TRUMP ANY WORSE THAN WASHINGTON AND JEFFERSON? THEY OWNED SLAVES. THEY ACTUALLY OWNED HUMAN BEINGS.
THAT'S A PRETTY LOW BAR DON'T YOU THINK? -NOT BEING A SLAVE OWNER?
"...Because it comes from China. It's not racist at all..." ...CLICK!
TRUMP SAID HE'D BRING JOBS BACK FOR CHRIST'S SAKE!
I GUESS I WISH I KNEW WHY YOU BELIEVED HIM.
NOT BEING THE WORST... DOESN'T MAKE TRUMP GREAT, OR EVEN GOOD.
TRUMP SAID ALL THE THINGS HILLARY WOULDN'T.
BUT HE WAS LYING.
MARK? IF YOU HAD A SINGLE WISH FOR THE COUNTRY...
...I WISH THAT ONE DAY, EVERYBODY WHO EVER DID THAT STUPID THING WHEN THEY TUG AT THE CORNERS OF THEIR EYES???

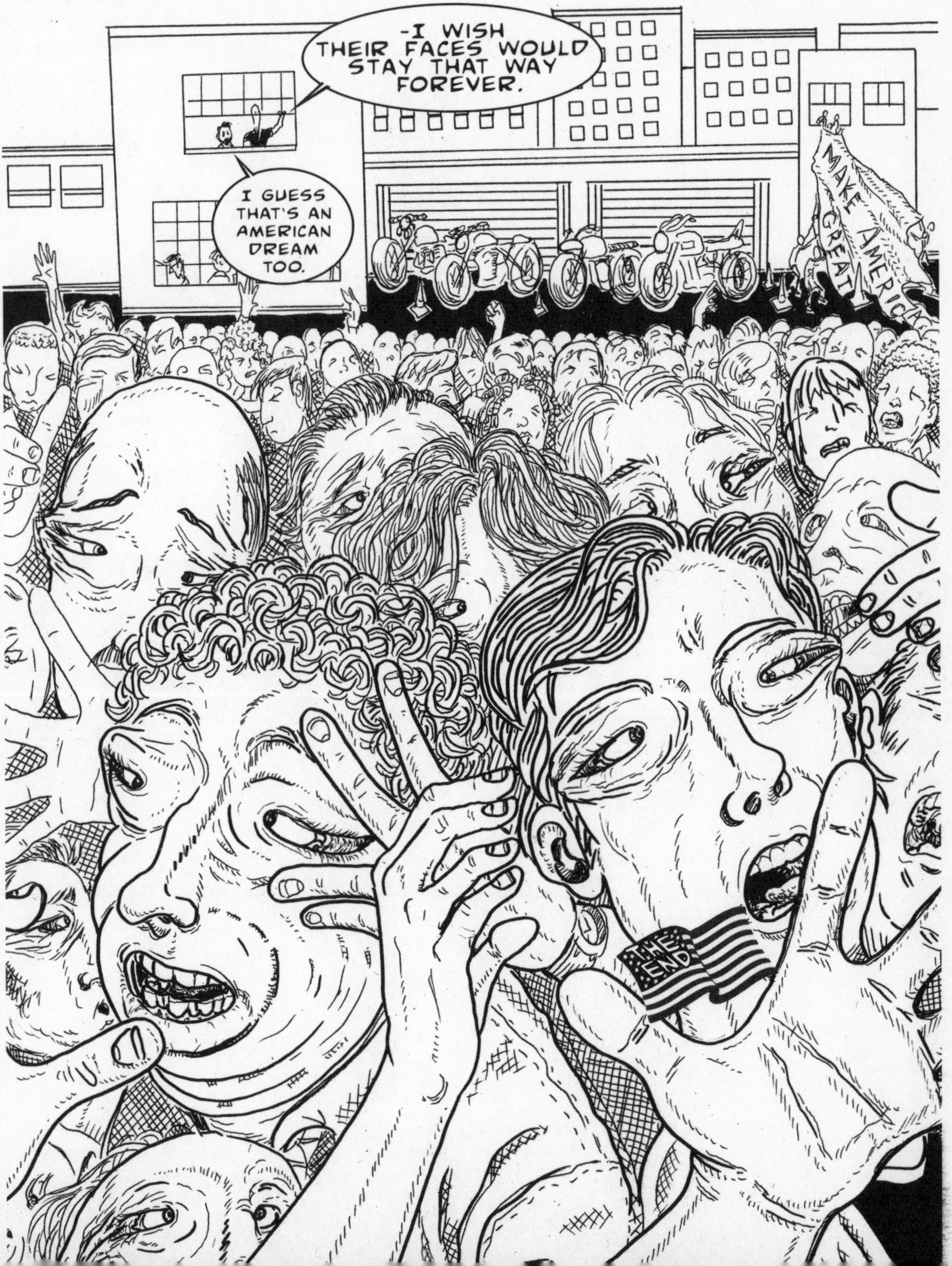
-I WISH THEIR FACES WOULD STAY THAT WAY FOREVER.
I GUESS THAT'S AN AMERICAN DREAM TOO.
MAKE AMERICA GREAT
THE END

LIFE WITH TRUMP

Dream of Feb. 13, 2017 by R.L.M.

DREAMING ABOUT TRUMP • *I can't stop drawing comics of my weird dreams about Donald Trump.* - Rebecca Migdal

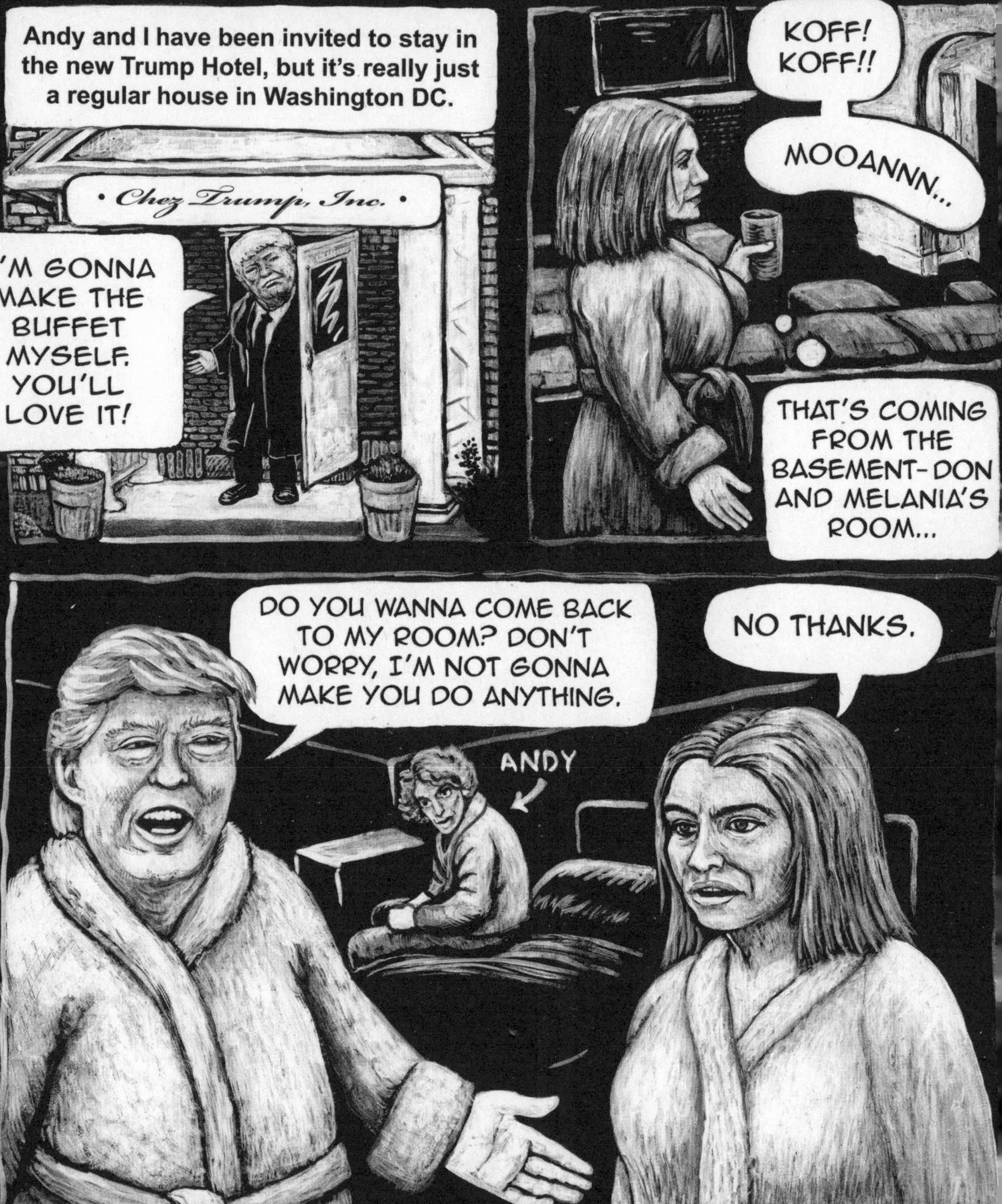

Andy and I have been invited to stay in the new Trump Hotel, but it's really just a regular house in Washington DC.
• Chez Trump, Inc. •
I'M GONNA MAKE THE BUFFET MYSELF. YOU'LL LOVE IT!
KOFF! KOFF!!
MOOANNN...
THAT'S COMING FROM THE BASEMENT- DON AND MELANIA'S ROOM...
DO YOU WANNA COME BACK TO MY ROOM? DON'T WORRY, I'M NOT GONNA MAKE YOU DO ANYTHING.
NO THANKS.
ANDY

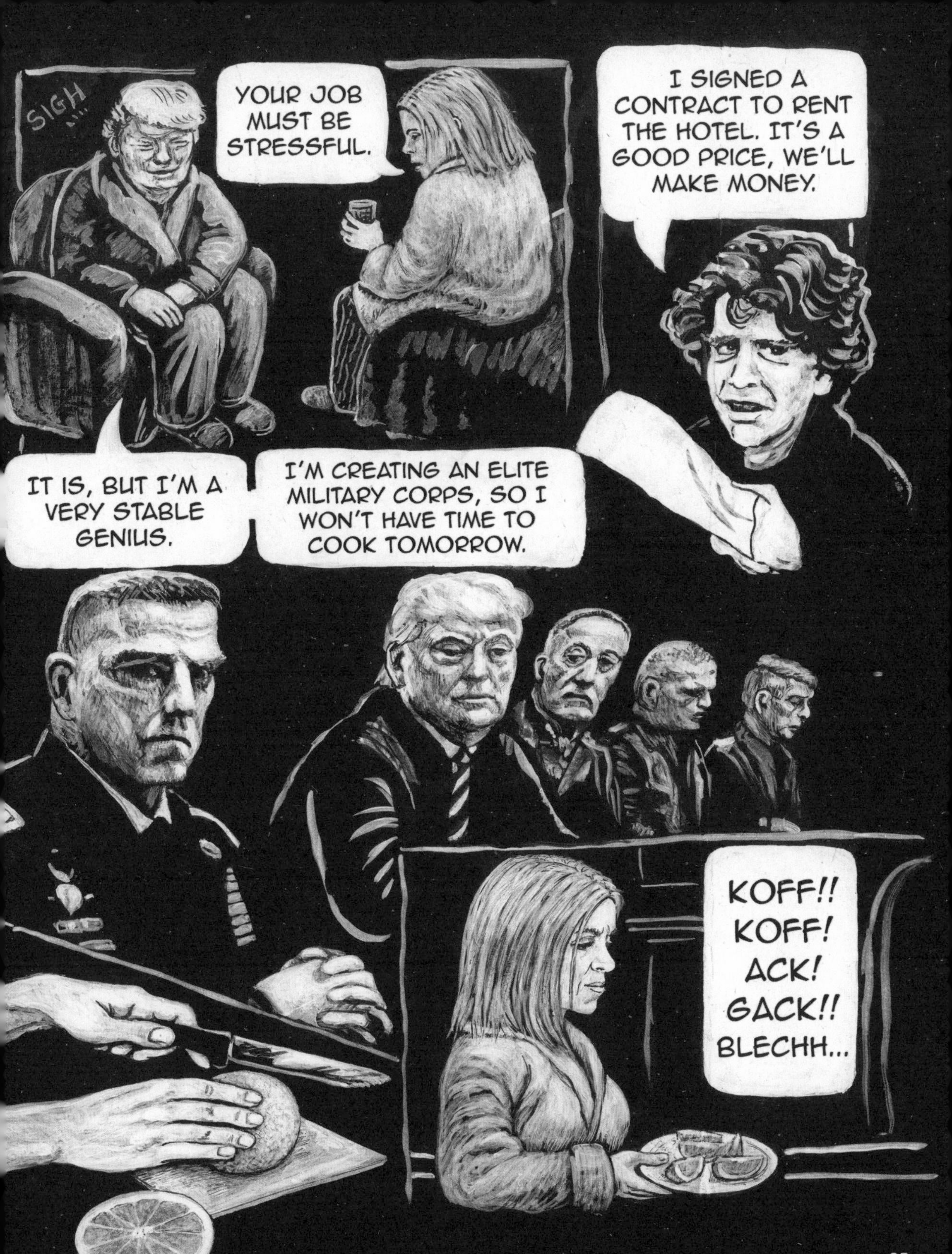
SIGH...
YOUR JOB MUST BE STRESSFUL.
I SIGNED A CONTRACT TO RENT THE HOTEL. IT'S A GOOD PRICE, WE'LL MAKE MONEY.
IT IS, BUT I'M A VERY STABLE GENIUS.
I'M CREATING AN ELITE MILITARY CORPS, SO I WON'T HAVE TIME TO COOK TOMORROW.
KOFF!! KOFF! ACK! GACK!! BLECHH...

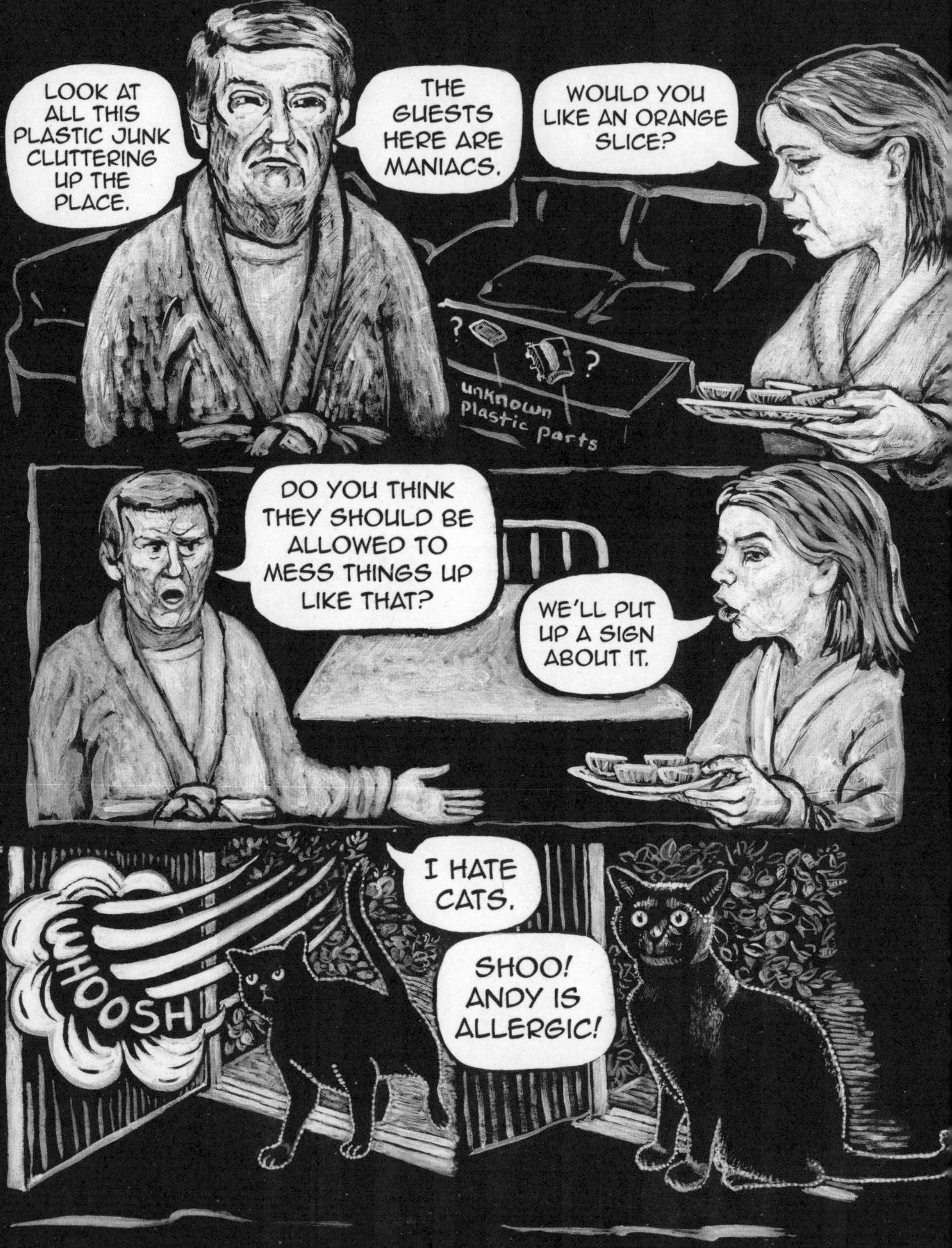
LOOK AT ALL THIS PLASTIC JUNK CLUTTERING UP THE PLACE.
THE GUESTS HERE ARE MANIACS.
WOULD YOU LIKE AN ORANGE SLICE?
unknown plastic parts
DO YOU THINK THEY SHOULD BE ALLOWED TO MESS THINGS UP LIKE THAT?
WE'LL PUT UP A SIGN ABOUT IT.
WHOOSH
I HATE CATS.
SHOO! ANDY IS ALLERGIC!

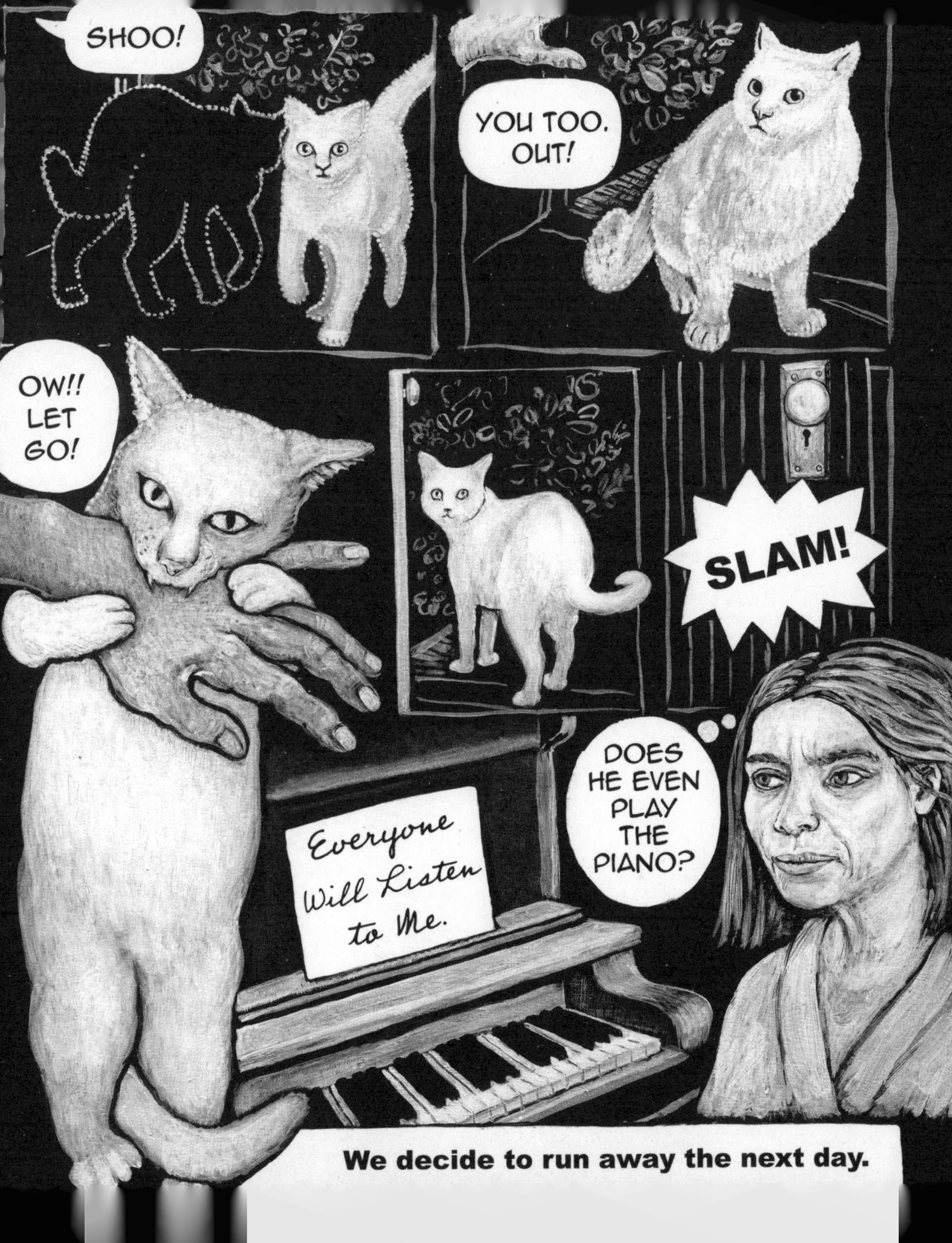
SHOO!
YOU TOO. OUT!
OW!! LET GO!
SLAM!
Everyone Will Listen to Me.
DOES HE EVEN PLAY THE PIANO?
We decide to run away the next day.

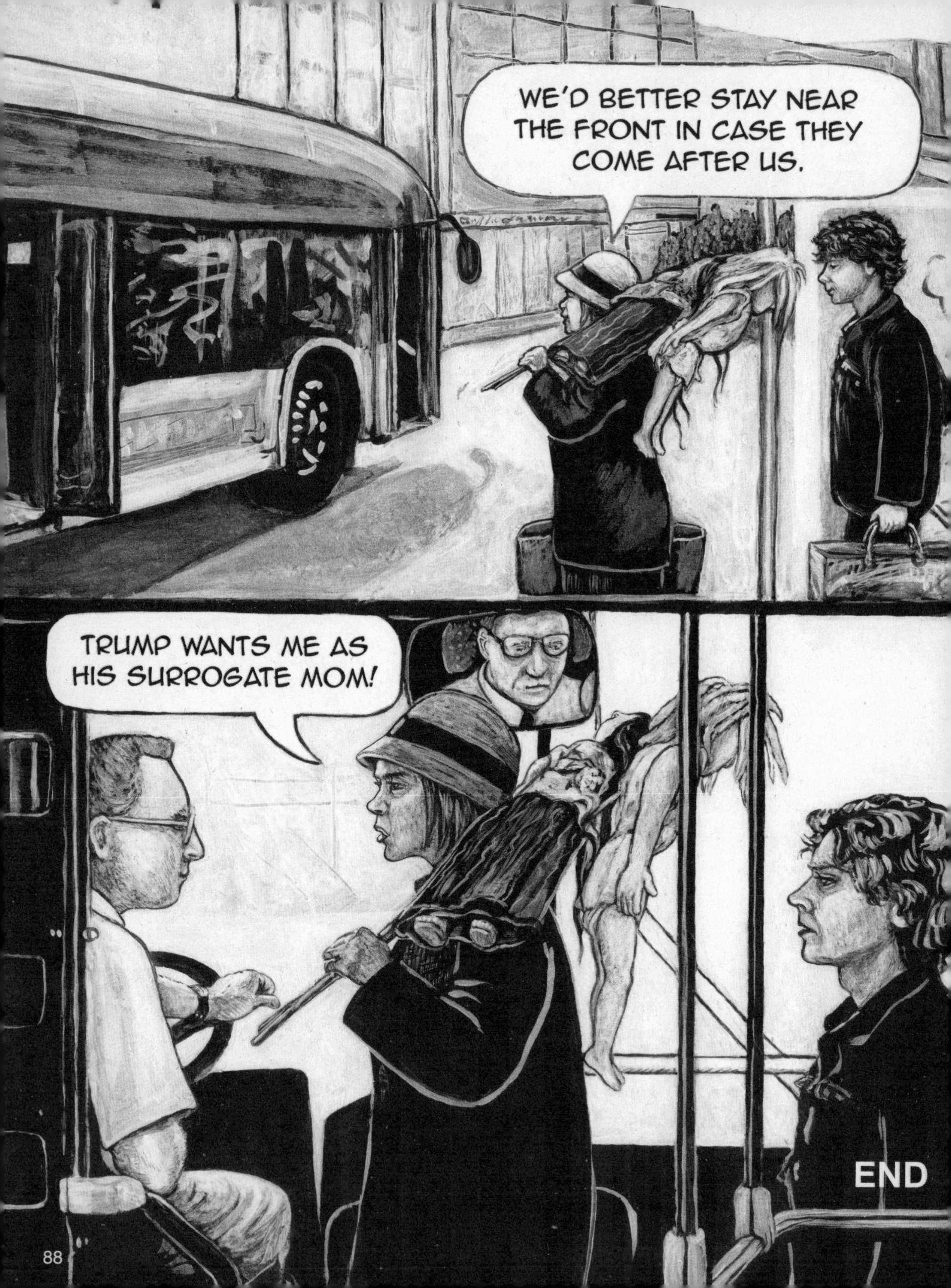
WE'D BETTER STAY NEAR THE FRONT IN CASE THEY COME AFTER US.
TRUMP WANTS ME AS HIS SURROGATE MOM!
END

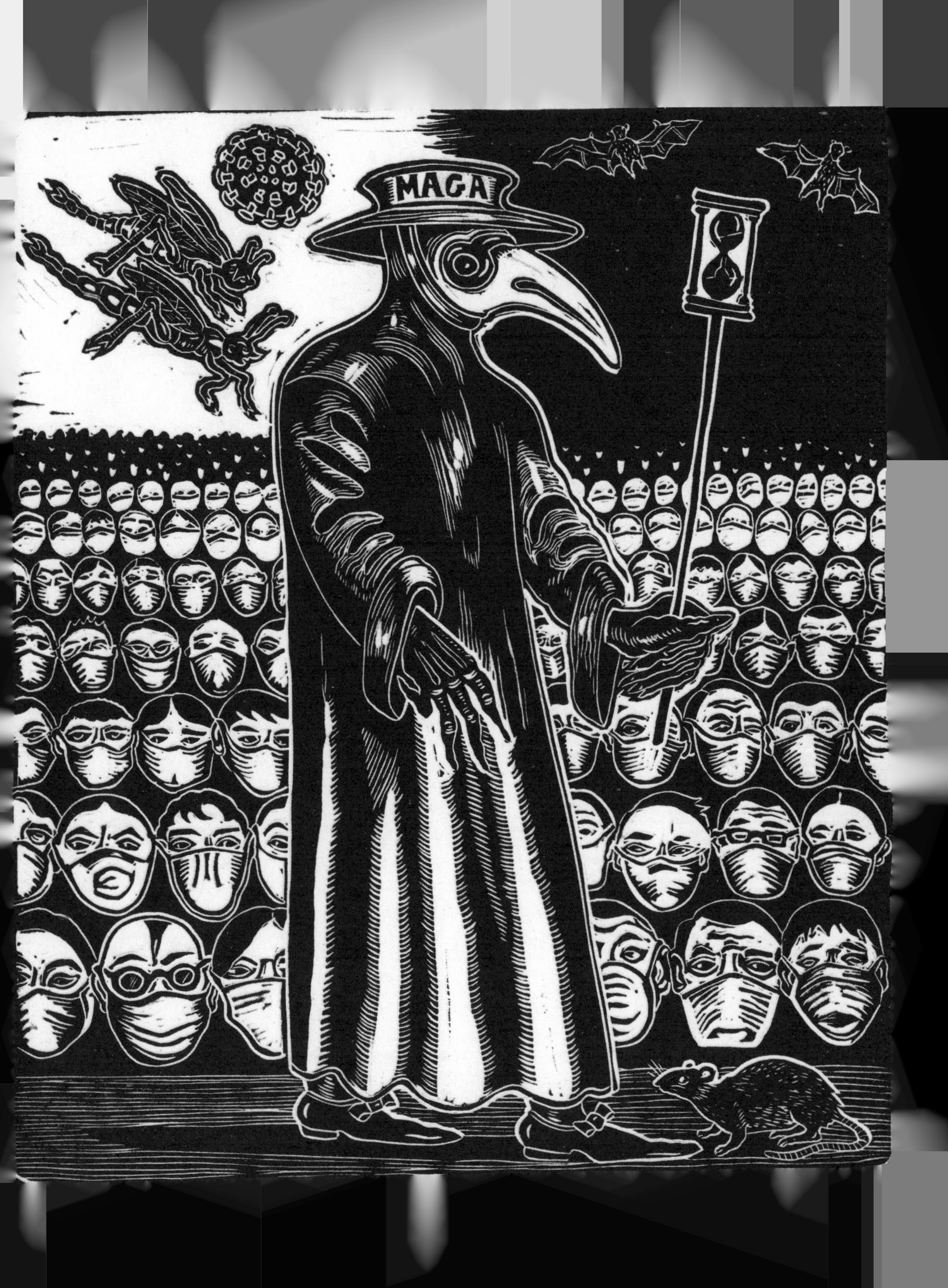
MAGA

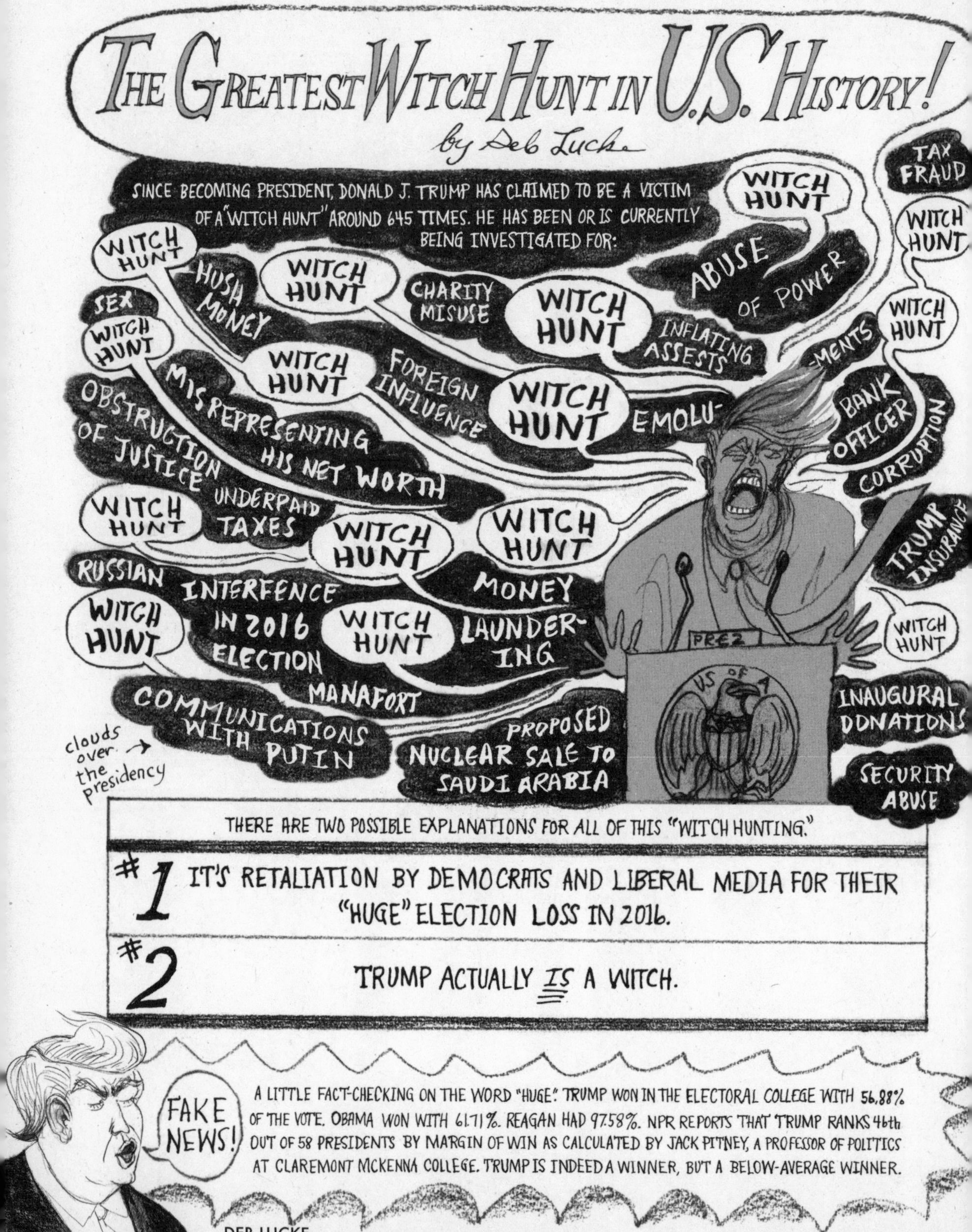
THE GREATEST WITCH HUNT IN U.S. HISTORY!
by Deb Lucke
SINCE BECOMING PRESIDENT, DONALD J. TRUMP HAS CLAIMED TO BE A VICTIM OF A "WITCH HUNT" AROUND 645 TIMES. HE HAS BEEN OR IS CURRENTLY BEING INVESTIGATED FOR:
WITCH HUNT
TAX FRAUD
WITCH HUNT
WITCH HUNT
HUSH MONEY
WITCH HUNT
CHARITY MISUSE
WITCH HUNT
ABUSE OF POWER
SEX
WITCH HUNT
INFLATING ASSESTS
WITCH HUNT
-MENTS
WITCH HUNT
FOREIGN INFLUENCE
WITCH HUNT
EMOLU-
MISREPRESENTING HIS NET WORTH
OBSTRUCTION OF JUSTICE
BANK OFFICER CORRUPTION
WITCH HUNT
UNDERPAID TAXES
WITCH HUNT
WITCH HUNT
TRUMP INSURANCE
RUSSIAN INTERFENCE IN 2016 ELECTION
MONEY LAUNDER-ING
WITCH HUNT
WITCH HUNT
WITCH HUNT
PREZ
US OF A
MANAFORT
COMMUNICATIONS WITH PUTIN
PROPOSED NUCLEAR SALE TO SAUDI ARABIA
INAUGURAL DONATIONS
SECURITY ABUSE
clouds over the presidency
THERE ARE TWO POSSIBLE EXPLANATIONS FOR ALL OF THIS "WITCH HUNTING."
#1 IT'S RETALIATION BY DEMOCRATS AND LIBERAL MEDIA FOR THEIR "HUGE" ELECTION LOSS IN 2016.
#2 TRUMP ACTUALLY IS A WITCH.
FAKE NEWS!
A LITTLE FACT-CHECKING ON THE WORD "HUGE." TRUMP WON IN THE ELECTORAL COLLEGE WITH 56.88% OF THE VOTE. OBAMA WON WITH 61.71%. REAGAN HAD 97.58%. NPR REPORTS THAT TRUMP RANKS 46th OUT OF 58 PRESIDENTS BY MARGIN OF WIN AS CALCULATED BY JACK PITNEY, A PROFESSOR OF POLITICS AT CLAREMONT MCKENNA COLLEGE. TRUMP IS INDEED A WINNER, BUT A BELOW-AVERAGE WINNER.

DEB LUCKE

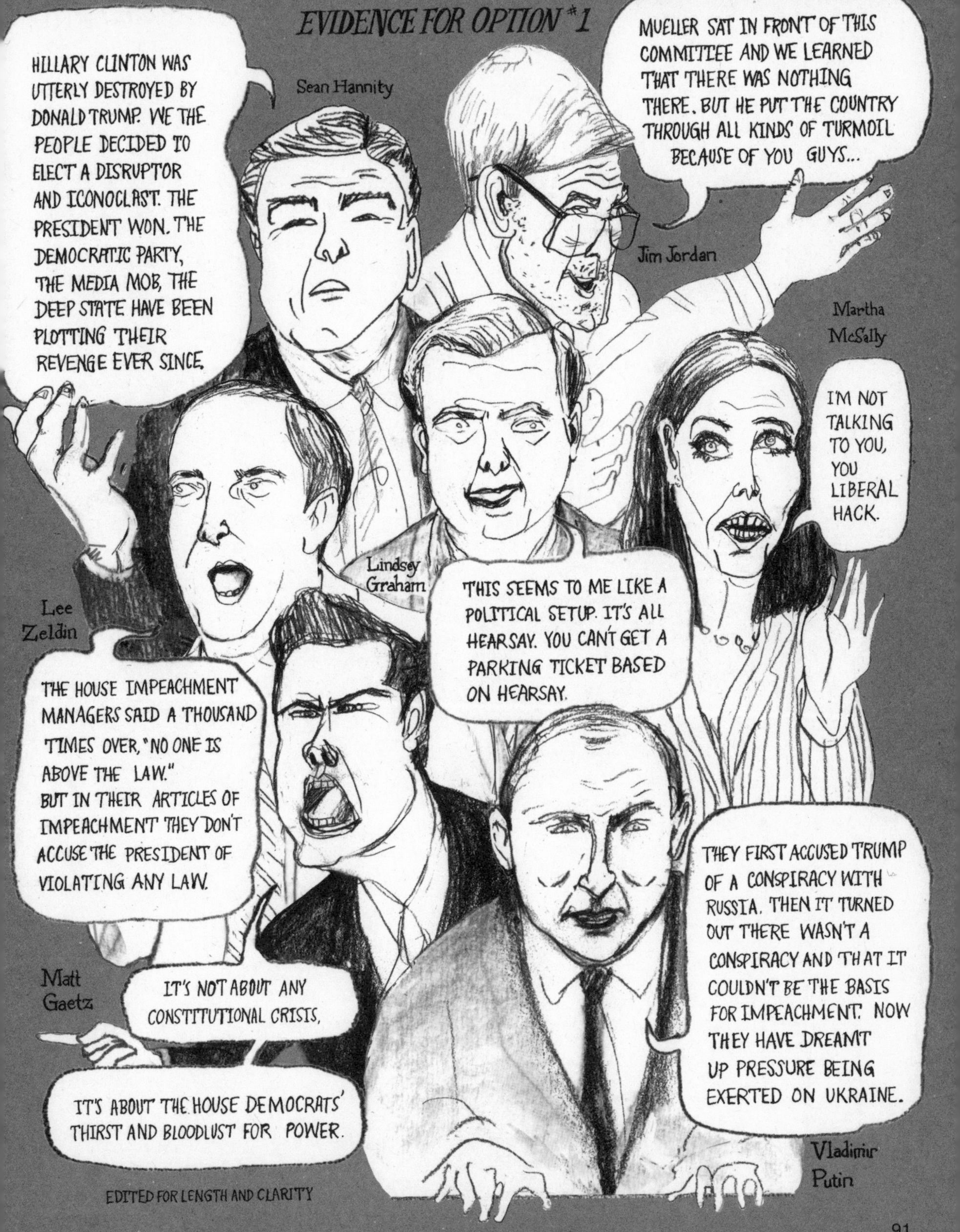
EVIDENCE FOR OPTION #1
HILLARY CLINTON WAS UTTERLY DESTROYED BY DONALD TRUMP. WE THE PEOPLE DECIDED TO ELECT A DISRUPTOR AND ICONOCLAST. THE PRESIDENT WON. THE DEMOCRATIC PARTY, THE MEDIA MOB, THE DEEP STATE HAVE BEEN PLOTTING THEIR REVENGE EVER SINCE.
Sean Hannity
MUELLER SAT IN FRONT OF THIS COMMITTEE AND WE LEARNED THAT THERE WAS NOTHING THERE. BUT HE PUT THE COUNTRY THROUGH ALL KINDS OF TURMOIL BECAUSE OF YOU GUYS...
Jim Jordan
Martha McSally
I'M NOT TALKING TO YOU, YOU LIBERAL HACK.
Lindsey Graham
THIS SEEMS TO ME LIKE A POLITICAL SETUP. IT'S ALL HEARSAY. YOU CAN'T GET A PARKING TICKET BASED ON HEARSAY.
Lee Zeldin
THE HOUSE IMPEACHMENT MANAGERS SAID A THOUSAND TIMES OVER, "NO ONE IS ABOVE THE LAW." BUT IN THEIR ARTICLES OF IMPEACHMENT THEY DON'T ACCUSE THE PRESIDENT OF VIOLATING ANY LAW.
THEY FIRST ACCUSED TRUMP OF A CONSPIRACY WITH RUSSIA. THEN IT TURNED OUT THERE WASN'T A CONSPIRACY AND THAT IT COULDN'T BE THE BASIS FOR IMPEACHMENT. NOW THEY HAVE DREAMT UP PRESSURE BEING EXERTED ON UKRAINE.
Matt Gaetz
IT'S NOT ABOUT ANY CONSTITUTIONAL CRISIS,
IT'S ABOUT THE HOUSE DEMOCRATS' THIRST AND BLOODLUST FOR POWER.
Vladimir Putin
EDITED FOR LENGTH AND CLARITY

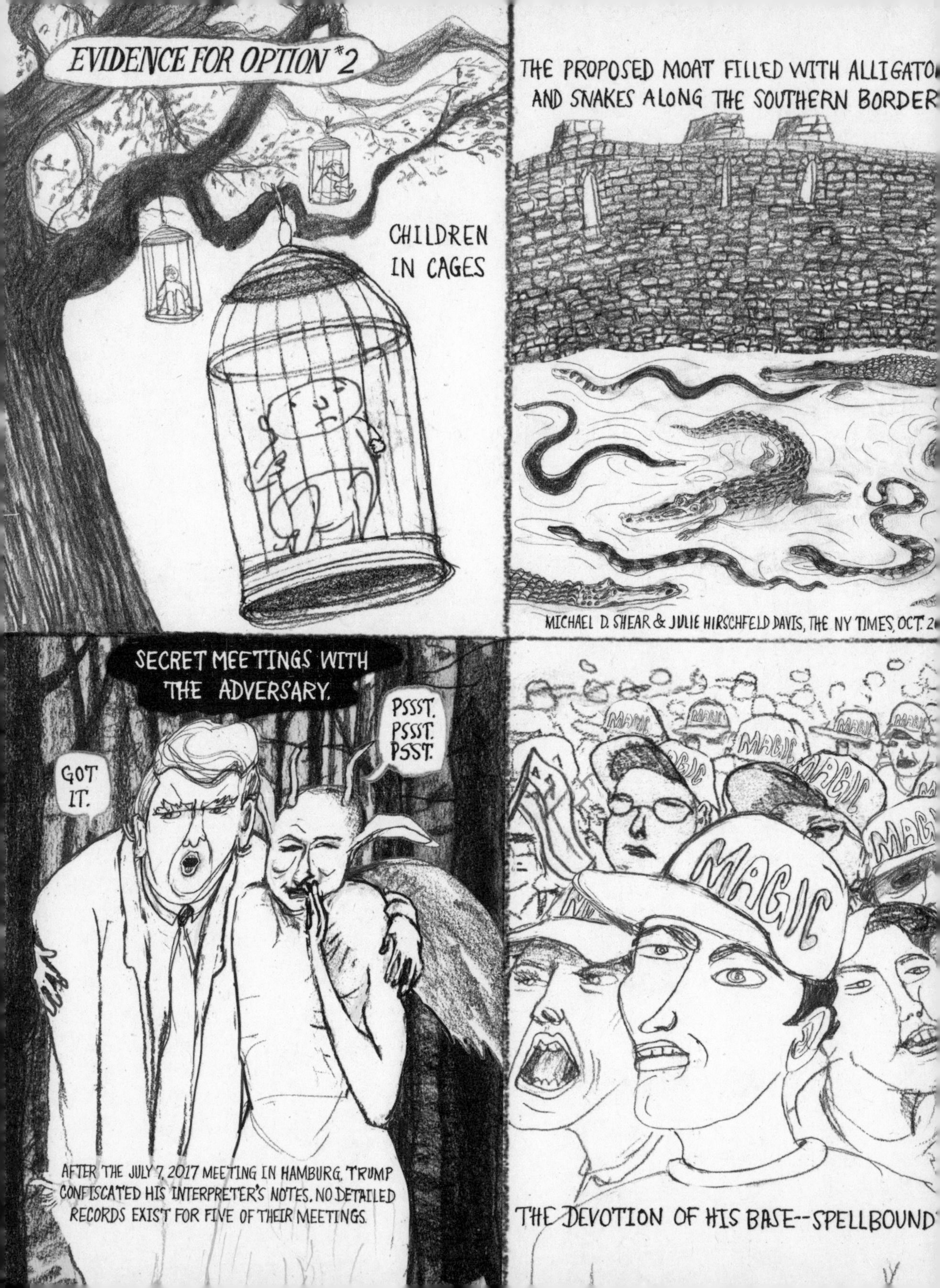
EVIDENCE FOR OPTION #2
CHILDREN IN CAGES
THE PROPOSED MOAT FILLED WITH ALLIGATO
AND SNAKES ALONG THE SOUTHERN BORDER
MICHAEL D. SHEAR & JULIE HIRSCHFELD DAVIS, THE NY TIMES, OCT. 2
SECRET MEETINGS WITH THE ADVERSARY.
PSSST. PSSST. PSST.
GOT IT.
AFTER THE JULY 7, 2017 MEETING IN HAMBURG, TRUMP CONFISCATED HIS INTERPRETER'S NOTES. NO DETAILED RECORDS EXIST FOR FIVE OF THEIR MEETINGS.
MAGIC
THE DEVOTION OF HIS BASE--SPELLBOUND

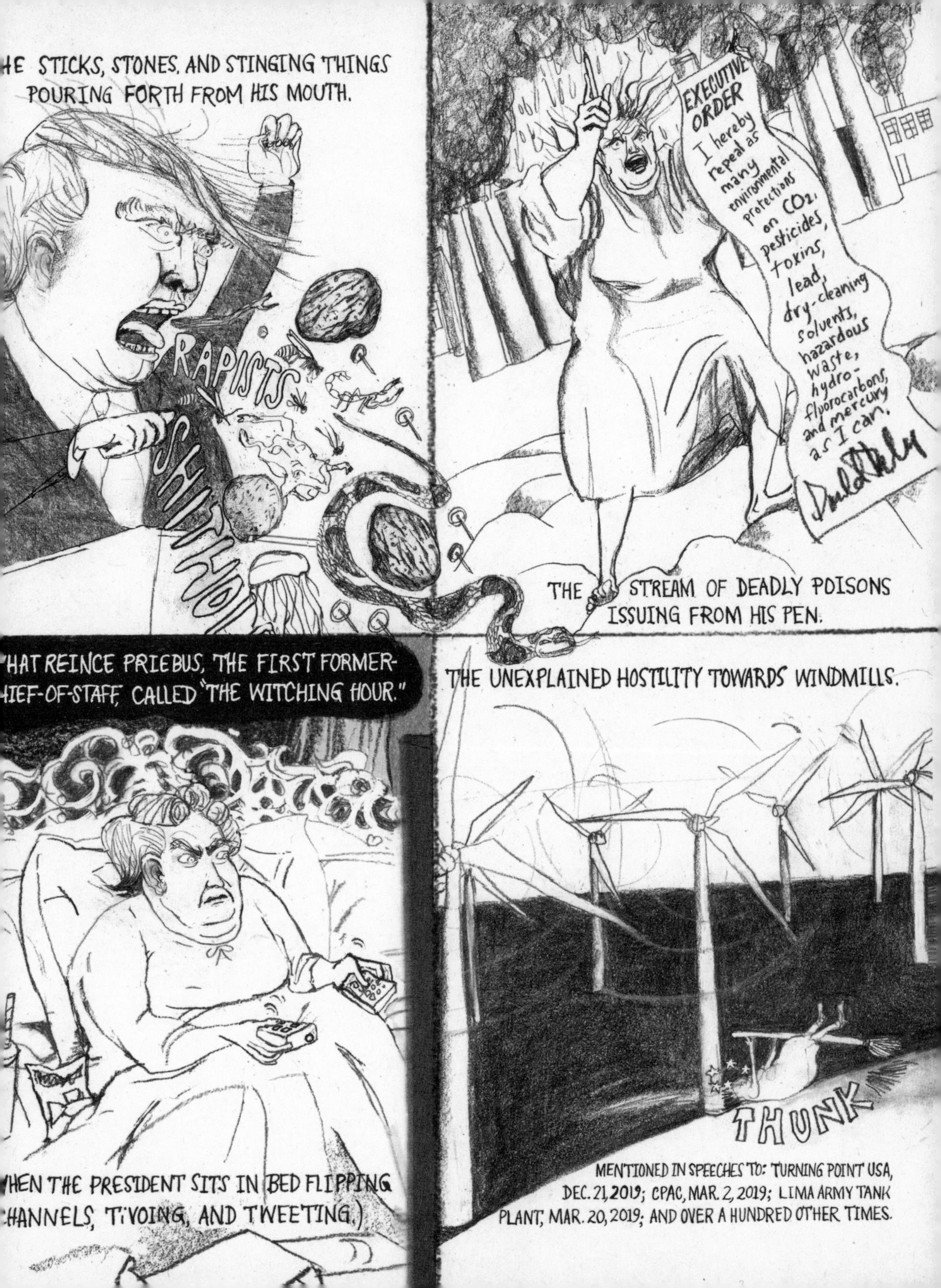
HE STICKS, STONES, AND STINGING THINGS POURING FORTH FROM HIS MOUTH.
RAPISTS
SHITHOL
EXECUTIVE ORDER
I hereby repeal as many environmental protections on CO2, pesticides, toxins, lead, dry-cleaning solvents, hazardous waste, hydro-fluorocarbons, and mercury as I can.
THE STREAM OF DEADLY POISONS ISSUING FROM HIS PEN.
HAT REINCE PRIEBUS, THE FIRST FORMER-HIEF-OF-STAFF, CALLED "THE WITCHING HOUR."
HEN THE PRESIDENT SITS IN BED FLIPPING HANNELS, TIVOING, AND TWEETING.)
THE UNEXPLAINED HOSTILITY TOWARDS WINDMILLS.
THUNK
MENTIONED IN SPEECHES TO: TURNING POINT USA, DEC. 21, 2019; CPAC, MAR. 2, 2019; LIMA ARMY TANK PLANT, MAR. 20, 2019; AND OVER A HUNDRED OTHER TIMES.

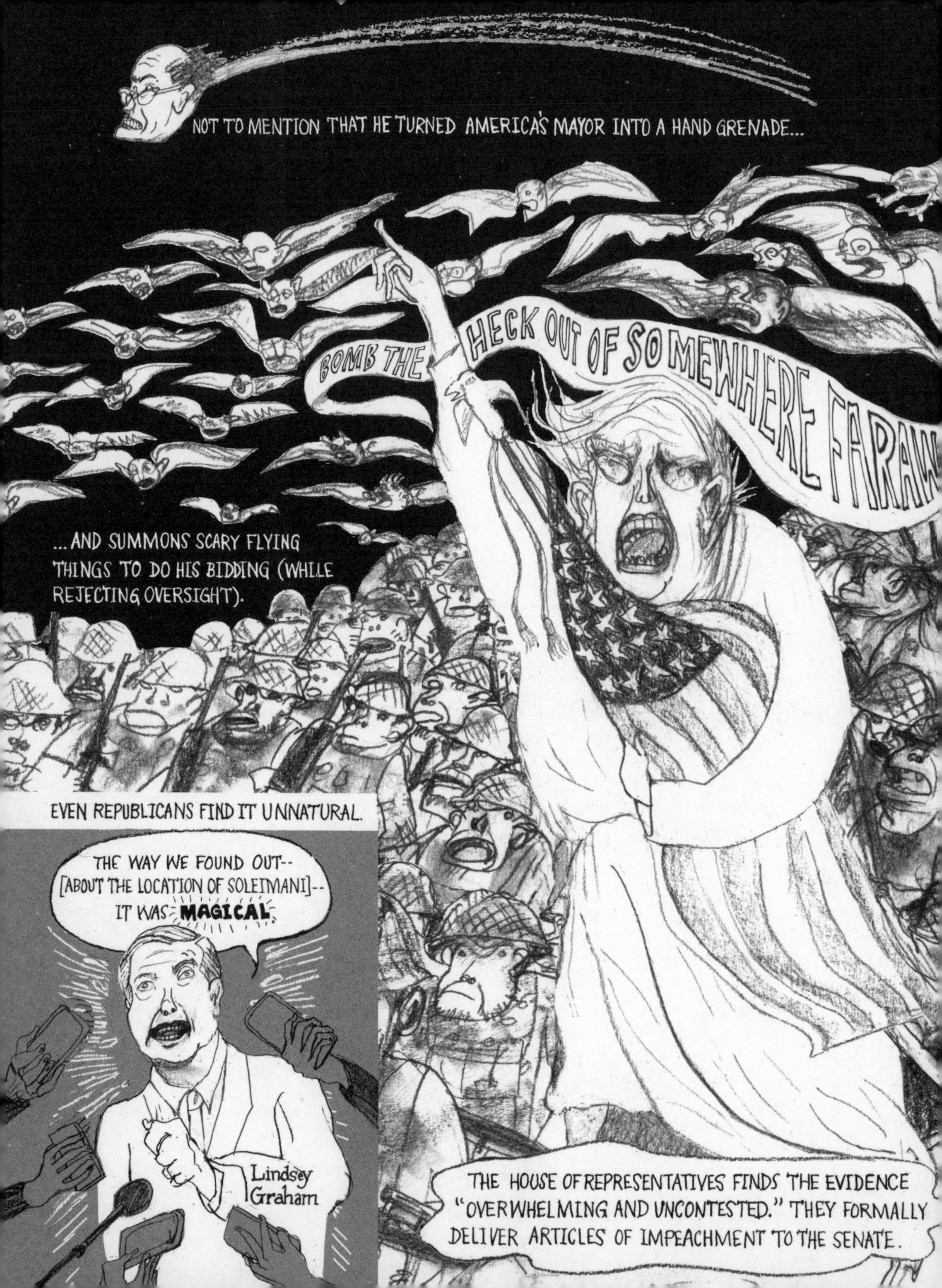
NOT TO MENTION THAT HE TURNED AMERICA'S MAYOR INTO A HAND GRENADE...
BOMB THE HECK OUT OF SOMEWHERE FARAW
...AND SUMMONS SCARY FLYING THINGS TO DO HIS BIDDING (WHILE REJECTING OVERSIGHT).
EVEN REPUBLICANS FIND IT UNNATURAL.
THE WAY WE FOUND OUT-- [ABOUT THE LOCATION OF SOLEIMANI]-- IT WAS MAGICAL.
Lindsey Graham
THE HOUSE OF REPRESENTATIVES FINDS THE EVIDENCE "OVERWHELMING AND UNCONTESTED." THEY FORMALLY DELIVER ARTICLES OF IMPEACHMENT TO THE SENATE.

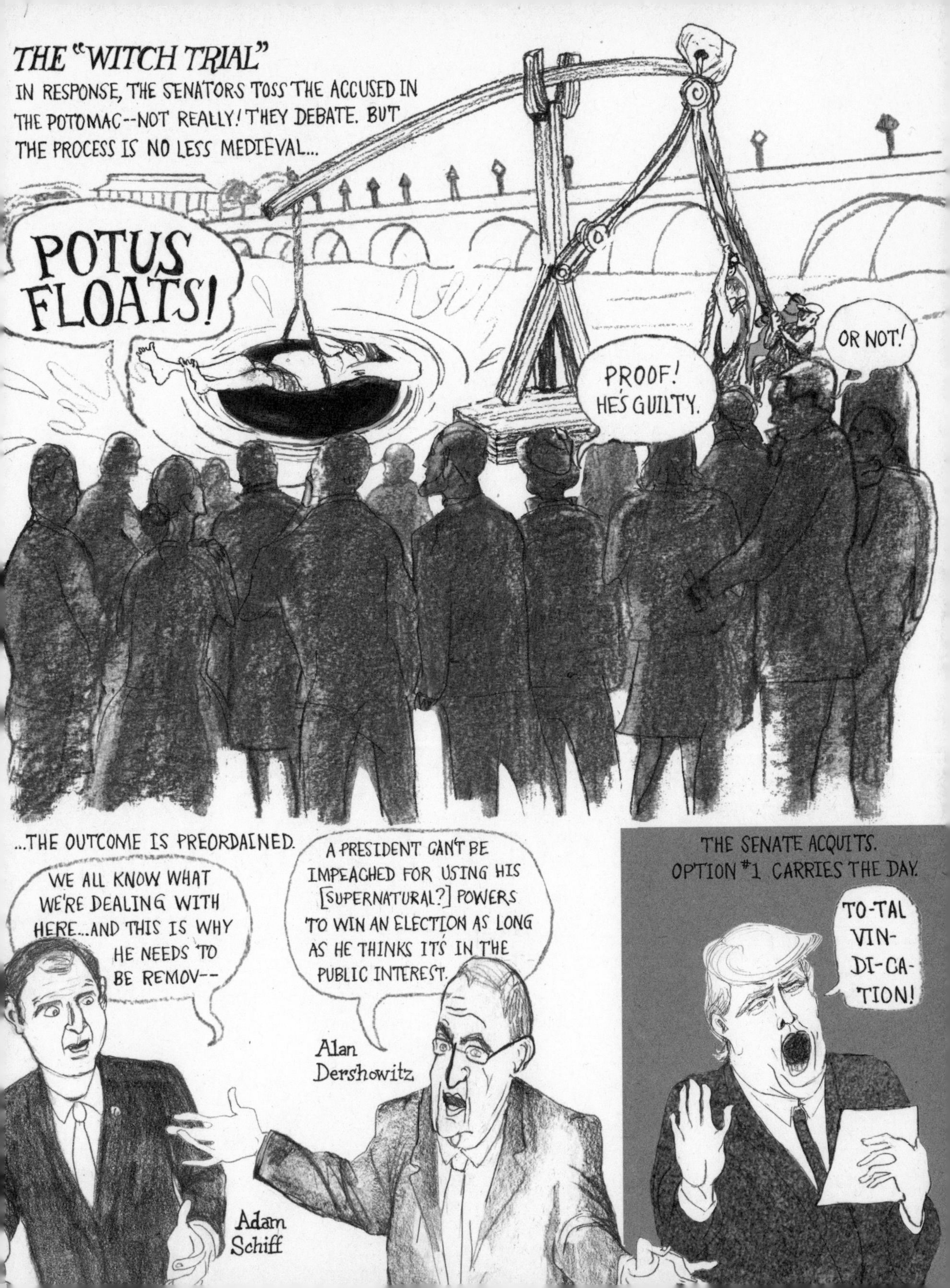
THE "WITCH TRIAL"
IN RESPONSE, THE SENATORS TOSS THE ACCUSED IN THE POTOMAC--NOT REALLY! THEY DEBATE. BUT THE PROCESS IS NO LESS MEDIEVAL...
POTUS FLOATS!
PROOF! HE'S GUILTY.
OR NOT!
...THE OUTCOME IS PREORDAINED.
WE ALL KNOW WHAT WE'RE DEALING WITH HERE...AND THIS IS WHY HE NEEDS TO BE REMOV--
A PRESIDENT CAN'T BE IMPEACHED FOR USING HIS [SUPERNATURAL?] POWERS TO WIN AN ELECTION AS LONG AS HE THINKS IT'S IN THE PUBLIC INTEREST.
Alan Dershowitz
Adam Schiff
THE SENATE ACQUITS. OPTION #1 CARRIES THE DAY.
TO-TAL VIN-DI-CA-TION!

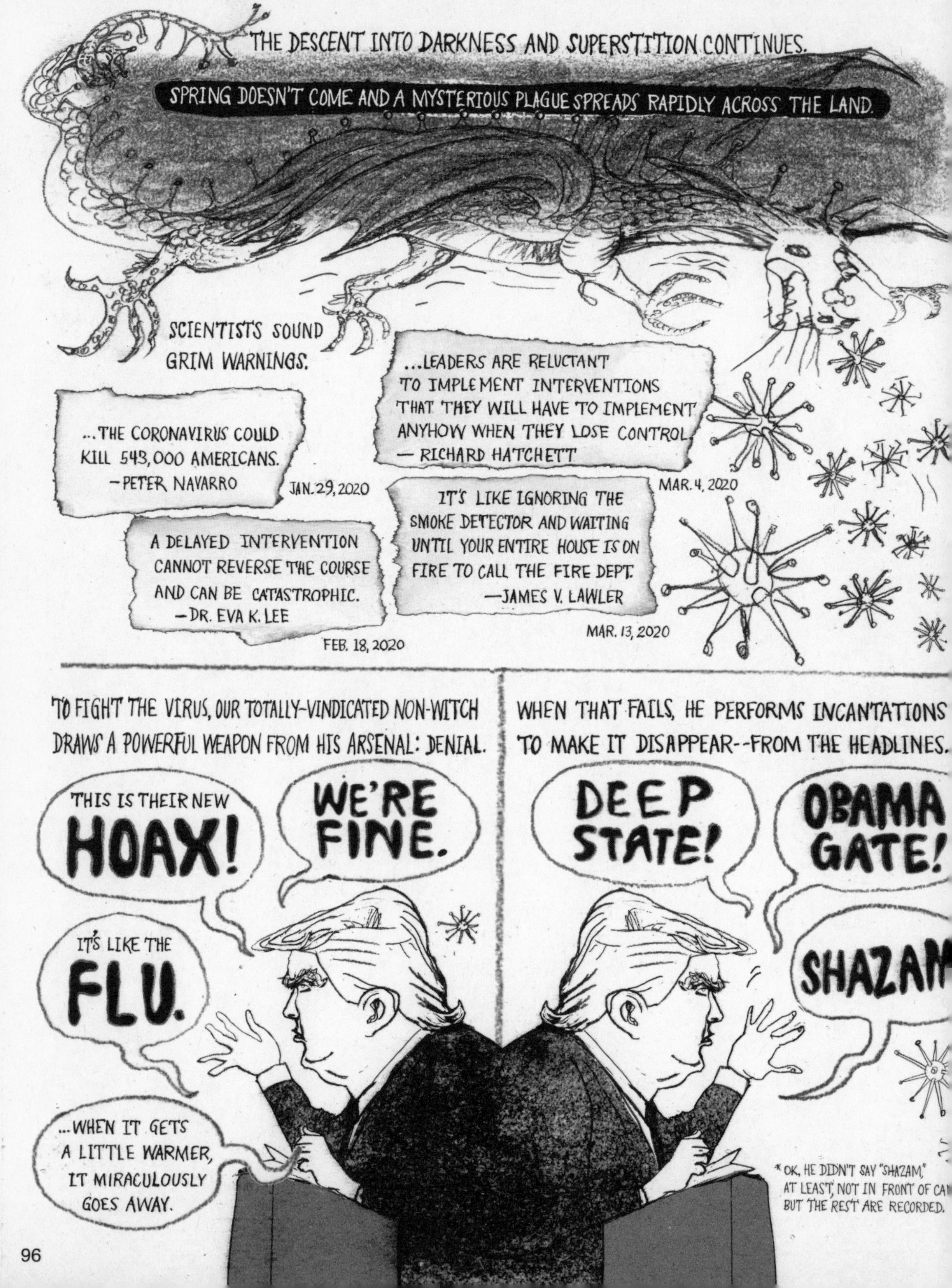
THE DESCENT INTO DARKNESS AND SUPERSTITION CONTINUES.
SPRING DOESN'T COME AND A MYSTERIOUS PLAGUE SPREADS RAPIDLY ACROSS THE LAND.
SCIENTISTS SOUND GRIM WARNINGS.
...THE CORONAVIRUS COULD KILL 543,000 AMERICANS. —PETER NAVARRO
JAN. 29, 2020
A DELAYED INTERVENTION CANNOT REVERSE THE COURSE AND CAN BE CATASTROPHIC. —DR. EVA K. LEE
FEB. 18, 2020
...LEADERS ARE RELUCTANT TO IMPLEMENT INTERVENTIONS THAT THEY WILL HAVE TO IMPLEMENT ANYHOW WHEN THEY LOSE CONTROL. — RICHARD HATCHETT
MAR. 4, 2020
IT'S LIKE IGNORING THE SMOKE DETECTOR AND WAITING UNTIL YOUR ENTIRE HOUSE IS ON FIRE TO CALL THE FIRE DEPT. —JAMES V. LAWLER
MAR. 13, 2020
TO FIGHT THE VIRUS, OUR TOTALLY-VINDICATED NON-WITCH DRAWS A POWERFUL WEAPON FROM HIS ARSENAL: DENIAL.
THIS IS THEIR NEW HOAX!
WE'RE FINE.
IT'S LIKE THE FLU.
...WHEN IT GETS A LITTLE WARMER, IT MIRACULOUSLY GOES AWAY.
WHEN THAT FAILS, HE PERFORMS INCANTATIONS TO MAKE IT DISAPPEAR--FROM THE HEADLINES.
DEEP STATE!
OBAMA GATE!
SHAZAM
* OK, HE DIDN'T SAY "SHAZAM," AT LEAST, NOT IN FRONT OF CA
BUT THE REST ARE RECORDED.

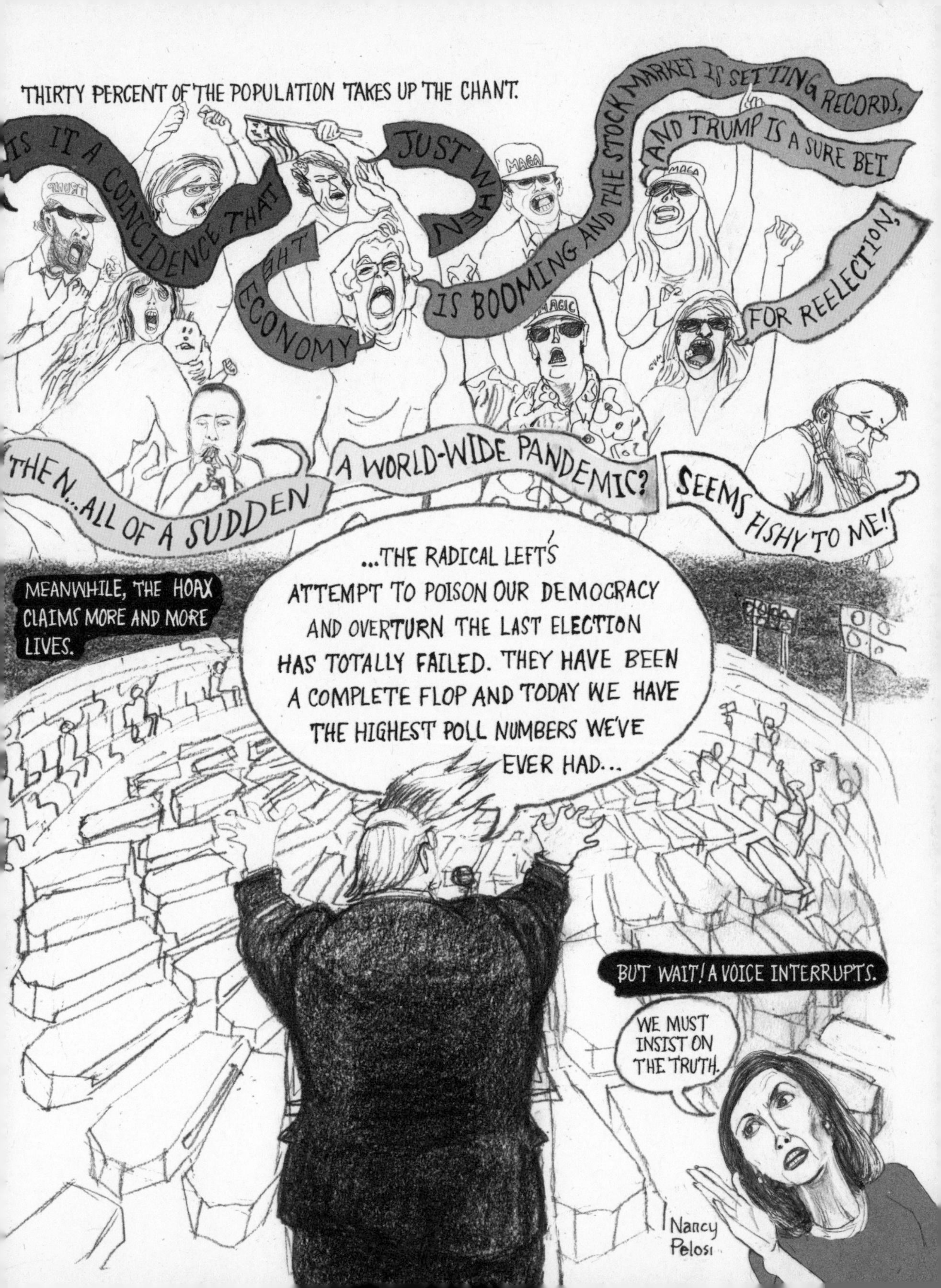
THIRTY PERCENT OF THE POPULATION TAKES UP THE CHANT.
IS IT A COINCIDENCE THAT JUST WHEN THE ECONOMY IS BOOMING AND THE STOCK MARKET IS SETTING RECORDS, AND TRUMP IS A SURE BET FOR REELECTION,
THEN... ALL OF A SUDDEN A WORLD-WIDE PANDEMIC? SEEMS FISHY TO ME!
MEANWHILE, THE HOAX CLAIMS MORE AND MORE LIVES.
...THE RADICAL LEFT'S ATTEMPT TO POISON OUR DEMOCRACY AND OVERTURN THE LAST ELECTION HAS TOTALLY FAILED. THEY HAVE BEEN A COMPLETE FLOP AND TODAY WE HAVE THE HIGHEST POLL NUMBERS WE'VE EVER HAD...
BUT WAIT! A VOICE INTERRUPTS.
WE MUST INSIST ON THE TRUTH.
Nancy Pelosi

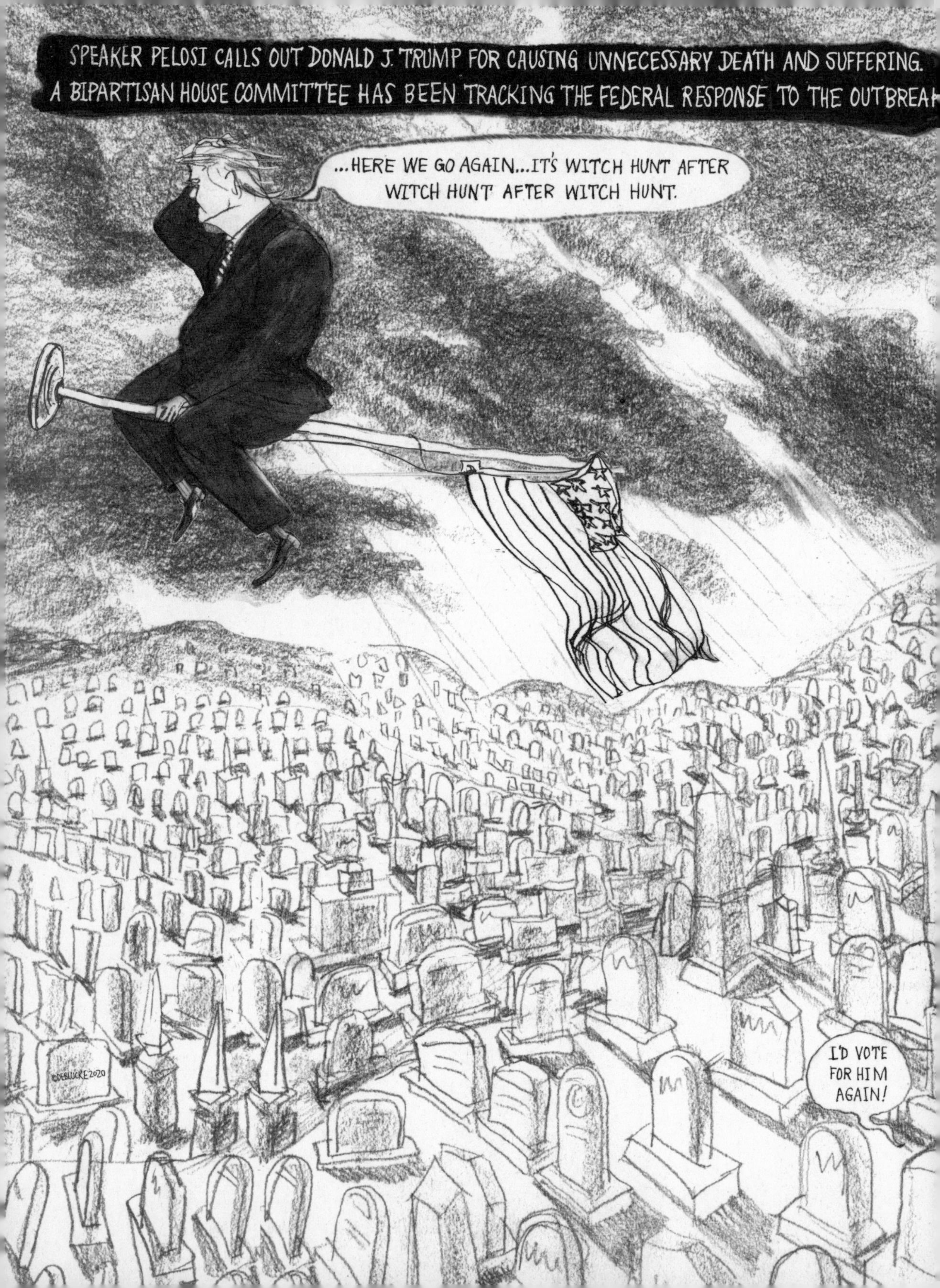
SPEAKER PELOSI CALLS OUT DONALD J. TRUMP FOR CAUSING UNNECESSARY DEATH AND SUFFERING.
A BIPARTISAN HOUSE COMMITTEE HAS BEEN TRACKING THE FEDERAL RESPONSE TO THE OUTBREAK
...HERE WE GO AGAIN...IT'S WITCH HUNT AFTER WITCH HUNT AFTER WITCH HUNT.
I'D VOTE FOR HIM AGAIN!
©DEBLUCKE 2020

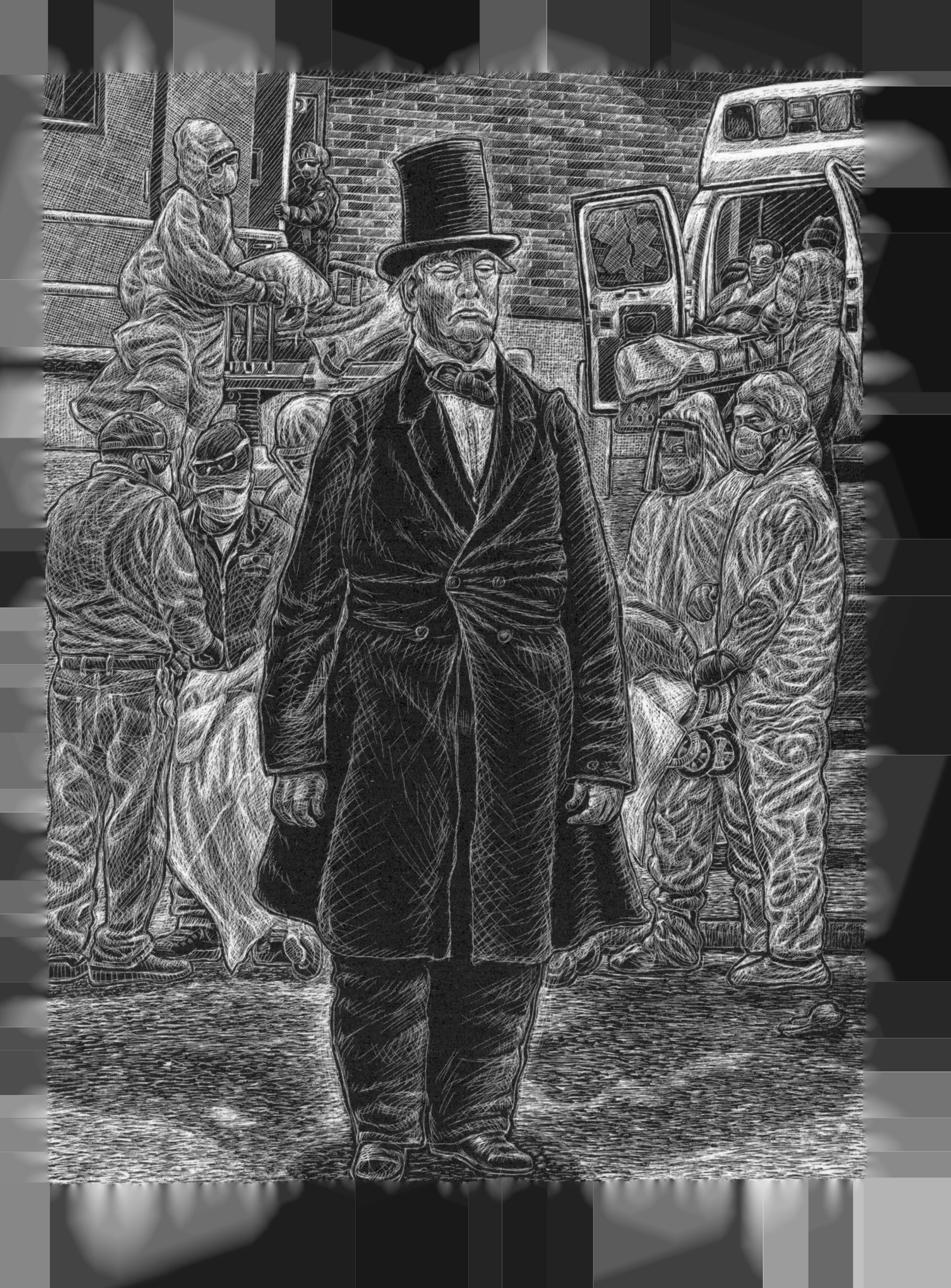

APOCALYPSE OF IGNORANCE

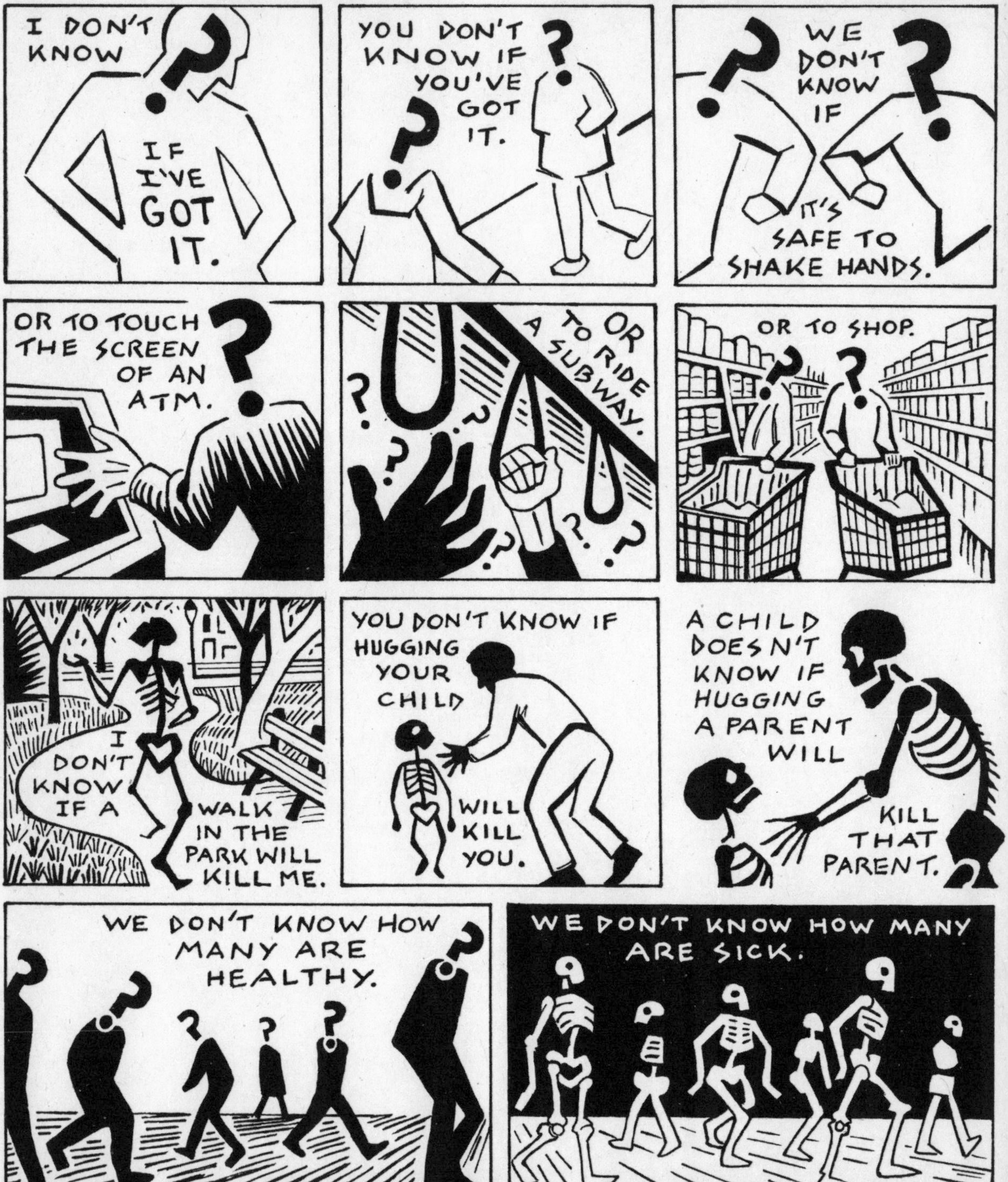

I DON'T KNOW
IF I'VE GOT IT.
YOU DON'T KNOW IF YOU'VE GOT IT.
WE DON'T KNOW IF
IT'S SAFE TO SHAKE HANDS.
OR TO TOUCH THE SCREEN OF AN ATM.
OR TO RIDE A SUBWAY.
OR TO SHOP.
I DON'T KNOW IF A
WALK IN THE PARK WILL KILL ME.
YOU DON'T KNOW IF HUGGING YOUR CHILD
WILL KILL YOU.
A CHILD DOESN'T KNOW IF HUGGING A PARENT WILL
KILL THAT PARENT.
WE DON'T KNOW HOW MANY ARE HEALTHY.
WE DON'T KNOW HOW MANY ARE SICK.

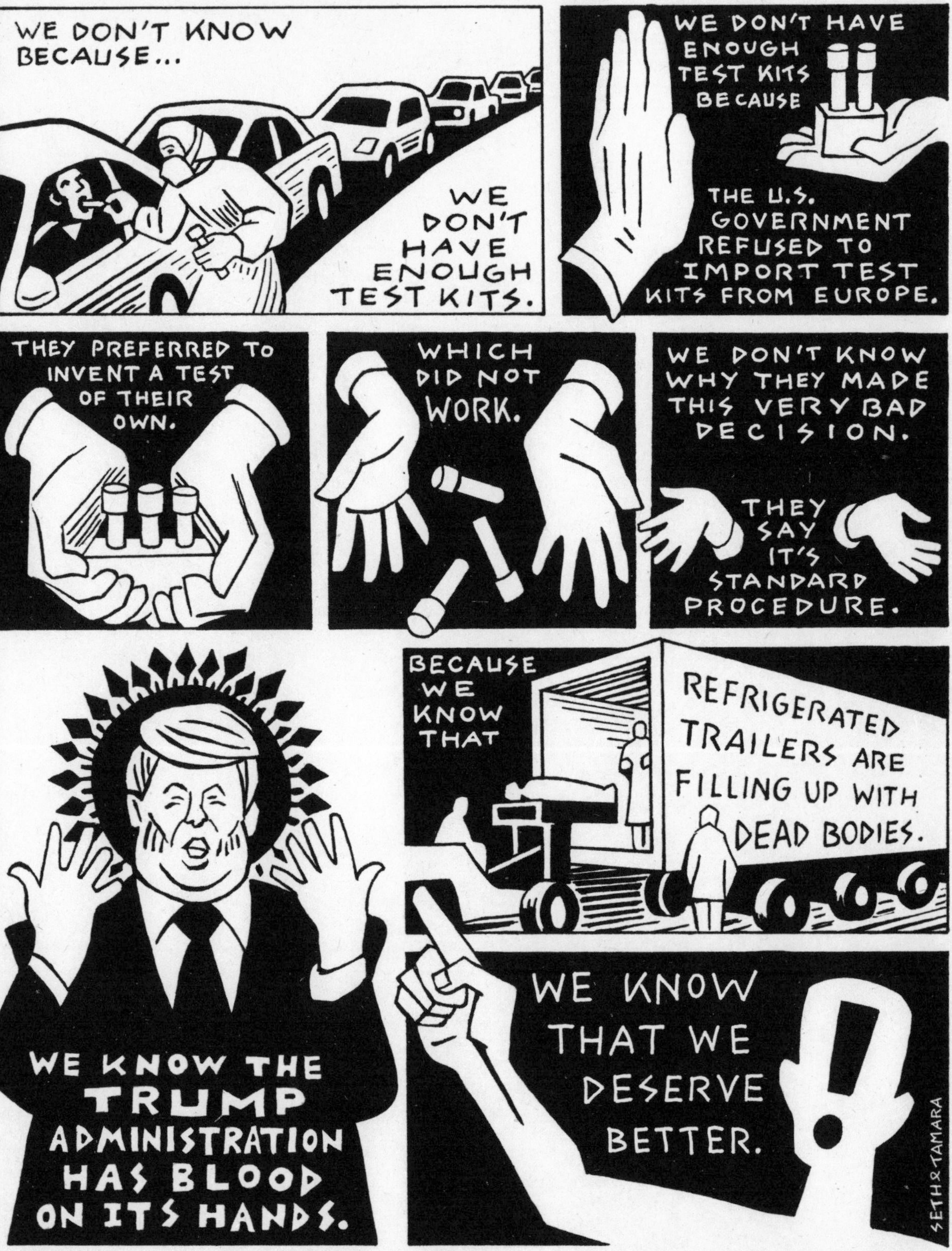
WE DON'T KNOW BECAUSE...
WE DON'T HAVE ENOUGH TEST KITS.
WE DON'T HAVE ENOUGH TEST KITS BECAUSE
THE U.S. GOVERNMENT REFUSED TO IMPORT TEST KITS FROM EUROPE.
THEY PREFERRED TO INVENT A TEST OF THEIR OWN.
WHICH DID NOT WORK.
WE DON'T KNOW WHY THEY MADE THIS VERY BAD DECISION.
THEY SAY IT'S STANDARD PROCEDURE.
WE KNOW THE TRUMP ADMINISTRATION HAS BLOOD ON ITS HANDS.
BECAUSE WE KNOW THAT
REFRIGERATED TRAILERS ARE FILLING UP WITH DEAD BODIES.
WE KNOW THAT WE DESERVE BETTER.
SETH & TAMARA

WRITTEN IN MARCH OF 2020 WHEN WE DID NOT KNOW.

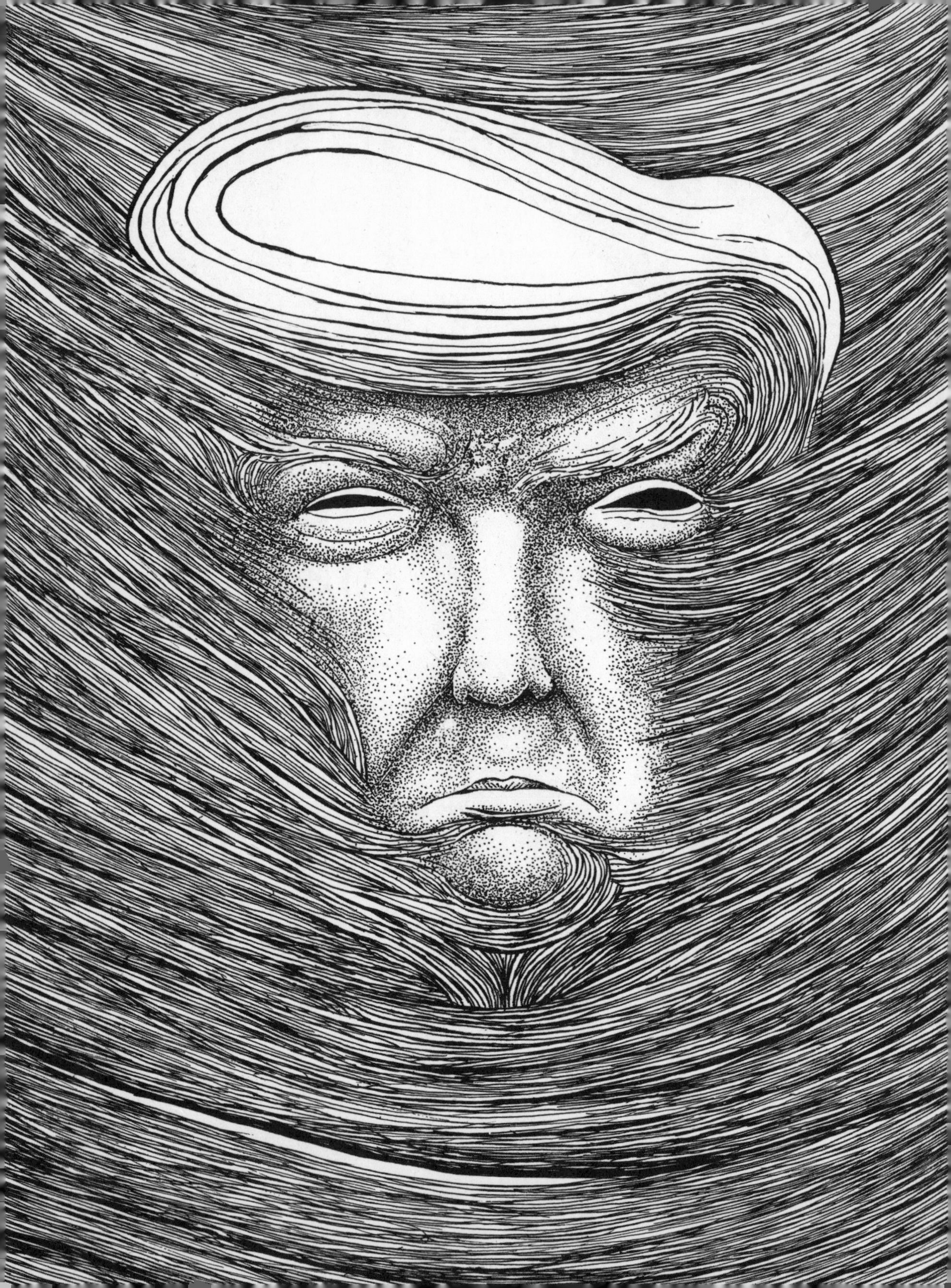

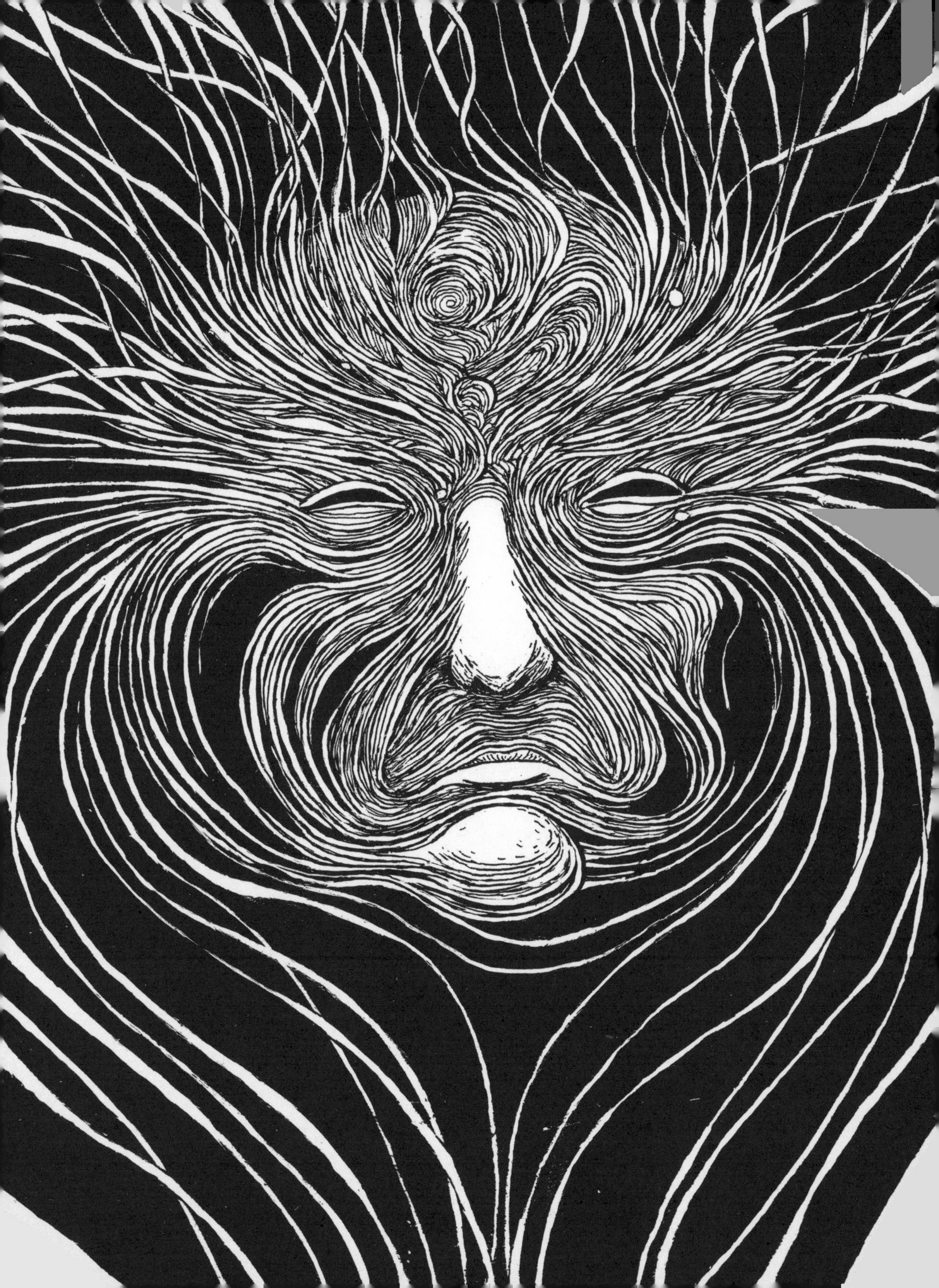

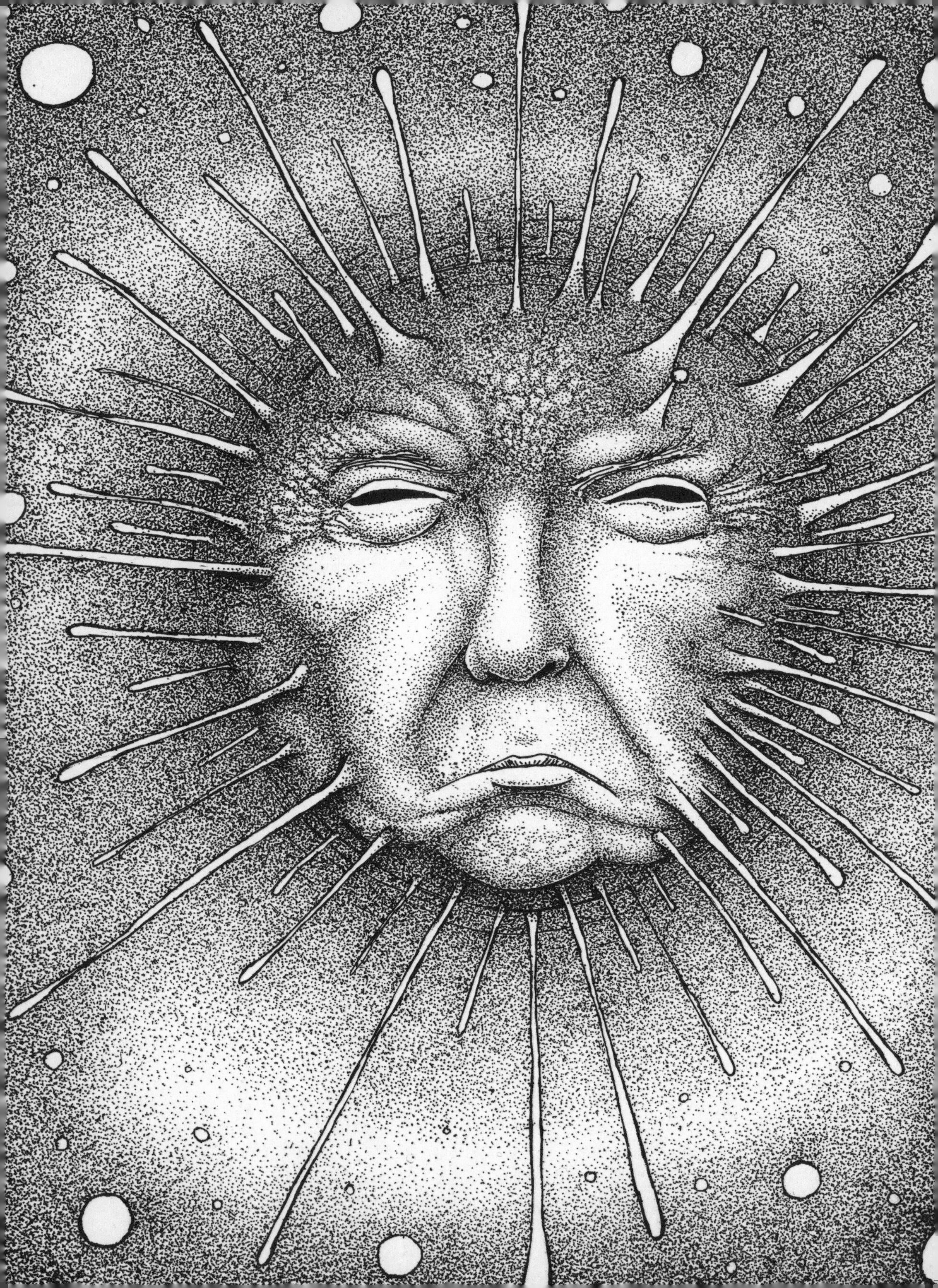

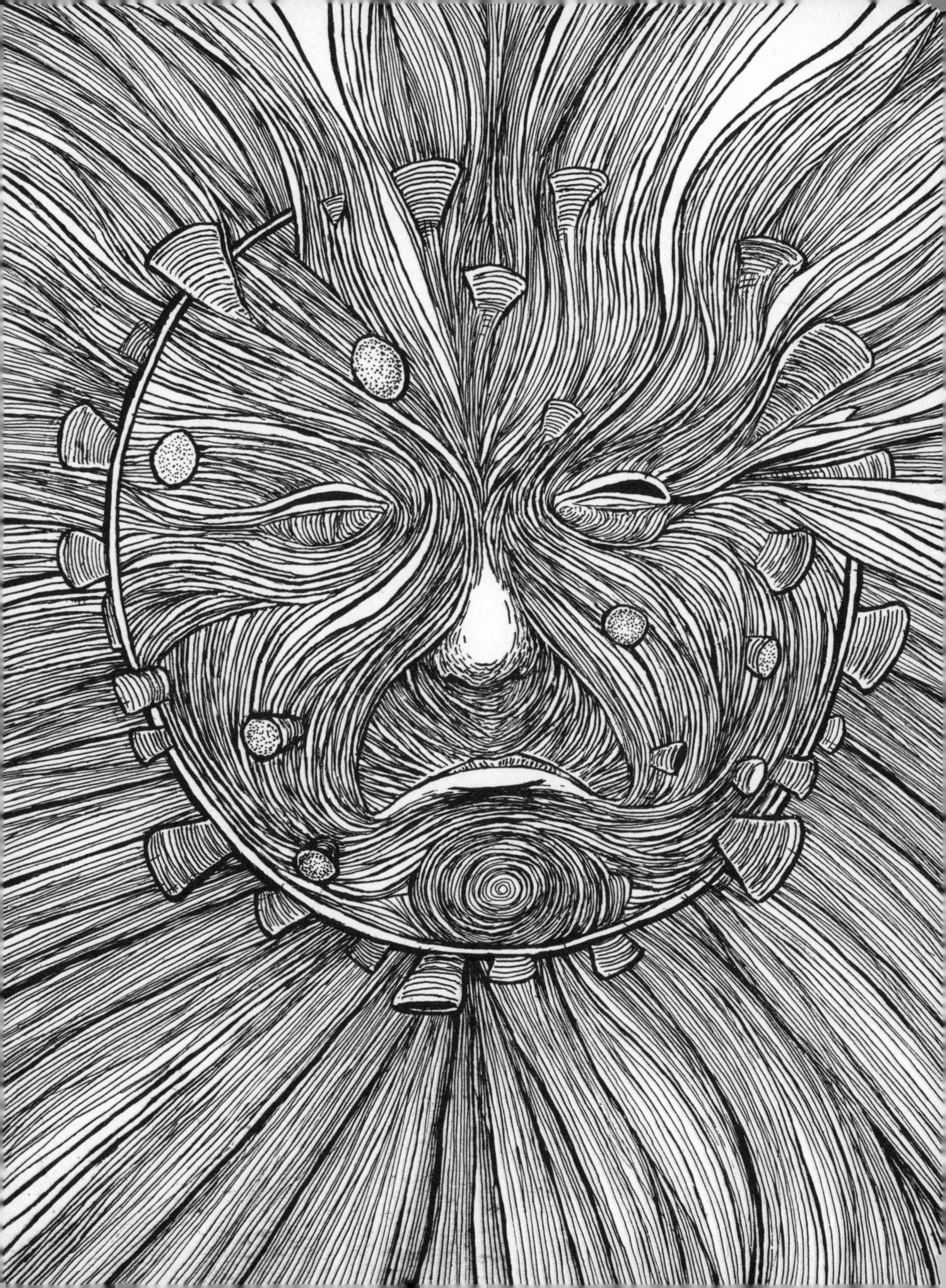

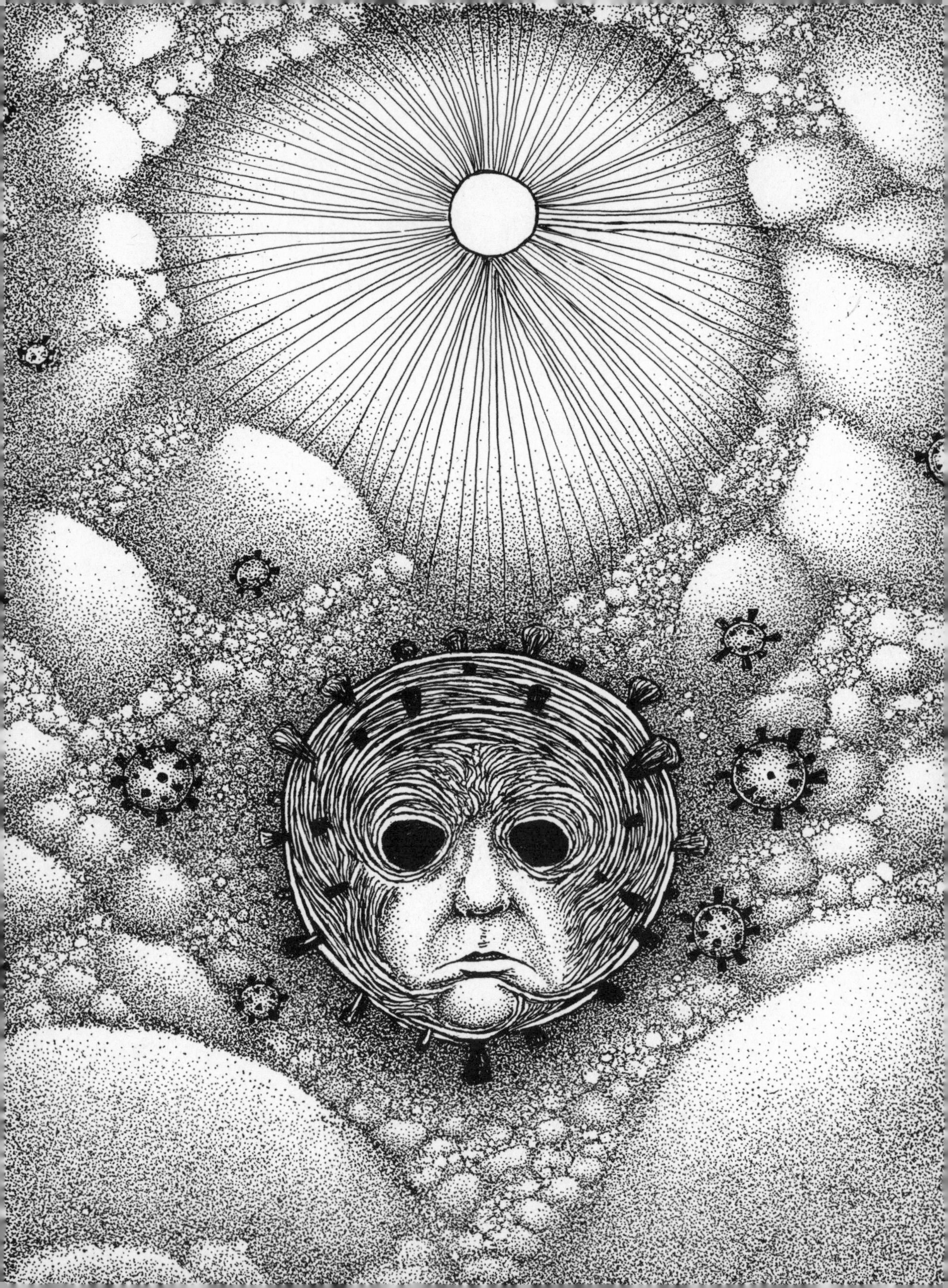

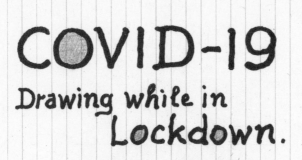

COVID-19
Drawing while in Lockdown.

Anton van Dalen

EAST VILLAGE, N.Y.C./ EAST MORICHES, L.I.

MARCH, 2020

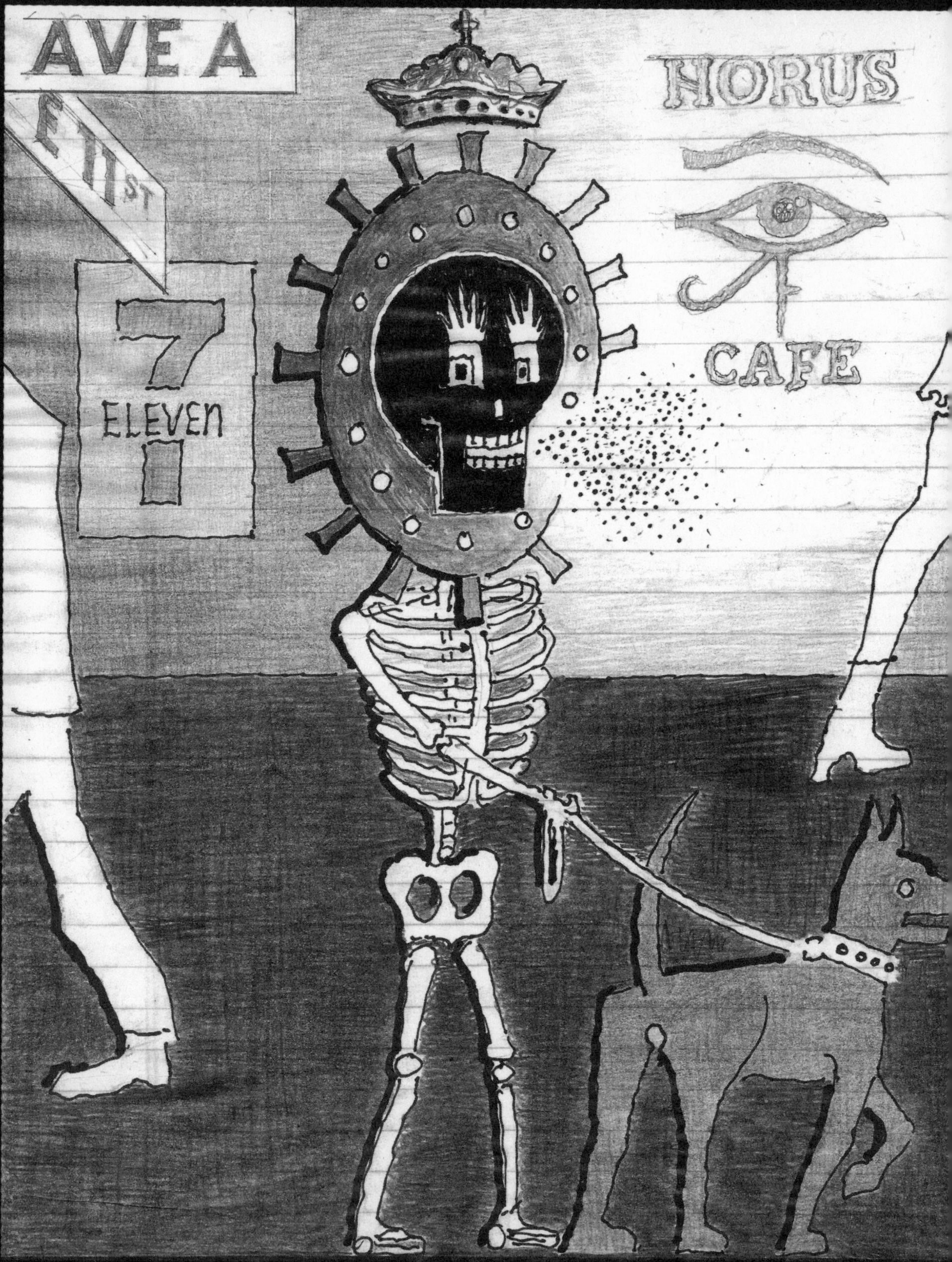
AVE A
E 11 ST
7
ELEVEN
HORUS
CAFE

Since March I have worked to put my learning about Covid-19 on paper. Much went through my mind. These times challenge us all to the very extreme. Then the Coronavirus blew up and unleashed its poisonous cloud everywhere. At once my hesitation vanished, the subject found me, our entire fragile world of today. I've always worked from a perspective beginning with home, then street, neighborhood, city, world. I wanted my visuals to center on the East Village, began my drawings at my Avenue A home. But then my children and friends thought, because of my age, 81, I should get out of the city.

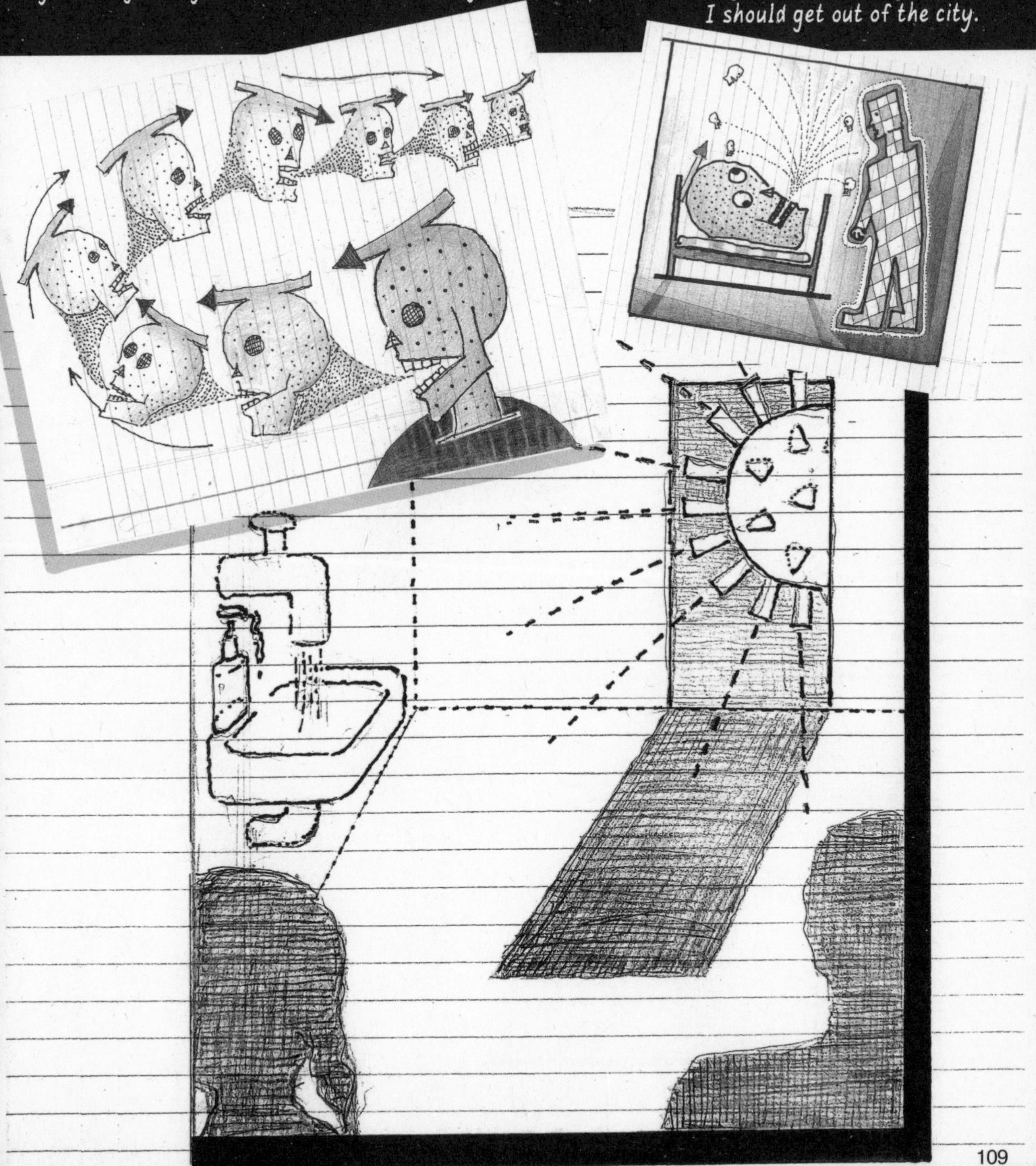

I came to understand that I should listen to them and retreat to the country side of Long Island. Through their generosity I was able to turn my scribbles into accessible drawings.

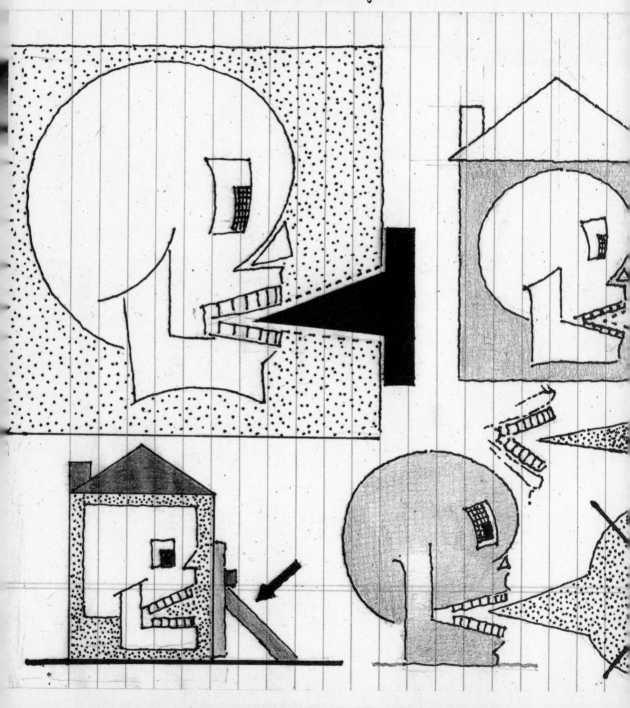

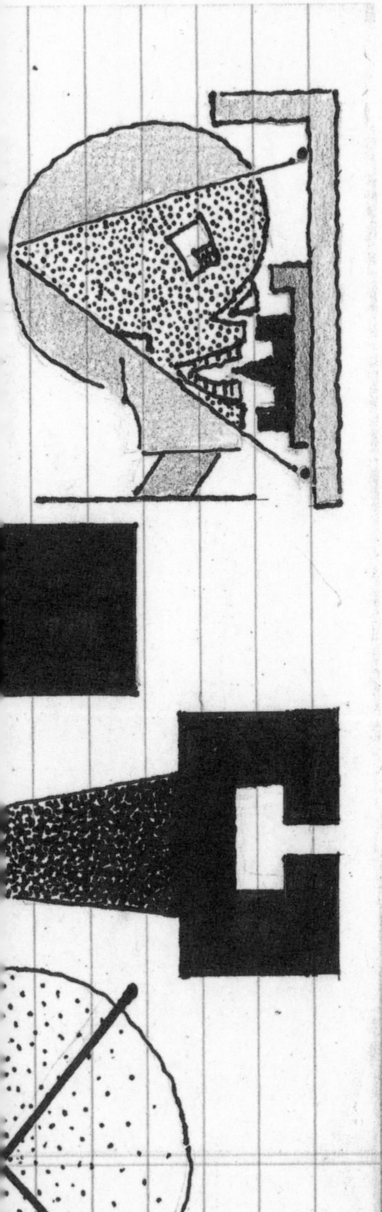

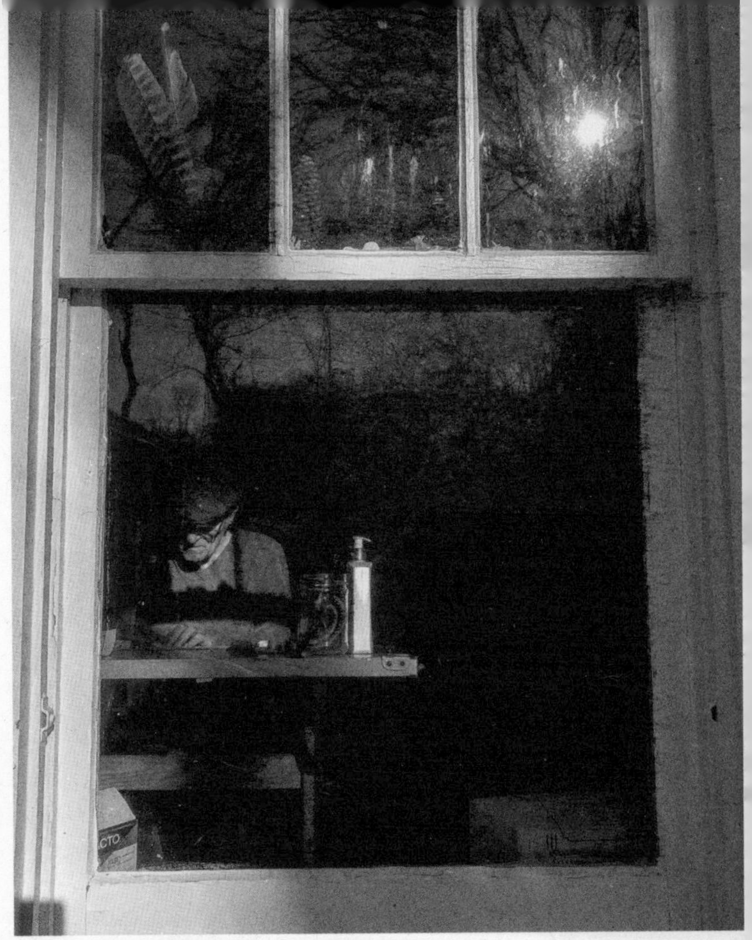

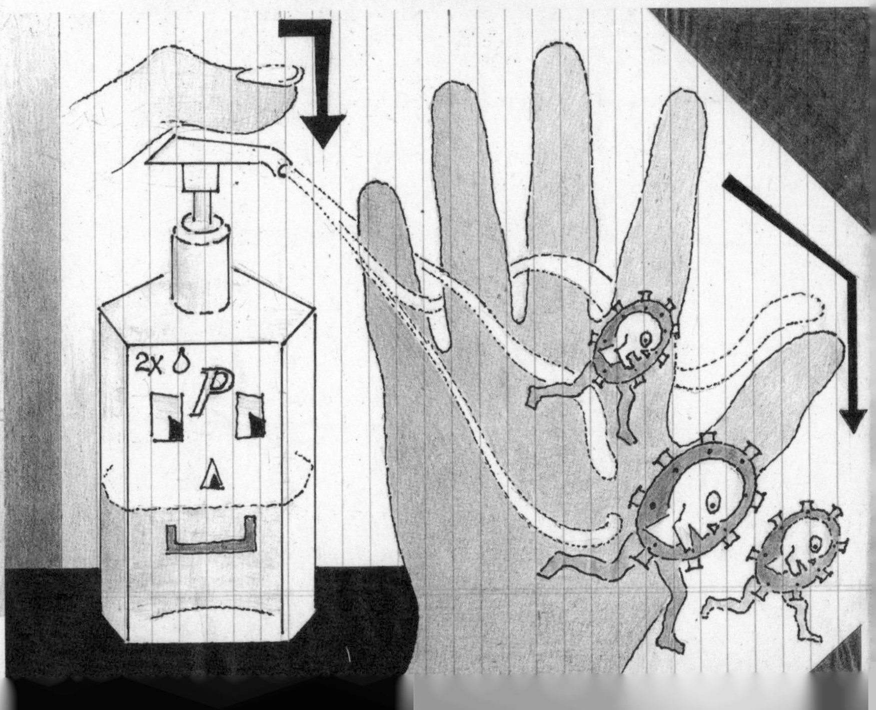

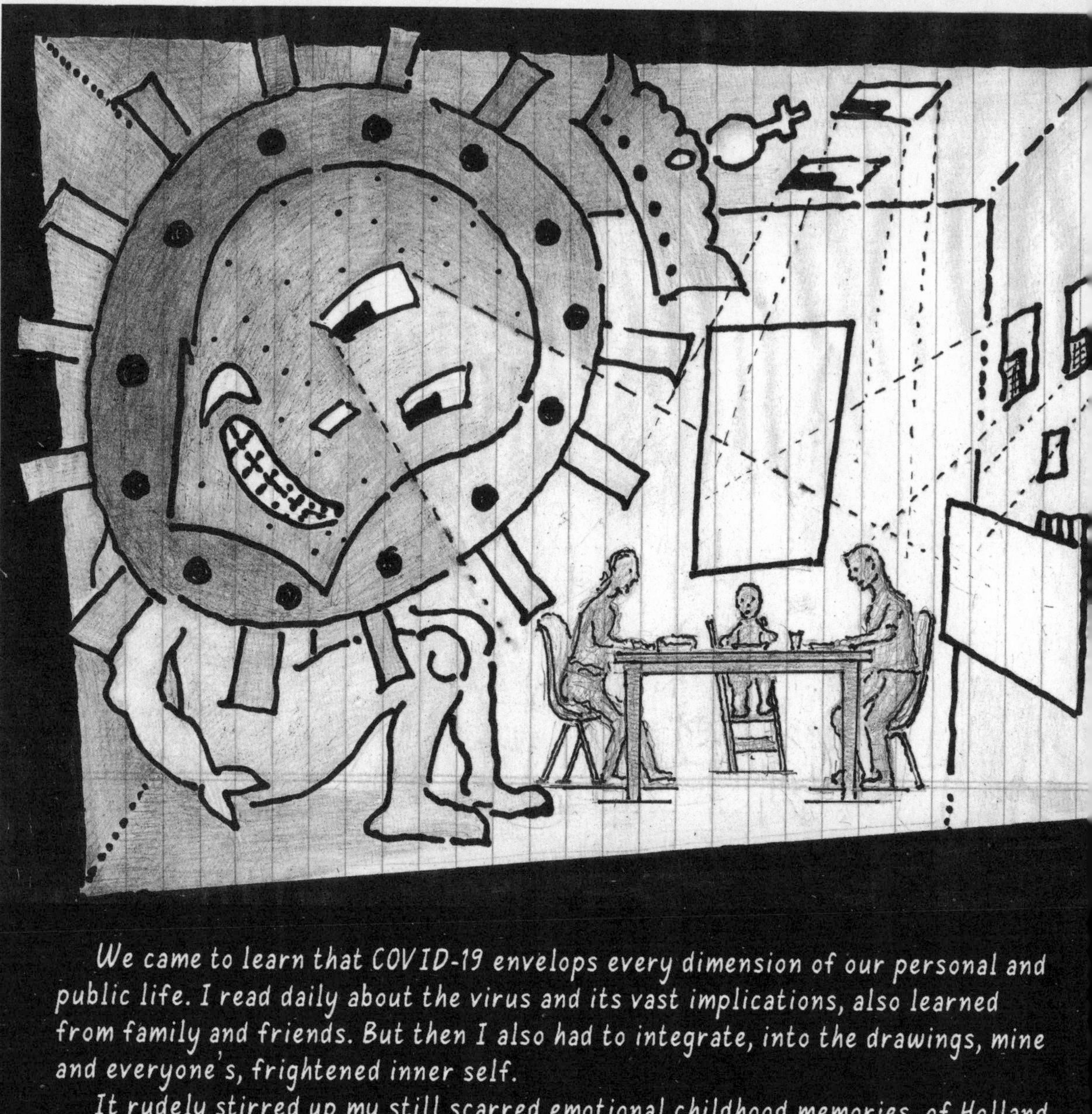

We came to learn that COVID-19 envelops every dimension of our personal and public life. I read daily about the virus and its vast implications, also learned from family and friends. But then I also had to integrate, into the drawings, mine and everyone's, frightened inner self.

It rudely stirred up my still scarred emotional childhood memories, of Holland during WW2, as military language has come to be used more and more to describe our naked vulnerabilities.

Yet, throughout I was worried about being appropriately thoughtful about this most serious matter. I was concerned not to be frivolous or satirical, but rather, to keep the subject big and myself small.

Having grown up with Dutch culture, its pictorial history gives me broad points of reference, with its tradition of a human narrative, from observation, and in the

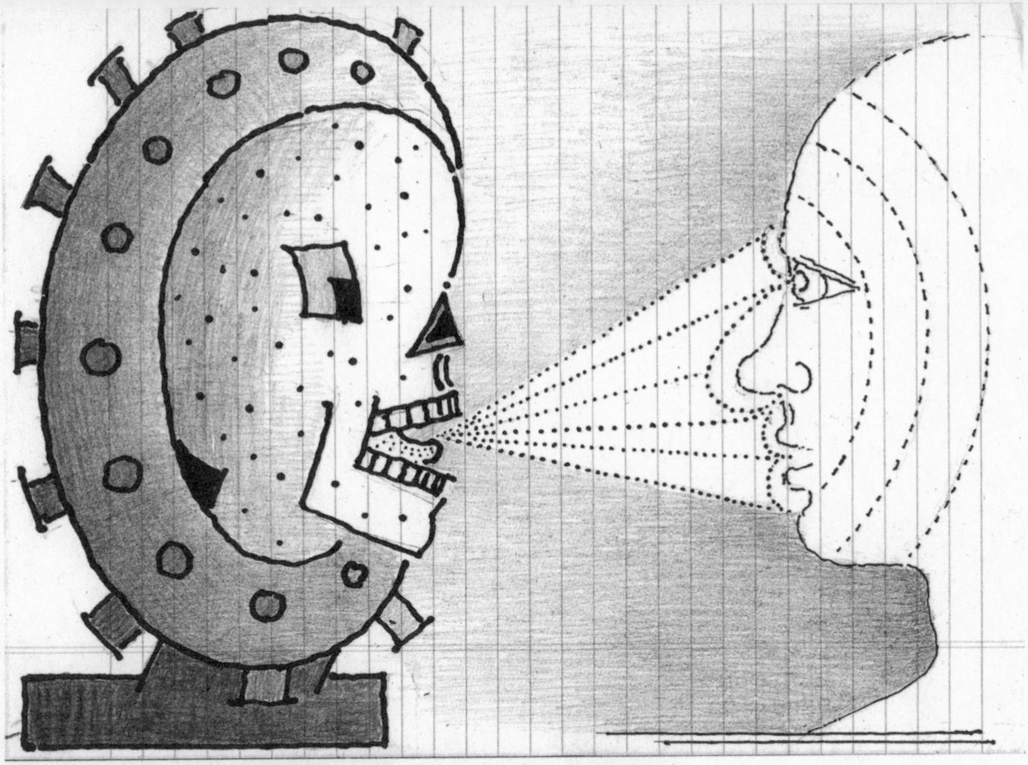

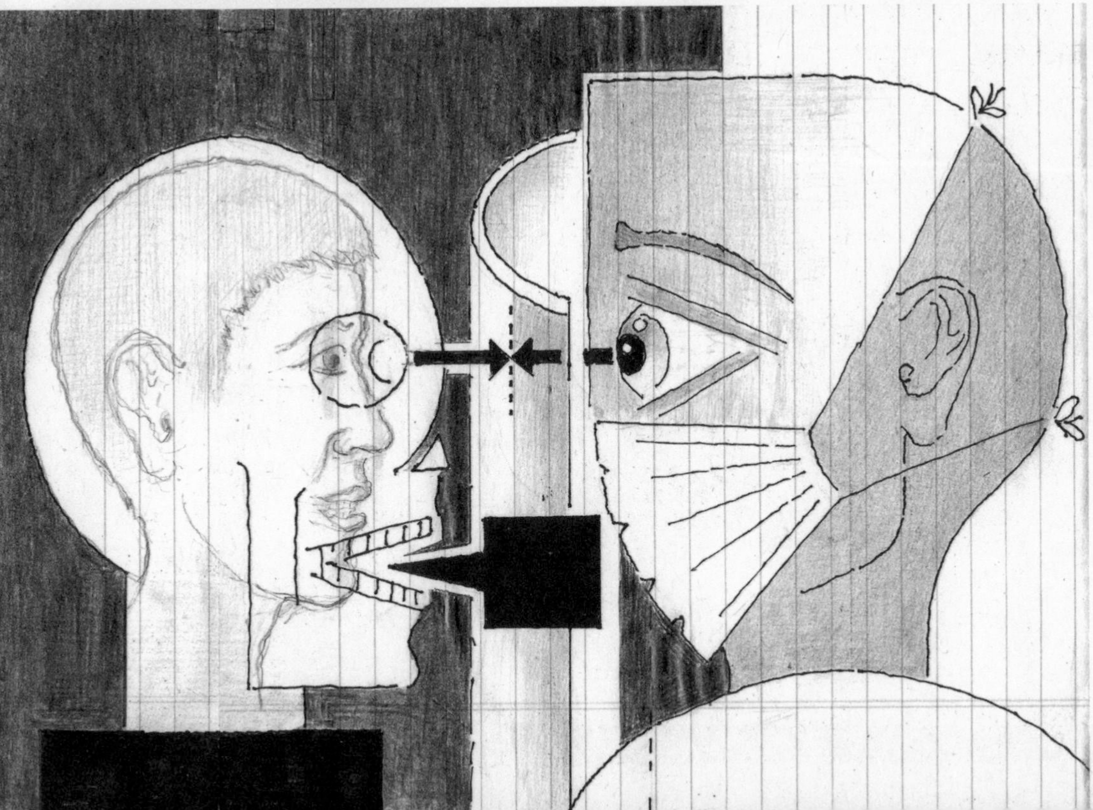

Ten days ago I returned to my NYC home. I'm not going out at all, but safely home with family help. And (it being Spring) pairing up 24 of my pigeons as they are starting up their family again! Now my pigeon rooftop coop resounds like a joyous orchestra of the natural world.

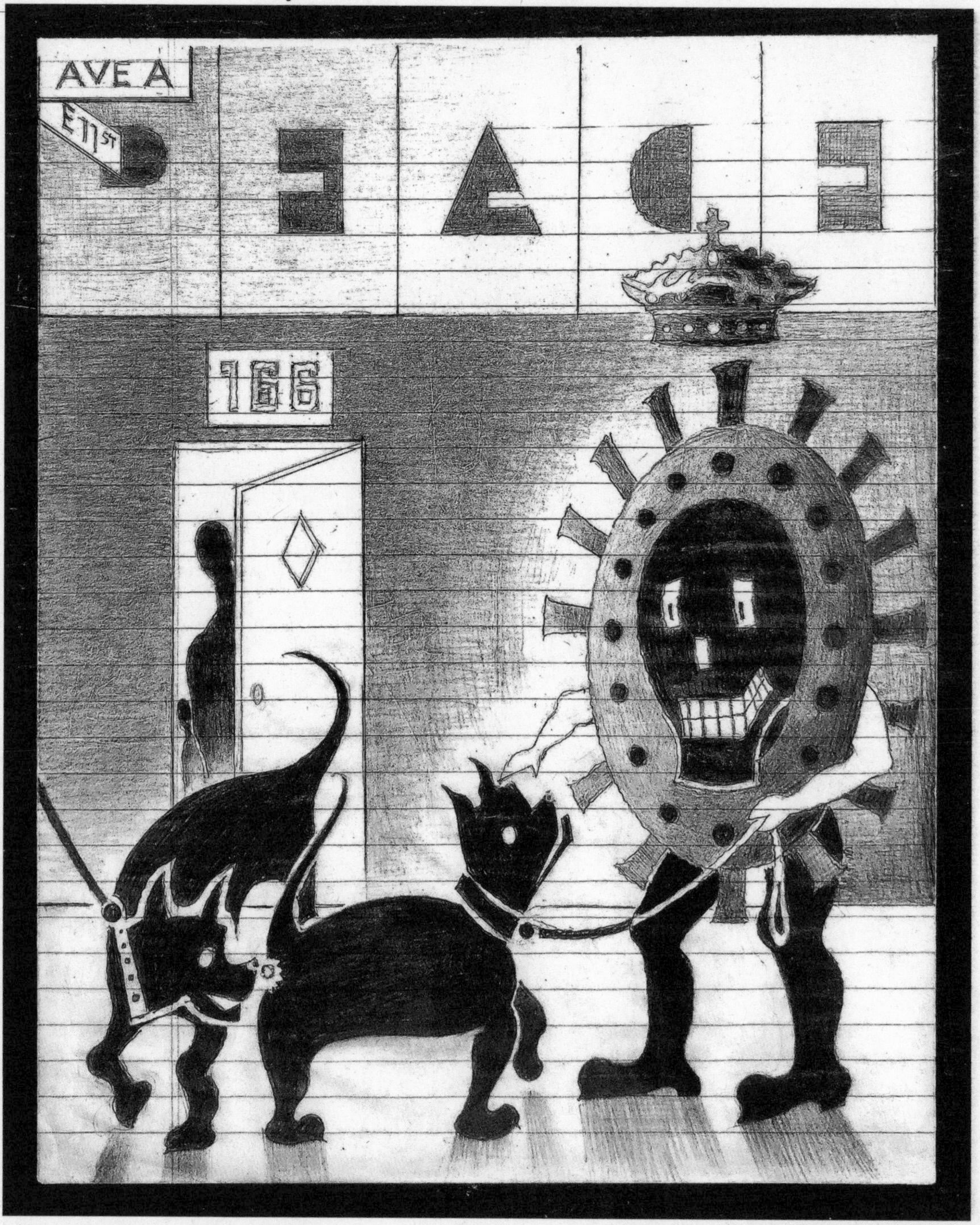

AVE A
E 11st
166

Life goes on, sad and beautiful.

A Safe Investment

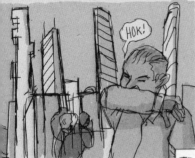

HE 9,000 UNSOLD LUXURY CONDOS
CATTERED THROUGHOUT THE CITY...
HOK!
HAVE BEEN SUBDIVIDED...
AND CONVERTED INTO INTENSIVE CARE UNITS.
HESE UNITS ARE SOLD TO PRIVATE
EALTH INSURANCE COMPANIES WHO
TURN LEASE THEM OUT...
EMERGENCY
NO NEED TO WAIT ON LINE.
TO CRITICALLY ILL PEOPLE WHO CAN NOT FIND A VACANT HOSPITAL BED DURING THE PANDEMIC.
THERE'S A DAILY $6,000. COVID-COPAY
Naiad HEALTH SIGN UP
SAVE YOUR LOVED ONES.
CAN WE AFFORD THIS?
THE SUDDEN WINDFALL HELPS REAL ESTATE DEVELOPERS OFFSET THEIR LOSSES.
TRAMPLE PROPERTY GROUP
B & Bs, HOSPITAL ROOMS, WHAT'S THE DIFFERENCE?
THEY'RE QUIET, SHORT-TERM LESSEES.
HE UNITS ARE STAFFED BY PRISON
NMATES PAID $1.25 AN HOUR FOR THE
HAZARDOUS DUTY.
THIS ONE IS READY TO CHECK OUT.
CLIC FLAP, FLAP CLIC
THOUSANDS OF VINTAGE VENTILATORS ARE BARELY KEPT RUNNING 24/7.
VETERANS HEALTH ADMINISTRATION HOSPITAL 1980.
THE EVENING SKYLINE ONCE AGAIN BECKONS WOULDBE OLIGARCHS LOOKING FOR A SAFE INVESTMENT.
©BEN KATCHOR

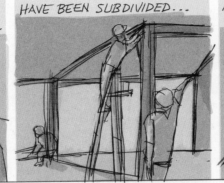

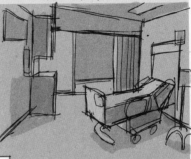

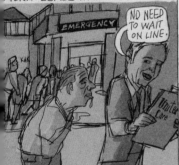

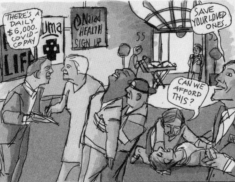

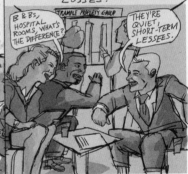

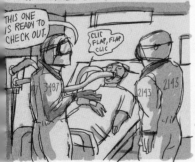

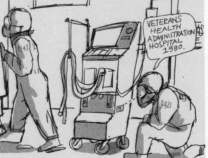

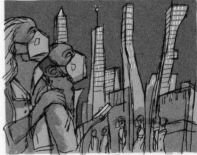

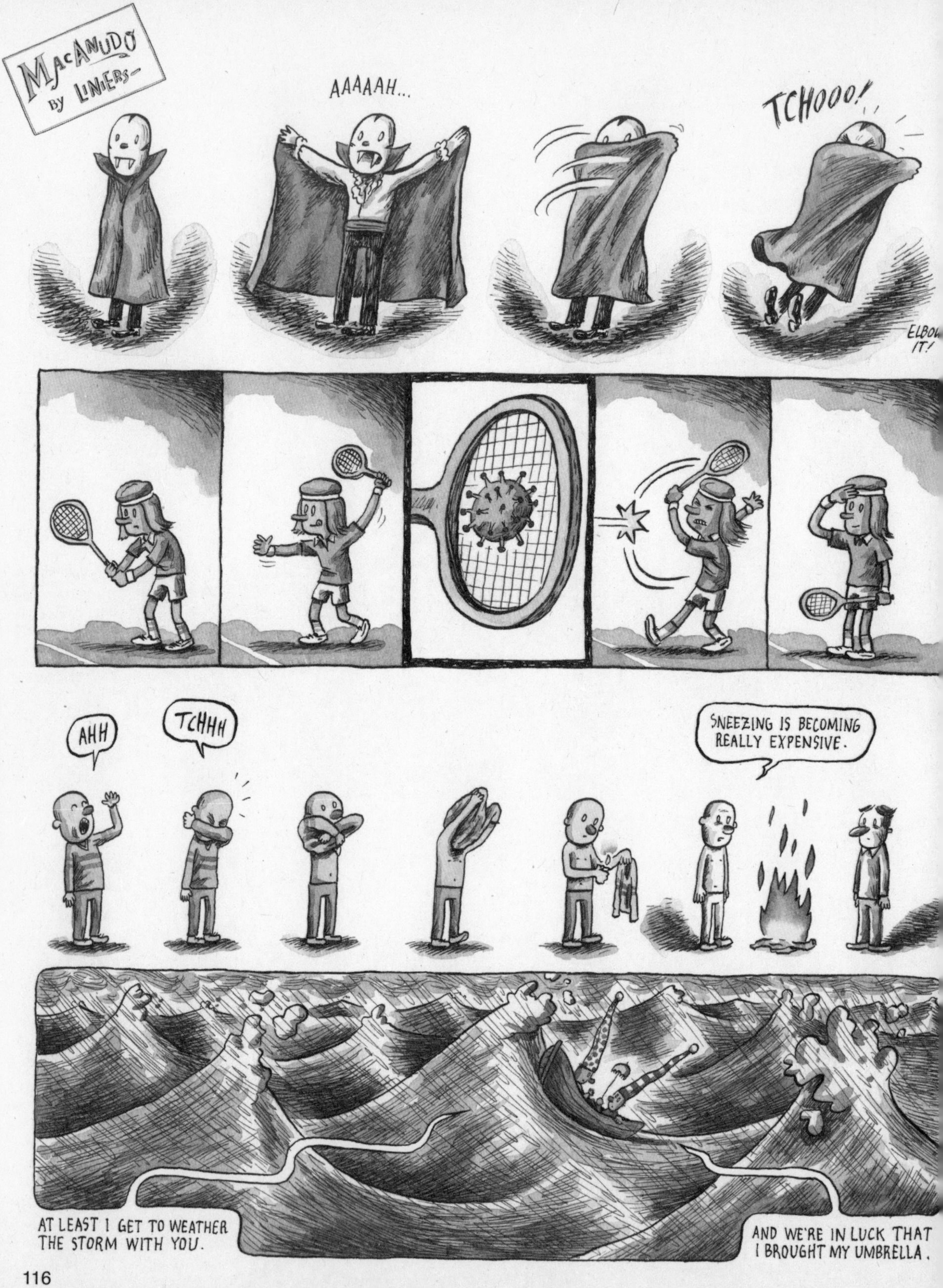
MACANUDO
BY LINIERS
AAAAAH...
TCHOOO!
ELBOW IT!
AHH
TCHHH
SNEEZING IS BECOMING REALLY EXPENSIVE.
AT LEAST I GET TO WEATHER THE STORM WITH YOU.
AND WE'RE IN LUCK THAT I BROUGHT MY UMBRELLA.

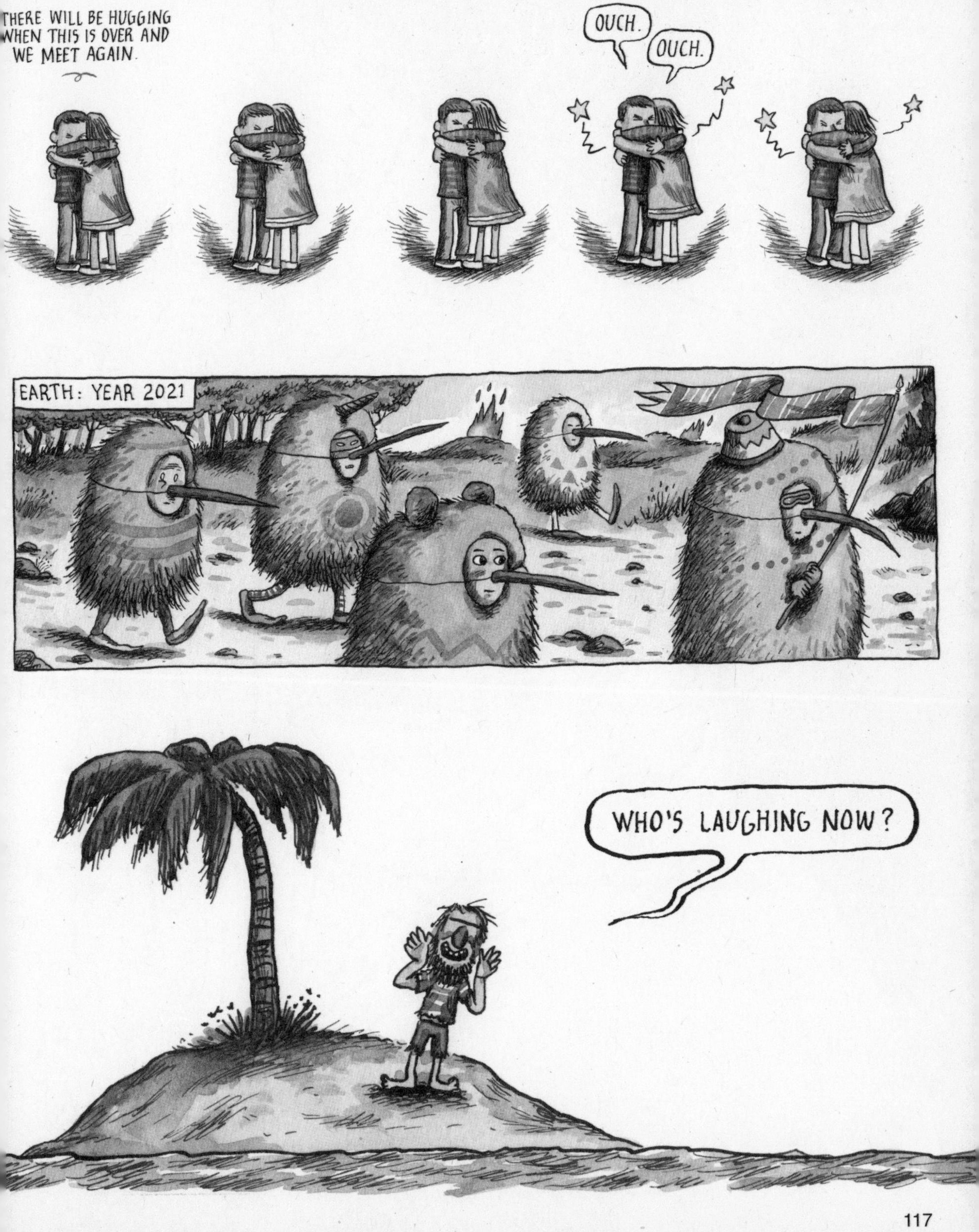

THERE WILL BE HUGGING WHEN THIS IS OVER AND WE MEET AGAIN.
OUCH.
OUCH.
EARTH: YEAR 2021
WHO'S LAUGHING NOW?

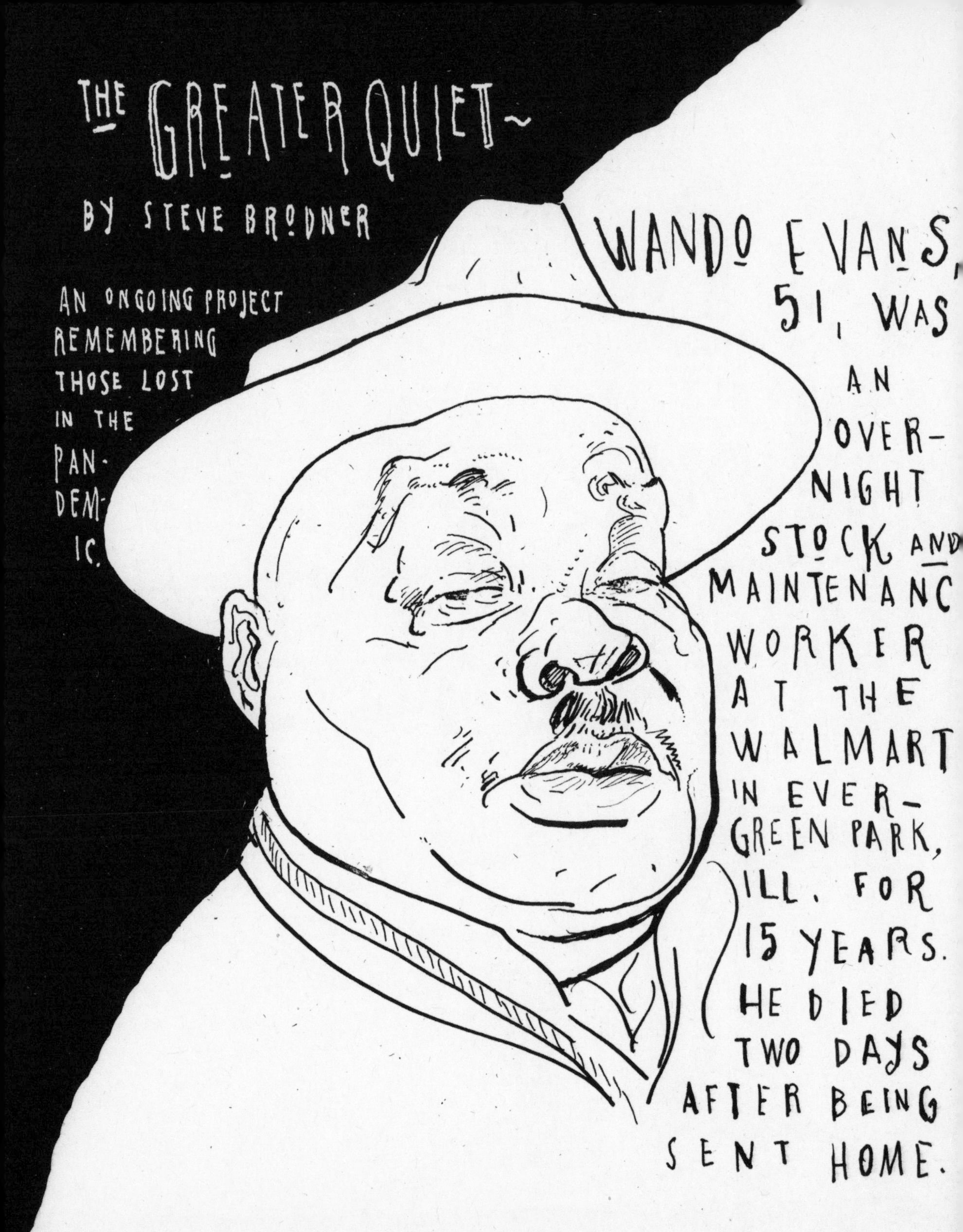
THE GREATER QUIET~
BY STEVE BRODNER
AN ONGOING PROJECT REMEMBERING THOSE LOST IN THE PAN-DEM-IC.
WANDO EVANS, 51, WAS AN OVER-NIGHT STOCK AND MAINTENANC WORKER AT THE WALMART IN EVER-GREEN PARK, ILL. FOR 15 YEARS. HE DIED TWO DAYS AFTER BEING SENT HOME.

CELIA
LARDIZABEL
MARCOS,

NURSE AT HOLLYWOOD PRESBYTERIAN HOSPITAL, DIED AFTER TRYING TO RESUSCITATE A COVID-19 PATIENT. SHE WORKED WITHOUT PROPER EQUIPMENT, DUE TO A SHORTAGE AT THE HOSPITAL. SHE CONTRACTED THE VIRUS AND DIED ON APRIL 17. SHE GAVE UP HER LIFE TO SAVE A PATIENT. SHE WAS 61.

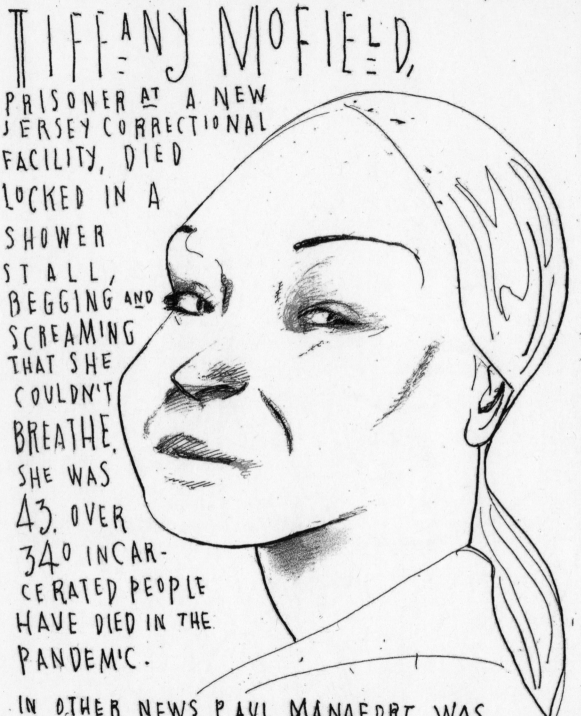

TIFFANY MOFIELD,

PRISONER AT A NEW JERSEY CORRECTIONAL FACILITY, DIED LOCKED IN A SHOWER STALL, BEGGING AND SCREAMING THAT SHE COULDN'T BREATHE. SHE WAS 43. OVER 340 INCARCERATED PEOPLE HAVE DIED IN THE PANDEMIC.

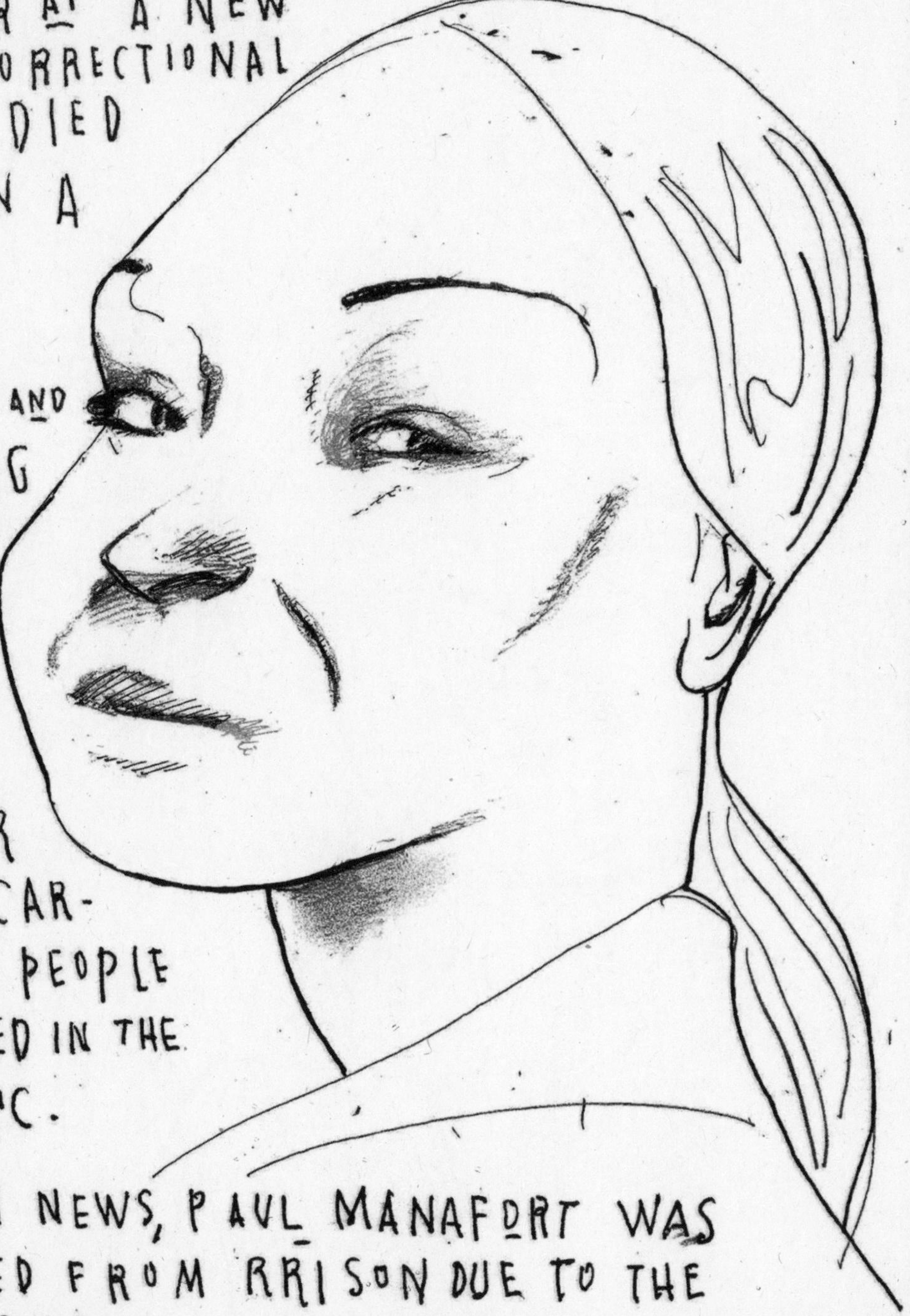

IN OTHER NEWS, PAUL MANAFORT WAS RELEASED FROM PRISON DUE TO THE OUTBREAK.

LEILANI JORDAN, 27,
WAS A GIANT FOOD
GROCERY CLERK IN
LARGO, MD.
SHE KEPT
WORKING,
DESPITE
THE RISK,
AS OTHERS
AT THE
STORE
FAILED
TO
SHOW
UP.
SHE
TOLD
HER
MOTHER:
"I'M GOING
TO STILL
GO TO WORK.
I WANT TO HELP."

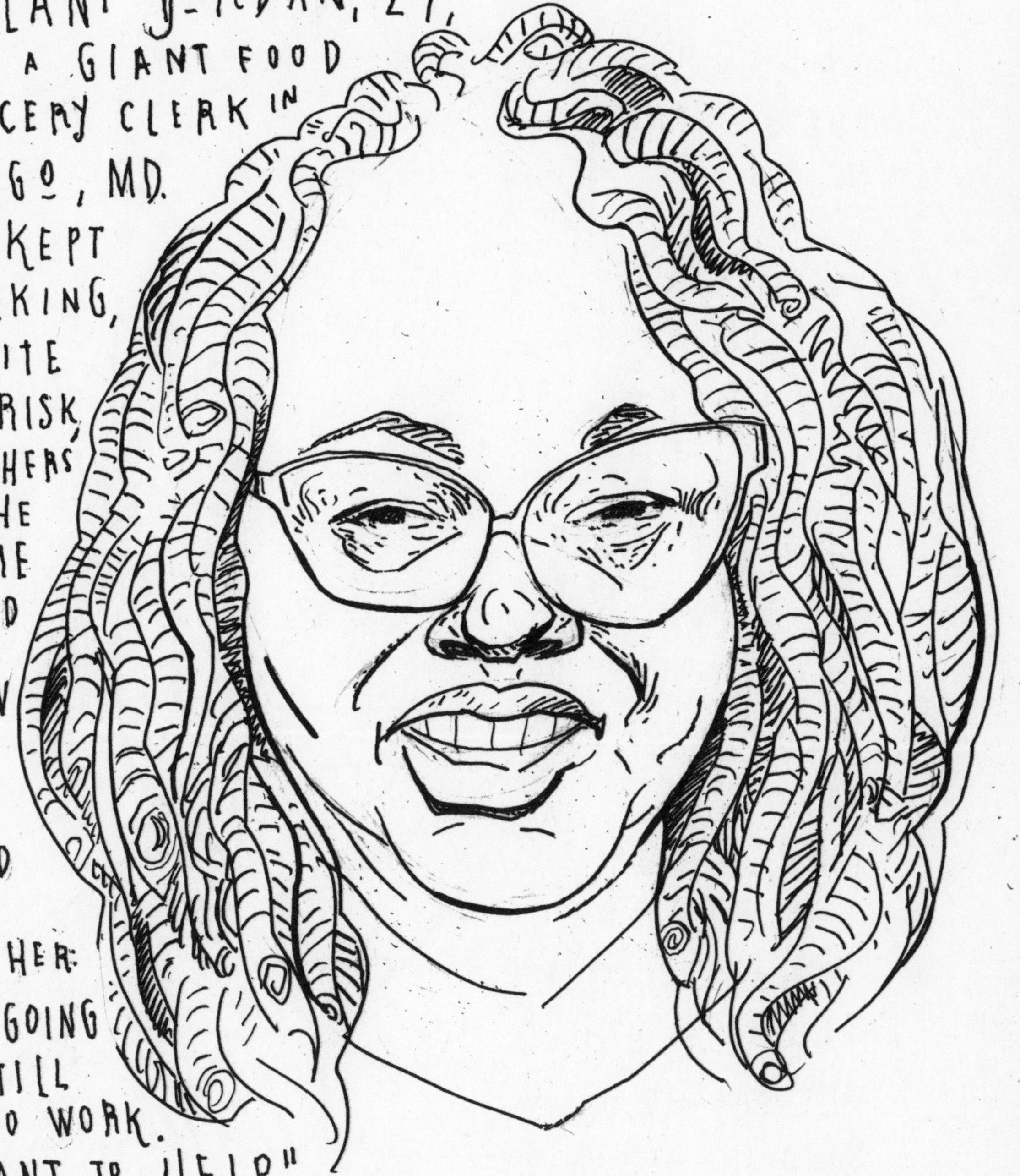

LEO DELA CRUZ, AGE UNKNOWN WAS A GERIATRIC PSYCHIATRIST AT CHRIST HOSPITAL IN JERSEY CITY, NJ. "HE WAS A GOOD PERSON, A SWEET MAN THAT WAS LOVED BY EVERYONE", THE HOSPITAL'S TUCKER WOODS AND MARIE DUFFY SAID IN A STATEMENT.

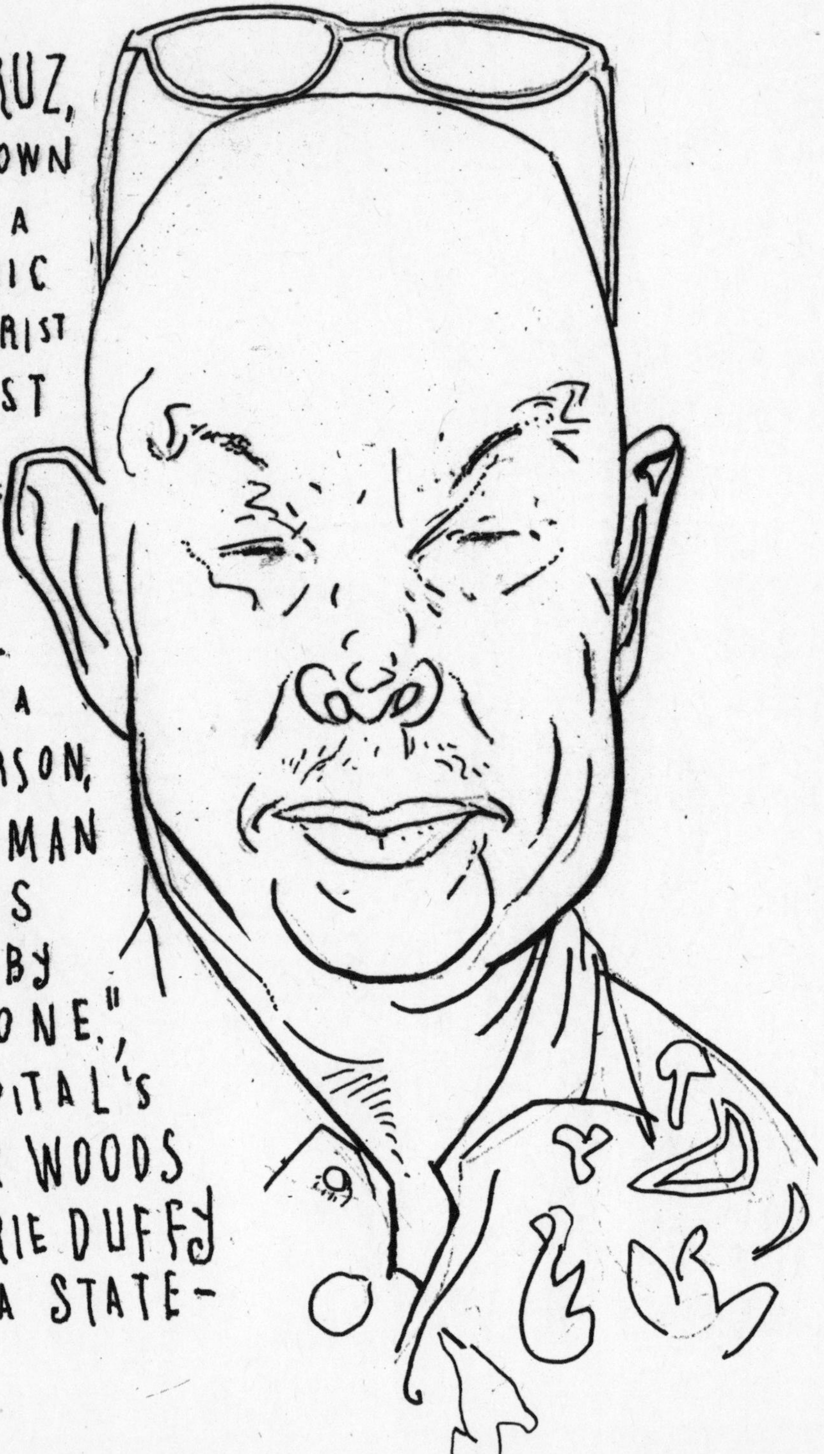

PRISCILLA CARROW, 65, WAS A CO-ORDINATING MANAGER AT ELMHURST HOSPITAL IN QUEENS. SHE WAS TOLD TO SELF-QUARANTINE AFTER SHE WAS EXPOSED TO A PATIENT WITH THE VIRUS. SHE WAS PLANNING TO RETIRE THIS YEAR.

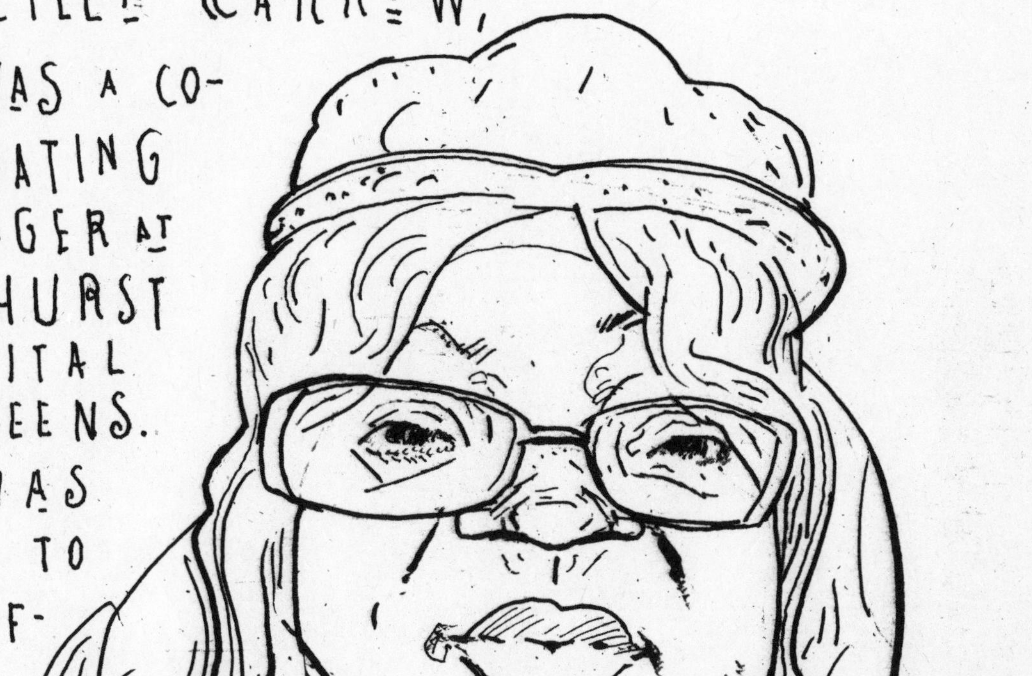

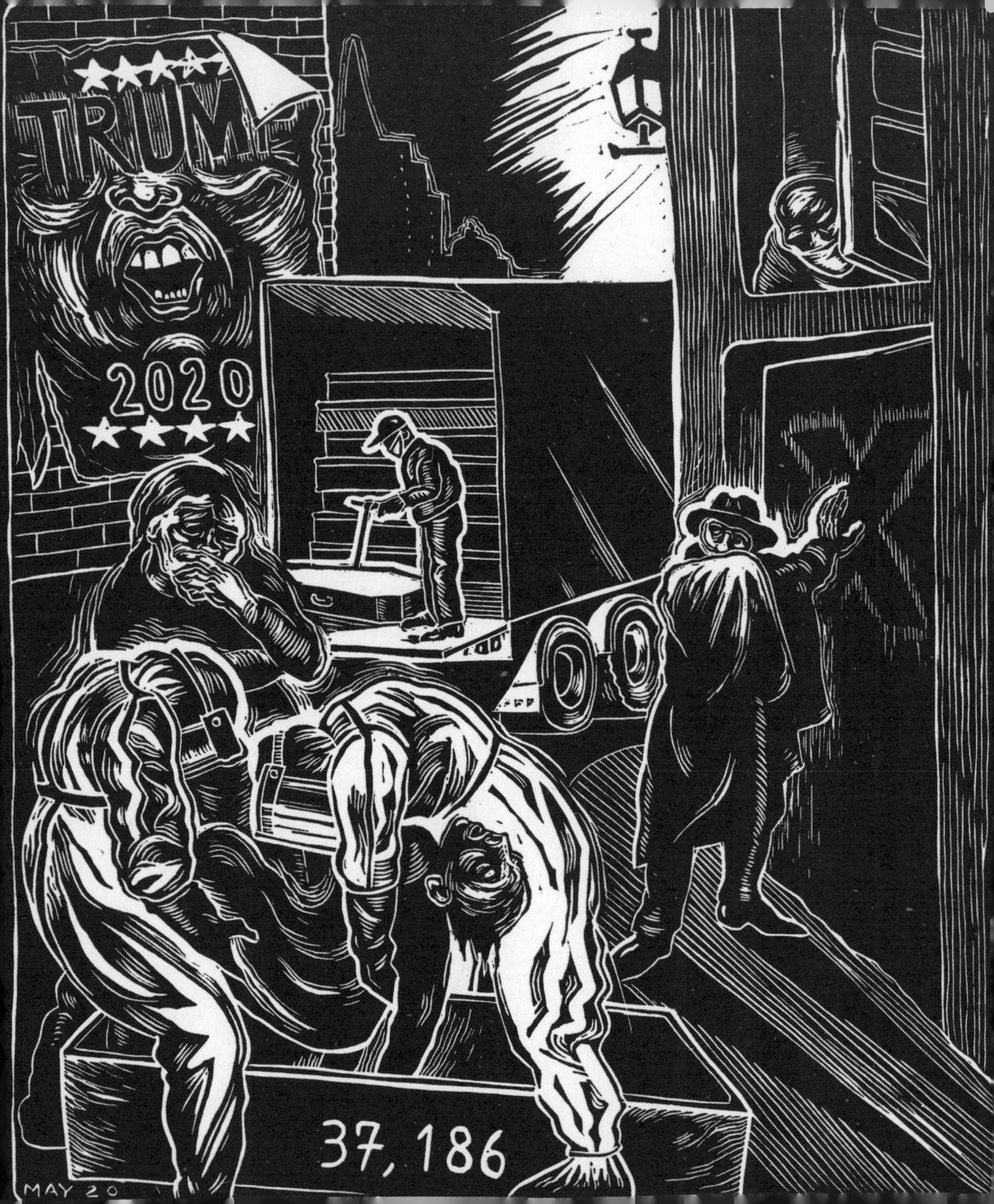
TRUM
2020
37, 186
MAY 20

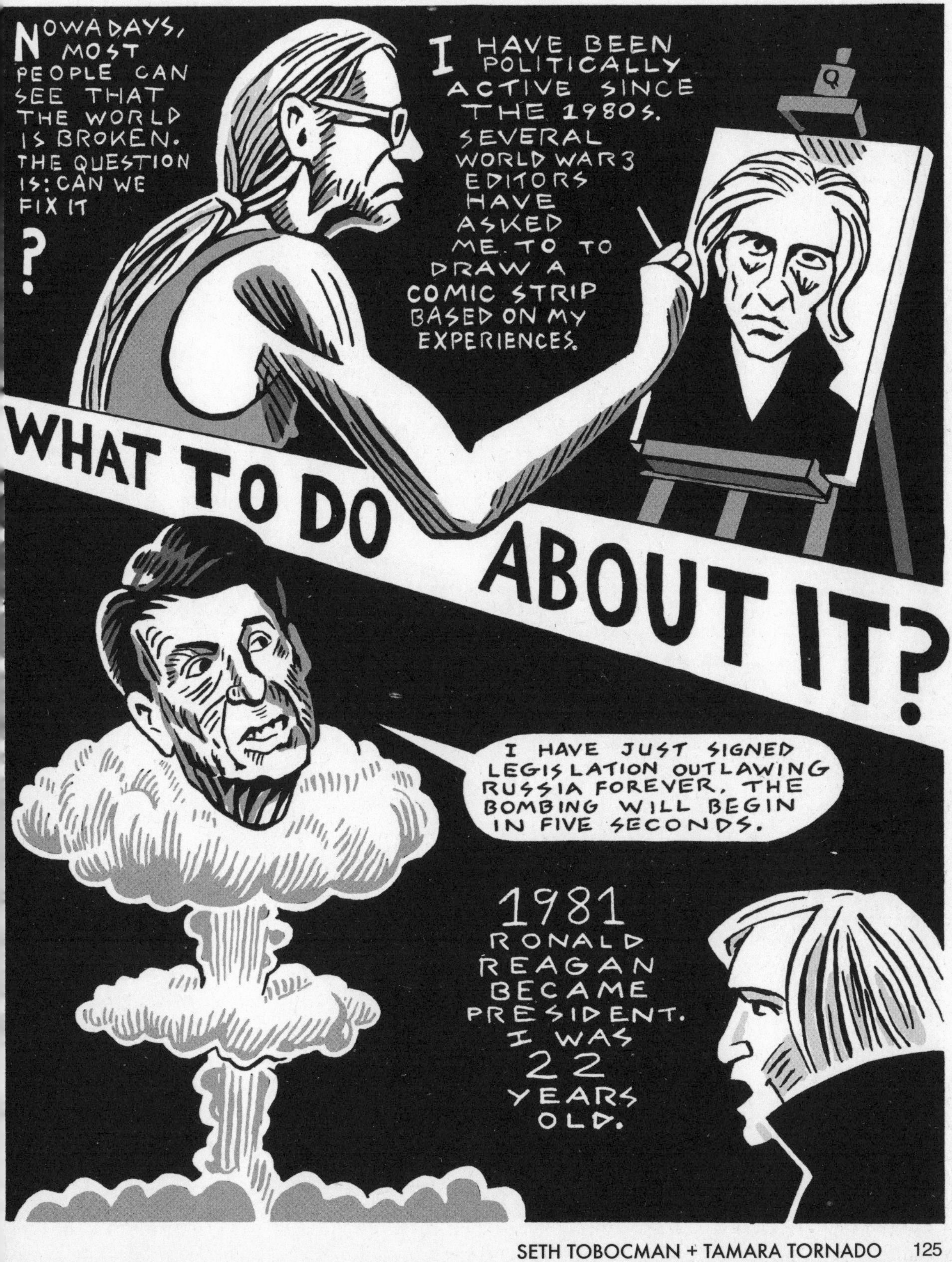

NOWADAYS, MOST PEOPLE CAN SEE THAT THE WORLD IS BROKEN. THE QUESTION IS: CAN WE FIX IT ?
I HAVE BEEN POLITICALLY ACTIVE SINCE THE 1980s. SEVERAL WORLD WAR 3 EDITORS HAVE ASKED ME TO TO DRAW A COMIC STRIP BASED ON MY EXPERIENCES.
Q
WHAT TO DO ABOUT IT?
I HAVE JUST SIGNED LEGISLATION OUTLAWING RUSSIA FOREVER. THE BOMBING WILL BEGIN IN FIVE SECONDS.
1981 RONALD REAGAN BECAME PRESIDENT. I WAS 22 YEARS OLD.

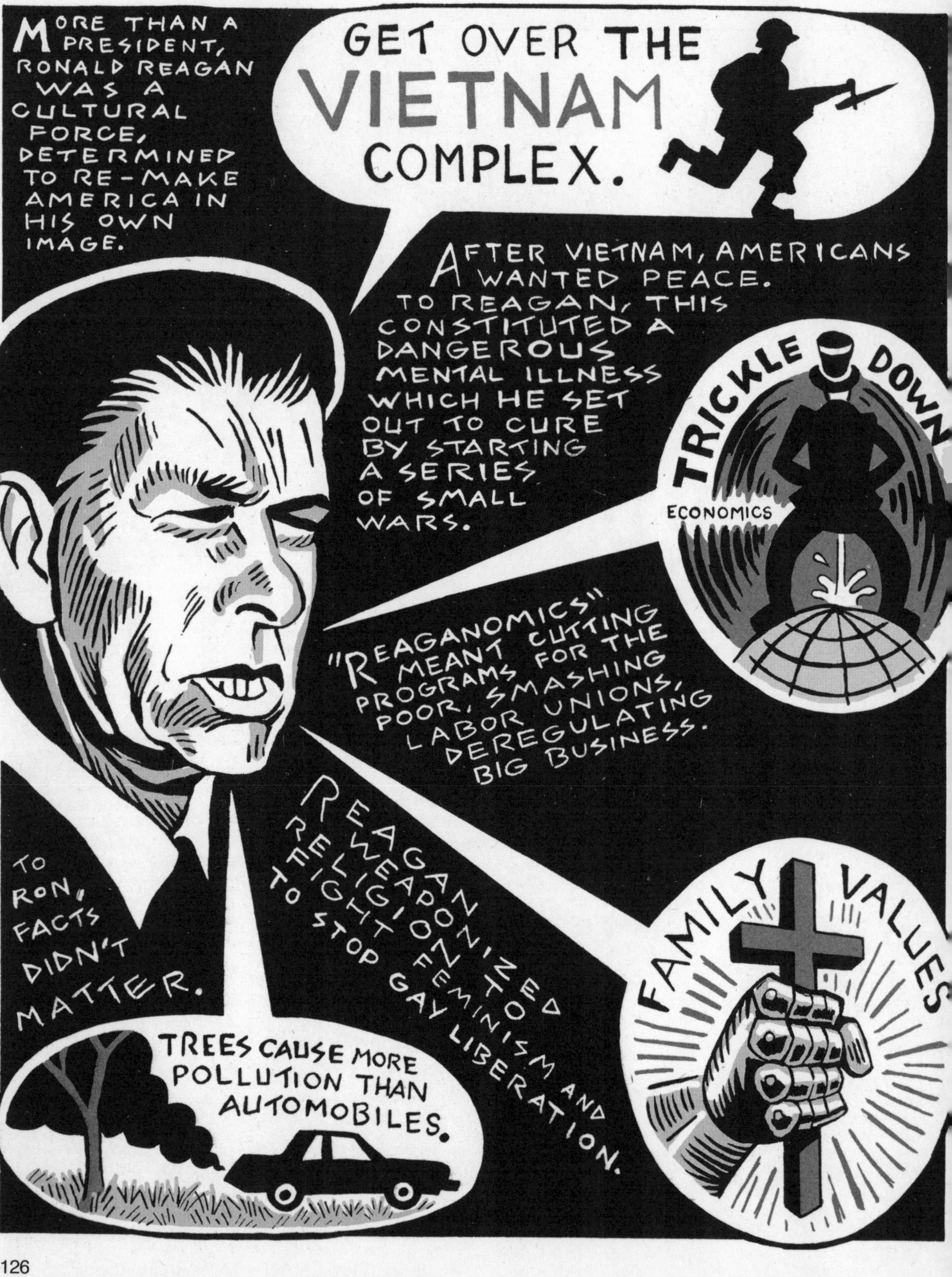
MORE THAN A PRESIDENT, RONALD REAGAN WAS A CULTURAL FORCE, DETERMINED TO RE-MAKE AMERICA IN HIS OWN IMAGE.
GET OVER THE VIETNAM COMPLEX.
AFTER VIETNAM, AMERICANS WANTED PEACE. TO REAGAN, THIS CONSTITUTED A DANGEROUS MENTAL ILLNESS WHICH HE SET OUT TO CURE BY STARTING A SERIES OF SMALL WARS.
TRICKLE DOWN
ECONOMICS
"REAGANOMICS" MEANT CUTTING PROGRAMS FOR THE POOR, SMASHING LABOR UNIONS, DEREGULATING BIG BUSINESS.
REAGAN WEAPONIZED RELIGION TO FIGHT FEMINISM AND TO STOP GAY LIBERATION.
FAMILY VALUES
TO RON, FACTS DIDN'T MATTER.
TREES CAUSE MORE POLLUTION THAN AUTOMOBILES.

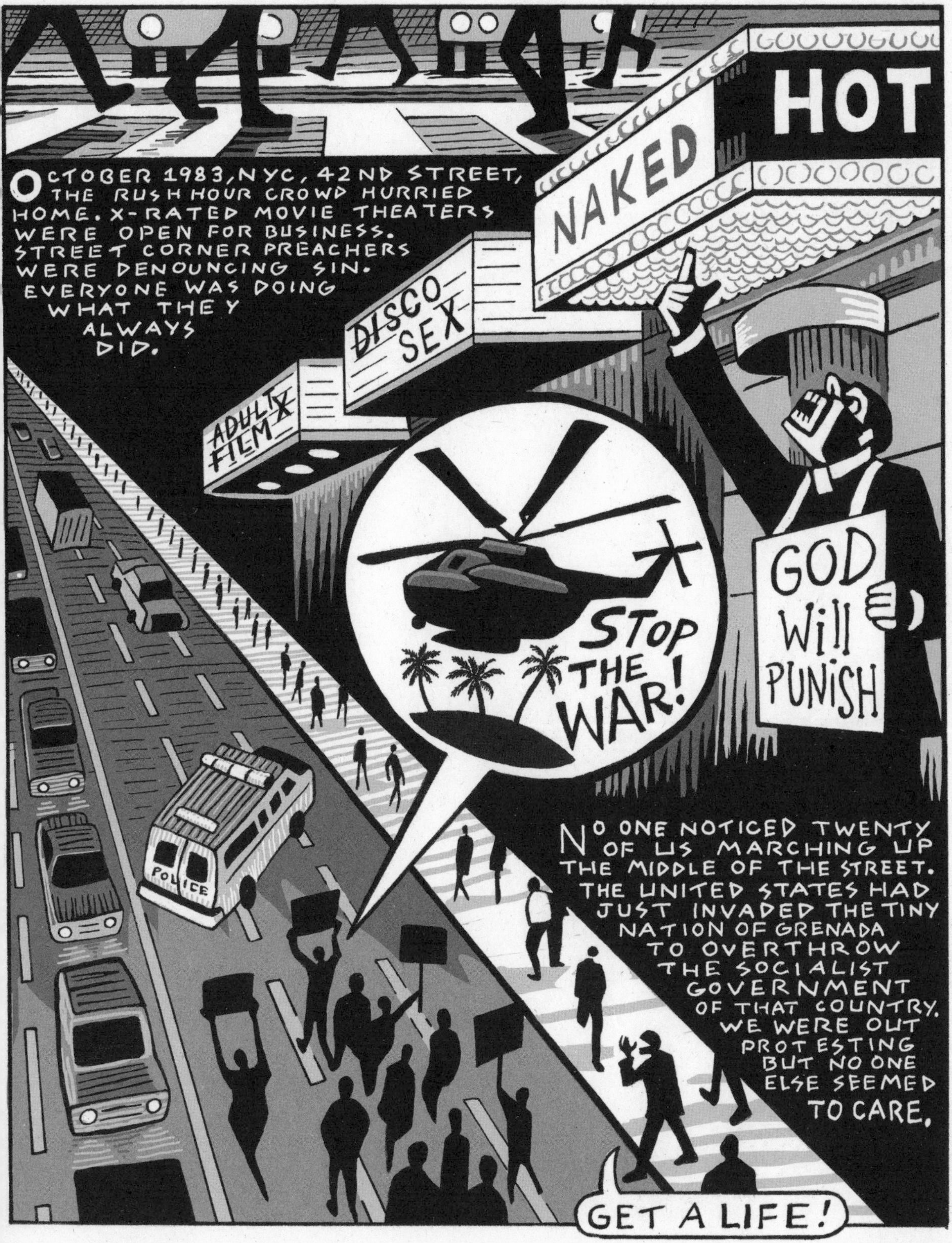
HOT
NAKED
OCTOBER 1983, NYC, 42ND STREET, THE RUSH HOUR CROWD HURRIED HOME. X-RATED MOVIE THEATERS WERE OPEN FOR BUSINESS. STREET CORNER PREACHERS WERE DENOUNCING SIN. EVERYONE WAS DOING WHAT THEY ALWAYS DID.
DISCO SEX
ADULT FILM X
GOD WILL PUNISH
STOP THE WAR!
POLICE
NO ONE NOTICED TWENTY OF US MARCHING UP THE MIDDLE OF THE STREET. THE UNITED STATES HAD JUST INVADED THE TINY NATION OF GRENADA TO OVERTHROW THE SOCIALIST GOVERNMENT OF THAT COUNTRY. WE WERE OUT PROTESTING BUT NO ONE ELSE SEEMED TO CARE.
GET A LIFE!

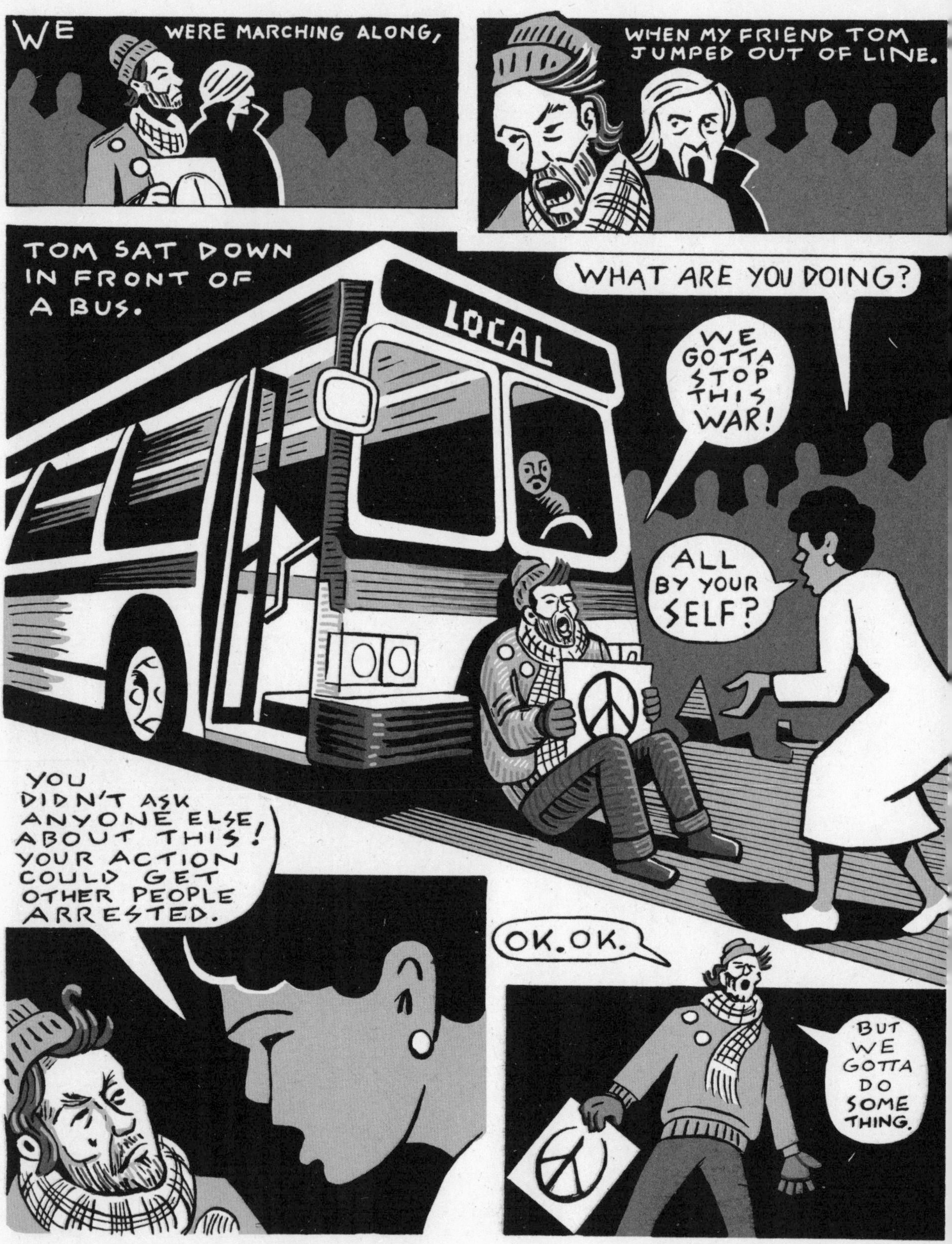
WE WERE MARCHING ALONG,
WHEN MY FRIEND TOM JUMPED OUT OF LINE.
TOM SAT DOWN IN FRONT OF A BUS.
LOCAL
WHAT ARE YOU DOING?
WE GOTTA STOP THIS WAR!
ALL BY YOUR SELF?
YOU DIDN'T ASK ANYONE ELSE ABOUT THIS! YOUR ACTION COULD GET OTHER PEOPLE ARRESTED.
OK.OK.
BUT WE GOTTA DO SOME THING.

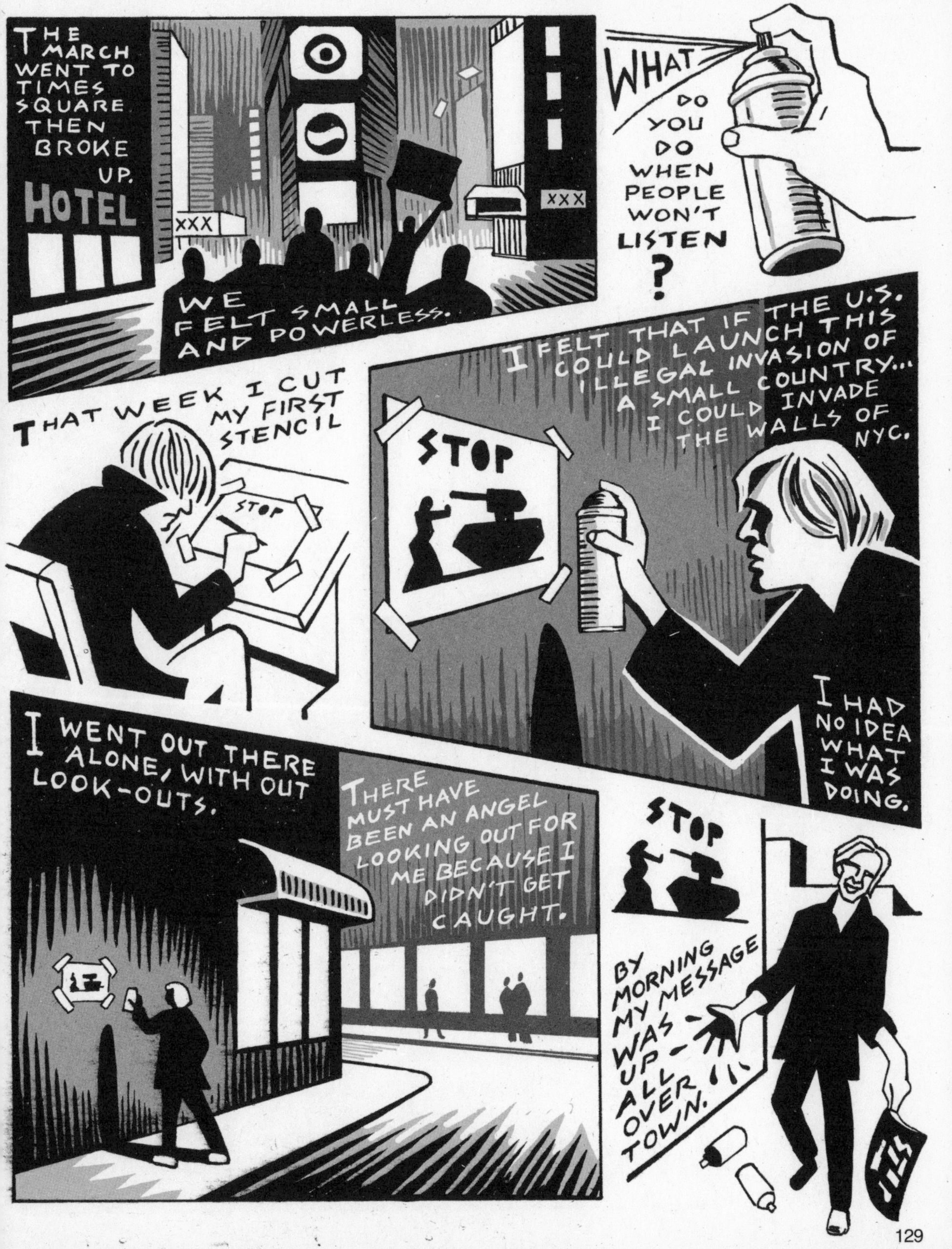

THE MARCH WENT TO TIMES SQUARE THEN BROKE UP.
HOTEL
XXX
XXX
WE FELT SMALL AND POWERLESS.
WHAT DO YOU DO WHEN PEOPLE WON'T LISTEN?
I FELT THAT IF THE U.S. COULD LAUNCH THIS ILLEGAL INVASION OF A SMALL COUNTRY... I COULD INVADE THE WALLS OF NYC.
THAT WEEK I CUT MY FIRST STENCIL
STOP
STOP
I HAD NO IDEA WHAT I WAS DOING.
I WENT OUT THERE ALONE, WITH OUT LOOK-OUTS.
THERE MUST HAVE BEEN AN ANGEL LOOKING OUT FOR ME BECAUSE I DIDN'T GET CAUGHT.
STOP
BY MORNING MY MESSAGE WAS UP ALL OVER TOWN.

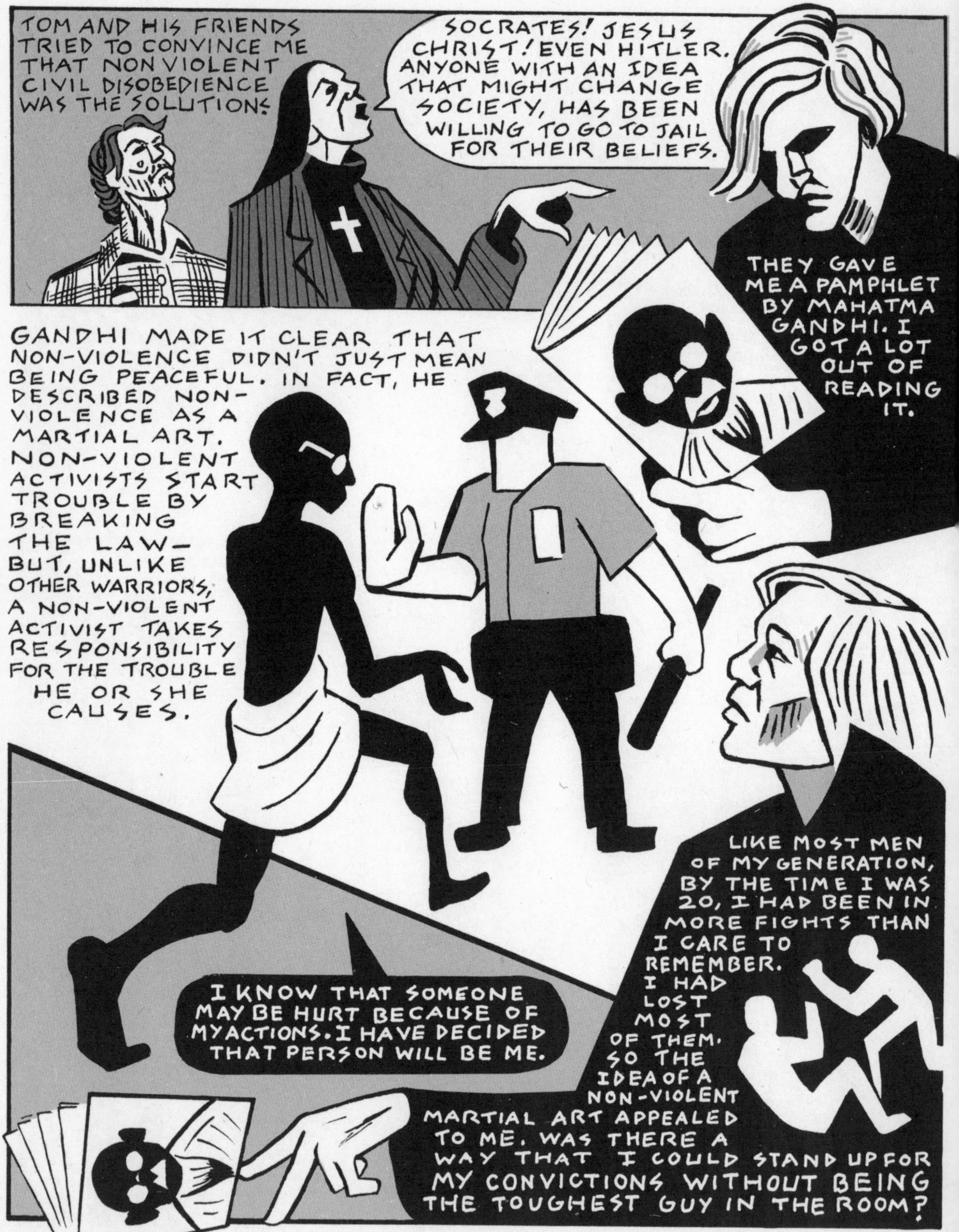

TOM AND HIS FRIENDS TRIED TO CONVINCE ME THAT NON VIOLENT CIVIL DISOBEDIENCE WAS THE SOLUTION:
SOCRATES! JESUS CHRIST! EVEN HITLER. ANYONE WITH AN IDEA THAT MIGHT CHANGE SOCIETY, HAS BEEN WILLING TO GO TO JAIL FOR THEIR BELIEFS.
THEY GAVE ME A PAMPHLET BY MAHATMA GANDHI. I GOT A LOT OUT OF READING IT.
GANDHI MADE IT CLEAR THAT NON-VIOLENCE DIDN'T JUST MEAN BEING PEACEFUL. IN FACT, HE DESCRIBED NON-VIOLENCE AS A MARTIAL ART. NON-VIOLENT ACTIVISTS START TROUBLE BY BREAKING THE LAW— BUT, UNLIKE OTHER WARRIORS, A NON-VIOLENT ACTIVIST TAKES RESPONSIBILITY FOR THE TROUBLE HE OR SHE CAUSES.
I KNOW THAT SOMEONE MAY BE HURT BECAUSE OF MY ACTIONS. I HAVE DECIDED THAT PERSON WILL BE ME.
LIKE MOST MEN OF MY GENERATION, BY THE TIME I WAS 20, I HAD BEEN IN MORE FIGHTS THAN I CARE TO REMEMBER. I HAD LOST MOST OF THEM. SO THE IDEA OF A NON-VIOLENT MARTIAL ART APPEALED TO ME. WAS THERE A WAY THAT I COULD STAND UP FOR MY CONVICTIONS WITHOUT BEING THE TOUGHEST GUY IN THE ROOM?

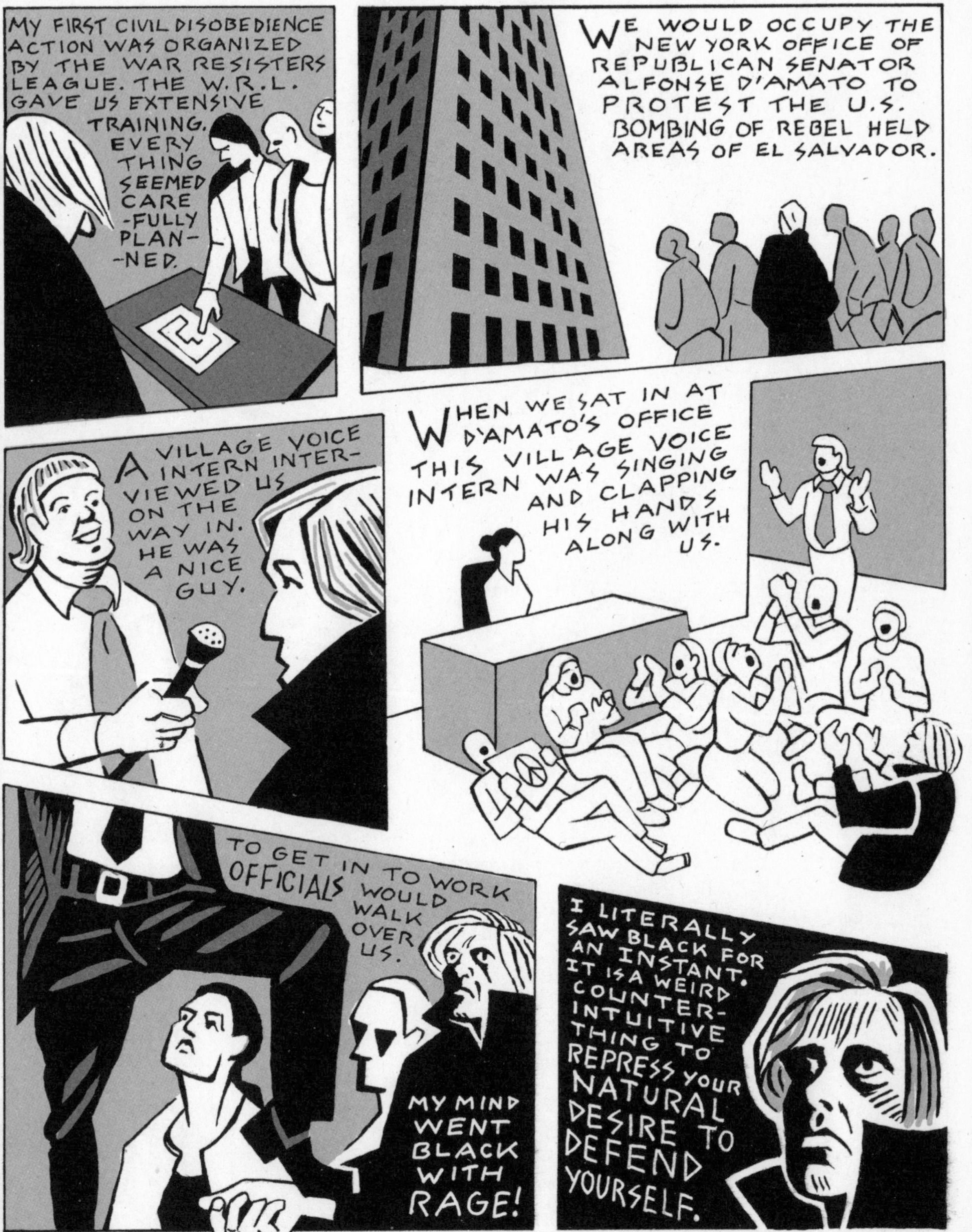
MY FIRST CIVIL DISOBEDIENCE ACTION WAS ORGANIZED BY THE WAR RESISTERS LEAGUE. THE W.R.L. GAVE US EXTENSIVE TRAINING. EVERYTHING SEEMED CARE-FULLY PLAN--NED.
WE WOULD OCCUPY THE NEW YORK OFFICE OF REPUBLICAN SENATOR ALFONSE D'AMATO TO PROTEST THE U.S. BOMBING OF REBEL HELD AREAS OF EL SALVADOR.
A VILLAGE VOICE INTERN INTER-VIEWED US ON THE WAY IN. HE WAS A NICE GUY.
WHEN WE SAT IN AT D'AMATO'S OFFICE THIS VILLAGE VOICE INTERN WAS SINGING AND CLAPPING HIS HANDS ALONG WITH US.
TO GET IN TO WORK OFFICIALS WOULD WALK OVER US.
MY MIND WENT BLACK WITH RAGE!
I LITERALLY SAW BLACK FOR AN INSTANT. IT IS A WEIRD COUNTER-INTUITIVE THING TO REPRESS YOUR NATURAL DESIRE TO DEFEND YOURSELF.

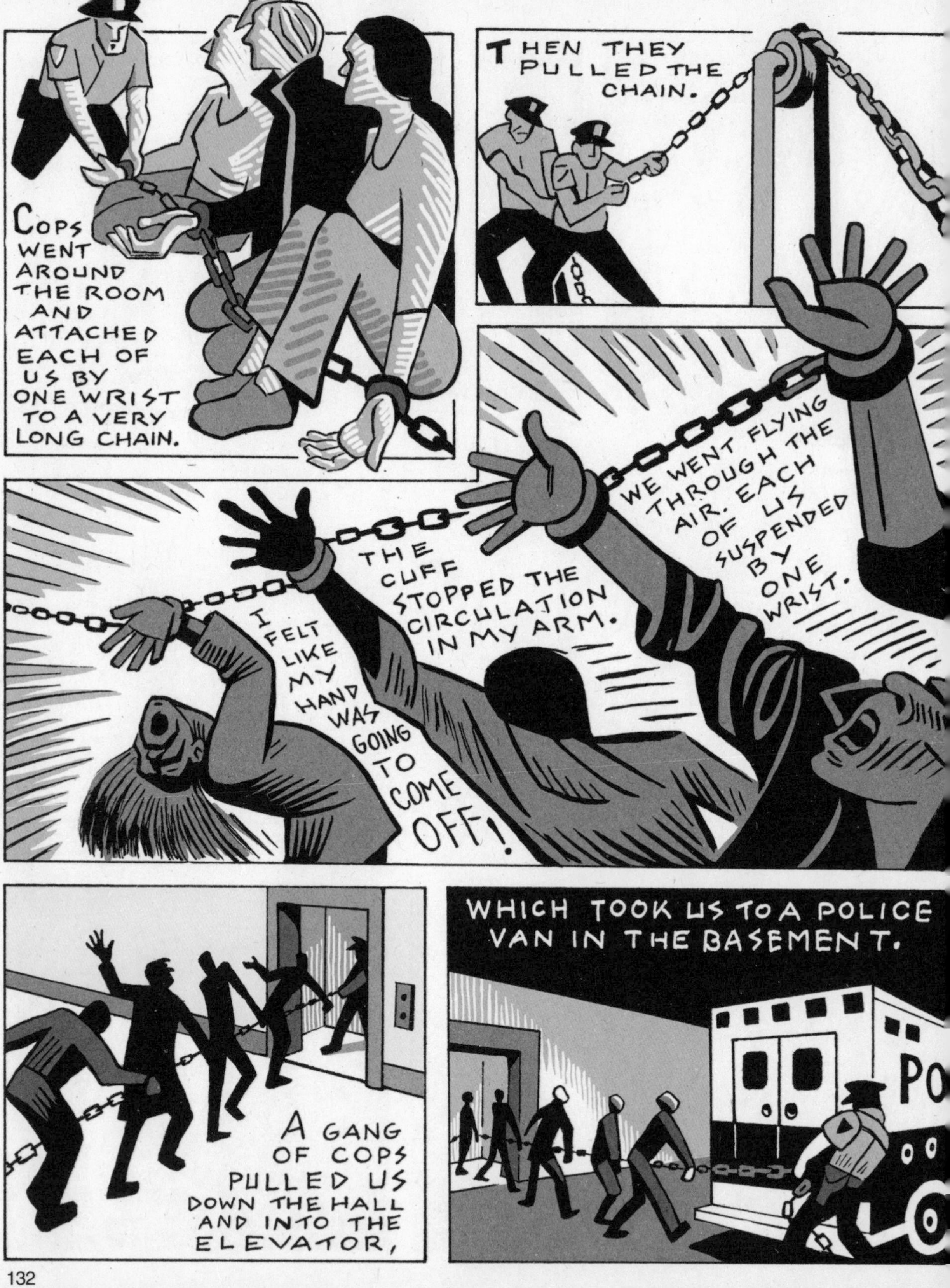
COPS WENT AROUND THE ROOM AND ATTACHED EACH OF US BY ONE WRIST TO A VERY LONG CHAIN.
THEN THEY PULLED THE CHAIN.
WE WENT FLYING THROUGH THE AIR. EACH OF US SUSPENDED BY ONE WRIST.
THE CUFF STOPPED THE CIRCULATION IN MY ARM.
I FELT LIKE MY HAND WAS GOING TO COME OFF!
A GANG OF COPS PULLED US DOWN THE HALL AND INTO THE ELEVATOR,
WHICH TOOK US TO A POLICE VAN IN THE BASEMENT.
PO

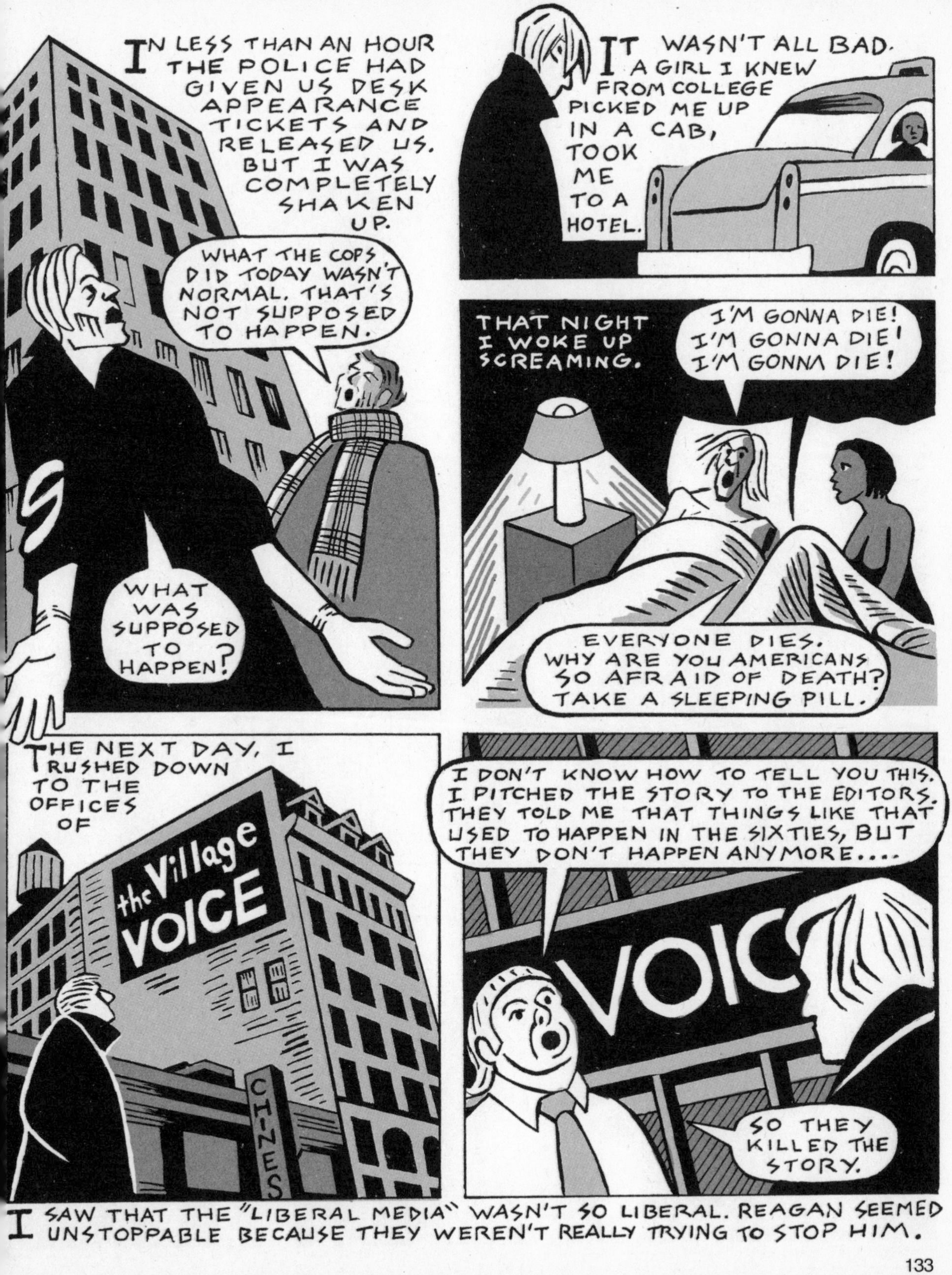
IN LESS THAN AN HOUR THE POLICE HAD GIVEN US DESK APPEARANCE TICKETS AND RELEASED US. BUT I WAS COMPLETELY SHAKEN UP.
WHAT THE COPS DID TODAY WASN'T NORMAL. THAT'S NOT SUPPOSED TO HAPPEN.
WHAT WAS SUPPOSED TO HAPPEN?
IT WASN'T ALL BAD. A GIRL I KNEW FROM COLLEGE PICKED ME UP IN A CAB, TOOK ME TO A HOTEL.
THAT NIGHT I WOKE UP SCREAMING.
I'M GONNA DIE! I'M GONNA DIE! I'M GONNA DIE!
EVERYONE DIES. WHY ARE YOU AMERICANS SO AFRAID OF DEATH? TAKE A SLEEPING PILL.
THE NEXT DAY, I RUSHED DOWN TO THE OFFICES OF
the Village VOICE
CHINES
I DON'T KNOW HOW TO TELL YOU THIS. I PITCHED THE STORY TO THE EDITORS. THEY TOLD ME THAT THINGS LIKE THAT USED TO HAPPEN IN THE SIXTIES, BUT THEY DON'T HAPPEN ANYMORE....
VOIC
SO THEY KILLED THE STORY.
I SAW THAT THE "LIBERAL MEDIA" WASN'T SO LIBERAL. REAGAN SEEMED UNSTOPPABLE BECAUSE THEY WEREN'T REALLY TRYING TO STOP HIM.

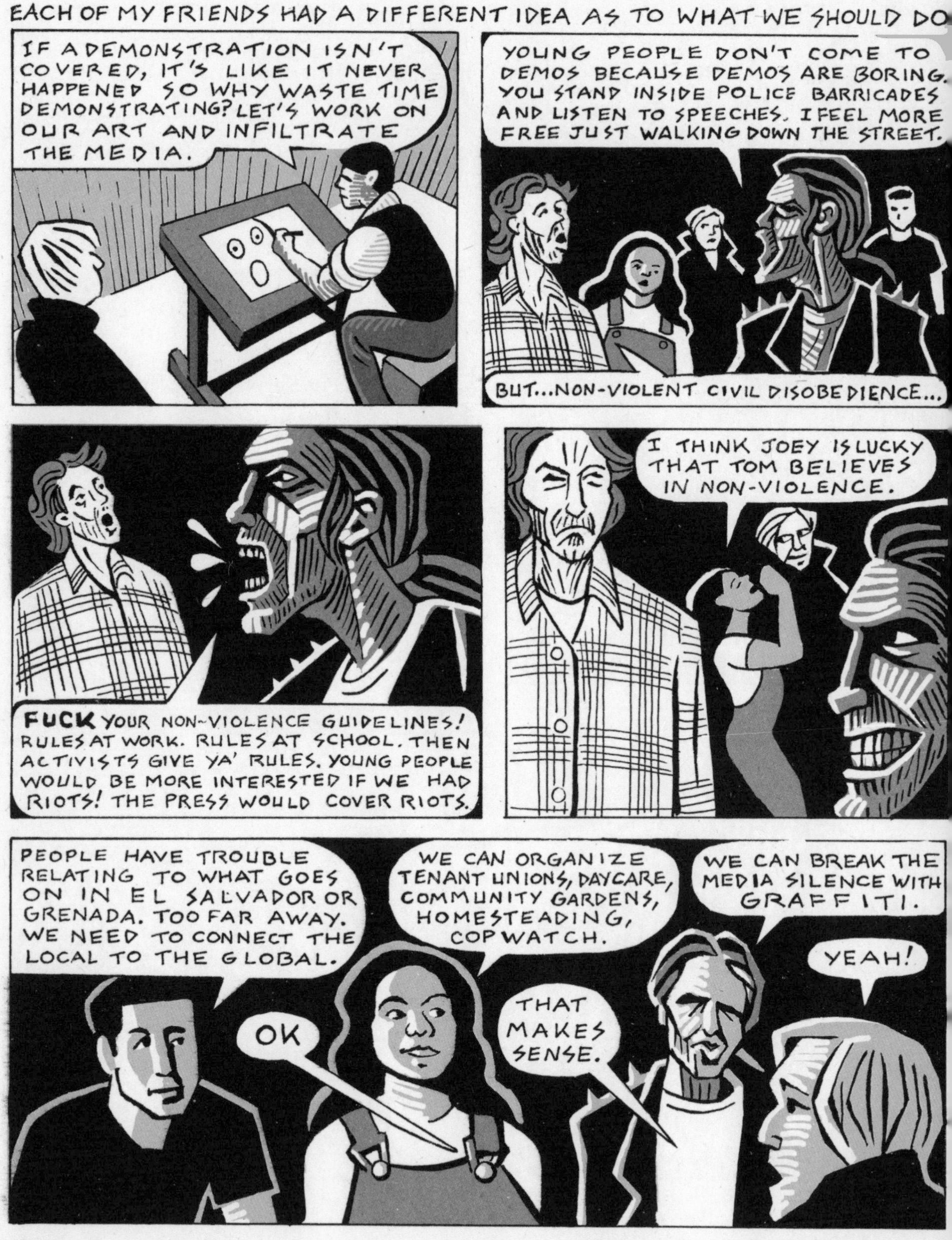
EACH OF MY FRIENDS HAD A DIFFERENT IDEA AS TO WHAT WE SHOULD DO
IF A DEMONSTRATION ISN'T COVERED, IT'S LIKE IT NEVER HAPPENED SO WHY WASTE TIME DEMONSTRATING? LET'S WORK ON OUR ART AND INFILTRATE THE MEDIA.
YOUNG PEOPLE DON'T COME TO DEMOS BECAUSE DEMOS ARE BORING. YOU STAND INSIDE POLICE BARRICADES AND LISTEN TO SPEECHES. I FEEL MORE FREE JUST WALKING DOWN THE STREET.
BUT...NON-VIOLENT CIVIL DISOBEDIENCE...
FUCK YOUR NON-VIOLENCE GUIDELINES! RULES AT WORK. RULES AT SCHOOL. THEN ACTIVISTS GIVE YA' RULES. YOUNG PEOPLE WOULD BE MORE INTERESTED IF WE HAD RIOTS! THE PRESS WOULD COVER RIOTS.
I THINK JOEY IS LUCKY THAT TOM BELIEVES IN NON-VIOLENCE.
PEOPLE HAVE TROUBLE RELATING TO WHAT GOES ON IN EL SALVADOR OR GRENADA. TOO FAR AWAY. WE NEED TO CONNECT THE LOCAL TO THE GLOBAL.
OK
WE CAN ORGANIZE TENANT UNIONS, DAYCARE, COMMUNITY GARDENS, HOMESTEADING, COPWATCH.
THAT MAKES SENSE.
WE CAN BREAK THE MEDIA SILENCE WITH GRAFFITI.
YEAH!

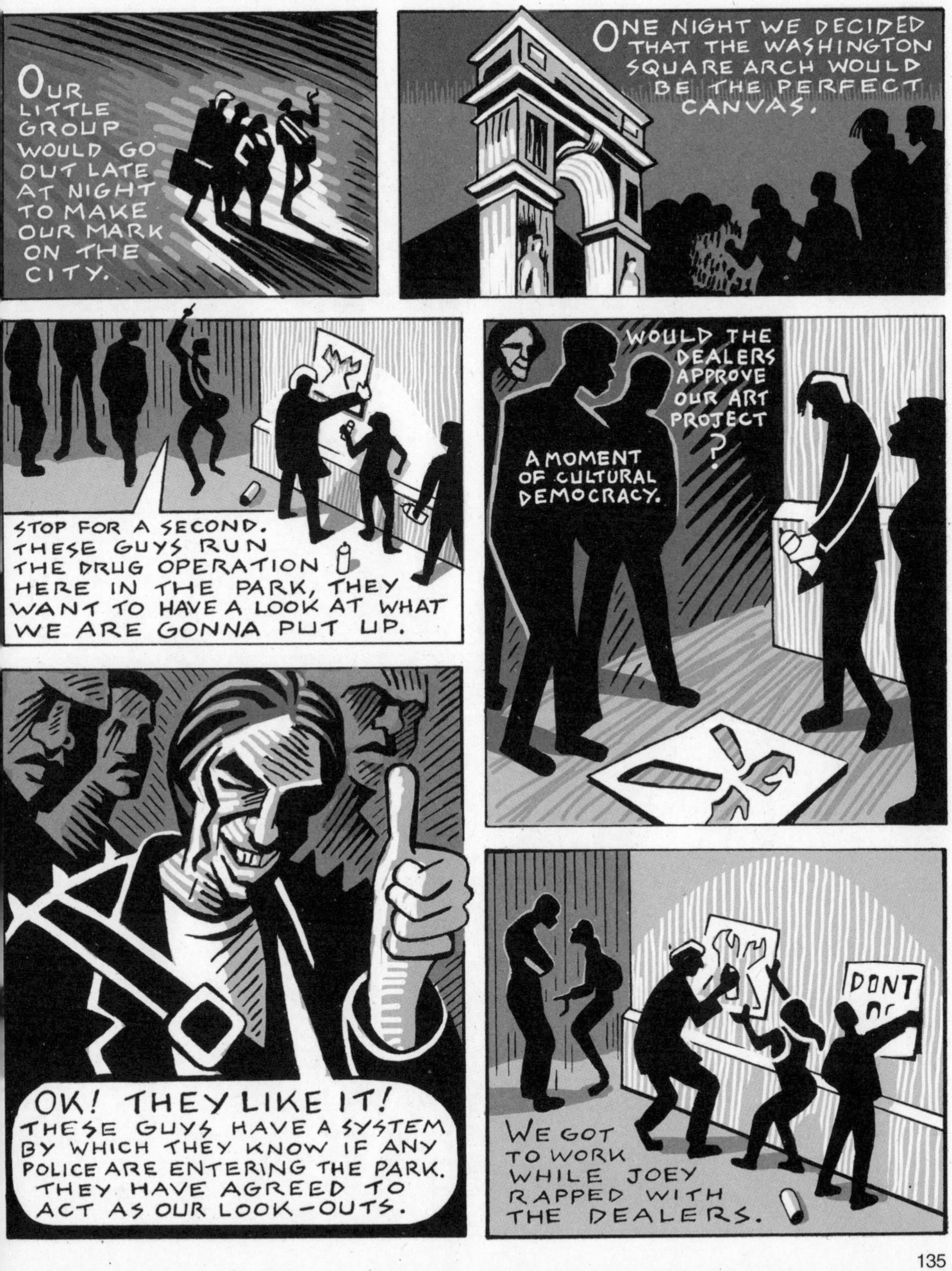

OUR LITTLE GROUP WOULD GO OUT LATE AT NIGHT TO MAKE OUR MARK ON THE CITY.
ONE NIGHT WE DECIDED THAT THE WASHINGTON SQUARE ARCH WOULD BE THE PERFECT CANVAS.
STOP FOR A SECOND. THESE GUYS RUN THE DRUG OPERATION HERE IN THE PARK, THEY WANT TO HAVE A LOOK AT WHAT WE ARE GONNA PUT UP.
WOULD THE DEALERS APPROVE OUR ART PROJECT ?
A MOMENT OF CULTURAL DEMOCRACY.
OK! THEY LIKE IT! THESE GUYS HAVE A SYSTEM BY WHICH THEY KNOW IF ANY POLICE ARE ENTERING THE PARK. THEY HAVE AGREED TO ACT AS OUR LOOK-OUTS.
WE GOT TO WORK WHILE JOEY RAPPED WITH THE DEALERS.
DONT

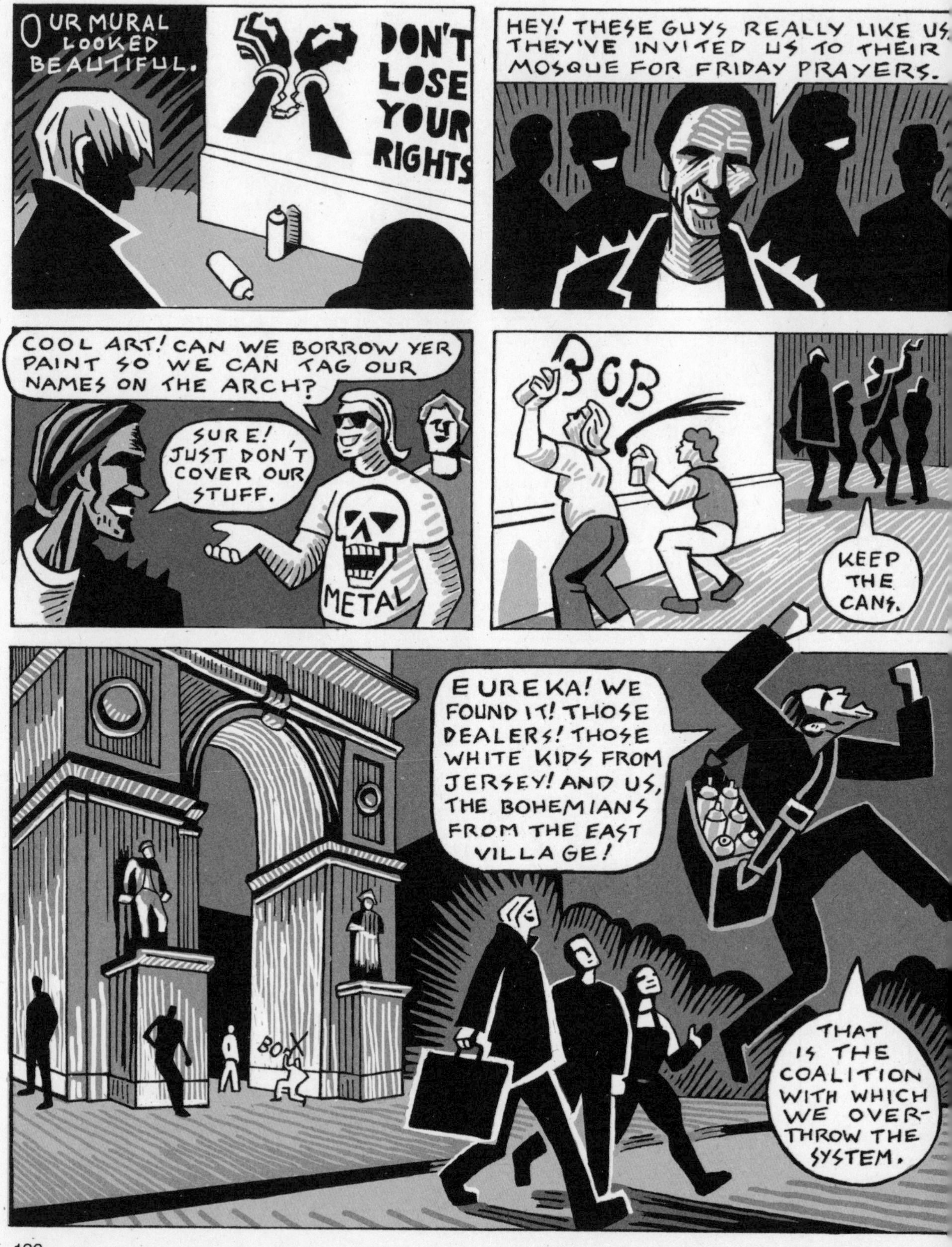
OUR MURAL LOOKED BEAUTIFUL.
DON'T LOSE YOUR RIGHTS
HEY! THESE GUYS REALLY LIKE US. THEY'VE INVITED US TO THEIR MOSQUE FOR FRIDAY PRAYERS.
COOL ART! CAN WE BORROW YER PAINT SO WE CAN TAG OUR NAMES ON THE ARCH?
SURE! JUST DON'T COVER OUR STUFF.
METAL
BOB
KEEP THE CANS.
EUREKA! WE FOUND IT! THOSE DEALERS! THOSE WHITE KIDS FROM JERSEY! AND US, THE BOHEMIANS FROM THE EAST VILLAGE!
THAT IS THE COALITION WITH WHICH WE OVER-THROW THE SYSTEM.

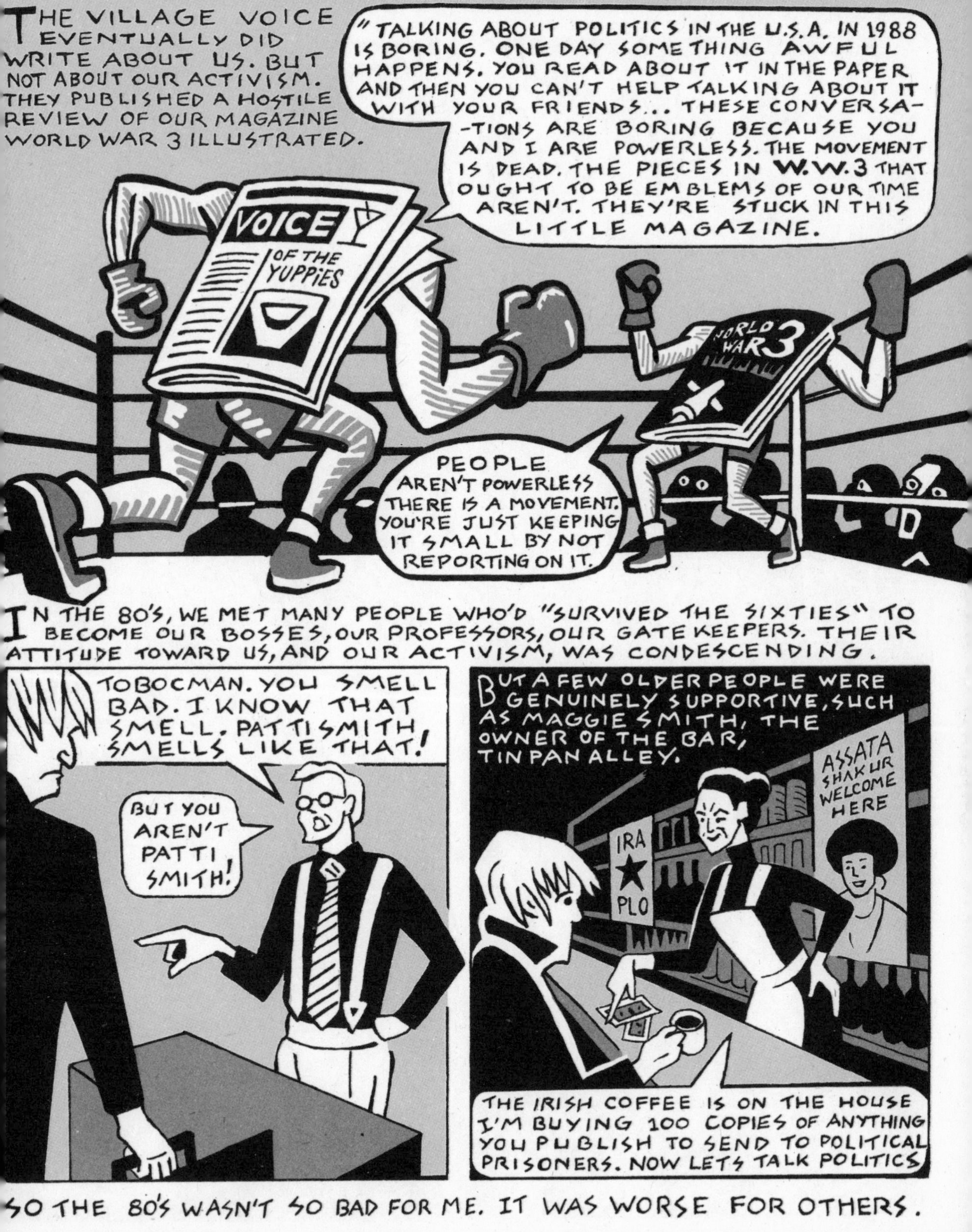
THE VILLAGE VOICE EVENTUALLY DID WRITE ABOUT US. BUT NOT ABOUT OUR ACTIVISM. THEY PUBLISHED A HOSTILE REVIEW OF OUR MAGAZINE WORLD WAR 3 ILLUSTRATED.
"TALKING ABOUT POLITICS IN THE U.S.A. IN 1988 IS BORING. ONE DAY SOMETHING AWFUL HAPPENS. YOU READ ABOUT IT IN THE PAPER AND THEN YOU CAN'T HELP TALKING ABOUT IT WITH YOUR FRIENDS... THESE CONVERSA--TIONS ARE BORING BECAUSE YOU AND I ARE POWERLESS. THE MOVEMENT IS DEAD. THE PIECES IN W.W.3 THAT OUGHT TO BE EMBLEMS OF OUR TIME AREN'T. THEY'RE STUCK IN THIS LITTLE MAGAZINE.
VOICE
OF THE YUPPIES
WORLD WAR 3
PEOPLE AREN'T POWERLESS THERE IS A MOVEMENT. YOU'RE JUST KEEPING IT SMALL BY NOT REPORTING ON IT.
IN THE 80'S, WE MET MANY PEOPLE WHO'D "SURVIVED THE SIXTIES" TO BECOME OUR BOSSES, OUR PROFESSORS, OUR GATEKEEPERS. THEIR ATTITUDE TOWARD US, AND OUR ACTIVISM, WAS CONDESCENDING.
TOBOCMAN. YOU SMELL BAD. I KNOW THAT SMELL. PATTI SMITH SMELLS LIKE THAT!
BUT YOU AREN'T PATTI SMITH!
BUT A FEW OLDER PEOPLE WERE GENUINELY SUPPORTIVE, SUCH AS MAGGIE SMITH, THE OWNER OF THE BAR, TIN PAN ALLEY.
ASSATA SHAKUR WELCOME HERE
IRA
PLO
THE IRISH COFFEE IS ON THE HOUSE I'M BUYING 100 COPIES OF ANYTHING YOU PUBLISH TO SEND TO POLITICAL PRISONERS. NOW LETS TALK POLITICS
SO THE 80'S WASN'T SO BAD FOR ME. IT WAS WORSE FOR OTHERS.

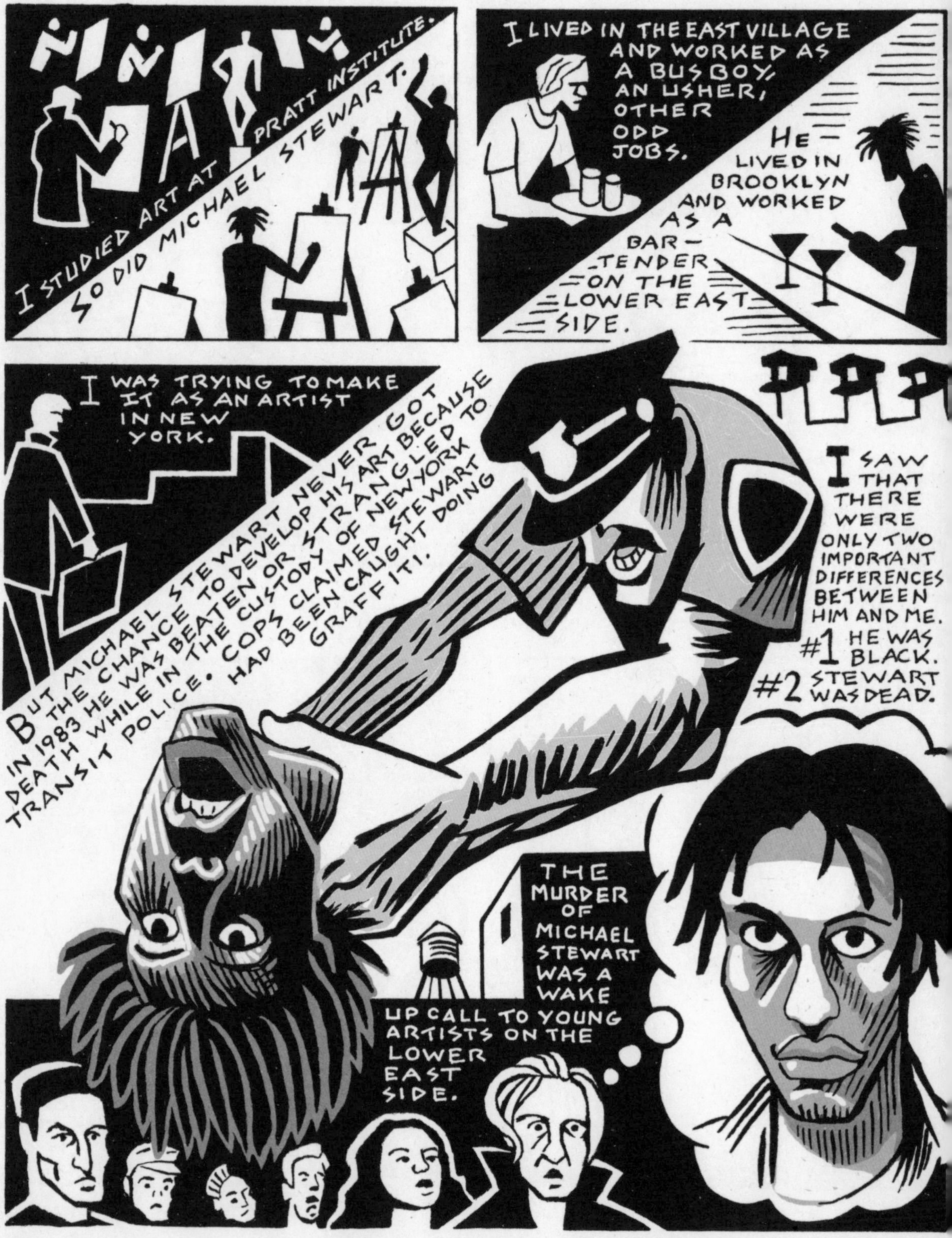
I NEVER MET HIM BUT...
I STUDIED ART AT PRATT INSTITUTE.
SO DID MICHAEL STEWART.
I LIVED IN THE EAST VILLAGE AND WORKED AS A BUSBOY, AN USHER, OTHER ODD JOBS.
HE LIVED IN BROOKLYN AND WORKED AS A BAR-TENDER ON THE LOWER EAST SIDE.
I WAS TRYING TO MAKE IT AS AN ARTIST IN NEW YORK.
BUT MICHAEL STEWART NEVER GOT THE CHANCE TO DEVELOP HIS ART BECAUSE IN 1983 HE WAS BEATEN OR STRANGLED TO DEATH WHILE IN THE CUSTODY OF NEW YORK TRANSIT POLICE. COPS CLAIMED STEWART HAD BEEN CAUGHT DOING GRAFFITI.
I SAW THAT THERE WERE ONLY TWO IMPORTANT DIFFERENCES BETWEEN HIM AND ME.
#1 HE WAS BLACK.
#2 STEWART WAS DEAD.
THE MURDER OF MICHAEL STEWART WAS A WAKE UP CALL TO YOUNG ARTISTS ON THE LOWER EAST SIDE.

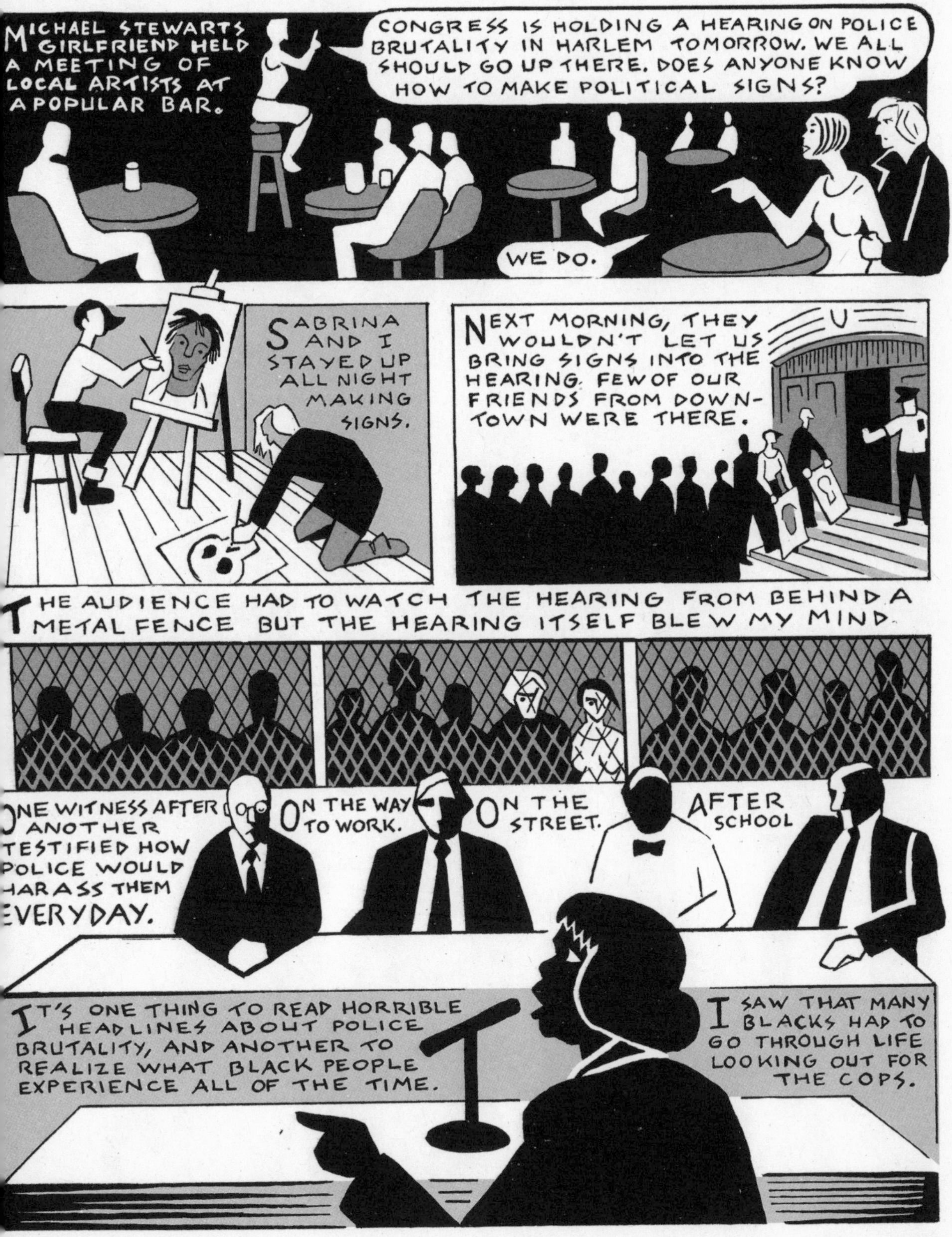
MICHAEL STEWARTS GIRLFRIEND HELD A MEETING OF LOCAL ARTISTS AT A POPULAR BAR.
CONGRESS IS HOLDING A HEARING ON POLICE BRUTALITY IN HARLEM TOMORROW. WE ALL SHOULD GO UP THERE. DOES ANYONE KNOW HOW TO MAKE POLITICAL SIGNS?
WE DO.
SABRINA AND I STAYED UP ALL NIGHT MAKING SIGNS.
NEXT MORNING, THEY WOULDN'T LET US BRING SIGNS INTO THE HEARING. FEW OF OUR FRIENDS FROM DOWNTOWN WERE THERE.
THE AUDIENCE HAD TO WATCH THE HEARING FROM BEHIND A METAL FENCE BUT THE HEARING ITSELF BLEW MY MIND.
ONE WITNESS AFTER ANOTHER TESTIFIED HOW POLICE WOULD HARASS THEM EVERYDAY.
ON THE WAY TO WORK.
ON THE STREET.
AFTER SCHOOL
IT'S ONE THING TO READ HORRIBLE HEADLINES ABOUT POLICE BRUTALITY, AND ANOTHER TO REALIZE WHAT BLACK PEOPLE EXPERIENCE ALL OF THE TIME.
I SAW THAT MANY BLACKS HAD TO GO THROUGH LIFE LOOKING OUT FOR THE COPS.

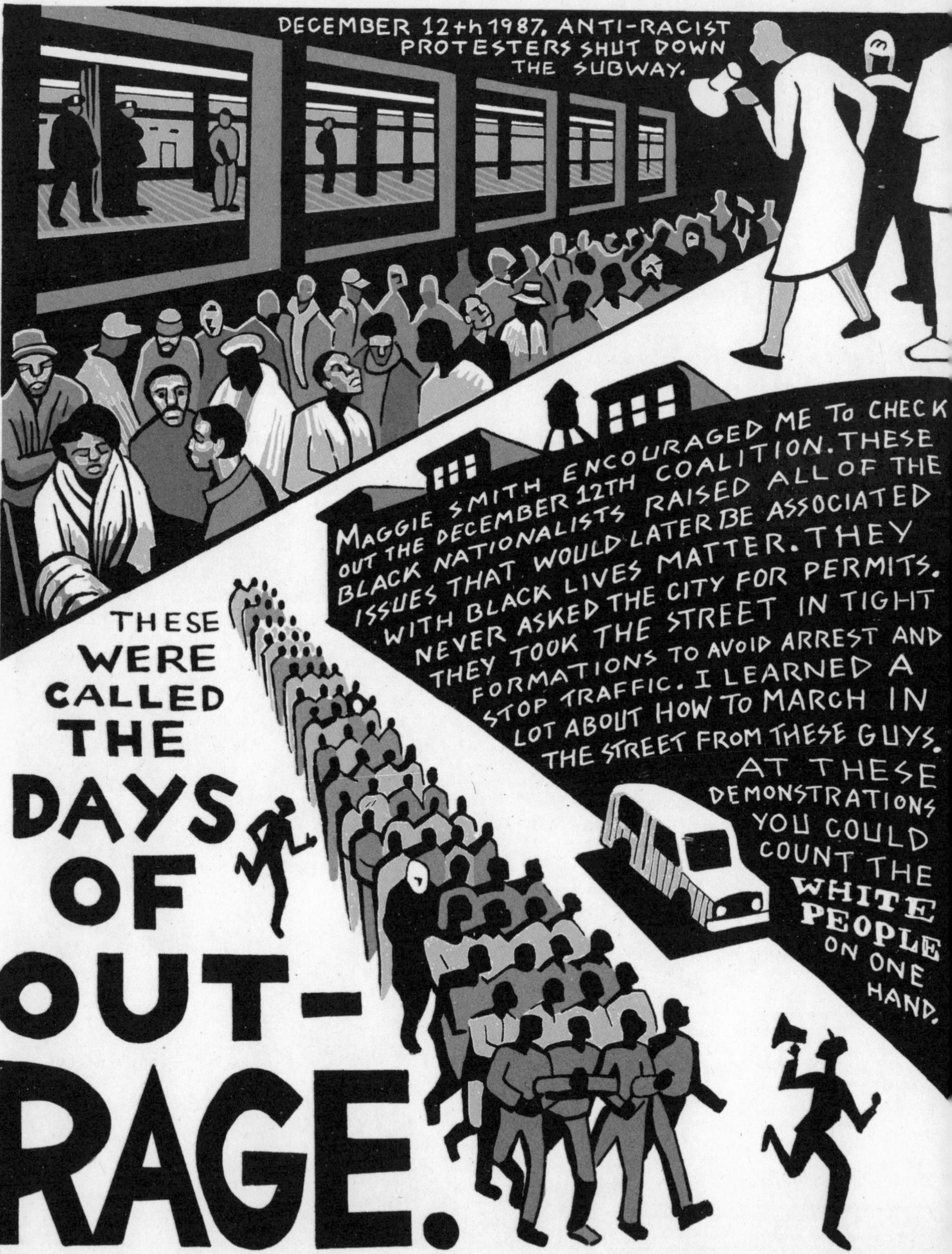

DECEMBER 12th 1987, ANTI-RACIST PROTESTERS SHUT DOWN THE SUBWAY.
MAGGIE SMITH ENCOURAGED ME TO CHECK OUT THE DECEMBER 12TH COALITION. THESE BLACK NATIONALISTS RAISED ALL OF THE ISSUES THAT WOULD LATER BE ASSOCIATED WITH BLACK LIVES MATTER. THEY NEVER ASKED THE CITY FOR PERMITS. THEY TOOK THE STREET IN TIGHT FORMATIONS TO AVOID ARREST AND STOP TRAFFIC. I LEARNED A LOT ABOUT HOW TO MARCH IN THE STREET FROM THESE GUYS.
AT THESE DEMONSTRATIONS YOU COULD COUNT THE WHITE PEOPLE ON ONE HAND.
THESE WERE CALLED THE DAYS OF OUT-RAGE.

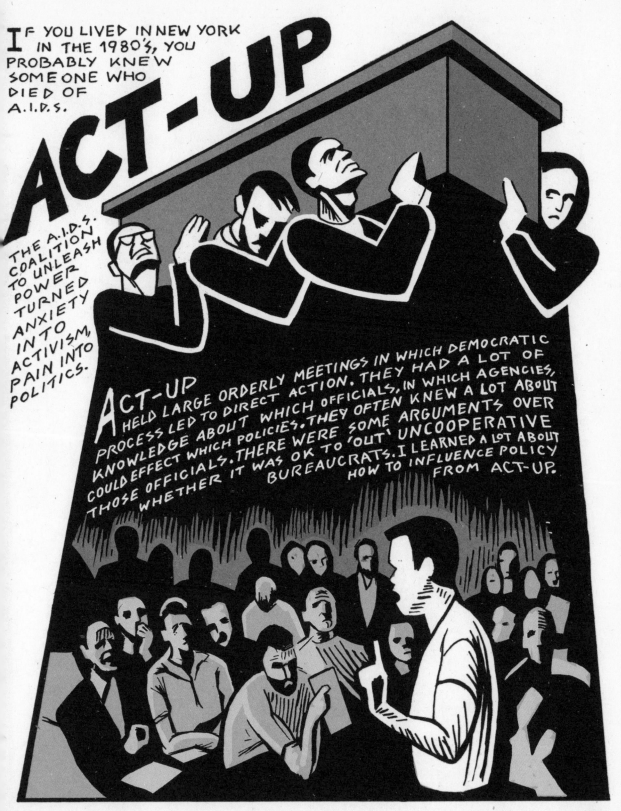

IF YOU LIVED IN NEW YORK IN THE 1980's, YOU PROBABLY KNEW SOME ONE WHO DIED OF A.I.D.S.

ACT-UP

THE A.I.D.S. COALITION TO UNLEASH POWER TURNED ANXIETY INTO ACTIVISM, PAIN INTO POLITICS.

ACT-UP HELD LARGE ORDERLY MEETINGS IN WHICH DEMOCRATIC PROCESS LED TO DIRECT ACTION. THEY HAD A LOT OF KNOWLEDGE ABOUT WHICH OFFICIALS, IN WHICH AGENCIES, COULD EFFECT WHICH POLICIES. THEY OFTEN KNEW A LOT ABOUT THOSE OFFICIALS. THERE WERE SOME ARGUMENTS OVER WHETHER IT WAS OK TO 'OUT' UNCOOPERATIVE BUREAUCRATS. I LEARNED A LOT ABOUT HOW TO INFLUENCE POLICY FROM ACT-UP.

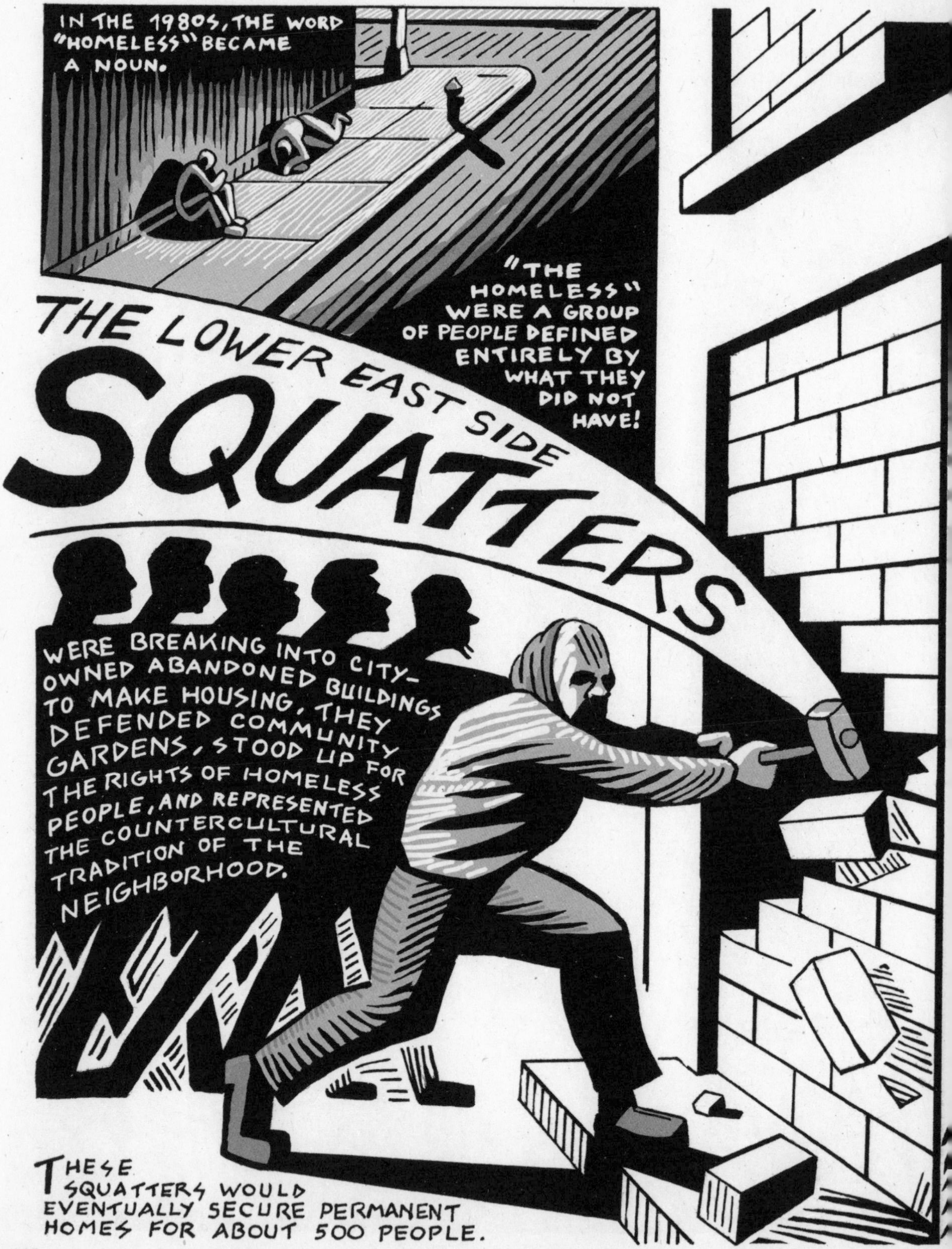

IN THE 1980s, THE WORD "HOMELESS" BECAME A NOUN.
"THE HOMELESS" WERE A GROUP OF PEOPLE DEFINED ENTIRELY BY WHAT THEY DID NOT HAVE!
THE LOWER EAST SIDE
SQUATTERS
WERE BREAKING INTO CITY-OWNED ABANDONED BUILDINGS TO MAKE HOUSING, THEY DEFENDED COMMUNITY GARDENS, STOOD UP FOR THE RIGHTS OF HOMELESS PEOPLE, AND REPRESENTED THE COUNTERCULTURAL TRADITION OF THE NEIGHBORHOOD.
THESE SQUATTERS WOULD EVENTUALLY SECURE PERMANENT HOMES FOR ABOUT 500 PEOPLE.

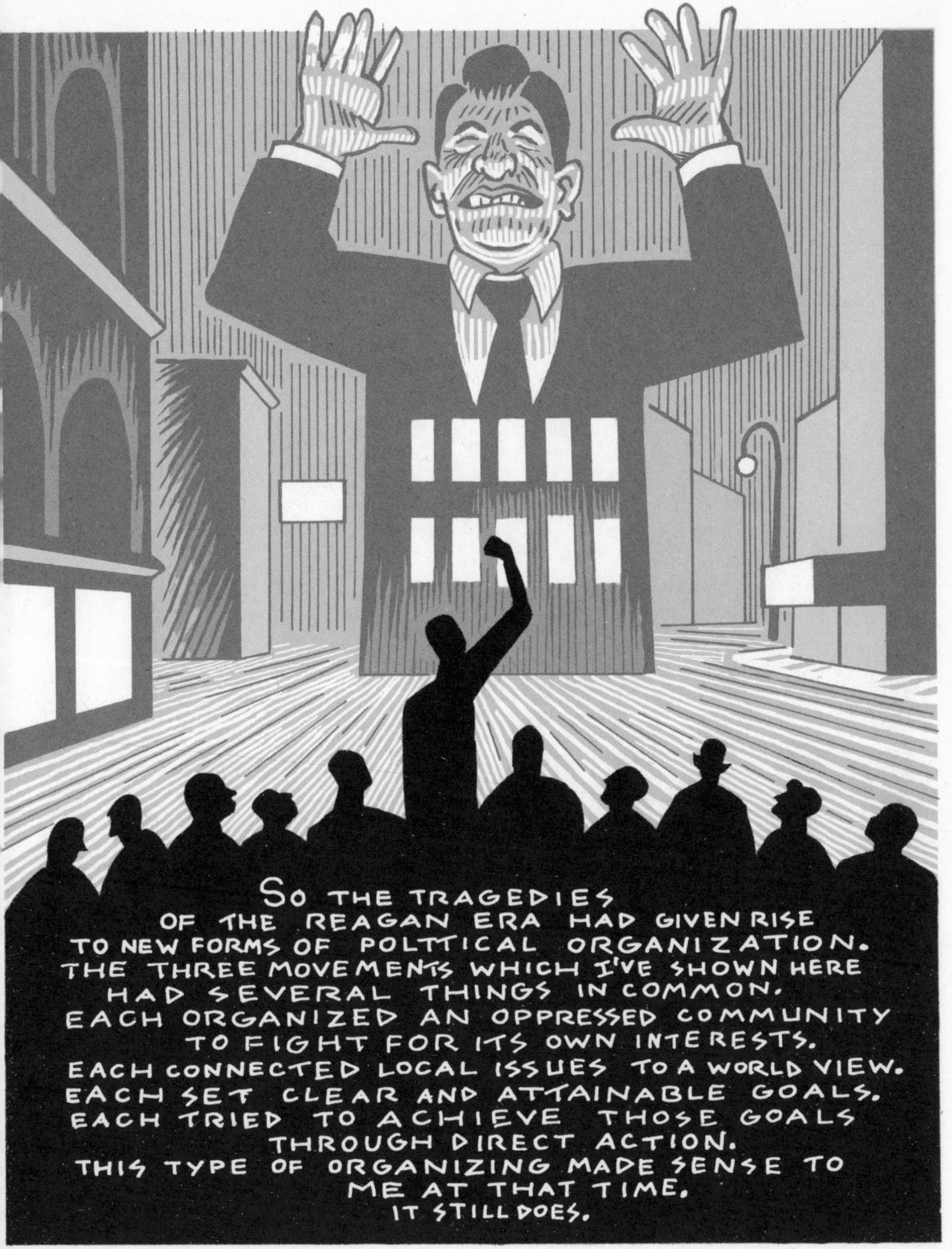
So the tragedies of the Reagan era had given rise to new forms of polttical organization. The three movements which I've shown here had several things in common. Each organized an oppressed community to fight for its own interests. Each connected local issues to a world view. Each set clear and attainable goals. Each tried to achieve those goals through direct action. This type of organizing made sense to me at that time. It still does.

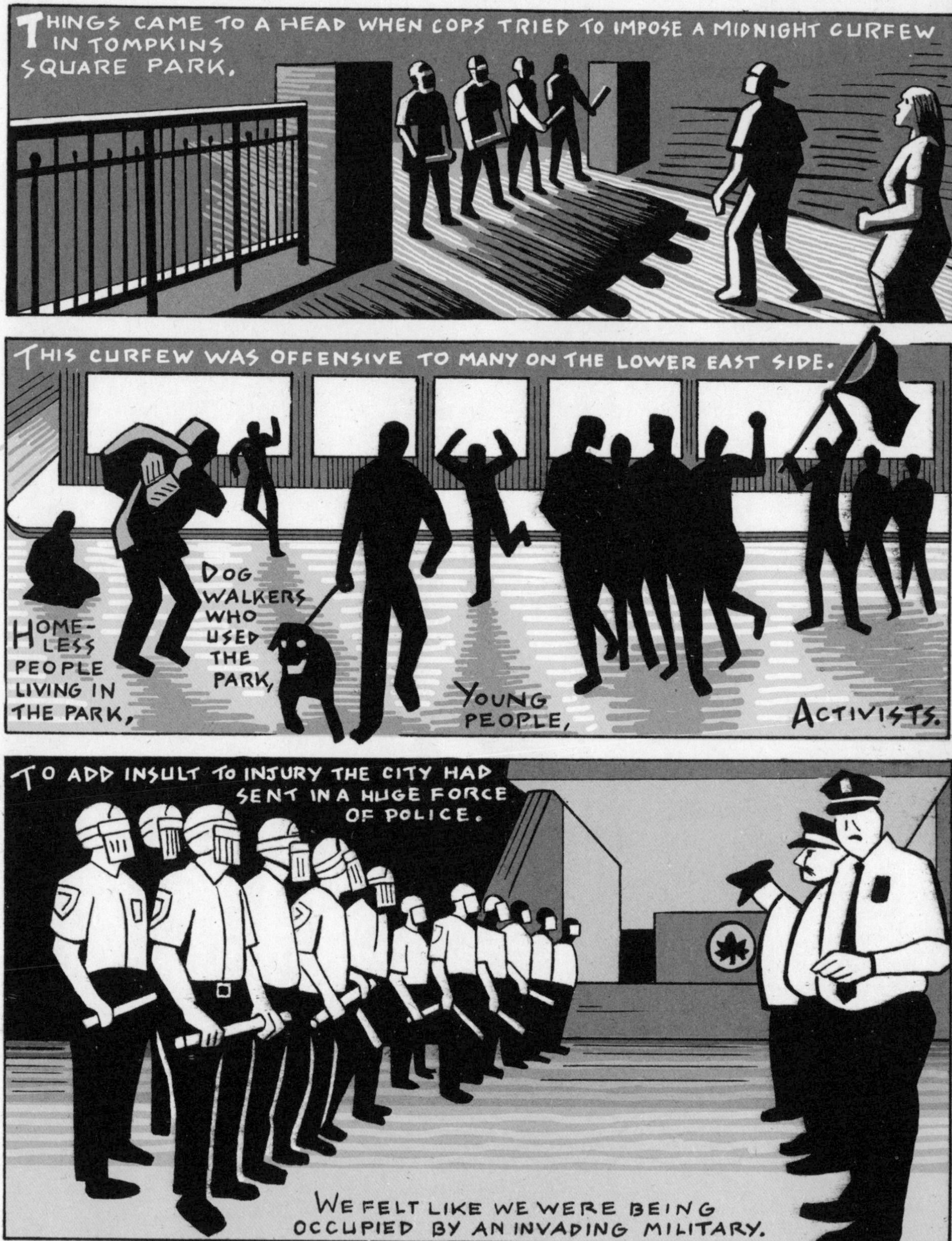
THINGS CAME TO A HEAD WHEN COPS TRIED TO IMPOSE A MIDNIGHT CURFEW IN TOMPKINS SQUARE PARK.
THIS CURFEW WAS OFFENSIVE TO MANY ON THE LOWER EAST SIDE.
HOMELESS PEOPLE LIVING IN THE PARK,
DOG WALKERS WHO USED THE PARK,
YOUNG PEOPLE,
ACTIVISTS.
TO ADD INSULT TO INJURY THE CITY HAD SENT IN A HUGE FORCE OF POLICE.
WE FELT LIKE WE WERE BEING OCCUPIED BY AN INVADING MILITARY.

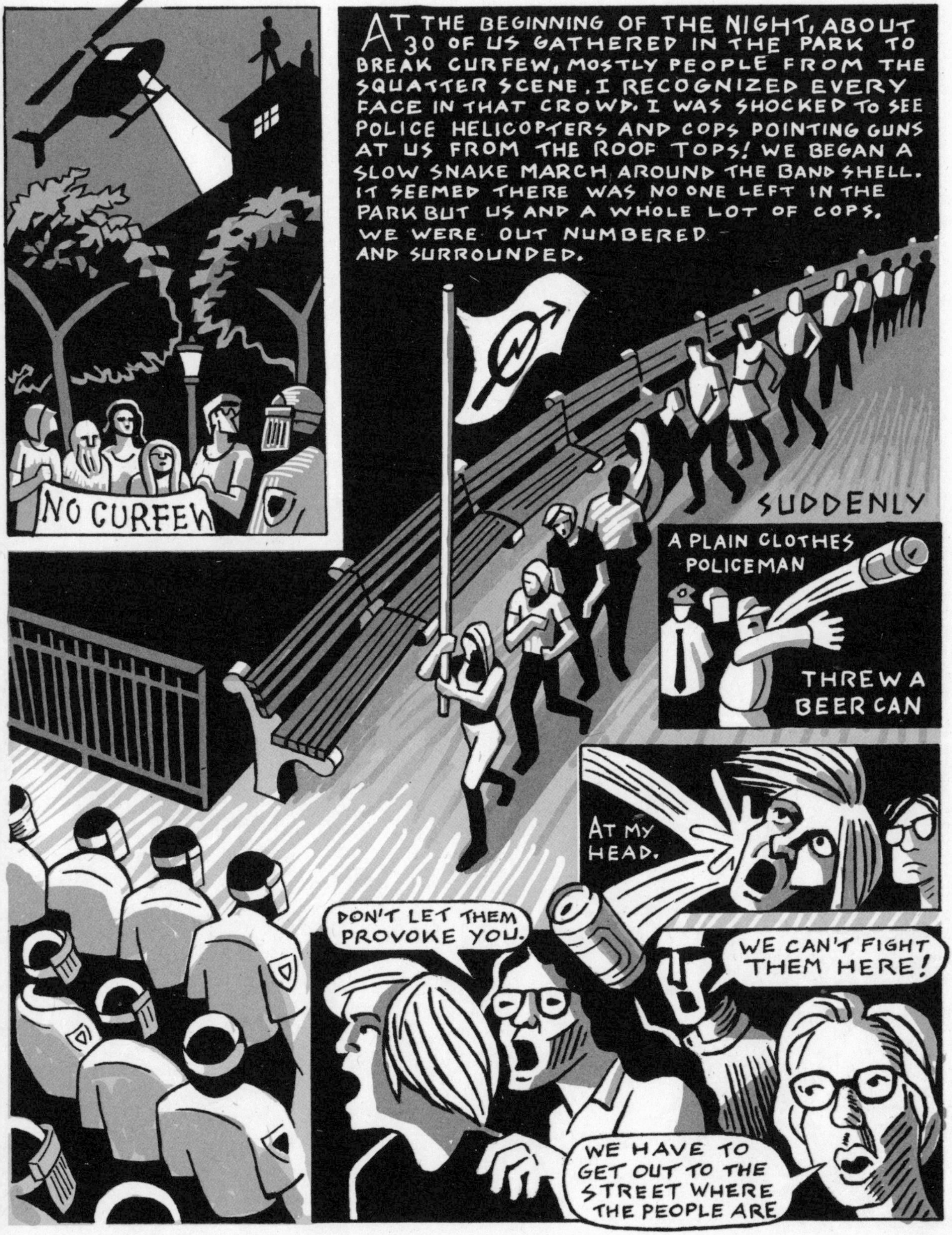

AT THE BEGINNING OF THE NIGHT, ABOUT 30 OF US GATHERED IN THE PARK TO BREAK CURFEW, MOSTLY PEOPLE FROM THE SQUATTER SCENE. I RECOGNIZED EVERY FACE IN THAT CROWD. I WAS SHOCKED TO SEE POLICE HELICOPTERS AND COPS POINTING GUNS AT US FROM THE ROOF TOPS! WE BEGAN A SLOW SNAKE MARCH AROUND THE BAND SHELL. IT SEEMED THERE WAS NO ONE LEFT IN THE PARK BUT US AND A WHOLE LOT OF COPS. WE WERE OUT NUMBERED AND SURROUNDED.
NO CURFEW
SUDDENLY
A PLAIN CLOTHES POLICEMAN
THREW A BEER CAN
AT MY HEAD.
DON'T LET THEM PROVOKE YOU.
WE CAN'T FIGHT THEM HERE!
WE HAVE TO GET OUT TO THE STREET WHERE THE PEOPLE ARE

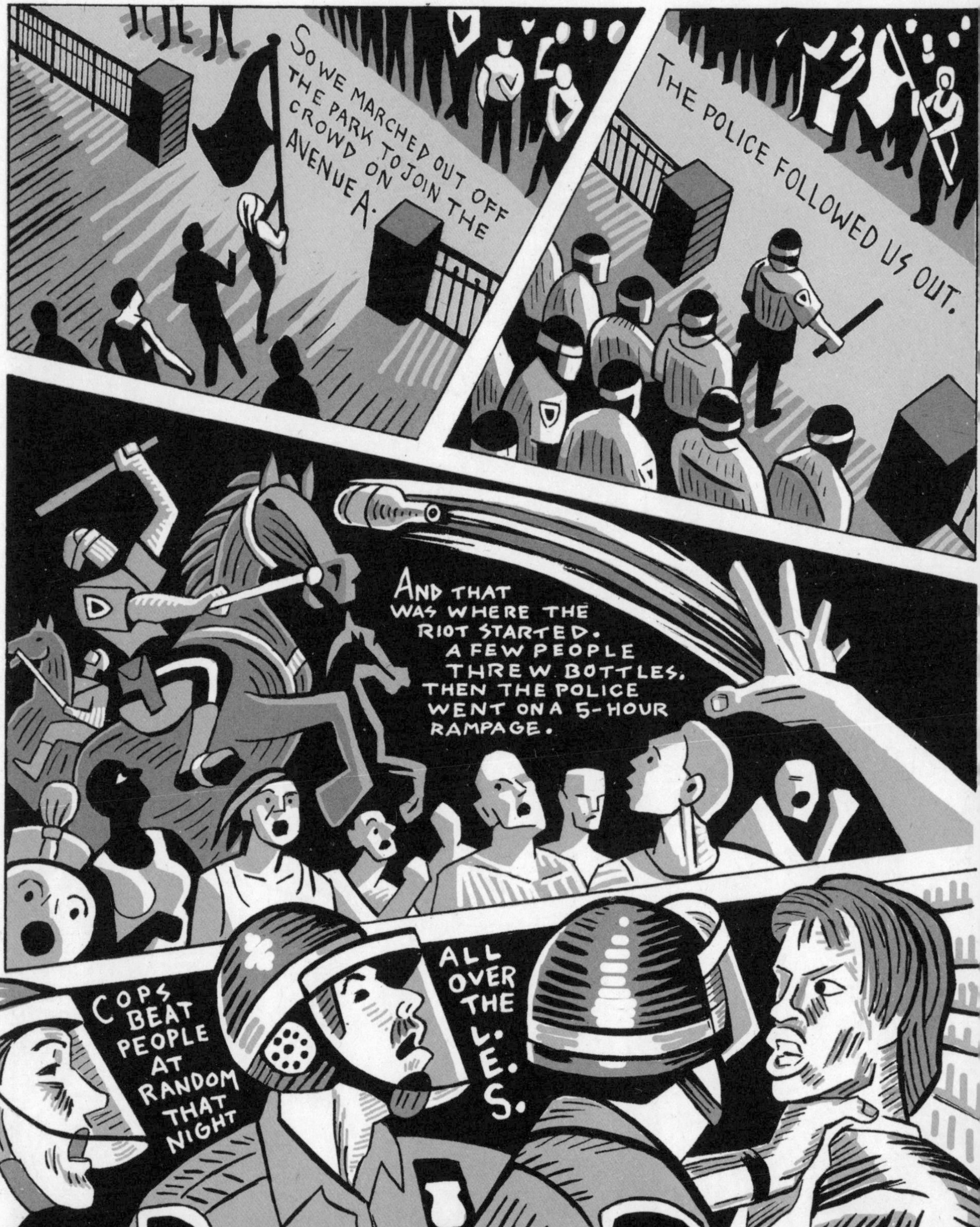

So we marched out off the park to join the crowd on Avenue A.
The police followed us out.
And that was where the riot started. A few people threw bottles. Then the police went on a 5-hour rampage.
Cops beat people at random that night
All over the L.E.S.

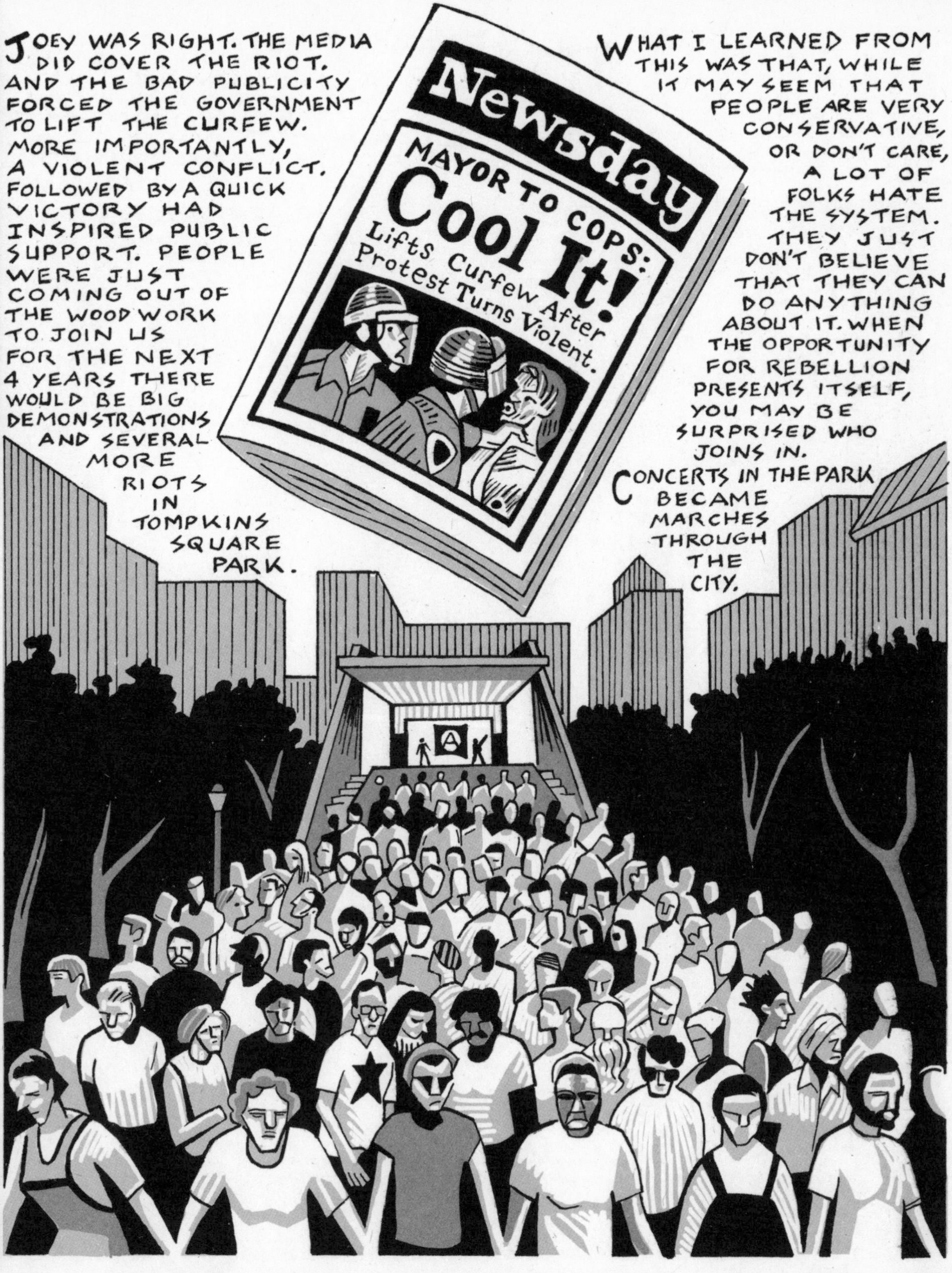
JOEY WAS RIGHT. THE MEDIA DID COVER THE RIOT. AND THE BAD PUBLICITY FORCED THE GOVERNMENT TO LIFT THE CURFEW. MORE IMPORTANTLY, A VIOLENT CONFLICT, FOLLOWED BY A QUICK VICTORY HAD INSPIRED PUBLIC SUPPORT. PEOPLE WERE JUST COMING OUT OF THE WOODWORK TO JOIN US FOR THE NEXT 4 YEARS THERE WOULD BE BIG DEMONSTRATIONS AND SEVERAL MORE RIOTS IN TOMPKINS SQUARE PARK.
Newsday
MAYOR TO COPS: Cool It!
Lifts Curfew After Protest Turns Violent.
WHAT I LEARNED FROM THIS WAS THAT, WHILE IT MAY SEEM THAT PEOPLE ARE VERY CONSERVATIVE, OR DON'T CARE, A LOT OF FOLKS HATE THE SYSTEM. THEY JUST DON'T BELIEVE THAT THEY CAN DO ANYTHING ABOUT IT. WHEN THE OPPORTUNITY FOR REBELLION PRESENTS ITSELF, YOU MAY BE SURPRISED WHO JOINS IN.
CONCERTS IN THE PARK BECAME MARCHES THROUGH THE CITY.

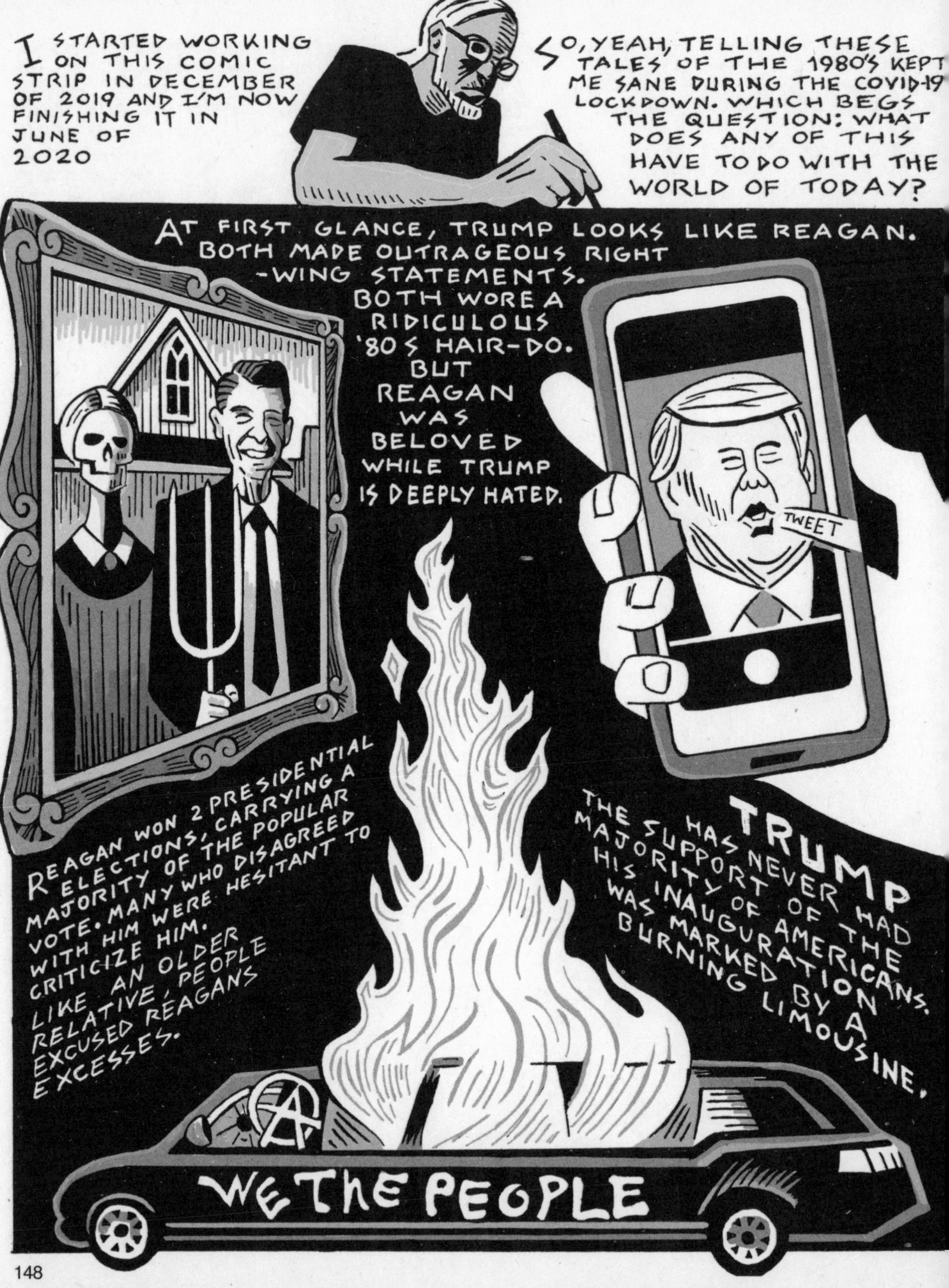
I STARTED WORKING ON THIS COMIC STRIP IN DECEMBER OF 2019 AND I'M NOW FINISHING IT IN JUNE OF 2020
SO, YEAH, TELLING THESE TALES OF THE 1980'S KEPT ME SANE DURING THE COVID-19 LOCKDOWN. WHICH BEGS THE QUESTION: WHAT DOES ANY OF THIS HAVE TO DO WITH THE WORLD OF TODAY?
AT FIRST GLANCE, TRUMP LOOKS LIKE REAGAN. BOTH MADE OUTRAGEOUS RIGHT-WING STATEMENTS. BOTH WORE A RIDICULOUS '80'S HAIR-DO. BUT REAGAN WAS BELOVED WHILE TRUMP IS DEEPLY HATED.
TWEET
REAGAN WON 2 PRESIDENTIAL ELECTIONS, CARRYING A MAJORITY OF THE POPULAR VOTE. MANY WHO DISAGREED WITH HIM WERE HESITANT TO CRITICIZE HIM. LIKE AN OLDER RELATIVE, PEOPLE EXCUSED REAGANS EXCESSES.
TRUMP HAS NEVER HAD THE SUPPORT OF THE MAJORITY OF AMERICANS. HIS INAUGURATION WAS MARKED BY A BURNING LIMOUSINE.
WE THE PEOPLE

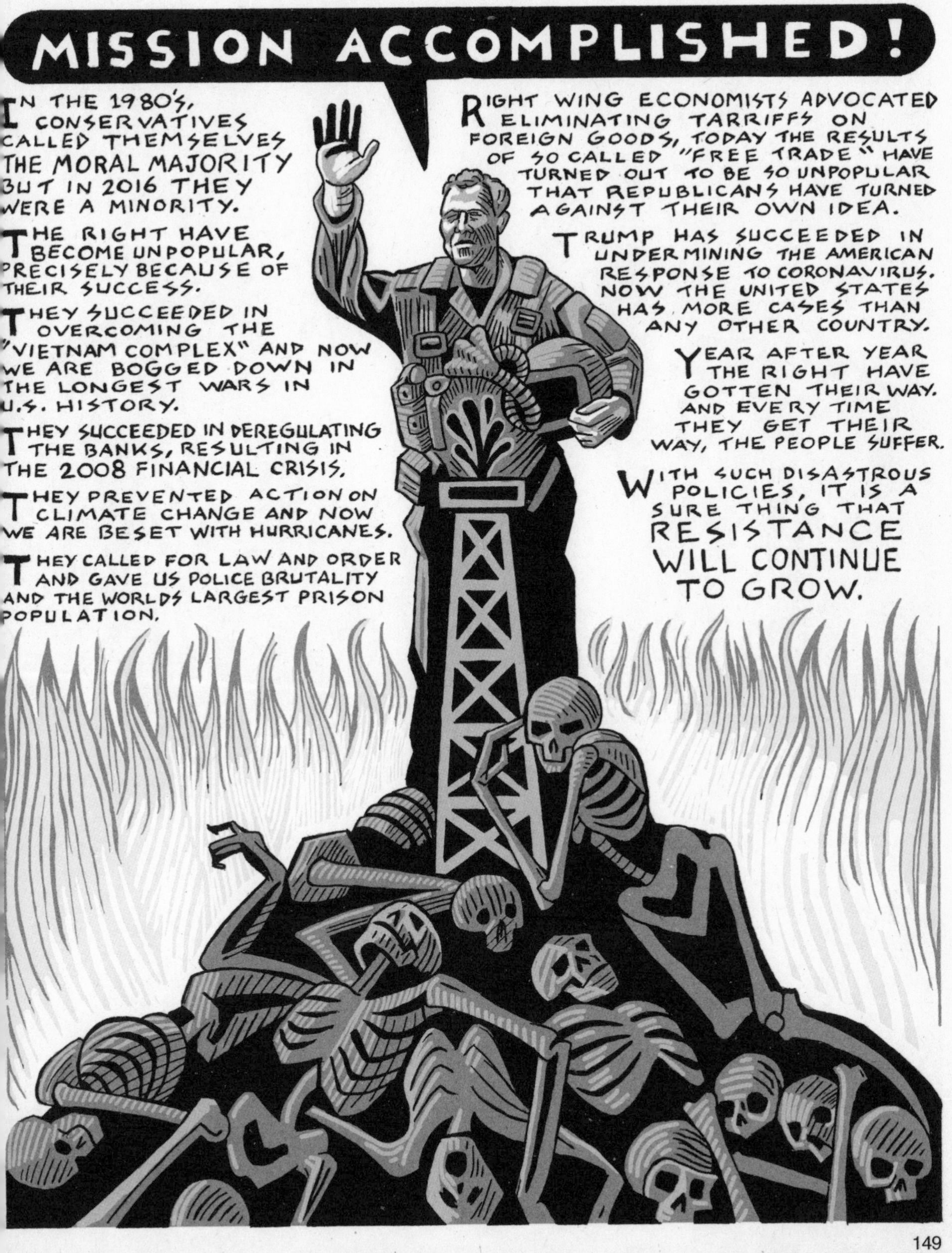
MISSION ACCOMPLISHED!
IN THE 1980'S, CONSERVATIVES CALLED THEMSELVES THE MORAL MAJORITY BUT IN 2016 THEY WERE A MINORITY.
THE RIGHT HAVE BECOME UNPOPULAR, PRECISELY BECAUSE OF THEIR SUCCESS.
THEY SUCCEEDED IN OVERCOMING THE "VIETNAM COMPLEX" AND NOW WE ARE BOGGED DOWN IN THE LONGEST WARS IN U.S. HISTORY.
THEY SUCCEEDED IN DEREGULATING THE BANKS, RESULTING IN THE 2008 FINANCIAL CRISIS.
THEY PREVENTED ACTION ON CLIMATE CHANGE AND NOW WE ARE BESET WITH HURRICANES.
THEY CALLED FOR LAW AND ORDER AND GAVE US POLICE BRUTALITY AND THE WORLDS LARGEST PRISON POPULATION.
RIGHT WING ECONOMISTS ADVOCATED ELIMINATING TARRIFFS ON FOREIGN GOODS, TODAY THE RESULTS OF SO CALLED "FREE TRADE" HAVE TURNED OUT TO BE SO UNPOPULAR THAT REPUBLICANS HAVE TURNED AGAINST THEIR OWN IDEA.
TRUMP HAS SUCCEEDED IN UNDERMINING THE AMERICAN RESPONSE TO CORONAVIRUS. NOW THE UNITED STATES HAS MORE CASES THAN ANY OTHER COUNTRY.
YEAR AFTER YEAR THE RIGHT HAVE GOTTEN THEIR WAY. AND EVERY TIME THEY GET THEIR WAY, THE PEOPLE SUFFER.
WITH SUCH DISASTROUS POLICIES, IT IS A SURE THING THAT RESISTANCE WILL CONTINUE TO GROW.

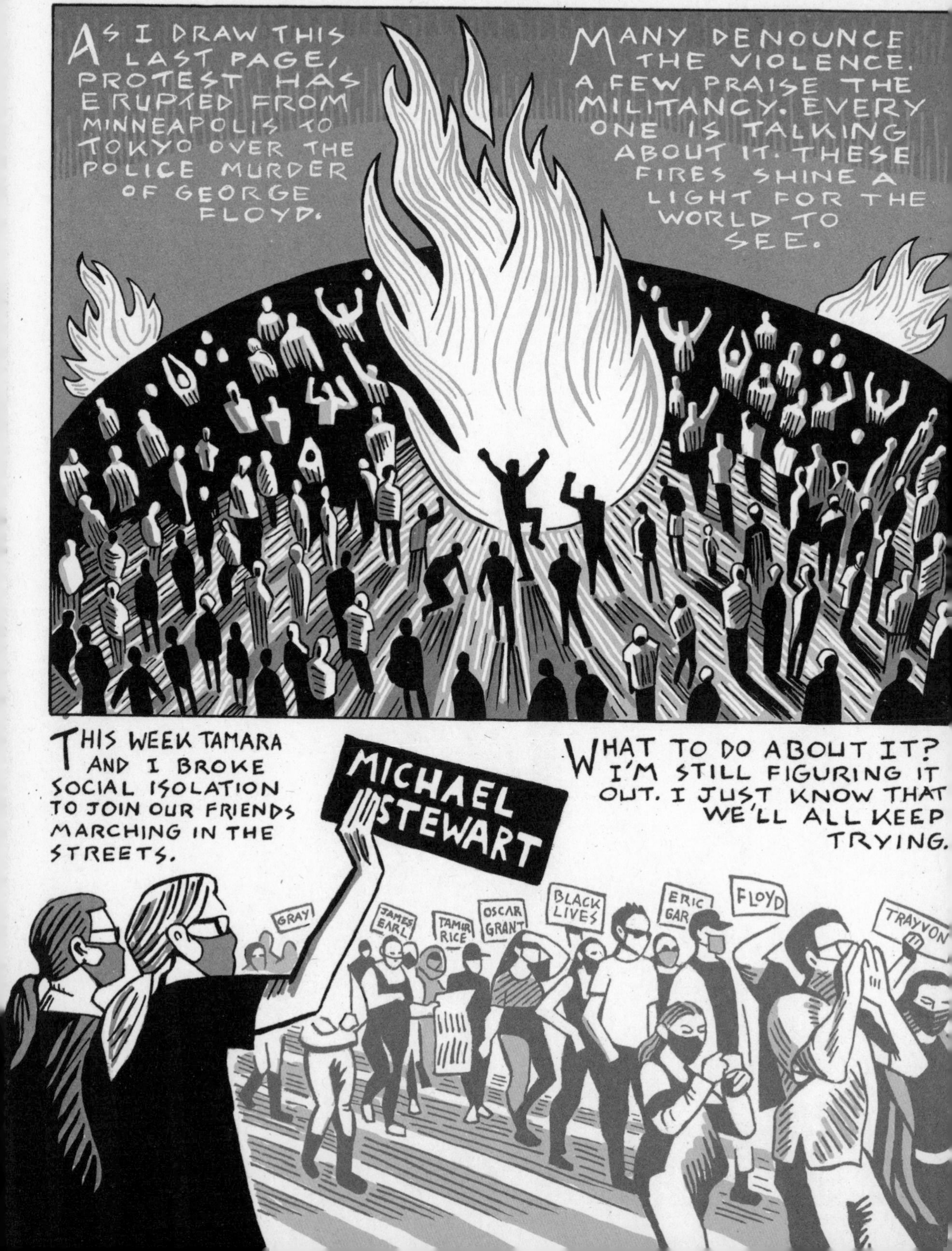
AS I DRAW THIS LAST PAGE, PROTEST HAS ERUPTED FROM MINNEAPOLIS TO TOKYO OVER THE POLICE MURDER OF GEORGE FLOYD.
MANY DENOUNCE THE VIOLENCE. A FEW PRAISE THE MILITANCY. EVERY ONE IS TALKING ABOUT IT. THESE FIRES SHINE A LIGHT FOR THE WORLD TO SEE.
THIS WEEK TAMARA AND I BROKE SOCIAL ISOLATION TO JOIN OUR FRIENDS MARCHING IN THE STREETS.
MICHAEL STEWART
WHAT TO DO ABOUT IT? I'M STILL FIGURING IT OUT. I JUST KNOW THAT WE'LL ALL KEEP TRYING.
GRAY
JAMES EARL
TAMIR RICE
OSCAR GRANT
BLACK LIVES
ERIC GAR
FLOYD
TRAYVON

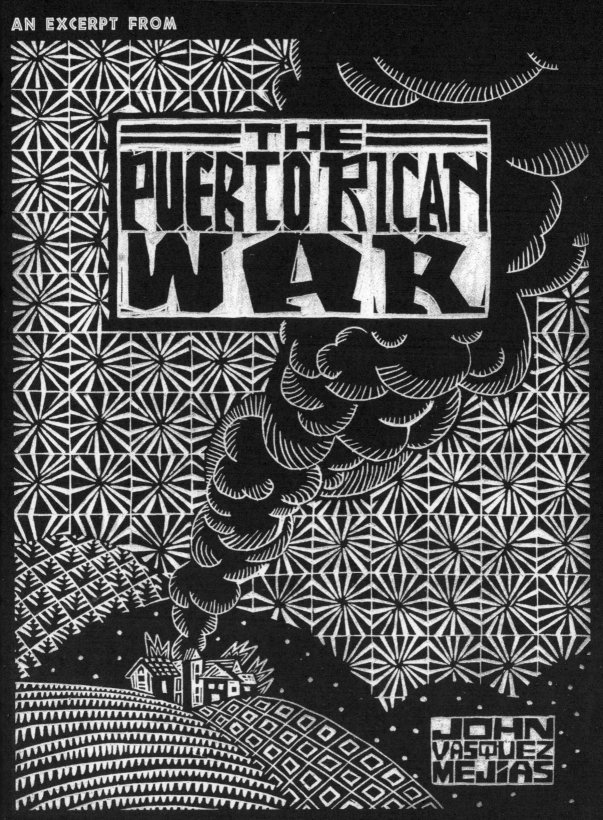

THE PUERTO RICAN WAR

JOHN VASQUEZ MEJIAS

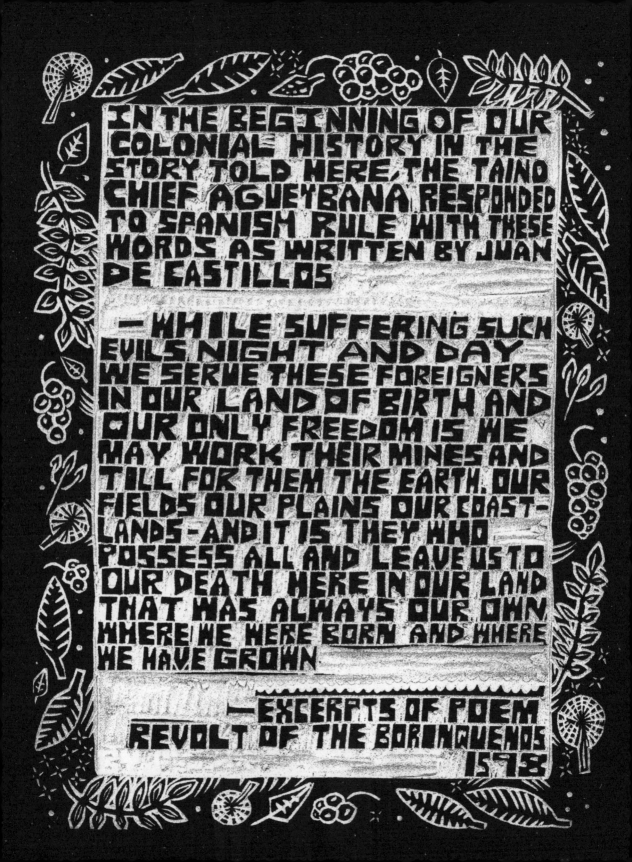

IN THE BEGINNING OF OUR
COLONIAL HISTORY IN THE
STORY TOLD HERE, THE TAINO
CHIEF AGUEYBANA RESPONDED
TO SPANISH RULE WITH THESE
WORDS AS WRITTEN BY JUAN
DE CASTILLOS

—WHILE SUFFERING SUCH
EVILS NIGHT AND DAY
WE SERVE THESE FOREIGNERS
IN OUR LAND OF BIRTH AND
OUR ONLY FREEDOM IS WE
MAY WORK THEIR MINES AND
TILL FOR THEM THE EARTH. OUR
FIELDS OUR PLAINS OUR COAST-
LANDS—AND IT IS THEY WHO
POSSESS ALL AND LEAVE US TO
OUR DEATH HERE IN OUR LAND
THAT WAS ALWAYS OUR OWN
WHERE WE WERE BORN AND WHERE
WE HAVE GROWN

—EXCERPTS OF POEM
REVOLT OF THE BORONQUENOS
1598

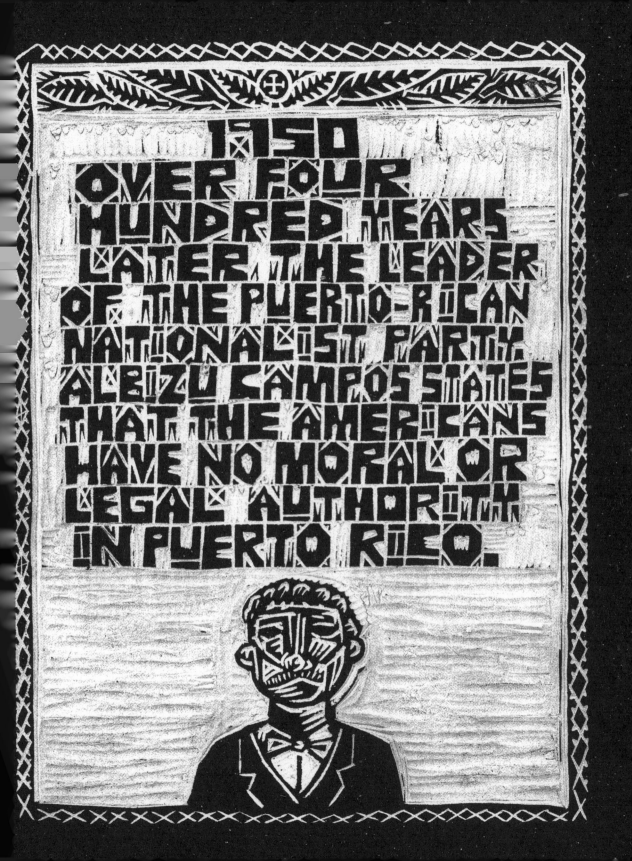

1750
OVER FOUR
HUNDRED YEARS
LATER THE LEADER
OF THE PUERTO-RICAN
NATIONALIST PARTY.
ALBIZU CAMPOS STATES
THAT THE AMERICANS
HAVE NO MORAL OR
LEGAL AUTHORITY
IN PUERTO RICO.

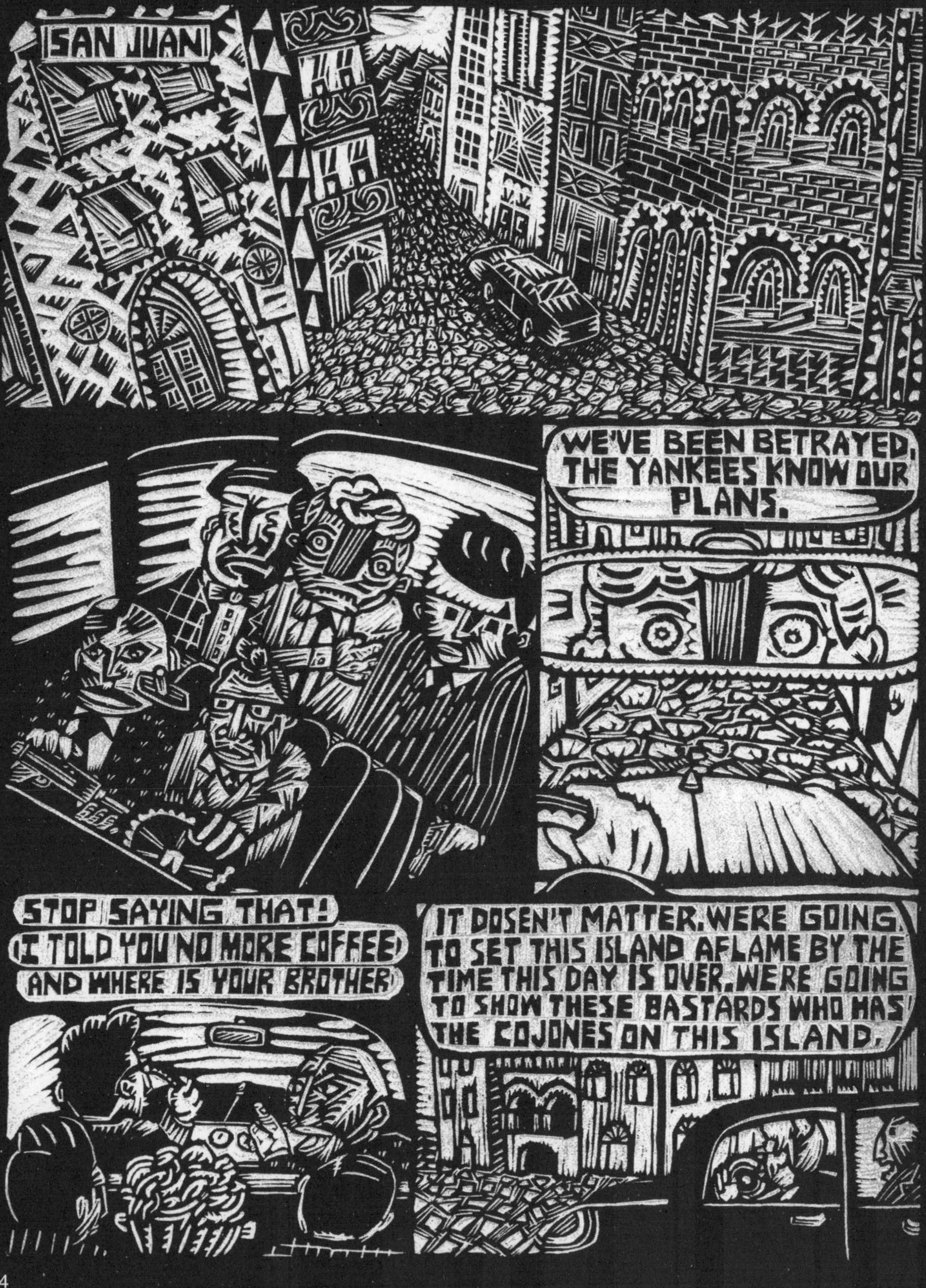
SAN JUAN
WE'VE BEEN BETRAYED. THE YANKEES KNOW OUR PLANS.
STOP SAYING THAT! I TOLD YOU NO MORE COFFEE AND WHERE IS YOUR BROTHER
IT DOSEN'T MATTER. WERE GOING TO SET THIS ISLAND AFLAME BY THE TIME THIS DAY IS OVER. WERE GOING TO SHOW THESE BASTARDS WHO HAS THE COJONES ON THIS ISLAND.

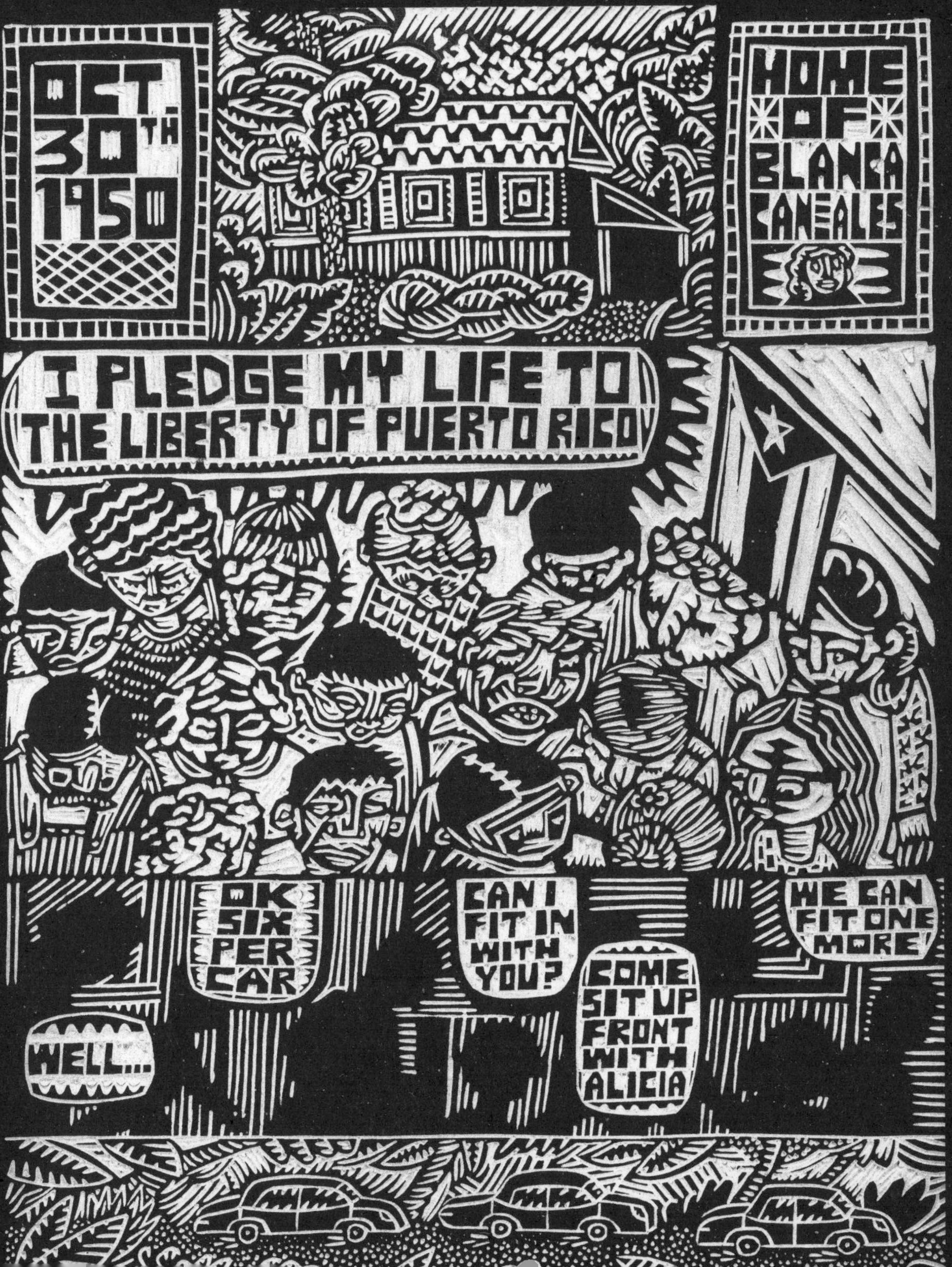
OCT. 30TH 1950
HOME OF BLANCA CANALES
I PLEDGE MY LIFE TO THE LIBERTY OF PUERTO RICO
OK SIX PER CAR
CAN I FIT IN WITH YOU?
WE CAN FIT ONE MORE
COME SIT UP FRONT WITH ALICIA
WELL...

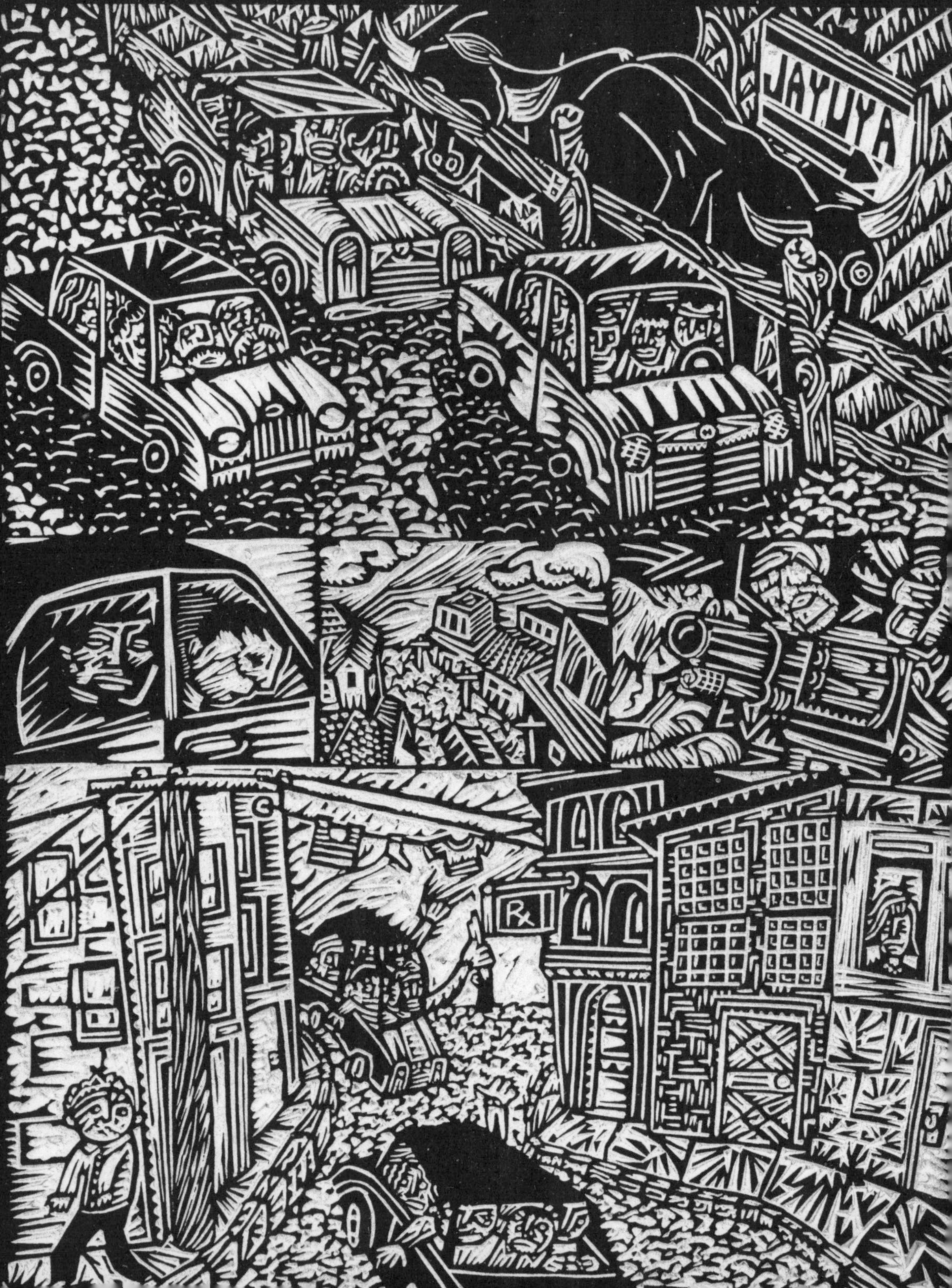
JAYUYA
Rx

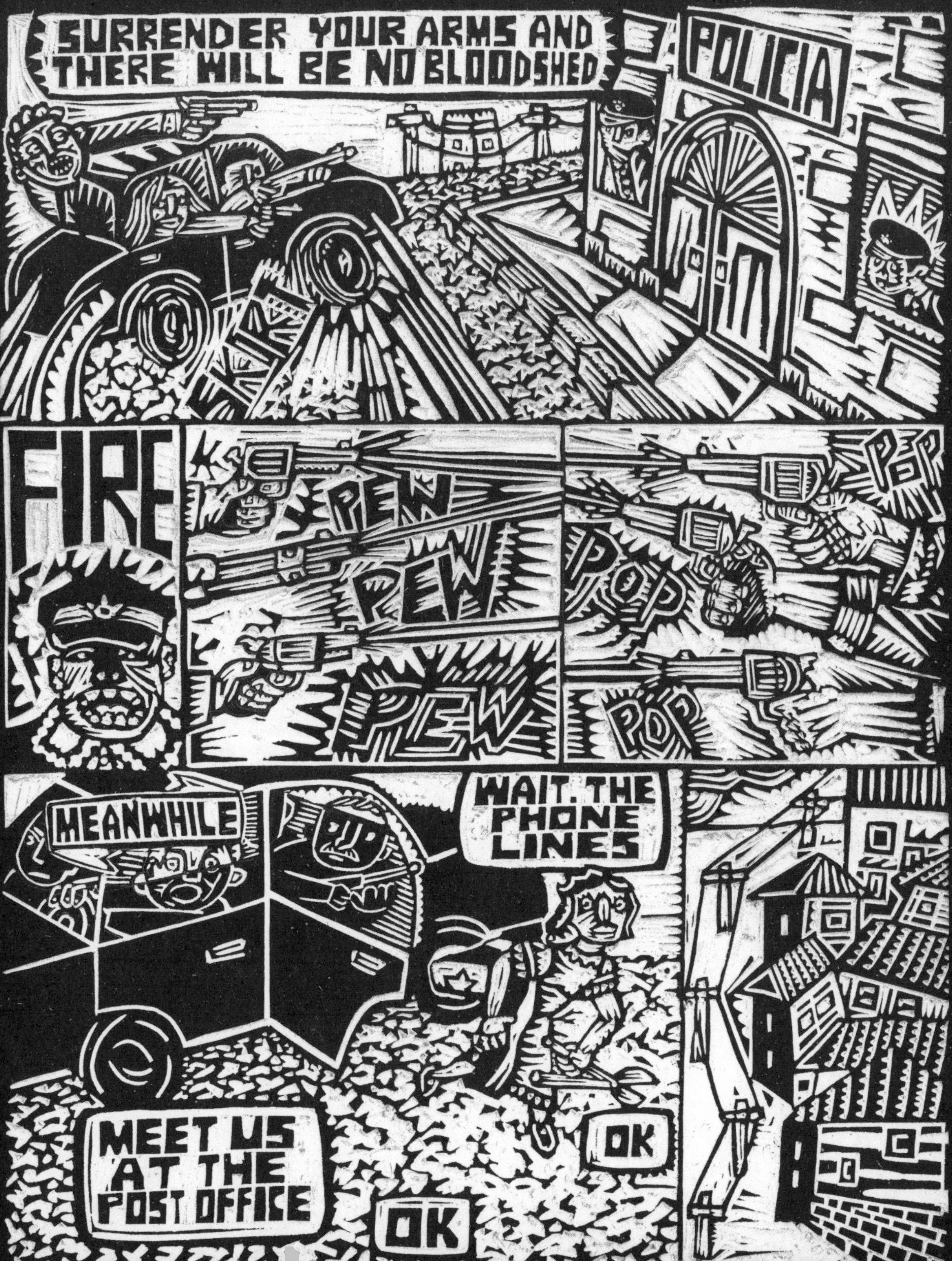
SURRENDER YOUR ARMS AND THERE WILL BE NO BLOODSHED
POLICIA
FIRE
PEW
PEW
PEW
POP
POP
POP
MEANWHILE
WAIT. THE PHONE LINES
MEET US AT THE POST OFFICE
OK
OK

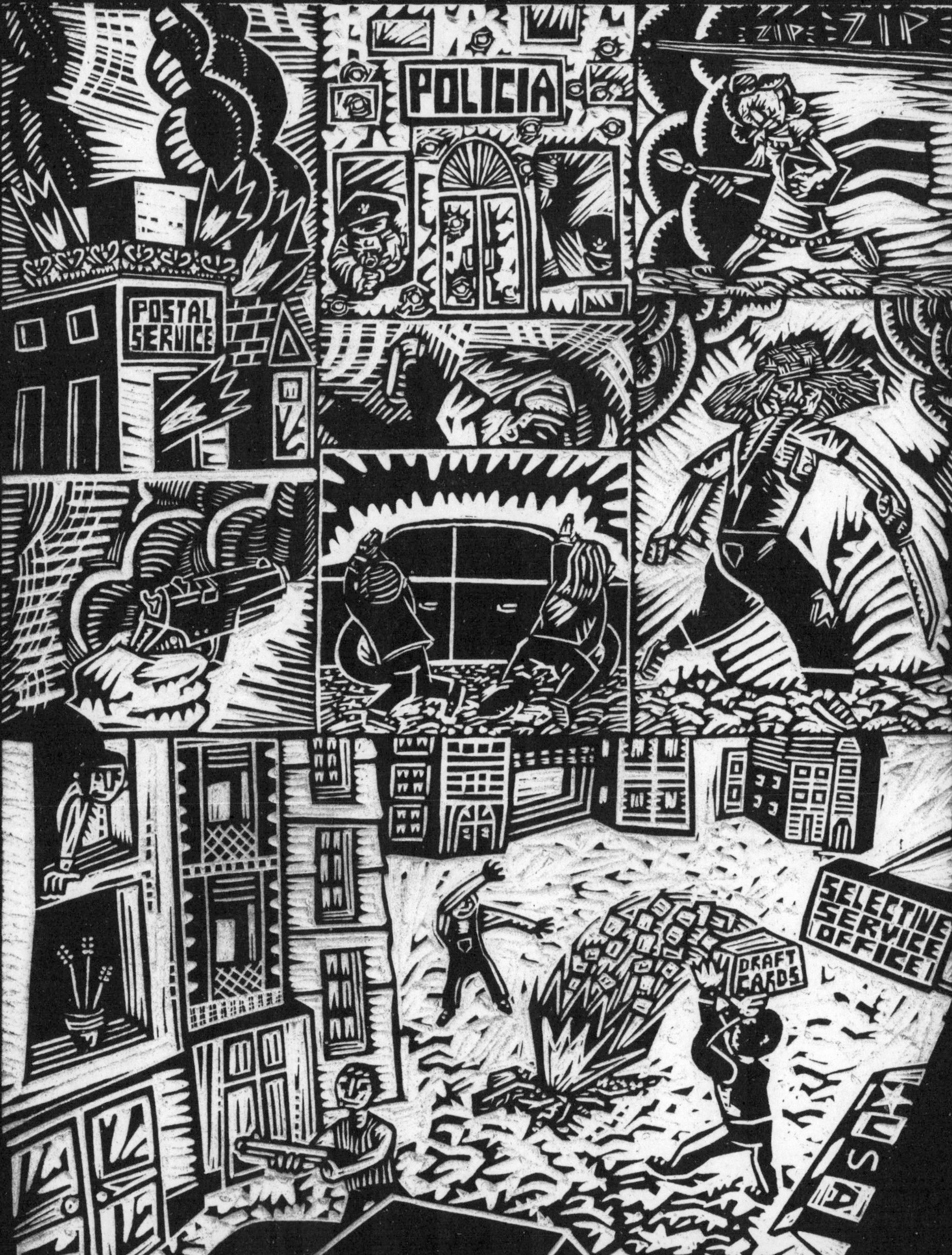
POSTAL SERVICE
POLICIA
ZIP ZIP
SELECTIVE SERVICE OFFICE
DRAFT CARDS

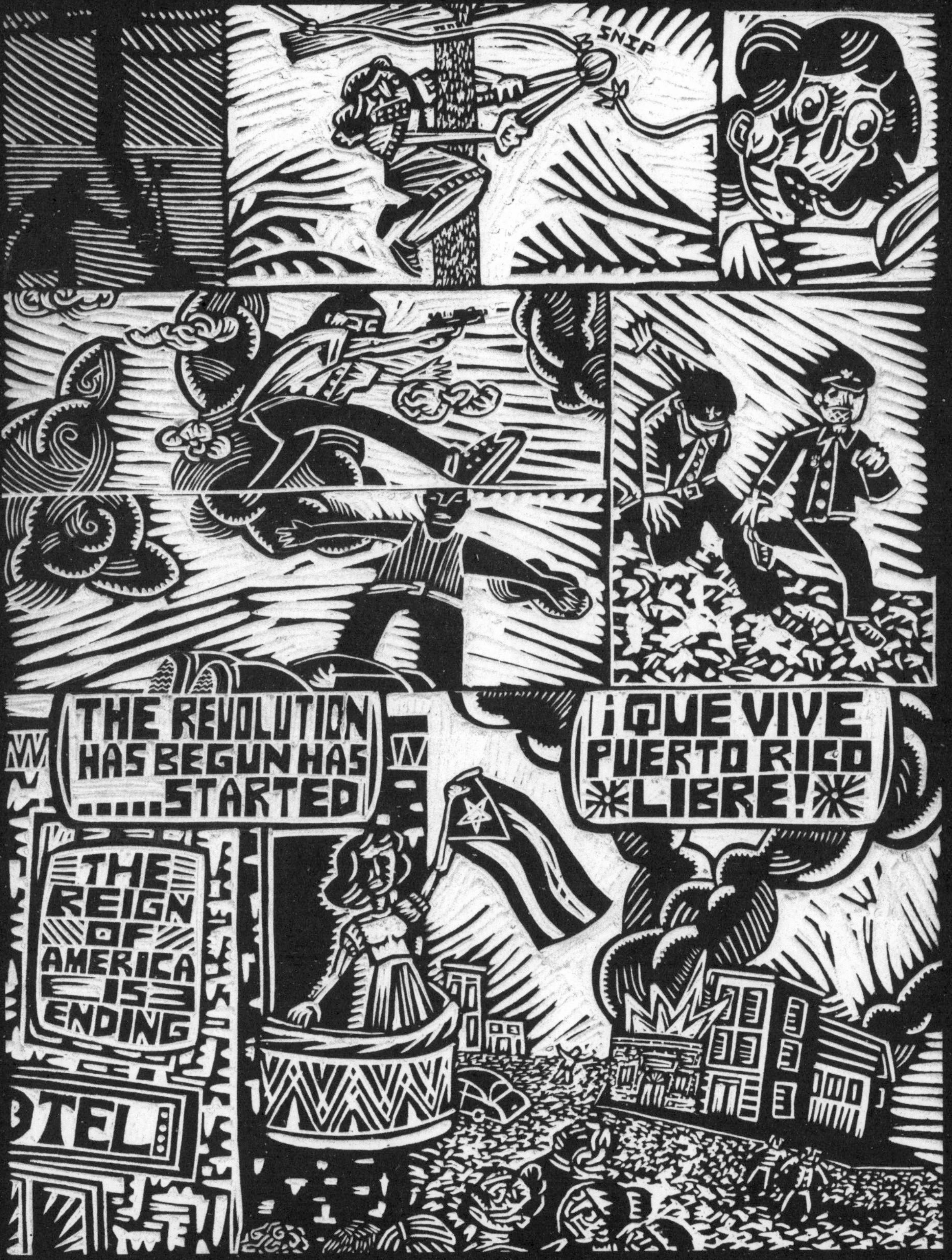
SNIP
THE REVOLUTION HAS BEGUN HAS ......STARTED
¡QUE VIVE PUERTO RICO LIBRE!
THE REIGN OF AMERICA IS ENDING
OTEL

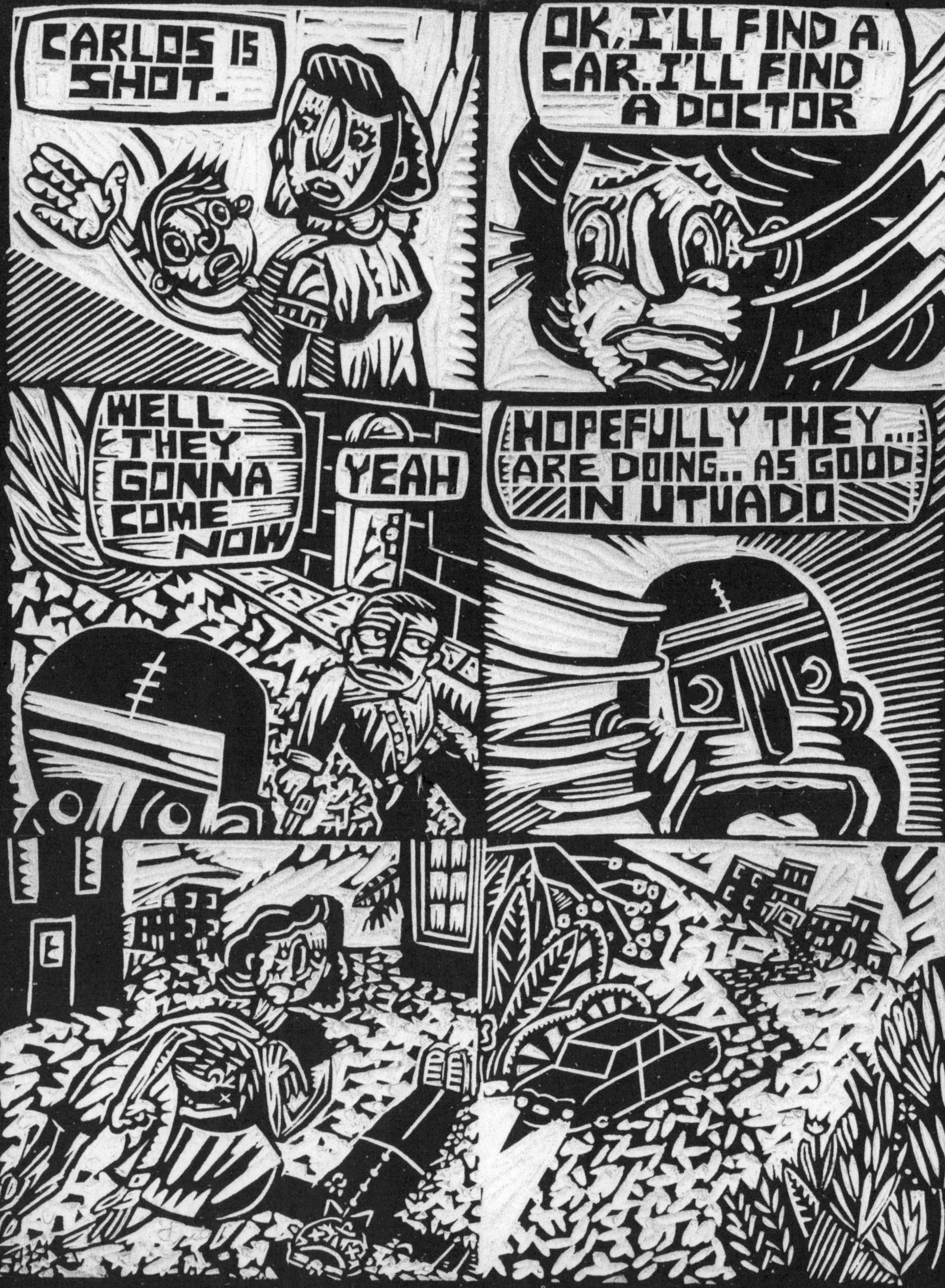
CARLOS IS SHOT.
OK, I'LL FIND A CAR. I'LL FIND A DOCTOR
WELL THEY GONNA COME NOW
YEAH
HOPEFULLY THEY... ARE DOING.. AS GOOD IN UTUADO

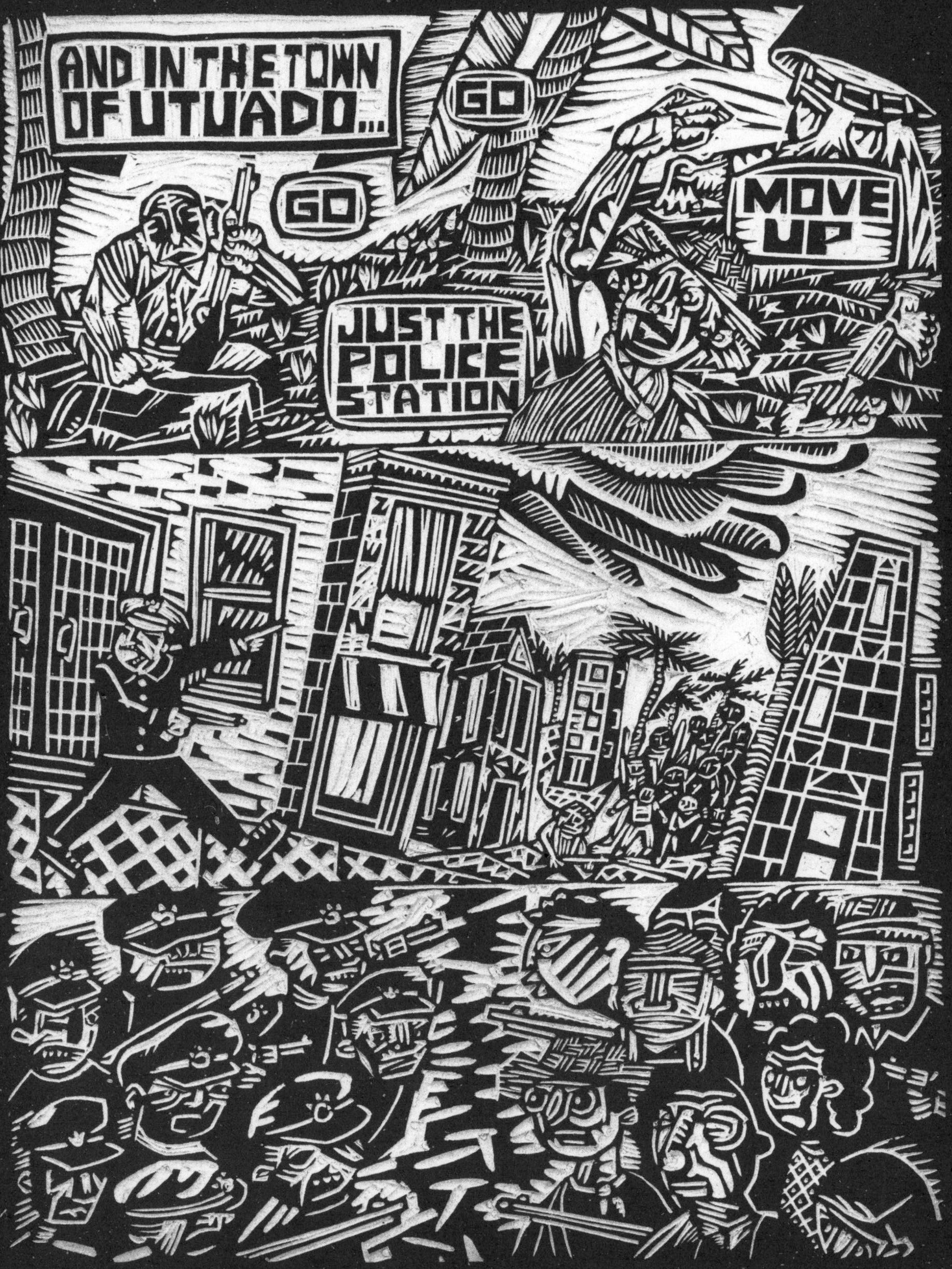
AND IN THE TOWN OF UTUADO...
GO
GO
JUST THE POLICE STATION
MOVE UP

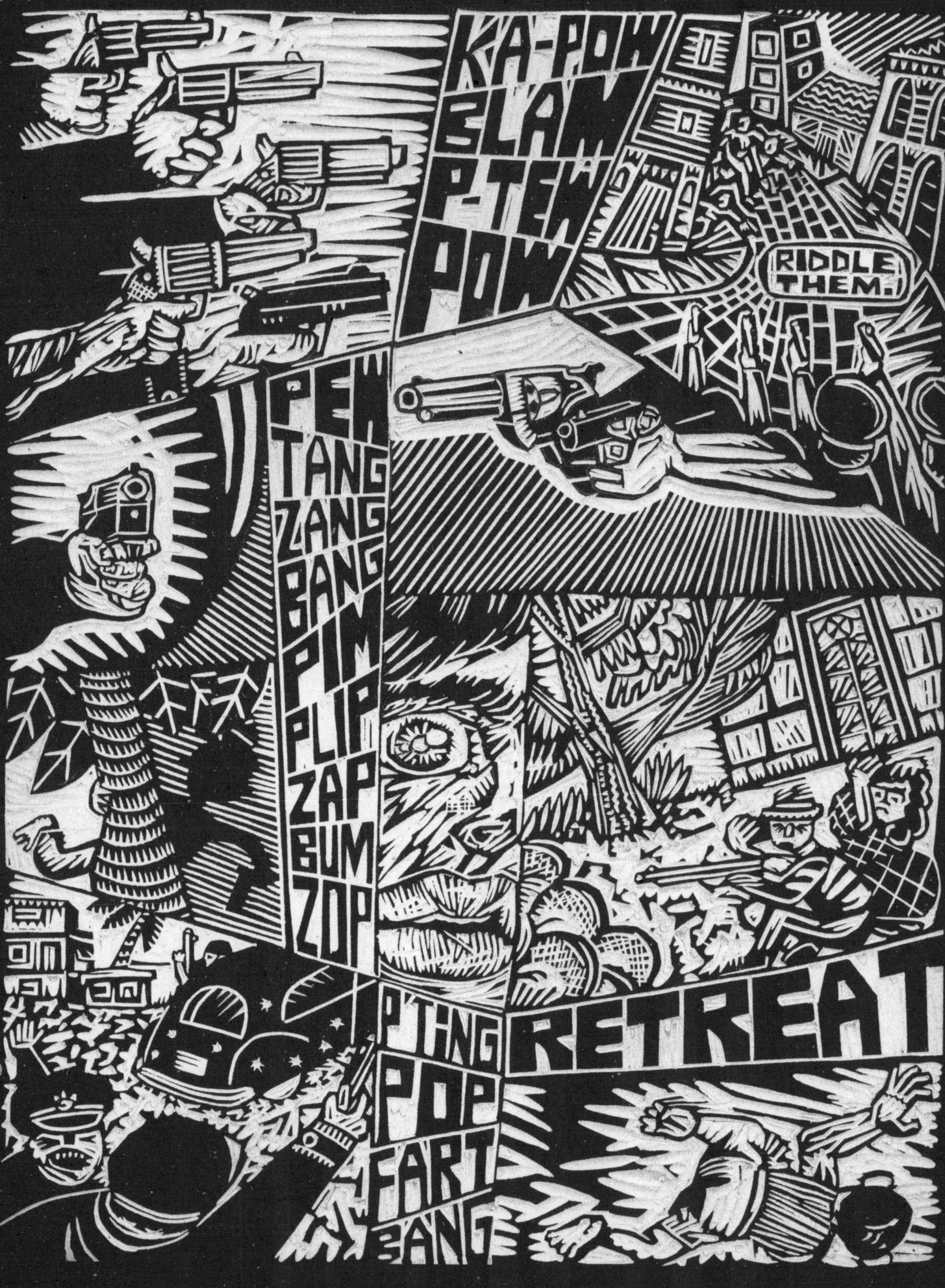
KA-POW
SLAM
P-TEW
POW
RIDDLE THEM.
PEW
TANG
ZANG
BANG
PIM
PLIP
ZAP
BUM
ZOP
P'TING
POP
FART
BANG
RETREAT

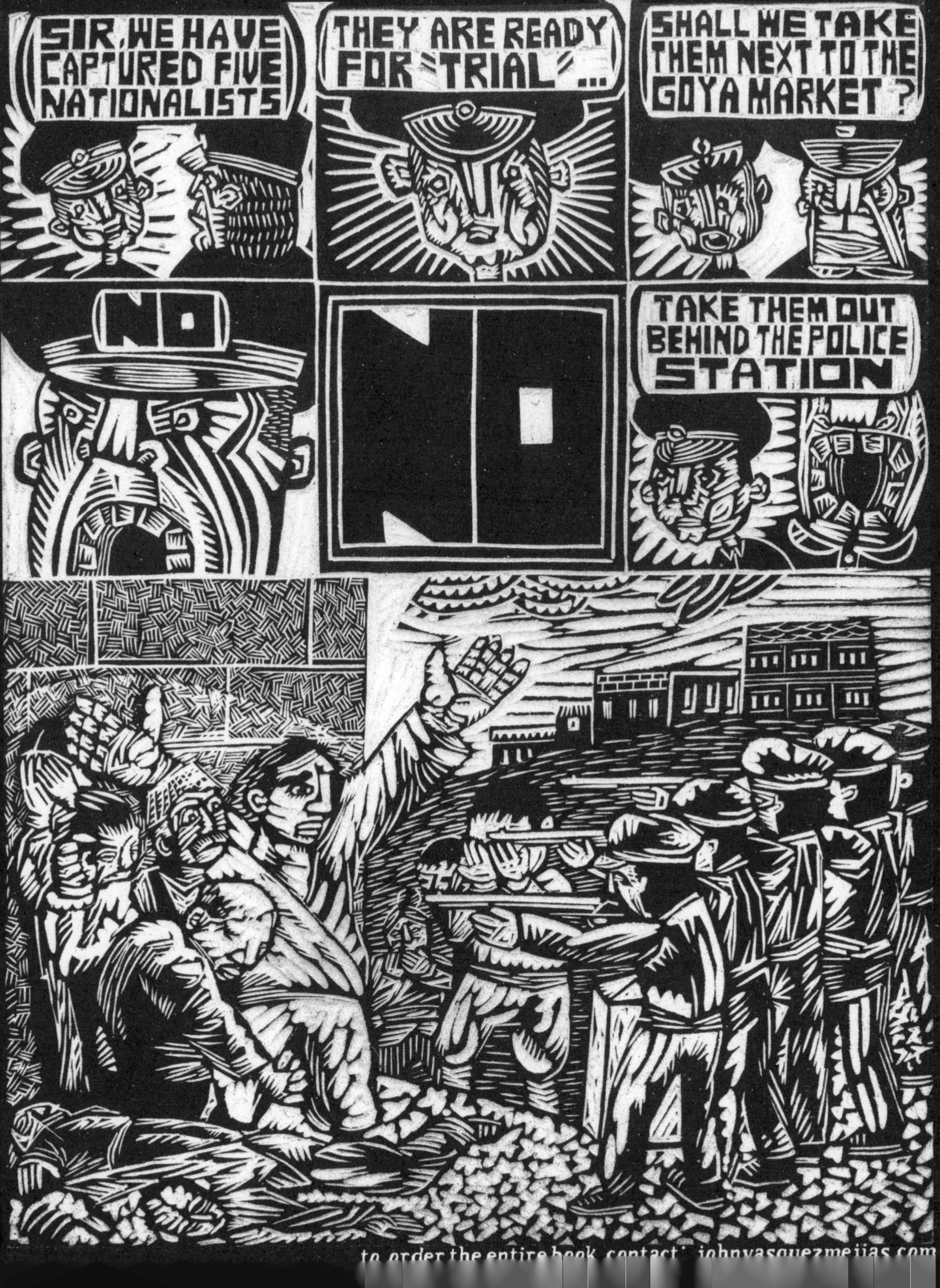
SIR, WE HAVE CAPTURED FIVE NATIONALISTS
THEY ARE READY FOR "TRIAL"...
SHALL WE TAKE THEM NEXT TO THE GOYA MARKET?
NO
NO
TAKE THEM OUT BEHIND THE POLICE STATION

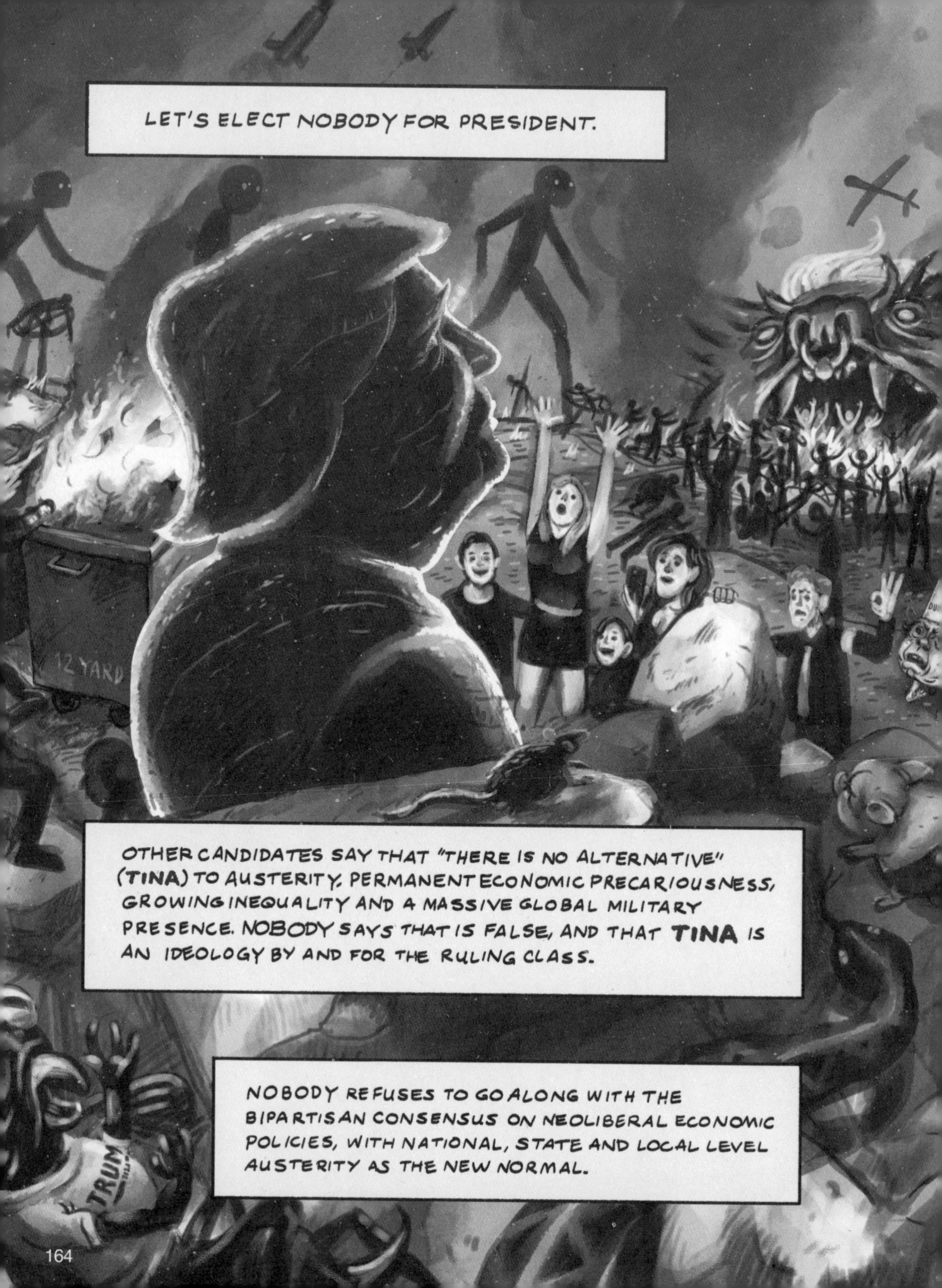
LET'S ELECT NOBODY FOR PRESIDENT.
12 YARD
OTHER CANDIDATES SAY THAT "THERE IS NO ALTERNATIVE" (TINA) TO AUSTERITY, PERMANENT ECONOMIC PRECARIOUSNESS, GROWING INEQUALITY AND A MASSIVE GLOBAL MILITARY PRESENCE. NOBODY SAYS THAT IS FALSE, AND THAT TINA IS AN IDEOLOGY BY AND FOR THE RULING CLASS.
NOBODY REFUSES TO GO ALONG WITH THE BIPARTISAN CONSENSUS ON NEOLIBERAL ECONOMIC POLICIES, WITH NATIONAL, STATE AND LOCAL LEVEL AUSTERITY AS THE NEW NORMAL.

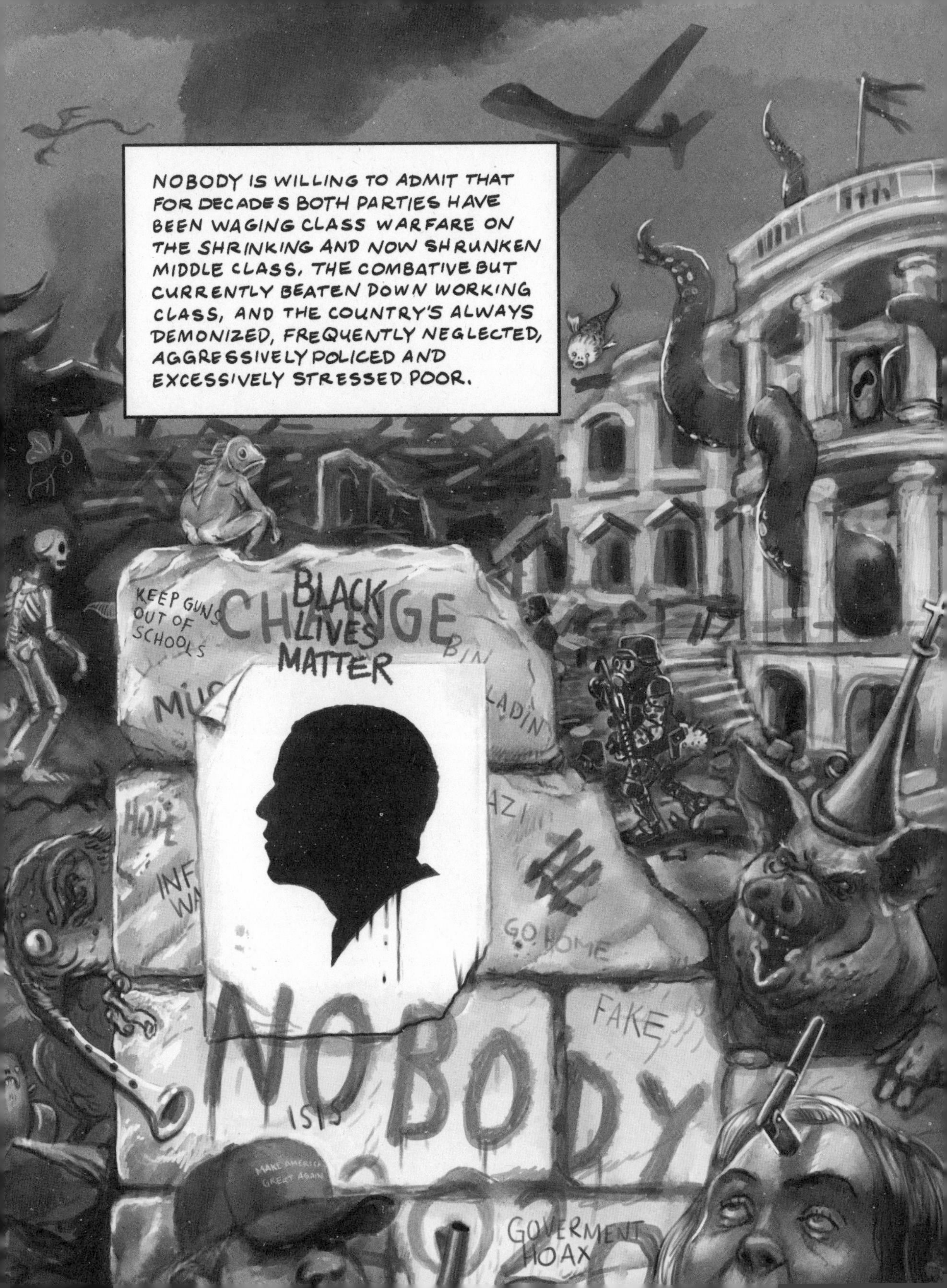
NOBODY IS WILLING TO ADMIT THAT FOR DECADES BOTH PARTIES HAVE BEEN WAGING CLASS WARFARE ON THE SHRINKING AND NOW SHRUNKEN MIDDLE CLASS, THE COMBATIVE BUT CURRENTLY BEATEN DOWN WORKING CLASS, AND THE COUNTRY'S ALWAYS DEMONIZED, FREQUENTLY NEGLECTED, AGGRESSIVELY POLICED AND EXCESSIVELY STRESSED POOR.
KEEP GUNS OUT OF SCHOOLS
CHANGE
BLACK LIVES MATTER
HOPE
GO HOME
FAKE
NOBODY
ISIS
MAKE AMERICA GREAT AGAIN
GOVERMENT HOAX

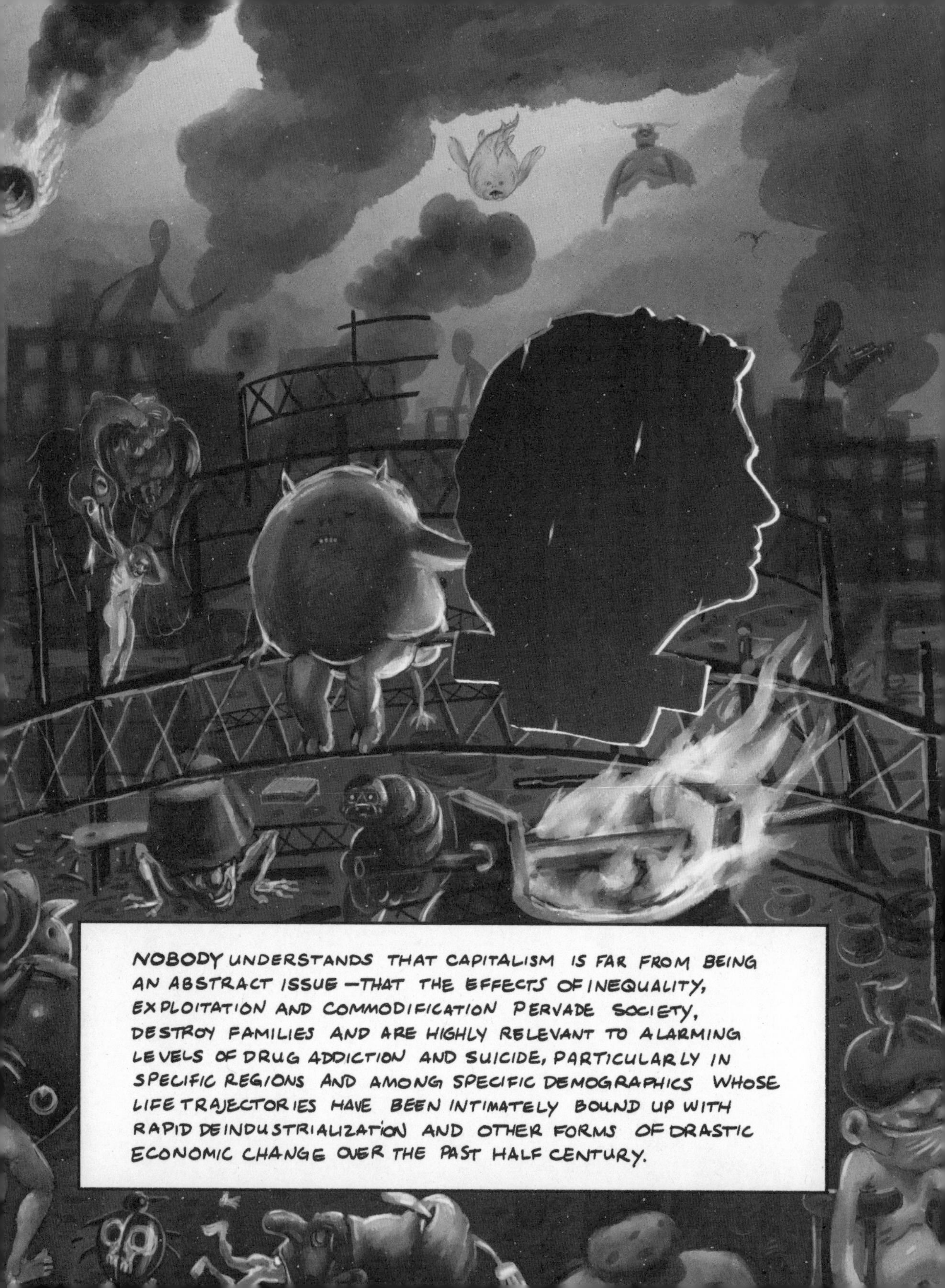
NOBODY UNDERSTANDS THAT CAPITALISM IS FAR FROM BEING AN ABSTRACT ISSUE—THAT THE EFFECTS OF INEQUALITY, EXPLOITATION AND COMMODIFICATION PERVADE SOCIETY, DESTROY FAMILIES AND ARE HIGHLY RELEVANT TO ALARMING LEVELS OF DRUG ADDICTION AND SUICIDE, PARTICULARLY IN SPECIFIC REGIONS AND AMONG SPECIFIC DEMOGRAPHICS WHOSE LIFE TRAJECTORIES HAVE BEEN INTIMATELY BOUND UP WITH RAPID DEINDUSTRIALIZATION AND OTHER FORMS OF DRASTIC ECONOMIC CHANGE OVER THE PAST HALF CENTURY.

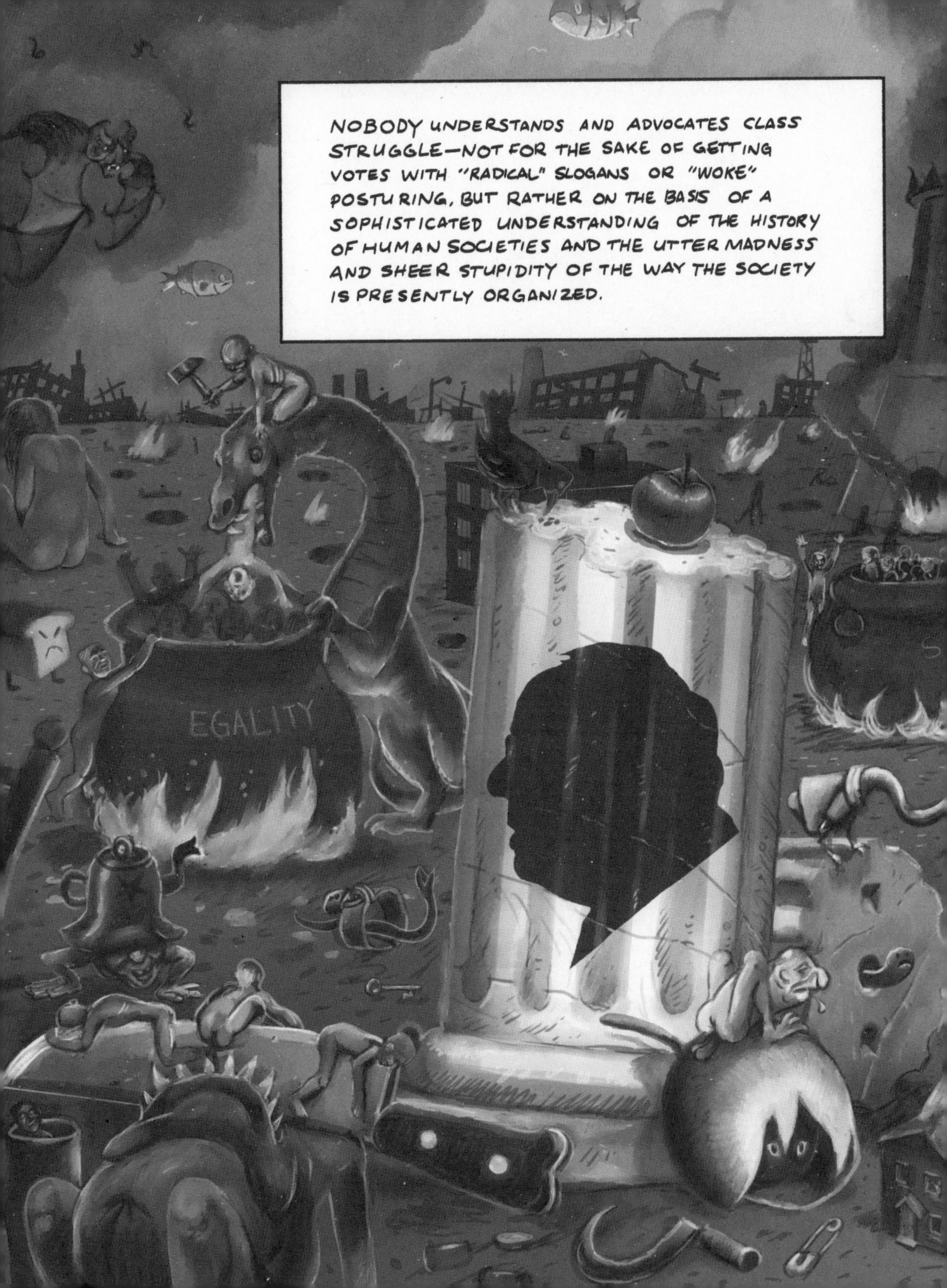
NOBODY UNDERSTANDS AND ADVOCATES CLASS STRUGGLE—NOT FOR THE SAKE OF GETTING VOTES WITH "RADICAL" SLOGANS OR "WOKE" POSTURING, BUT RATHER ON THE BASIS OF A SOPHISTICATED UNDERSTANDING OF THE HISTORY OF HUMAN SOCIETIES AND THE UTTER MADNESS AND SHEER STUPIDITY OF THE WAY THE SOCIETY IS PRESENTLY ORGANIZED.
EGALITY

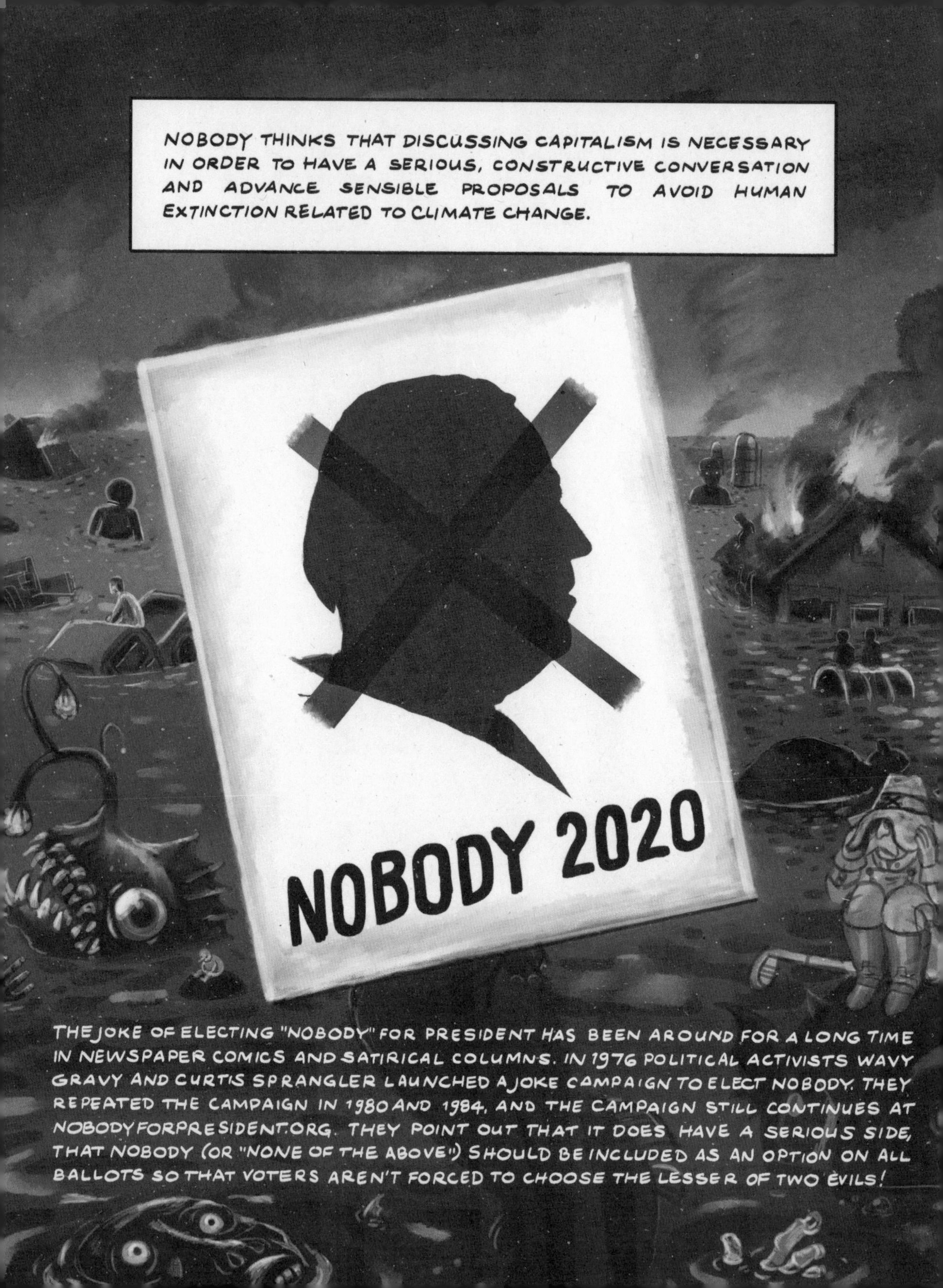
NOBODY THINKS THAT DISCUSSING CAPITALISM IS NECESSARY IN ORDER TO HAVE A SERIOUS, CONSTRUCTIVE CONVERSATION AND ADVANCE SENSIBLE PROPOSALS TO AVOID HUMAN EXTINCTION RELATED TO CLIMATE CHANGE.
NOBODY 2020
THE JOKE OF ELECTING "NOBODY" FOR PRESIDENT HAS BEEN AROUND FOR A LONG TIME IN NEWSPAPER COMICS AND SATIRICAL COLUMNS. IN 1976 POLITICAL ACTIVISTS WAVY GRAVY AND CURTIS SPRANGLER LAUNCHED A JOKE CAMPAIGN TO ELECT NOBODY. THEY REPEATED THE CAMPAIGN IN 1980 AND 1984, AND THE CAMPAIGN STILL CONTINUES AT NOBODYFORPRESIDENT.ORG. THEY POINT OUT THAT IT DOES HAVE A SERIOUS SIDE, THAT NOBODY (OR "NONE OF THE ABOVE") SHOULD BE INCLUDED AS AN OPTION ON ALL BALLOTS SO THAT VOTERS AREN'T FORCED TO CHOOSE THE LESSER OF TWO EVILS!

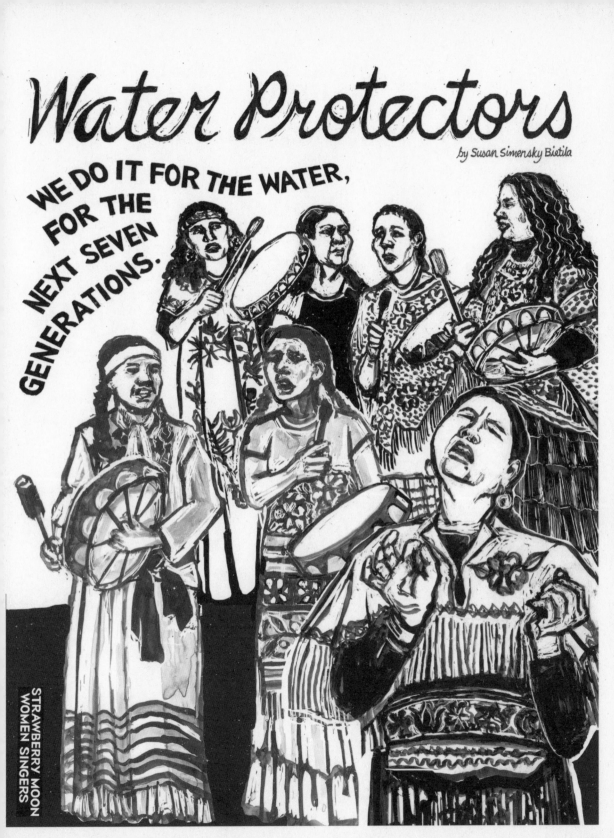

Water Protectors

by Susan Simensky Bietila

WE DO IT FOR THE WATER, FOR THE NEXT SEVEN GENERATIONS.

STRAWBERRY MOON WOMEN SINGERS

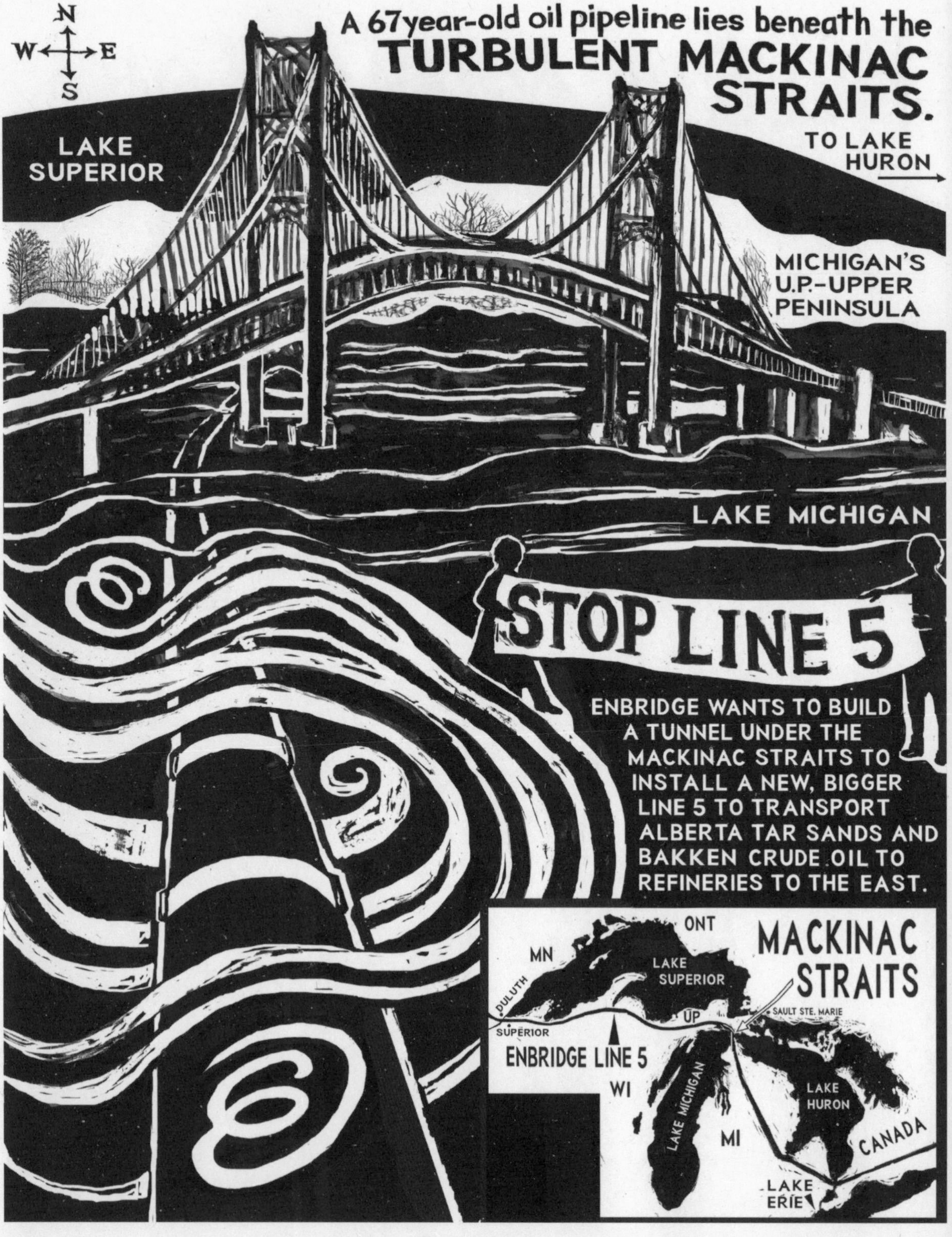
N
W
E
S
A 67 year-old oil pipeline lies beneath the
TURBULENT MACKINAC STRAITS.
LAKE SUPERIOR
TO LAKE HURON
MICHIGAN'S U.P.–UPPER PENINSULA
LAKE MICHIGAN
STOP LINE 5
ENBRIDGE WANTS TO BUILD A TUNNEL UNDER THE MACKINAC STRAITS TO INSTALL A NEW, BIGGER LINE 5 TO TRANSPORT ALBERTA TAR SANDS AND BAKKEN CRUDE OIL TO REFINERIES TO THE EAST.
ONT
MN
LAKE SUPERIOR
MACKINAC STRAITS
DULUTH
SUPERIOR
UP
SAULT STE. MARIE
ENBRIDGE LINE 5
WI
LAKE MICHIGAN
MI
LAKE HURON
CANADA
LAKE ERIE

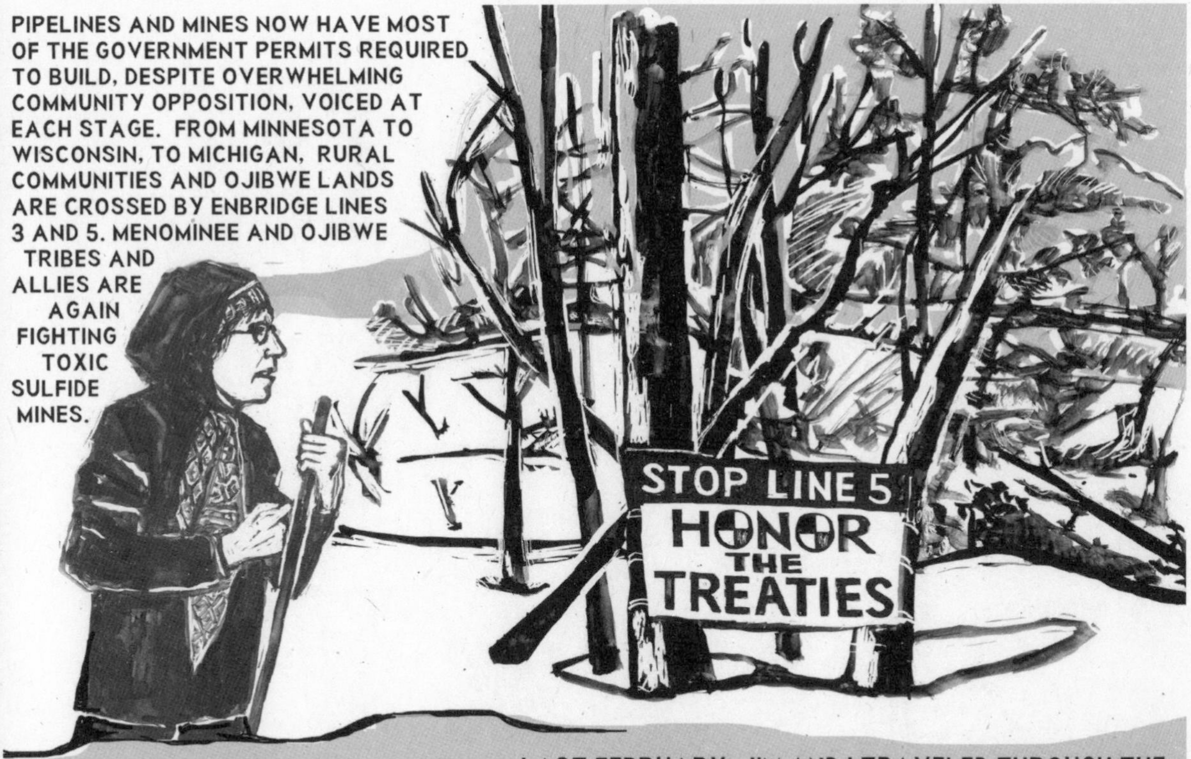
PIPELINES AND MINES NOW HAVE MOST OF THE GOVERNMENT PERMITS REQUIRED TO BUILD, DESPITE OVERWHELMING COMMUNITY OPPOSITION, VOICED AT EACH STAGE. FROM MINNESOTA TO WISCONSIN, TO MICHIGAN, RURAL COMMUNITIES AND OJIBWE LANDS ARE CROSSED BY ENBRIDGE LINES 3 AND 5. MENOMINEE AND OJIBWE TRIBES AND ALLIES ARE AGAIN FIGHTING TOXIC SULFIDE MINES.
STOP LINE 5
HONOR THE TREATIES

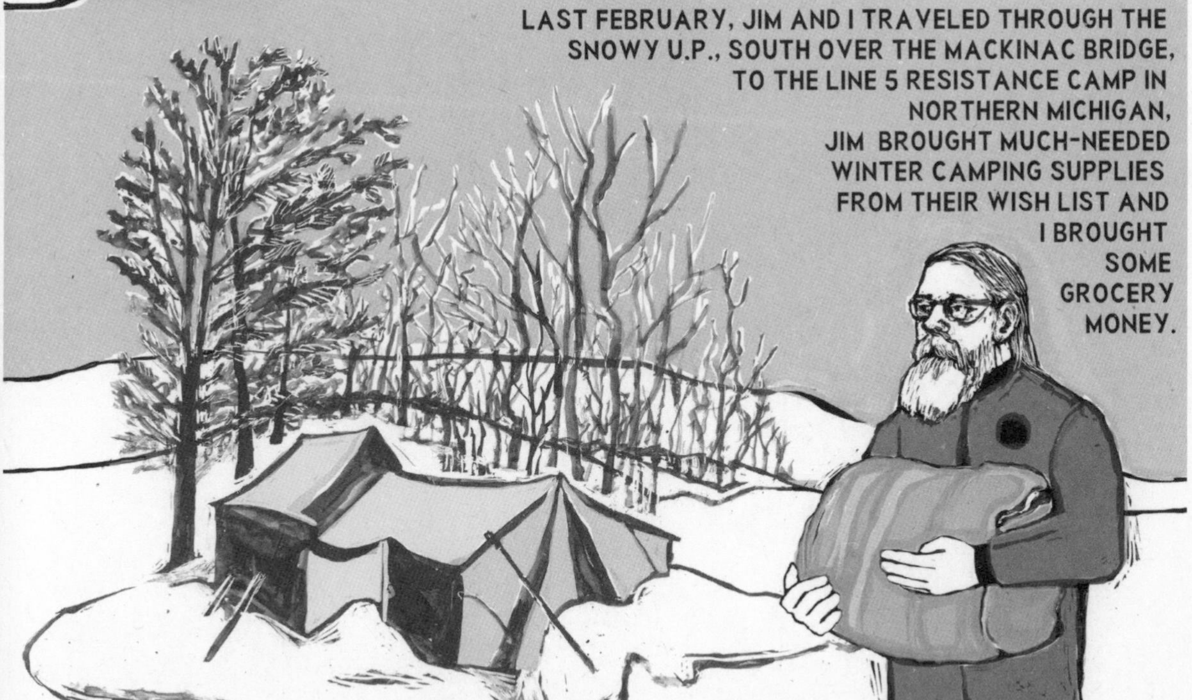
LAST FEBRUARY, JIM AND I TRAVELED THROUGH THE SNOWY U.P., SOUTH OVER THE MACKINAC BRIDGE, TO THE LINE 5 RESISTANCE CAMP IN NORTHERN MICHIGAN, JIM BROUGHT MUCH-NEEDED WINTER CAMPING SUPPLIES FROM THEIR WISH LIST AND I BROUGHT SOME GROCERY MONEY.

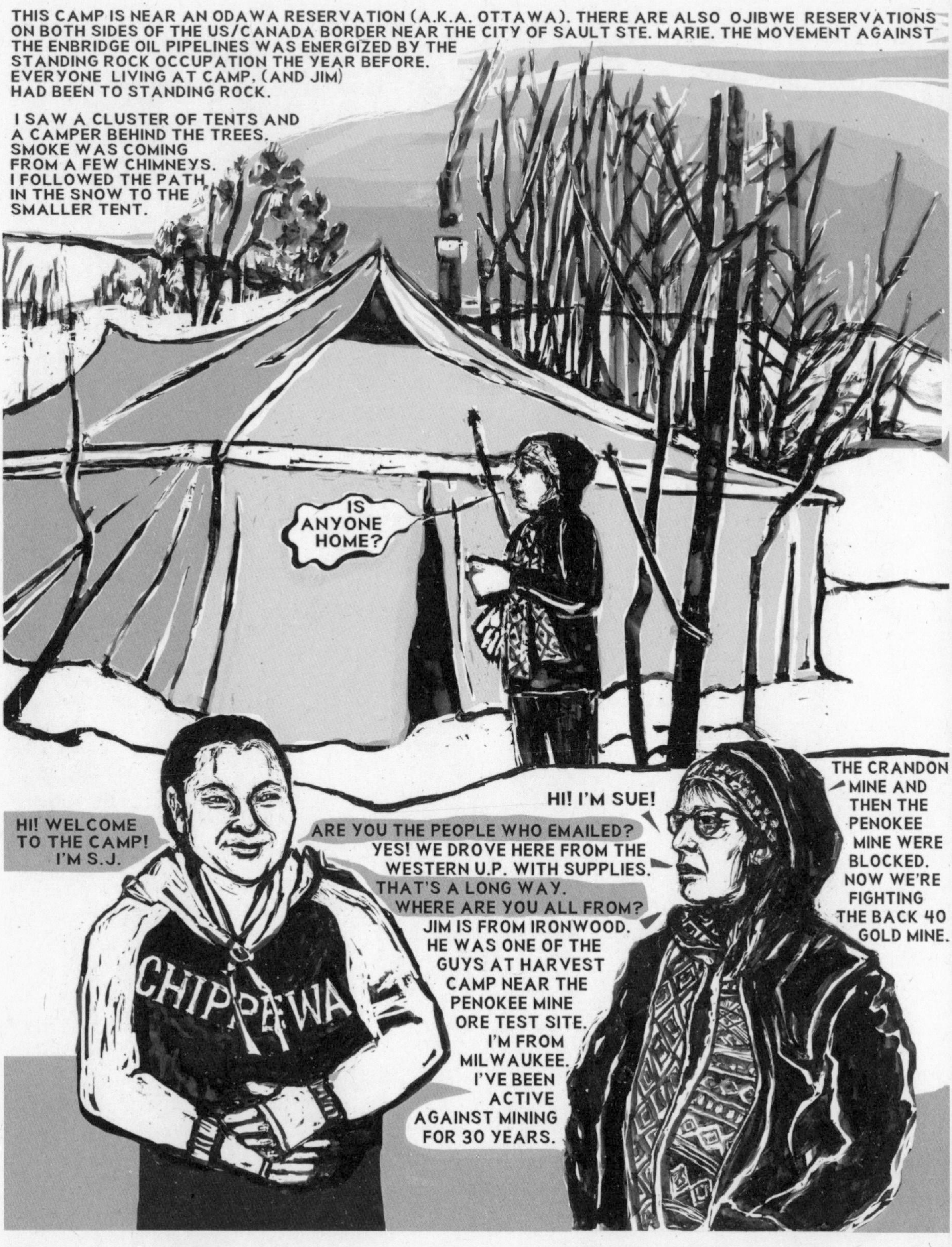
THIS CAMP IS NEAR AN ODAWA RESERVATION (A.K.A. OTTAWA). THERE ARE ALSO OJIBWE RESERVATIONS ON BOTH SIDES OF THE US/CANADA BORDER NEAR THE CITY OF SAULT STE. MARIE. THE MOVEMENT AGAINST THE ENBRIDGE OIL PIPELINES WAS ENERGIZED BY THE STANDING ROCK OCCUPATION THE YEAR BEFORE. EVERYONE LIVING AT CAMP, (AND JIM) HAD BEEN TO STANDING ROCK.
I SAW A CLUSTER OF TENTS AND A CAMPER BEHIND THE TREES. SMOKE WAS COMING FROM A FEW CHIMNEYS. I FOLLOWED THE PATH IN THE SNOW TO THE SMALLER TENT.
IS ANYONE HOME?
HI! WELCOME TO THE CAMP! I'M S.J.
HI! I'M SUE!
ARE YOU THE PEOPLE WHO EMAILED?
YES! WE DROVE HERE FROM THE WESTERN U.P. WITH SUPPLIES.
THAT'S A LONG WAY. WHERE ARE YOU ALL FROM?
JIM IS FROM IRONWOOD. HE WAS ONE OF THE GUYS AT HARVEST CAMP NEAR THE PENOKEE MINE ORE TEST SITE. I'M FROM MILWAUKEE. I'VE BEEN ACTIVE AGAINST MINING FOR 30 YEARS.
THE CRANDON MINE AND THEN THE PENOKEE MINE WERE BLOCKED. NOW WE'RE FIGHTING THE BACK 40 GOLD MINE.
CHIPPEWA

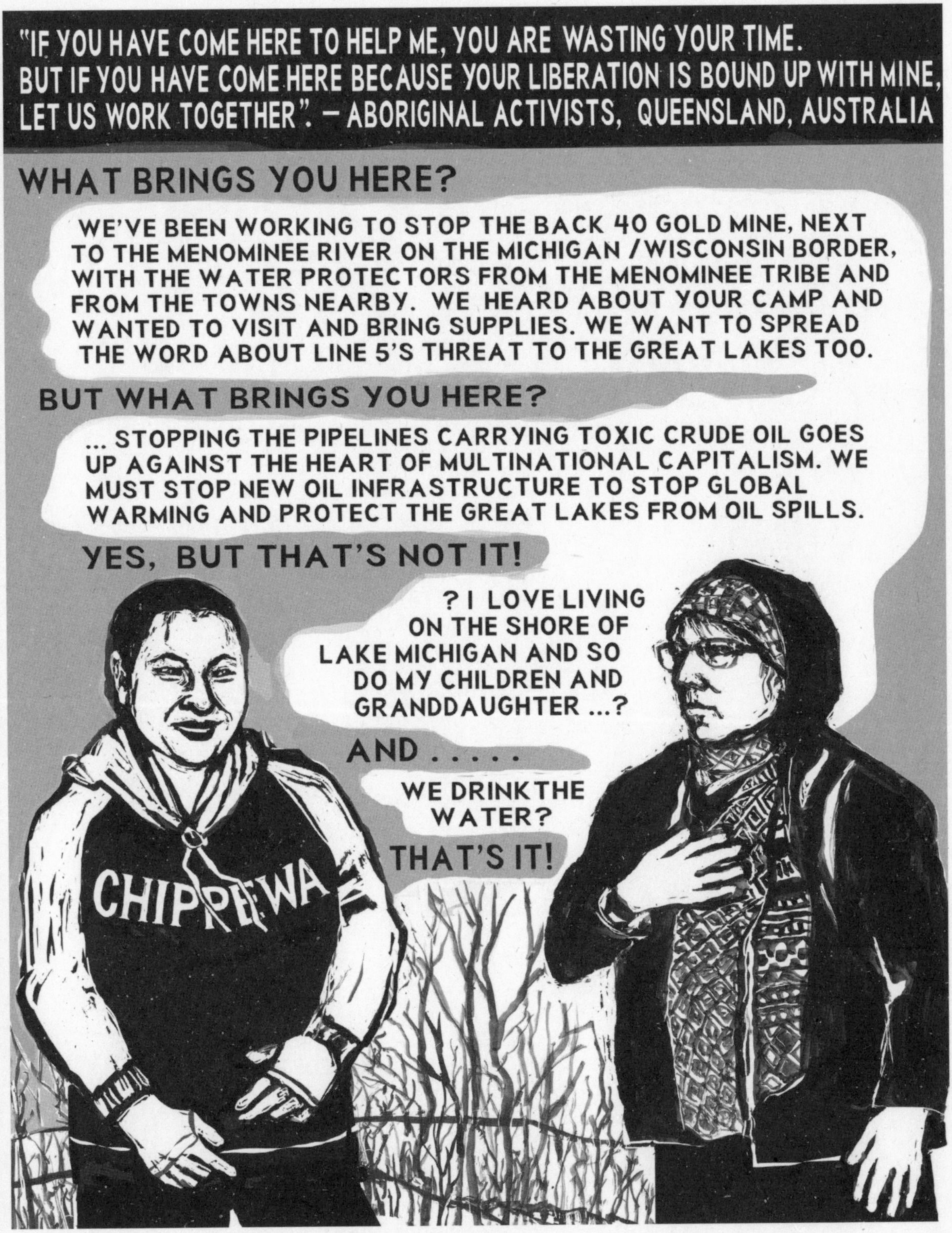
"IF YOU HAVE COME HERE TO HELP ME, YOU ARE WASTING YOUR TIME. BUT IF YOU HAVE COME HERE BECAUSE YOUR LIBERATION IS BOUND UP WITH MINE, LET US WORK TOGETHER". — ABORIGINAL ACTIVISTS, QUEENSLAND, AUSTRALIA
WHAT BRINGS YOU HERE?
WE'VE BEEN WORKING TO STOP THE BACK 40 GOLD MINE, NEXT TO THE MENOMINEE RIVER ON THE MICHIGAN /WISCONSIN BORDER, WITH THE WATER PROTECTORS FROM THE MENOMINEE TRIBE AND FROM THE TOWNS NEARBY. WE HEARD ABOUT YOUR CAMP AND WANTED TO VISIT AND BRING SUPPLIES. WE WANT TO SPREAD THE WORD ABOUT LINE 5'S THREAT TO THE GREAT LAKES TOO.
BUT WHAT BRINGS YOU HERE?
... STOPPING THE PIPELINES CARRYING TOXIC CRUDE OIL GOES UP AGAINST THE HEART OF MULTINATIONAL CAPITALISM. WE MUST STOP NEW OIL INFRASTRUCTURE TO STOP GLOBAL WARMING AND PROTECT THE GREAT LAKES FROM OIL SPILLS.
YES, BUT THAT'S NOT IT!
? I LOVE LIVING ON THE SHORE OF LAKE MICHIGAN AND SO DO MY CHILDREN AND GRANDDAUGHTER ...?
AND . . . . .
WE DRINK THE WATER?
THAT'S IT!
CHIPPEWA

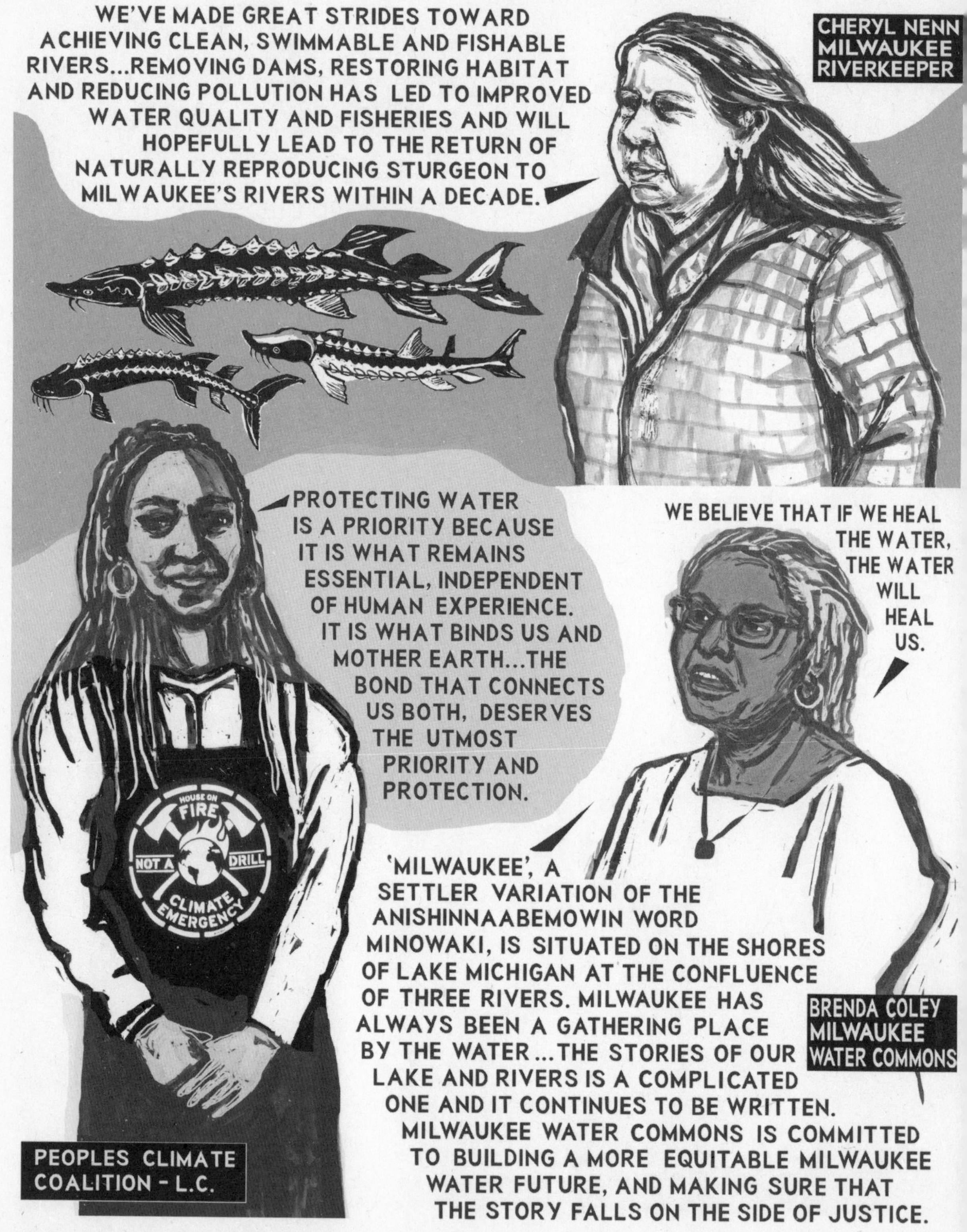

WE'VE MADE GREAT STRIDES TOWARD ACHIEVING CLEAN, SWIMMABLE AND FISHABLE RIVERS...REMOVING DAMS, RESTORING HABITAT AND REDUCING POLLUTION HAS LED TO IMPROVED WATER QUALITY AND FISHERIES AND WILL HOPEFULLY LEAD TO THE RETURN OF NATURALLY REPRODUCING STURGEON TO MILWAUKEE'S RIVERS WITHIN A DECADE.
CHERYL NENN MILWAUKEE RIVERKEEPER
PROTECTING WATER IS A PRIORITY BECAUSE IT IS WHAT REMAINS ESSENTIAL, INDEPENDENT OF HUMAN EXPERIENCE. IT IS WHAT BINDS US AND MOTHER EARTH...THE BOND THAT CONNECTS US BOTH, DESERVES THE UTMOST PRIORITY AND PROTECTION.
HOUSE ON FIRE NOT A DRILL CLIMATE EMERGENCY
PEOPLES CLIMATE COALITION - L.C.
WE BELIEVE THAT IF WE HEAL THE WATER, THE WATER WILL HEAL US.
'MILWAUKEE', A SETTLER VARIATION OF THE ANISHINNAABEMOWIN WORD MINOWAKI, IS SITUATED ON THE SHORES OF LAKE MICHIGAN AT THE CONFLUENCE OF THREE RIVERS. MILWAUKEE HAS ALWAYS BEEN A GATHERING PLACE BY THE WATER...THE STORIES OF OUR LAKE AND RIVERS IS A COMPLICATED ONE AND IT CONTINUES TO BE WRITTEN. MILWAUKEE WATER COMMONS IS COMMITTED TO BUILDING A MORE EQUITABLE MILWAUKEE WATER FUTURE, AND MAKING SURE THAT THE STORY FALLS ON THE SIDE OF JUSTICE.
BRENDA COLEY MILWAUKEE WATER COMMONS

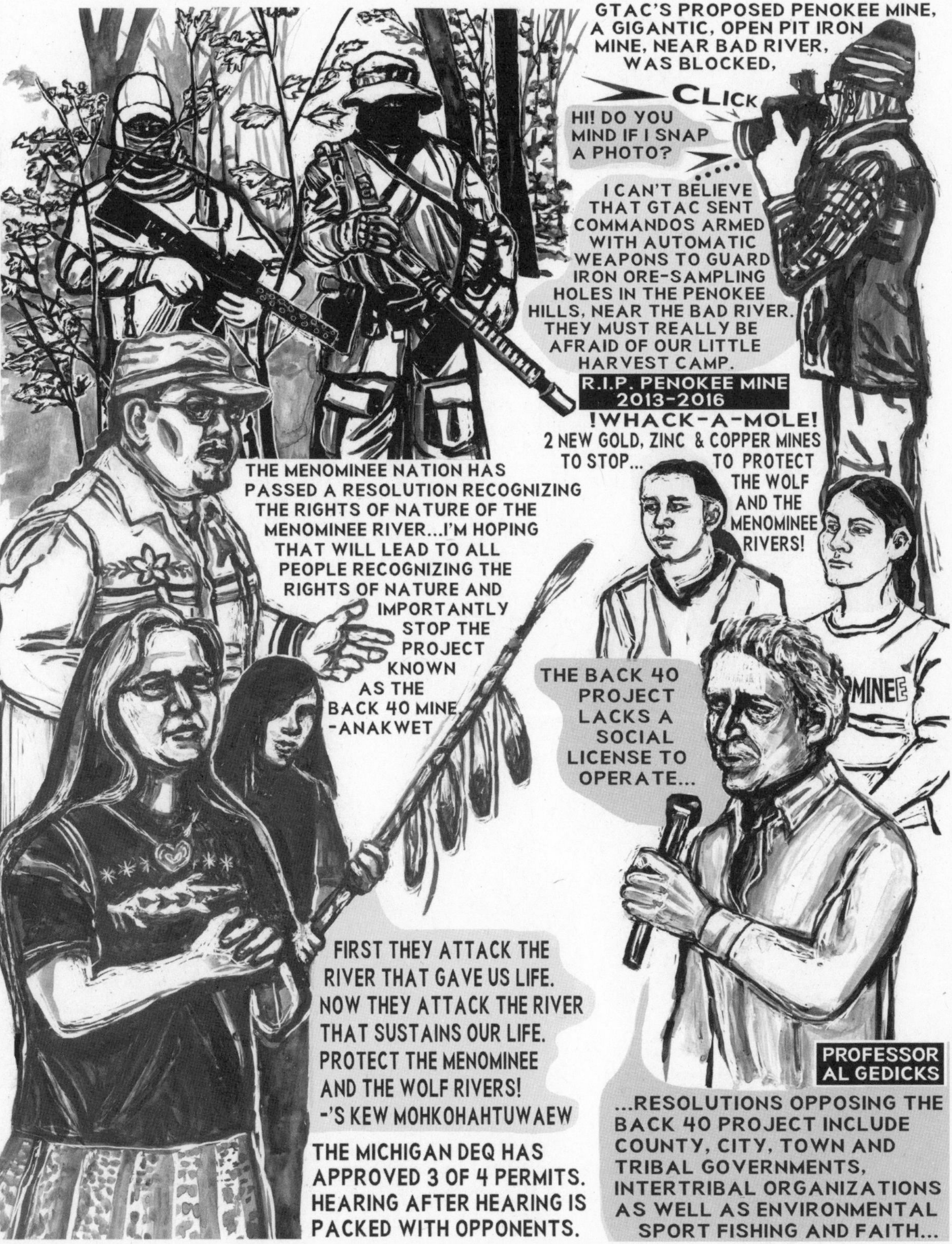
GTAC'S PROPOSED PENOKEE MINE, A GIGANTIC, OPEN PIT IRON MINE, NEAR BAD RIVER, WAS BLOCKED,
CLICK
HI! DO YOU MIND IF I SNAP A PHOTO?
I CAN'T BELIEVE THAT GTAC SENT COMMANDOS ARMED WITH AUTOMATIC WEAPONS TO GUARD IRON ORE-SAMPLING HOLES IN THE PENOKEE HILLS, NEAR THE BAD RIVER. THEY MUST REALLY BE AFRAID OF OUR LITTLE HARVEST CAMP.
R.I.P. PENOKEE MINE 2013-2016
!WHACK-A-MOLE!
2 NEW GOLD, ZINC & COPPER MINES TO STOP... TO PROTECT THE WOLF AND THE MENOMINEE RIVERS!
THE MENOMINEE NATION HAS PASSED A RESOLUTION RECOGNIZING THE RIGHTS OF NATURE OF THE MENOMINEE RIVER...I'M HOPING THAT WILL LEAD TO ALL PEOPLE RECOGNIZING THE RIGHTS OF NATURE AND IMPORTANTLY STOP THE PROJECT KNOWN AS THE BACK 40 MINE. -ANAKWET
THE BACK 40 PROJECT LACKS A SOCIAL LICENSE TO OPERATE...
FIRST THEY ATTACK THE RIVER THAT GAVE US LIFE. NOW THEY ATTACK THE RIVER THAT SUSTAINS OUR LIFE. PROTECT THE MENOMINEE AND THE WOLF RIVERS! -'S KEW MOHKOHAHTUWAEW
PROFESSOR AL GEDICKS
THE MICHIGAN DEQ HAS APPROVED 3 OF 4 PERMITS. HEARING AFTER HEARING IS PACKED WITH OPPONENTS.
...RESOLUTIONS OPPOSING THE BACK 40 PROJECT INCLUDE COUNTY, CITY, TOWN AND TRIBAL GOVERNMENTS, INTERTRIBAL ORGANIZATIONS AS WELL AS ENVIRONMENTAL SPORT FISHING AND FAITH...

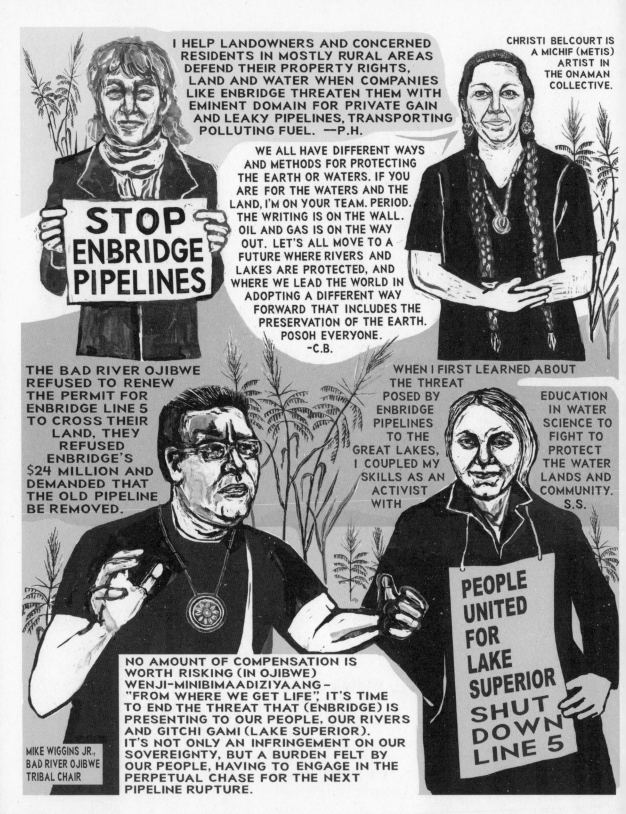

I HELP LANDOWNERS AND CONCERNED RESIDENTS IN MOSTLY RURAL AREAS DEFEND THEIR PROPERTY RIGHTS, LAND AND WATER WHEN COMPANIES LIKE ENBRIDGE THREATEN THEM WITH EMINENT DOMAIN FOR PRIVATE GAIN AND LEAKY PIPELINES, TRANSPORTING POLLUTING FUEL. —P.H.

STOP ENBRIDGE PIPELINES

CHRISTI BELCOURT IS A MICHIF (METIS) ARTIST IN THE ONAMAN COLLECTIVE.

WE ALL HAVE DIFFERENT WAYS AND METHODS FOR PROTECTING THE EARTH OR WATERS. IF YOU ARE FOR THE WATERS AND THE LAND, I'M ON YOUR TEAM. PERIOD. THE WRITING IS ON THE WALL. OIL AND GAS IS ON THE WAY OUT. LET'S ALL MOVE TO A FUTURE WHERE RIVERS AND LAKES ARE PROTECTED, AND WHERE WE LEAD THE WORLD IN ADOPTING A DIFFERENT WAY FORWARD THAT INCLUDES THE PRESERVATION OF THE EARTH. POSOH EVERYONE. —C.B.

THE BAD RIVER OJIBWE REFUSED TO RENEW THE PERMIT FOR ENBRIDGE LINE 5 TO CROSS THEIR LAND, THEY REFUSED ENBRIDGE'S $24 MILLION AND DEMANDED THAT THE OLD PIPELINE BE REMOVED.

WHEN I FIRST LEARNED ABOUT THE THREAT POSED BY ENBRIDGE PIPELINES TO THE GREAT LAKES, I COUPLED MY SKILLS AS AN ACTIVIST WITH EDUCATION IN WATER SCIENCE TO FIGHT TO PROTECT THE WATER LANDS AND COMMUNITY. S.S.

PEOPLE UNITED FOR LAKE SUPERIOR SHUT DOWN LINE 5

NO AMOUNT OF COMPENSATION IS WORTH RISKING (IN OJIBWE) WENJI-MINIBIMAADIZIYAANG – "FROM WHERE WE GET LIFE", IT'S TIME TO END THE THREAT THAT (ENBRIDGE) IS PRESENTING TO OUR PEOPLE, OUR RIVERS AND GITCHI GAMI (LAKE SUPERIOR). IT'S NOT ONLY AN INFRINGEMENT ON OUR SOVEREIGNTY, BUT A BURDEN FELT BY OUR PEOPLE, HAVING TO ENGAGE IN THE PERPETUAL CHASE FOR THE NEXT PIPELINE RUPTURE.

MIKE WIGGINS JR., BAD RIVER OJIBWE TRIBAL CHAIR

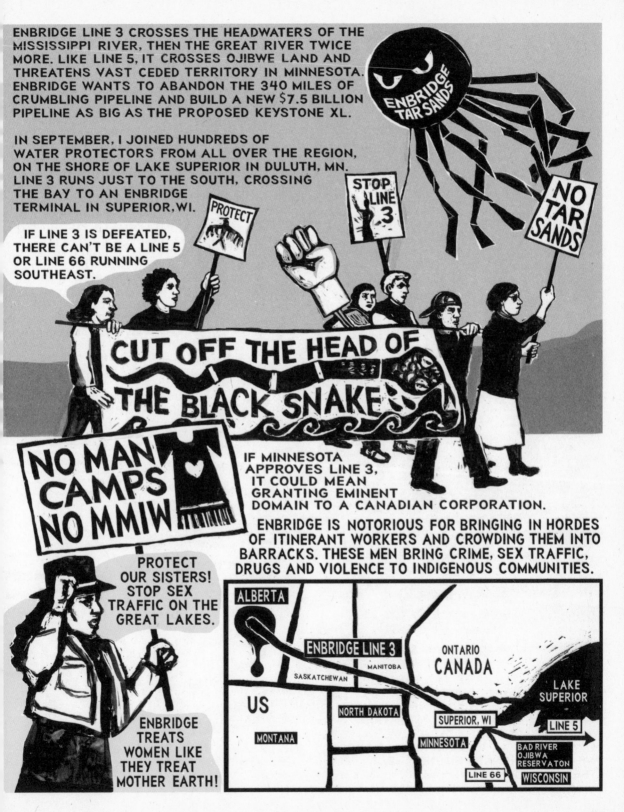

ENBRIDGE LINE 3 CROSSES THE HEADWATERS OF THE MISSISSIPPI RIVER, THEN THE GREAT RIVER TWICE MORE. LIKE LINE 5, IT CROSSES OJIBWE LAND AND THREATENS VAST CEDED TERRITORY IN MINNESOTA. ENBRIDGE WANTS TO ABANDON THE 340 MILES OF CRUMBLING PIPELINE AND BUILD A NEW $7.5 BILLION PIPELINE AS BIG AS THE PROPOSED KEYSTONE XL.

IN SEPTEMBER, I JOINED HUNDREDS OF WATER PROTECTORS FROM ALL OVER THE REGION, ON THE SHORE OF LAKE SUPERIOR IN DULUTH, MN. LINE 3 RUNS JUST TO THE SOUTH, CROSSING THE BAY TO AN ENBRIDGE TERMINAL IN SUPERIOR, WI.

IF LINE 3 IS DEFEATED, THERE CAN'T BE A LINE 5 OR LINE 66 RUNNING SOUTHEAST.

ENBRIDGE TAR SANDS

PROTECT

STOP LINE 3

NO TAR SANDS

CUT OFF THE HEAD OF THE BLACK SNAKE

NO MAN CAMPS NO MMIW

IF MINNESOTA APPROVES LINE 3, IT COULD MEAN GRANTING EMINENT DOMAIN TO A CANADIAN CORPORATION.

ENBRIDGE IS NOTORIOUS FOR BRINGING IN HORDES OF ITINERANT WORKERS AND CROWDING THEM INTO BARRACKS. THESE MEN BRING CRIME, SEX TRAFFIC, DRUGS AND VIOLENCE TO INDIGENOUS COMMUNITIES.

PROTECT OUR SISTERS! STOP SEX TRAFFIC ON THE GREAT LAKES.

ENBRIDGE TREATS WOMEN LIKE THEY TREAT MOTHER EARTH!

ALBERTA

ENBRIDGE LINE 3

SASKATCHEWAN

MANITOBA

ONTARIO CANADA

LAKE SUPERIOR

US

NORTH DAKOTA

SUPERIOR, WI

LINE 5

MONTANA

MINNESOTA

BAD RIVER OJIBWA RESERVATON

LINE 66

WISCONSIN

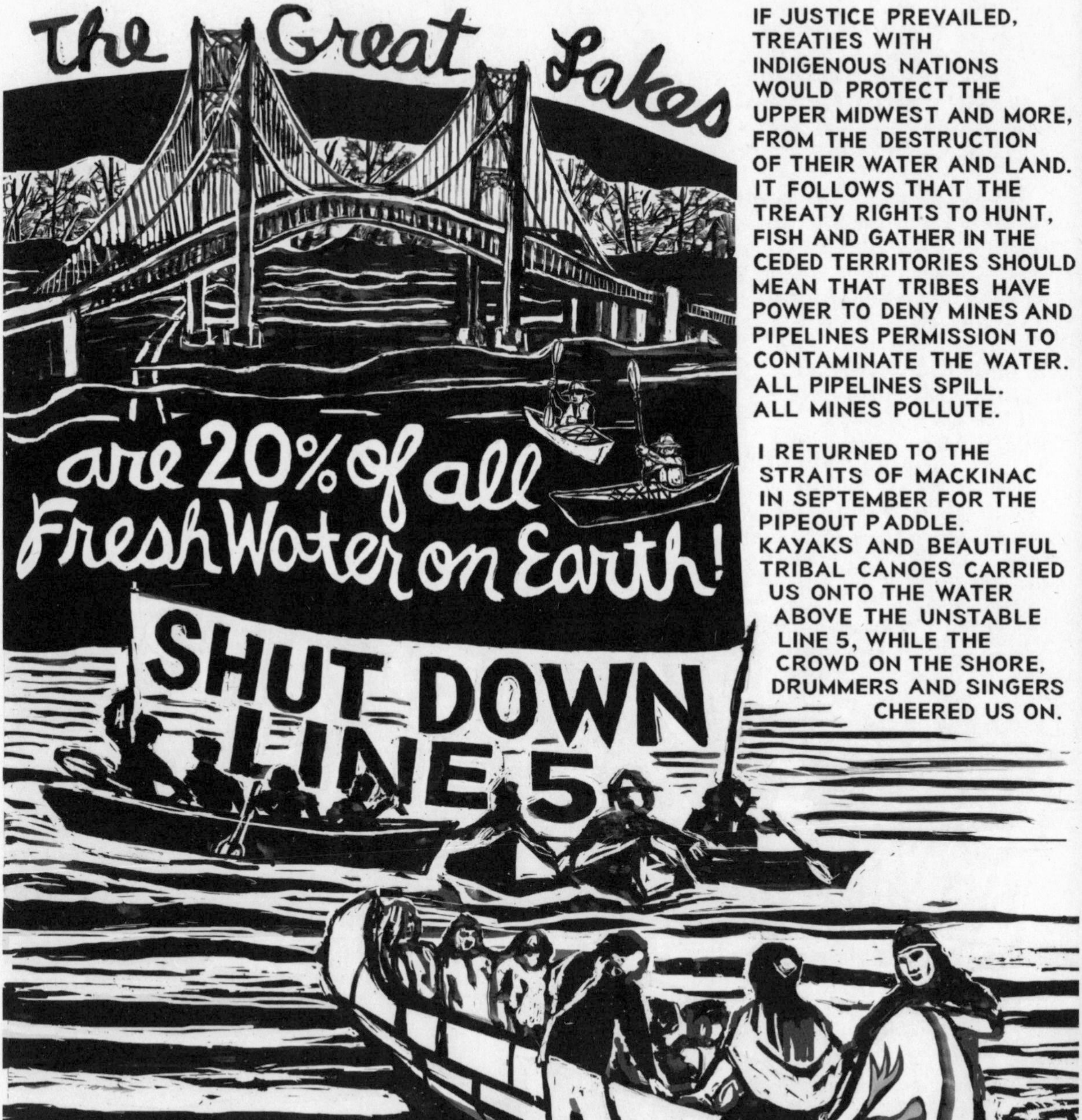
The Great Lakes
are 20% of all Fresh Water on Earth!
SHUT DOWN LINE 5

IF JUSTICE PREVAILED, TREATIES WITH INDIGENOUS NATIONS WOULD PROTECT THE UPPER MIDWEST AND MORE, FROM THE DESTRUCTION OF THEIR WATER AND LAND. IT FOLLOWS THAT THE TREATY RIGHTS TO HUNT, FISH AND GATHER IN THE CEDED TERRITORIES SHOULD MEAN THAT TRIBES HAVE POWER TO DENY MINES AND PIPELINES PERMISSION TO CONTAMINATE THE WATER. ALL PIPELINES SPILL. ALL MINES POLLUTE.

I RETURNED TO THE STRAITS OF MACKINAC IN SEPTEMBER FOR THE PIPEOUT PADDLE. KAYAKS AND BEAUTIFUL TRIBAL CANOES CARRIED US ONTO THE WATER ABOVE THE UNSTABLE LINE 5, WHILE THE CROWD ON THE SHORE, DRUMMERS AND SINGERS CHEERED US ON.

WHILE OUR LIVES ARE TRANSFORMED BY THE PANDEMIC, ENBRIDGE PUSHES AHEAD. INSTEAD OF LEARNING FROM THIS CATASTROPIC SITUATION, THEY ARE DOUBLING DOWN. GOVERNMENTS SUSPEND ENVIRONMENTAL PROTECTIONS TO EXPEDITE THE EXPANSION OF TOXIC INDUSTRIES. WE FACE 'ENHANCED ENFORCEMENT': FELONIES, JAIL TIME, AND FINES RIGGED TO PROTECT THESE FOREIGN-OWNED OIL PIPELINES, NOW REINVENTED AS 'CRITICAL INFRASTRUCTURE'. NEVERTHELESS, WE WILL CONTINUE TO PROTECT THE WATER AND PROTECT ONE ANOTHER.

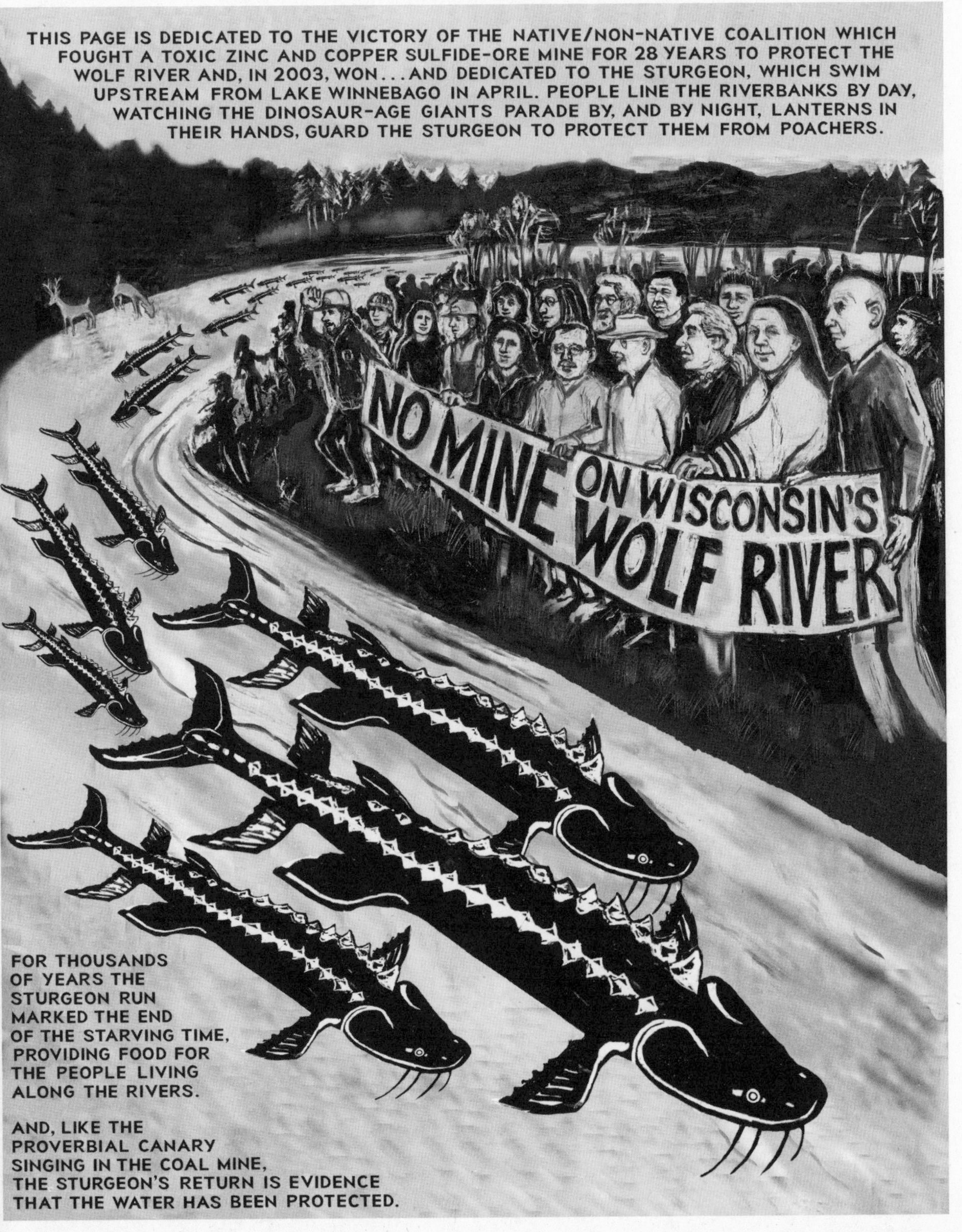
THIS PAGE IS DEDICATED TO THE VICTORY OF THE NATIVE/NON-NATIVE COALITION WHICH FOUGHT A TOXIC ZINC AND COPPER SULFIDE-ORE MINE FOR 28 YEARS TO PROTECT THE WOLF RIVER AND, IN 2003, WON...AND DEDICATED TO THE STURGEON, WHICH SWIM UPSTREAM FROM LAKE WINNEBAGO IN APRIL. PEOPLE LINE THE RIVERBANKS BY DAY, WATCHING THE DINOSAUR-AGE GIANTS PARADE BY, AND BY NIGHT, LANTERNS IN THEIR HANDS, GUARD THE STURGEON TO PROTECT THEM FROM POACHERS.
NO MINE ON WISCONSIN'S WOLF RIVER
FOR THOUSANDS OF YEARS THE STURGEON RUN MARKED THE END OF THE STARVING TIME, PROVIDING FOOD FOR THE PEOPLE LIVING ALONG THE RIVERS.
AND, LIKE THE PROVERBIAL CANARY SINGING IN THE COAL MINE, THE STURGEON'S RETURN IS EVIDENCE THAT THE WATER HAS BEEN PROTECTED.

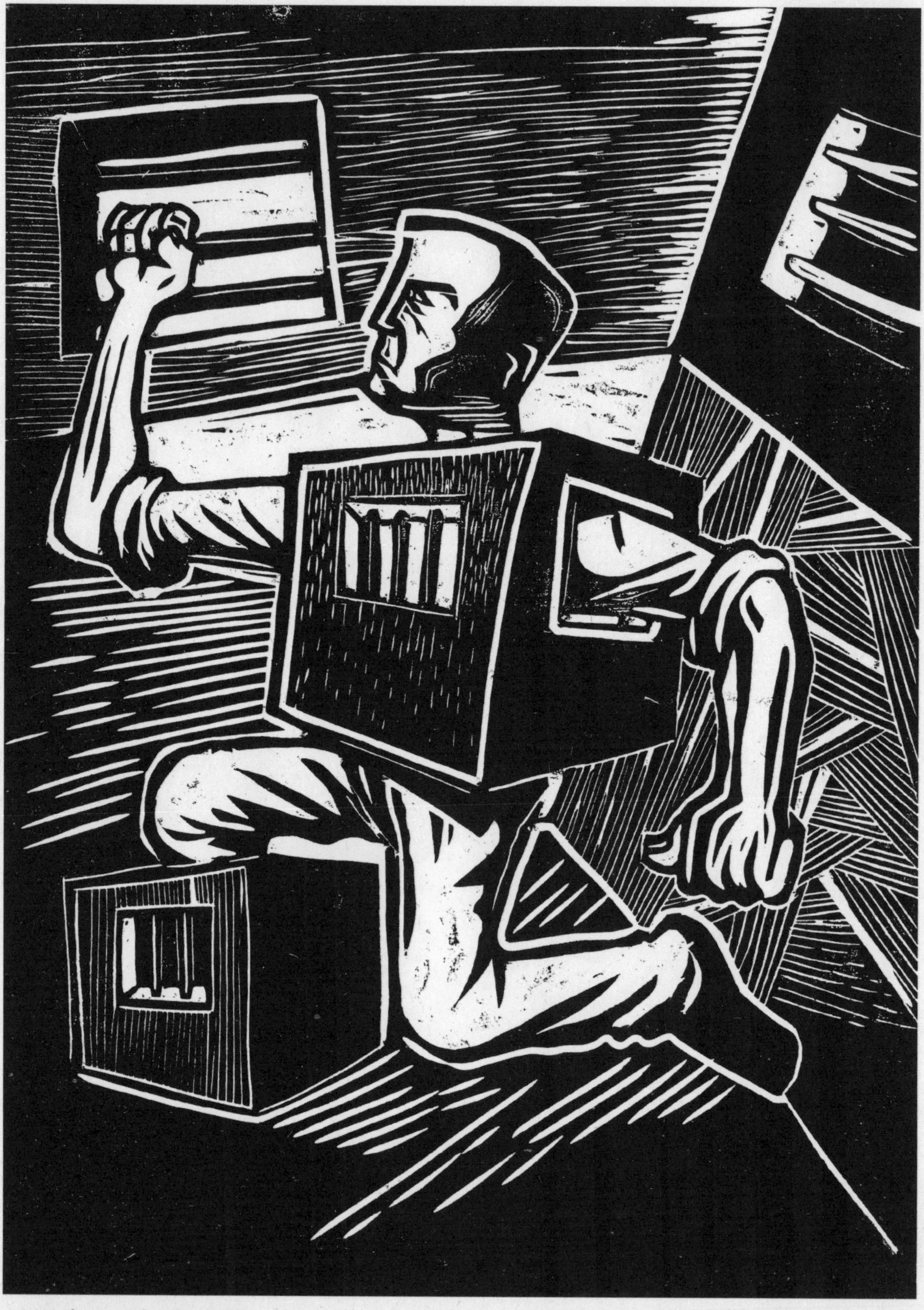

BREAKING FREE:

SPOTLIGHT ON ABO COMIX

EDITED AND COMPILED BY ETHAN HEITNER

ABO Comix logo by Elia

ABO Comix publishes comix by incarcerated queer people.

I spoke to one of the founders, Casper Cendre, at the end of April, as they were gathering material to publish a special anthology on COVID-19 in prisons. Their mailing list includes 135 prisoners across the United States, who identify in every imaginable way—Casper says that no-one needs to "prove their queerness," but demographic data is collected for grant funders.

This interview has been edited for length and clarity.

Ethan Heitner: Hi, how are you?

Casper Cendre: Doing pretty well. Went to the post office since our deadline was today, and there were 12 new submissions in our box. So we've got a lot of work to do in the next couple days, but it's good and I'm glad so many people want to share their experiences.

Do you have a lot of people helping?

It's for the most part me and my good friend Carla. We've got a couple other volunteers who will come in from time to time, or help with letter writing, or social media.

Our contributors are pretty heavily involved in the decision-making process, as much as humanly possible, because the mail system is slow. I would love our contributors to feel a lot more involved in the actual process of publishing the book and designing it and all that, but I haven't found a good way yet.

I hope that at some point we are able to start hiring on previously-incarcerated people. A lot of our contributors, it's really adorable, have sent us mock job applications. And they're like "I'm getting out in like a year! I would love if you consider me for a position!"

Like oh jeez, we're gonna have to start getting a lot more grant funding!

How did ABO Comix get started?

My friends 10 and Woof and I were hanging out together in a community garden here in Oakland, and we were just talking about comics and prisoner advocacy work. We had a spur of the moment idea that wouldn't it be cool if we asked prisoners about their experiences, and we had them create comics, and we compiled it into a cute little book. Like, wouldn't that be a fun project?

So we drew up this call for submissions poster, and we put that in the Black and Pink newsletter. Over the course of a year from that one call for submissions we received hundreds of letters. And we realized how big the interest and the need for this kind of project was, so then the three of us started working on answering letters and compiling artwork, and I got really, really invested in it, because I had already been looking for an artistic outlet to my activism for a long time.

My two co-founders worked on it with me for the first year pretty heavily and then had to drop off to pursue other stuff. But I really didn't want this to end, because I was so enjoying seeing the artwork that people were creating and how much it was helping them find healing.

As fun and as beautiful as this is, it's definitely traumatic at times. We hear about some of the worst things that can happen to human beings on a regular basis. So I think [10 and Woof] were feeling a little burnt out with it and had to step back to pursue other things.

Are most of your audience in queer radical spaces?

All of us who started this project at the time identified

Gabe Wyatt

I've been incarcerated for 20 years now and ABO is the first company (group of people) that truly cares about not only prisoners, but queer ones like myself. ABO was created to not only amplify my voice through my art, but work hard to keep us connected to our outside comrades who are fighting alongside us in our fight toward liberation and the ABOlition of the Prison Industrial Complex. On a personal note they have become family now and that means more to me than even publishing a comic...

I became an artist because of my love for the '60s BATMAN t.v. show (the reruns of course!!). The show got me into comics (Batman) and into the idea/dream of drawing comics. My Mom always encouraged me, but she was a single parent raising 3 kids so buying me art supplies was not even an option. So I drew on all my desks and textbooks at school. By the 7th grade I started actually making my own comics and not just drawing characters posing. Long summer days and weekends were spent alone creating my own worlds. It took me years before I outgrew superhero comics but after I discovered R.Crumb there was no going backwards. Discovering Underground Comix blew my teenage mind.

Comics became way more than entertainment or some cheap way to escape my reality. They became my only platform of self expression. Honestly, comics (my art) were my only means of proving to the world that I had any value.

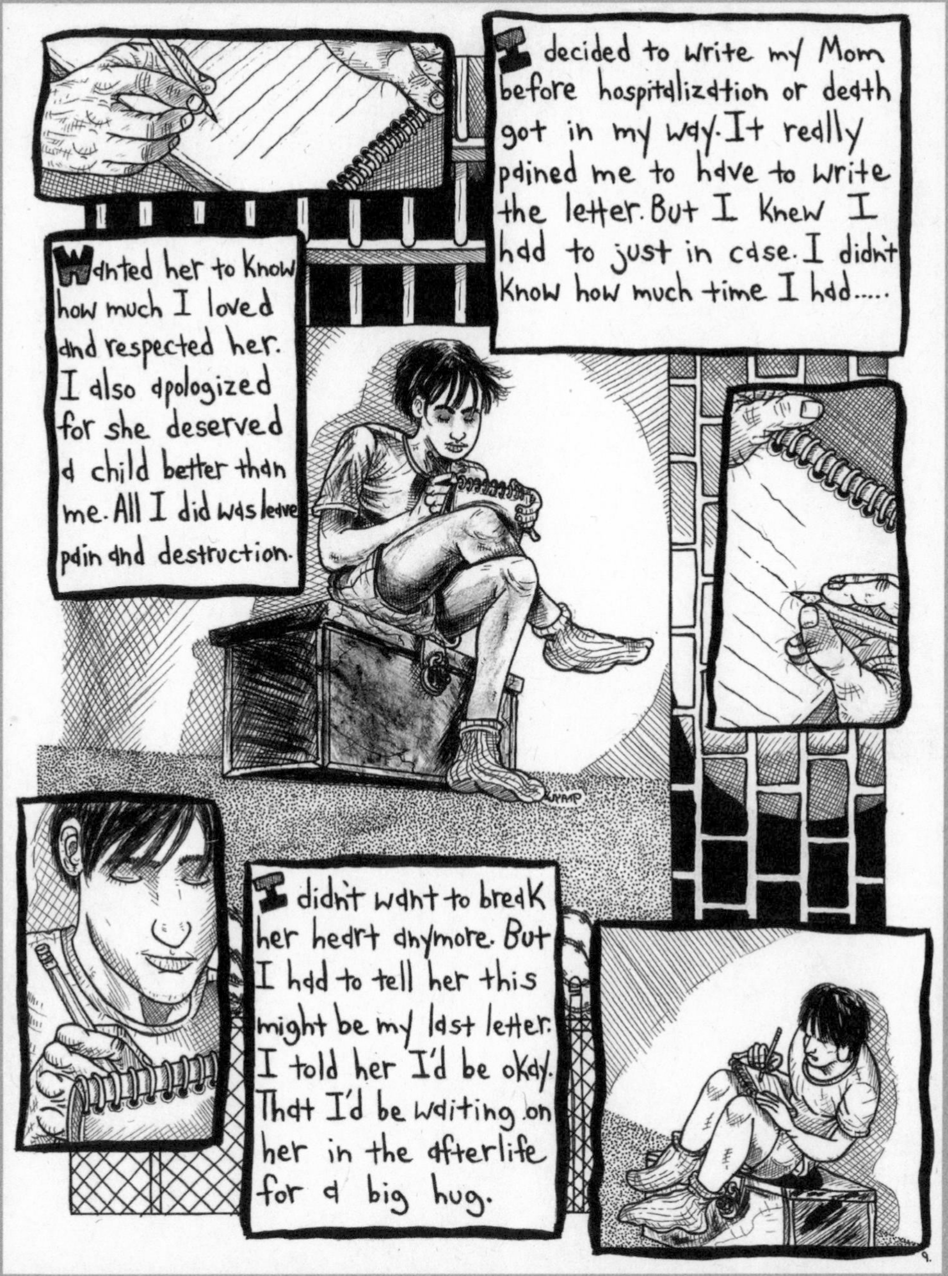
I decided to write my Mom before hospitalization or death got in my way. It really pained me to have to write the letter. But I knew I had to just in case. I didn't know how much time I had.....
Wanted her to know how much I loved and respected her. I also apologized for she deserved a child better than me. All I did was leave pain and destruction.
I didn't want to break her heart anymore. But I had to tell her this might be my last letter. I told her I'd be okay. That I'd be waiting on her in the afterlife for a big hug.
9.

With my comic art I'm not really trying to create pretty art, I'm more consumed with getting the ideas out. That's the important thing to me.

You can holler at me anytime for I usually respond the same day. (Us incarcerated comic artists don't have much of a social life to drag us away from the ole drawing board.)

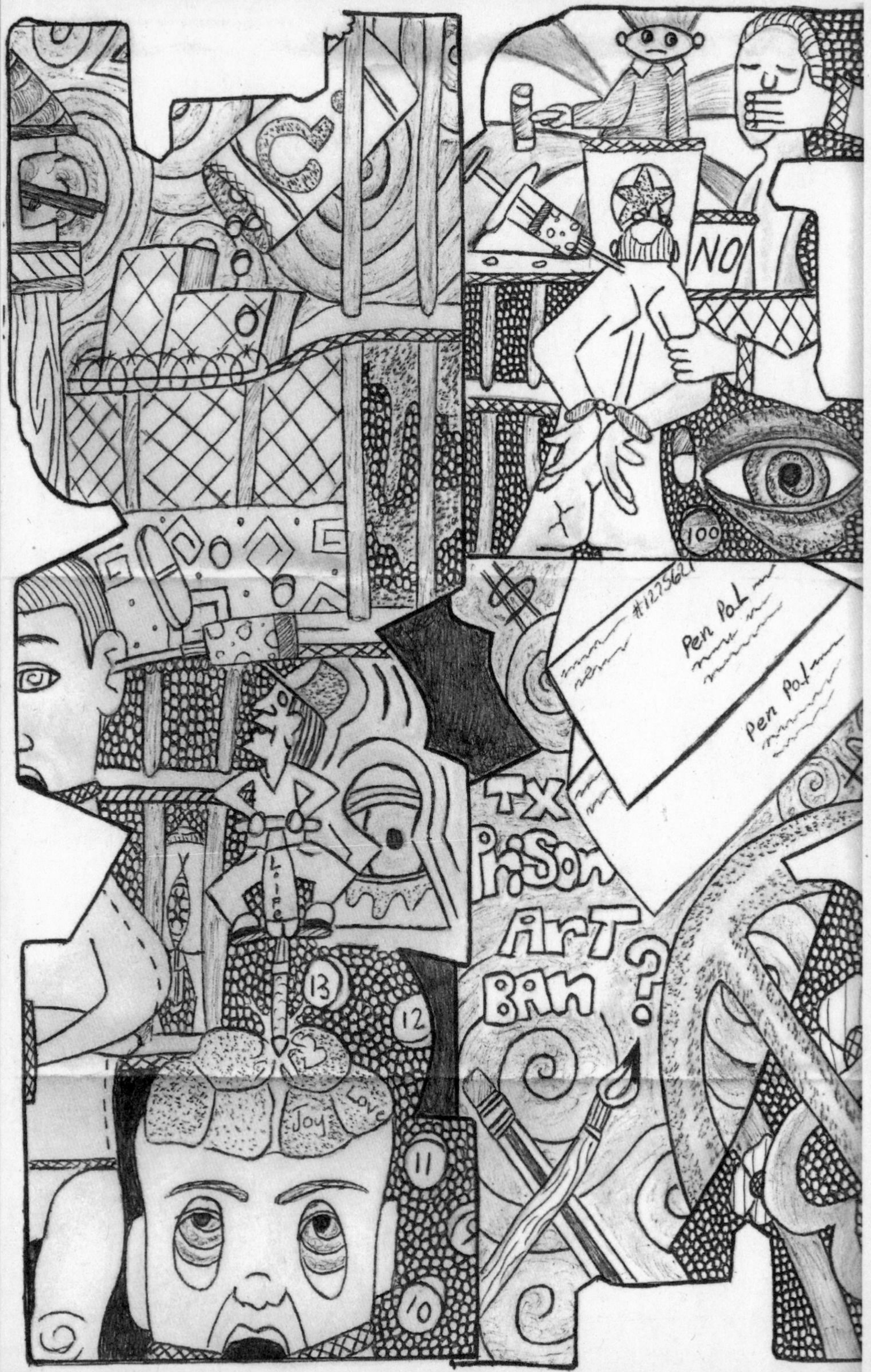
NO
100
#1275621
Pen Pal
Pen Pal
TX Prison Art Ban?
Life
13
12
Joy
Love
11
10

Billy D. Thomas

I am involved because I am a mentally ill person doing capital life in a Texas state prison ... the art helps me vent and send out my cry for help.

I started doing cards for money on the inside, but my art is a part of my life and pain that I learned to share with others so they can come to understand I am not the beast the Fort Worth TX DA office made me out to look like.

If I can be healed so can others, but we have to stop spreading the sickness of our past. Then we will win this world.

as queer anarchists. And so we had very specific political leanings that definitely influenced our publications and our correspondence and stuff.

But having now had so much correspondence with people in prisons nationwide, with queer people all over the country who come from all sorts of different backgrounds, you've got a lot of leftists, of course, you've got a lot of liberal people, but then we also have centrists and we have conservatives, we've gotten mail from queer Republicans in prison who were writing in and were like, "I was so nervous to send you a letter, because I know this is sort of a leftist organization and I face a lot of backlash for my belief, especially being a queer person."

We want it to be an open conversation for anybody. Especially anybody who identifies as queer, to feel safe to be able to write into us and know that they're not going to receive judgment or backlash or any sort of gatekeeping on our end. Our mission is to help people tell their stories, especially from a queer perspective, no matter what that perspective is.

Do you ever feel like you get submissions that you wouldn't want to print either for political reasons or artistic reasons or any other reason?

There have been times where I have really gone back and forth on whether or not it was appropriate to print a submission. In the third anthology, we got a submission from a person who was convicted of having child pornography. And I was very, very conflicted on whether or not to include their submission, because it told a story of dealing with their own abuse and trauma, and then how that manifested in their life.

And I was like, we're gonna get a lot of backlash on this. I'm really scared to publish this. But, who am I to decide whose story is and is not important to tell? I want to help everybody tell their story. So we did include that submission. And we've received nothing but positive feedback about it.

We've turned some down just because they needed more love, like they needed some editing and reworking. But for the most part no matter what the artistic level is, I definitely try to publish it.

We started this project with the idea that this was going to be a prison comics project by and for queer prisoners. And for me to personally make that editorial decision of, I don't want to include this because it offends my delicate sensibilities, or whatever, is not the route I want to go down.

There's questions of taste and offensiveness but there's also turning something down because you think the artists can do something better.

I think a lot of times people find a lot of value in constructive feedback. Nobody really writes under the assumption that they're going to get published. But hearing feedback on your artwork, and hearing from somebody who's spent the time to really look and ingest and take it all in, people are generally so excited about that. They're like, nobody's ever encouraged me like this. Nobody's ever looked at my artwork for more than like 10 seconds.

What makes ABO Comix an abolitionist project?

I want to see a world where we don't have to lock people in cages, where we have better systems in place to deal with issues that contribute to what we as a society deem "criminal activity."

And working with this project, it's been really eye-opening to realize that the link spreading throughout everybody's stories really is trauma that has not been dealt with in a healthy and productive way. A lot of the stories that we receive incorporate scenes of childhood abuse, or relationship abuse, or psychological abuse, something to that extent, and realizing that this is the link that's running through the prison system. Of course, there are a lot of innocent people in prison, but there are a lot of people who are convicted of a crime that they did "commit."

For lack of a better cliche, hurt people, hurt people.

I find it extremely powerful what Mariame Kaba says, and I think she's quoting somebody else, maybe, "No one enters into the system of violence the first time as a perpetrator."

Joanlisa Red Cloud-Featherston

Everyone hears what goes on in mens' prisons, but not in womens' prisons.

Lo and behold I created "In The Hen House," based on what I have personally gone through, or what others have throughout the years.

My main media is pen and ink, or a plain #2 pencil. I love to have others listen to me, but I have a stutter complex, in a sense. I get lost for words at times when I try to get my point across. So I put it on paper and draw my thoughts down.

I do want to explore more into my artwork and express myself freely in that aspect as well, so if you know of anyone that would love for me to draw for them, please let me know …

This place has a lot of tension and chaos all around here right now. This pandemic is really starting to get to everyone. Take care and stay safe.

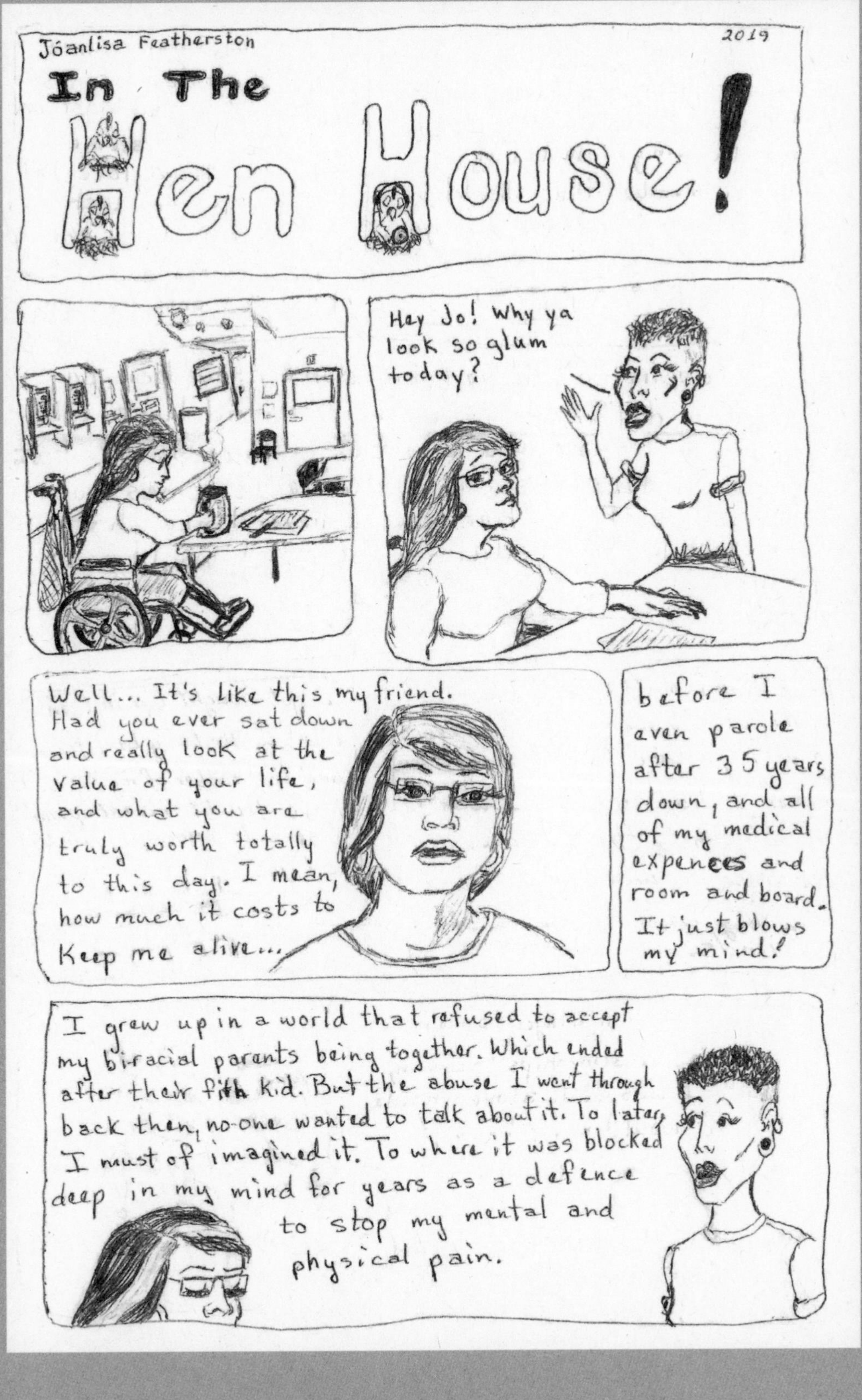
Jóanlisa Featherston
2019
In The Hen House!
Hey Jo! Why ya look so glum today?
Well... It's like this my friend. Had you ever sat down and really look at the value of your life, and what you are truly worth totally to this day. I mean, how much it costs to Keep me alive...
before I even parole after 35 years down, and all of my medical expences and room and board. It just blows my mind!
I grew up in a world that refused to accept my biracial parents being together. Which ended after their fith kid. But the abuse I went through back then, no-one wanted to talk about it. To later, I must of imagined it. To where it was blocked deep in my mind for years as a defence to stop my mental and physical pain.

Johnny Nixon (Joanna)

My property, along with my phone book with all my contacts were taken by the COs and I was moved to another yard. A.B.O. reassured me during the hardest of times. I'm just barely recovering from that loss and my best advocate's passing (who also sold my work online). And afforded me the ability to support myself as I always had. They made me a part of A.B.O. They spoke to me like they know me. Maybe they do, from my work drawing, painting, and beading.

Above all and mainly, I am involved because Casper made me feel wanted. It's like it matters what me and my cohorts think and feel, and our art and expression has real value.

Drawing means the world to me. I definitely would end my life if I could no longer draw and commit art! Drawing prolifically allows me to speak in the oldest and only language spoken over the entire planet. I am understood by everyone, in every language, deeper than the written or spoken word. During a portion of my life (brain damage from viral encephalitis) it was the only way I could speak, resulting in a life prison term for an infraction regulatory violation.

The world I would fight for is a loving, forgiving and one that facilitates everyone's potential and highest standard of living. One that starts with abolishing the prison industrial complex, currently distorting and destroying every life involved. We live in the Buck Rogers era. We all know what to fight for. I'd just like to be a part of a grand effort to make it happen.

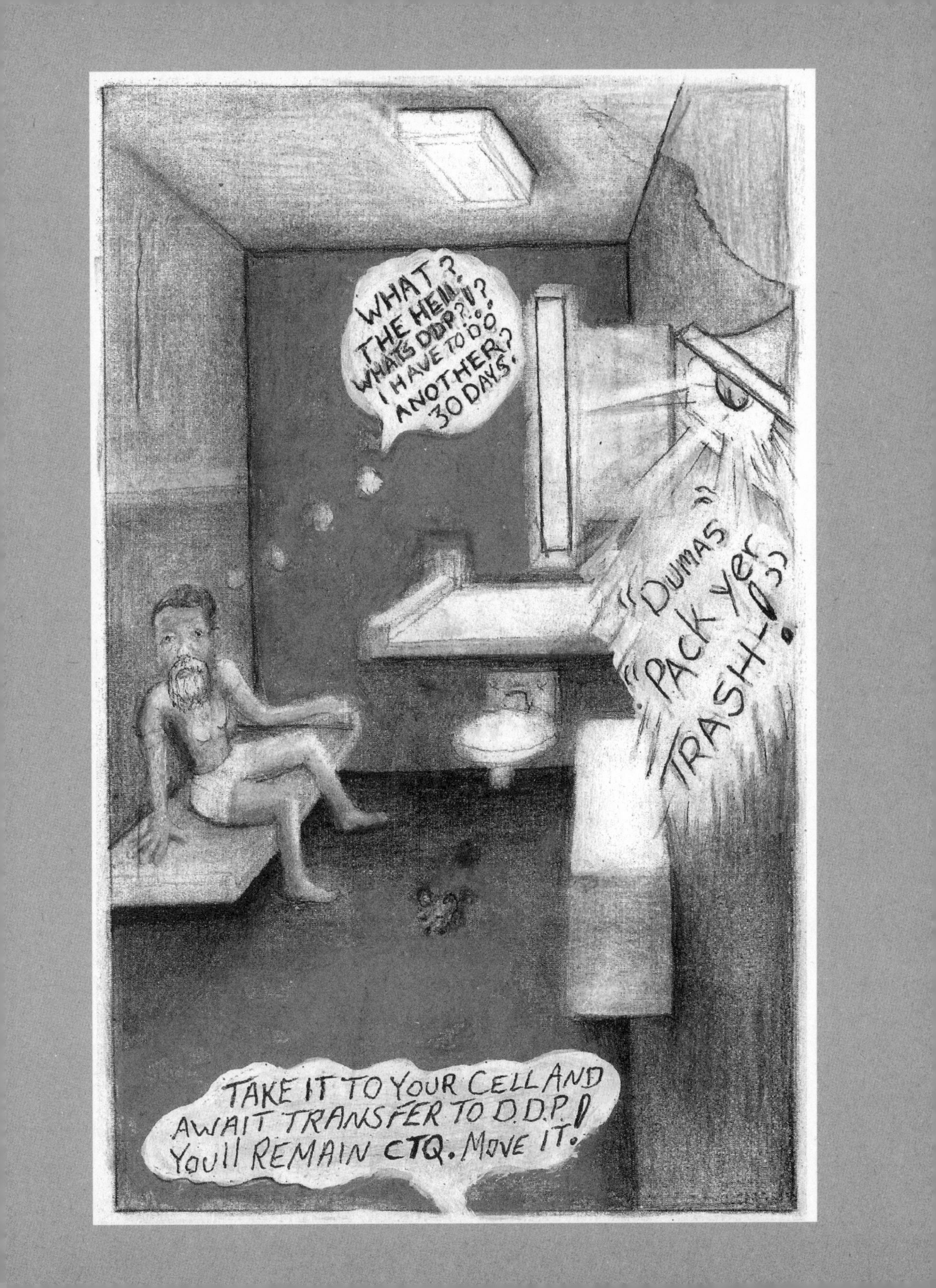
"Dumas"
"PACK yer TRASH!"
TAKE IT TO YOUR CELL AND AWAIT TRANSFER TO D.D.P.! YOU'LL REMAIN CTQ. MOVE IT!
WHAT?, THE HELL!?, WHATS DDP?!? I HAVE TO DO ANOTHER 30 DAYS?

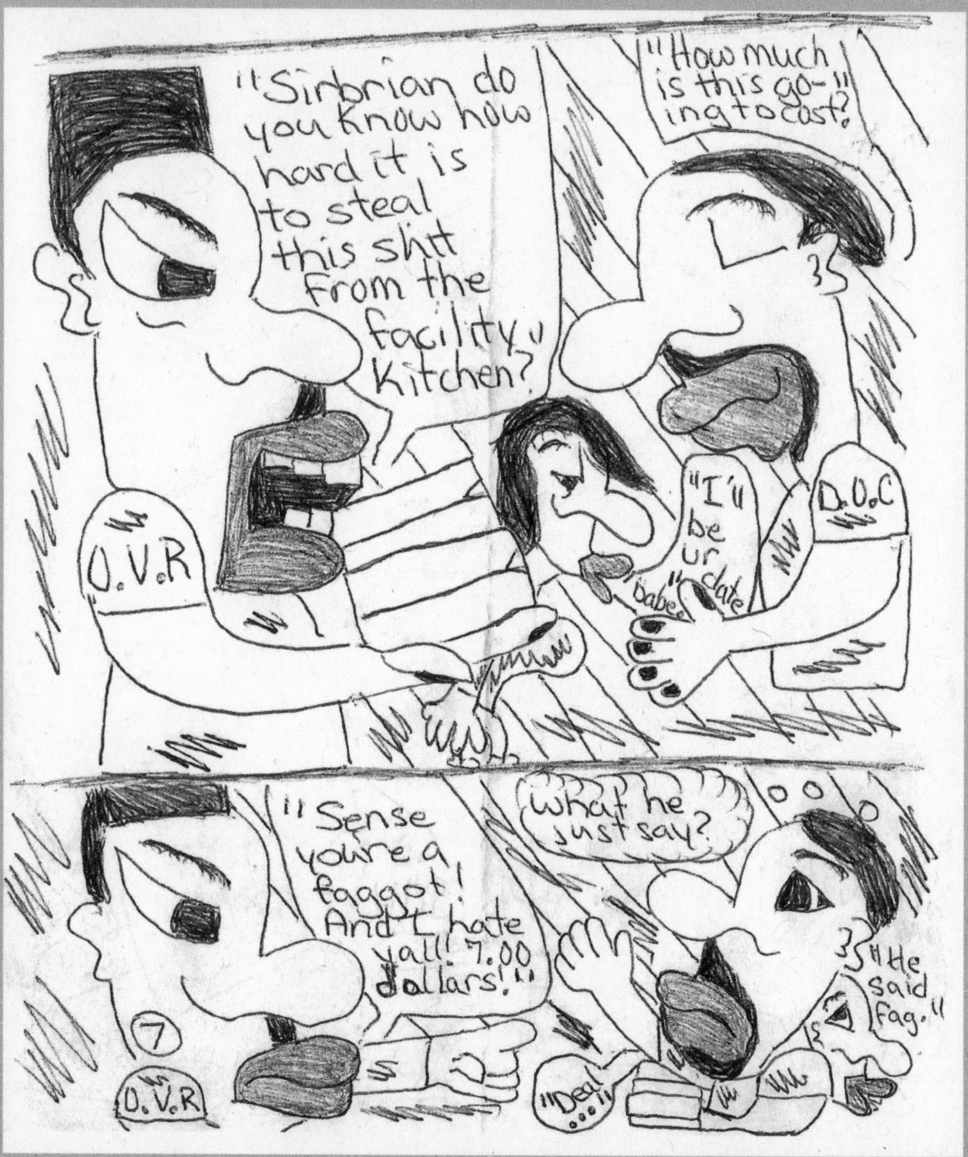
"Sirbrian do you know how hard it is to steal this shit from the facility kitchen?"
"How much is this go-ing to cost?"
"I'll be ur date babe"
O.V.R
D.O.C
"Sense you're a faggot! And I hate yall! 7.00 dollars!"
"What he just say?"
"He said fag."
"Deal..."
7
O.V.R

Sirbrian Spease

I wanted the world to see through a homo thug's eyes, that is why I continue my comic with ABO Comix called A Homo Thug Swagger, where I can tell the story of all the challenges that we go through being a openly gay couple in prison. A couple's love does not mean nothing if you cannot share it with the world.

I feel like that really speaks to the experiences I've heard as well. Because I don't think punitive measures are helping. We're not seeing the prison system help victims, we're not seeing the prison system help people who have committed harm. We're just seeing it punish and warehouse people.

Quite a few people in prison are not abolitionists, they have the perspective that like, "I did this, I deserve this." Or, "there are people in here who really should be isolated from society, people who should not be walking around in the general public," and I think that those perspectives are valid.

But where did this activity stem from in that person's life? If you go back in their timeline, and you ask them what happened before this crime that put you in prison, how did you get to this place? It almost always comes from a place of trauma.

This project, in a creative healing way, provides people an outlet to get in touch with their emotions and their perspectives and to really think about what has happened in their life that has led them to this point, and what other routes could have been taken. It encourages people to ask, what route can I take now?

You can buy comix and art, and become penpals with incarcerated artists, at abocomix.com and follow them @abocomix on social media. All proceeds support prisoners directly. All art used in this spotlight property of their respective creators, and is used with permission.

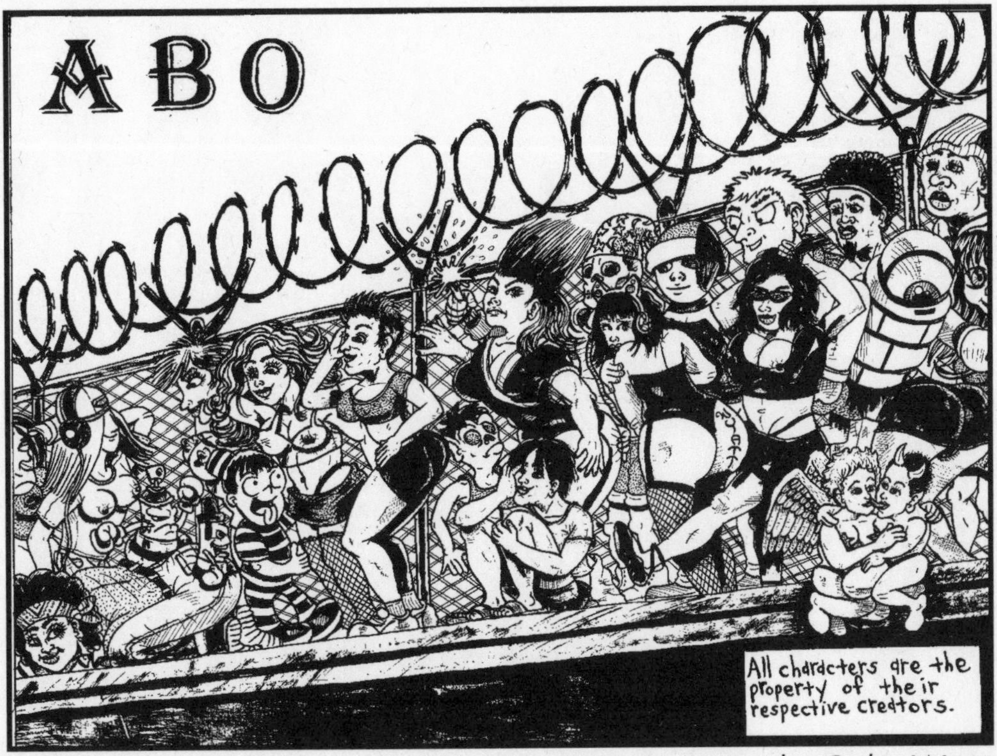
ABO
All characters are the property of their respective creators.

art by Gabe Wyatt

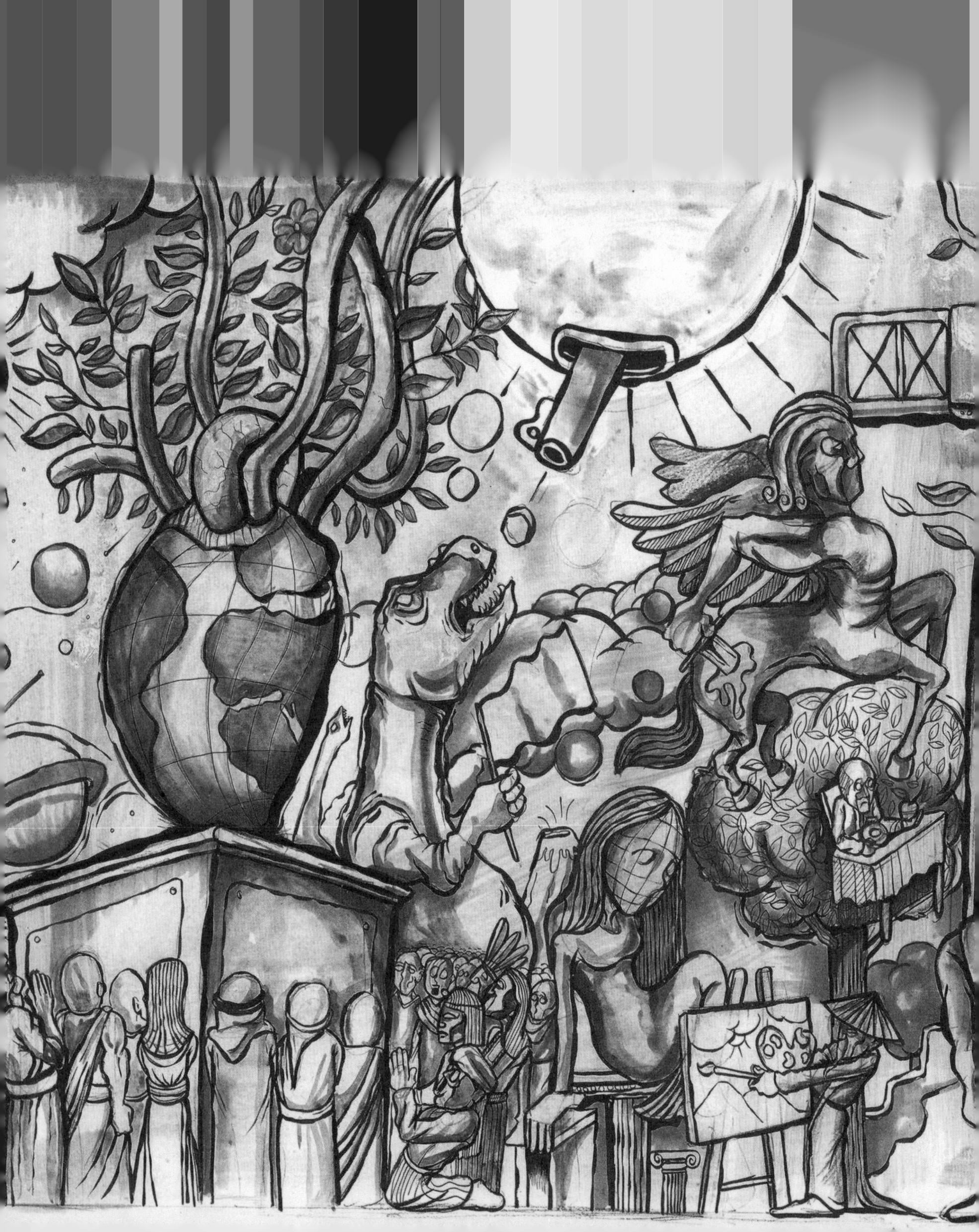

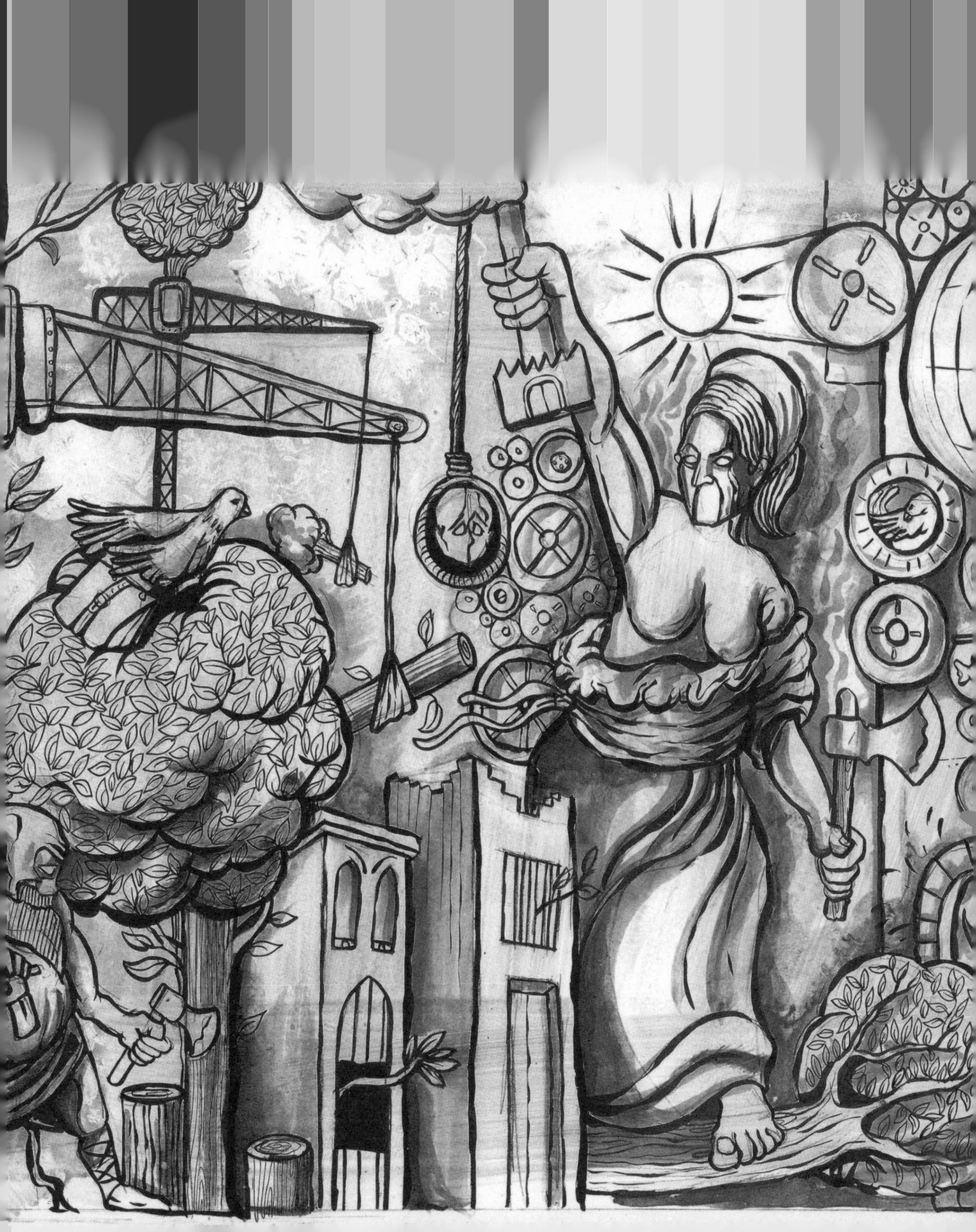

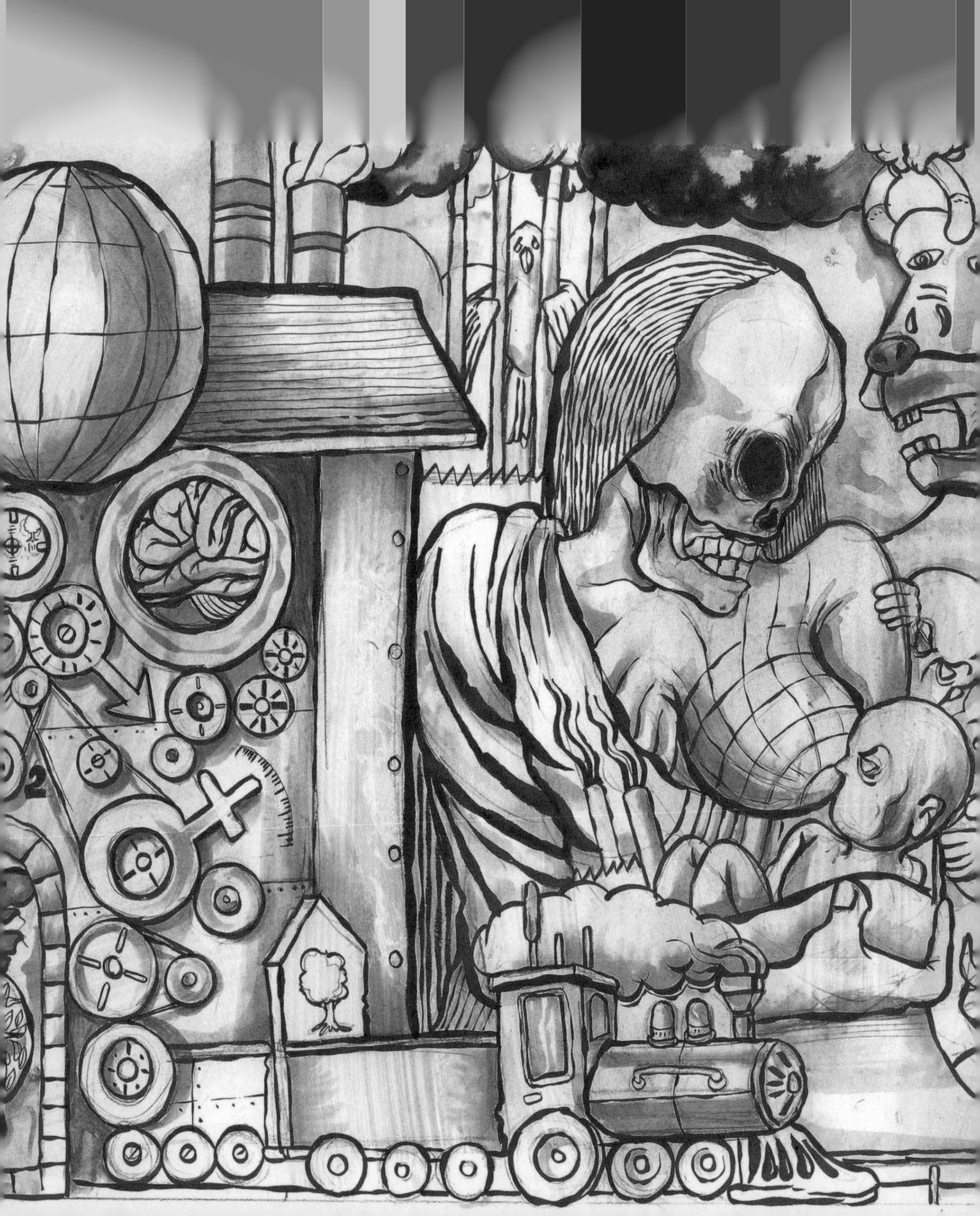

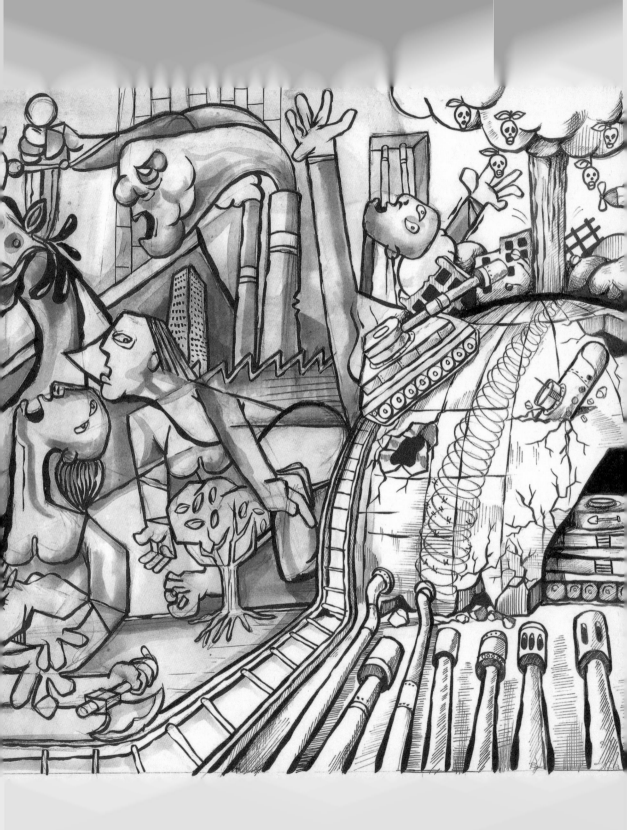

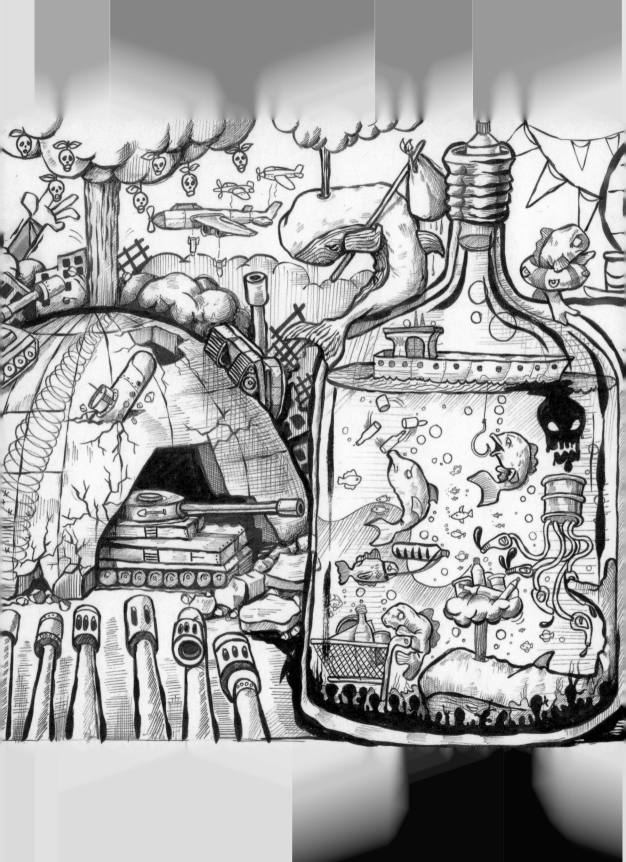

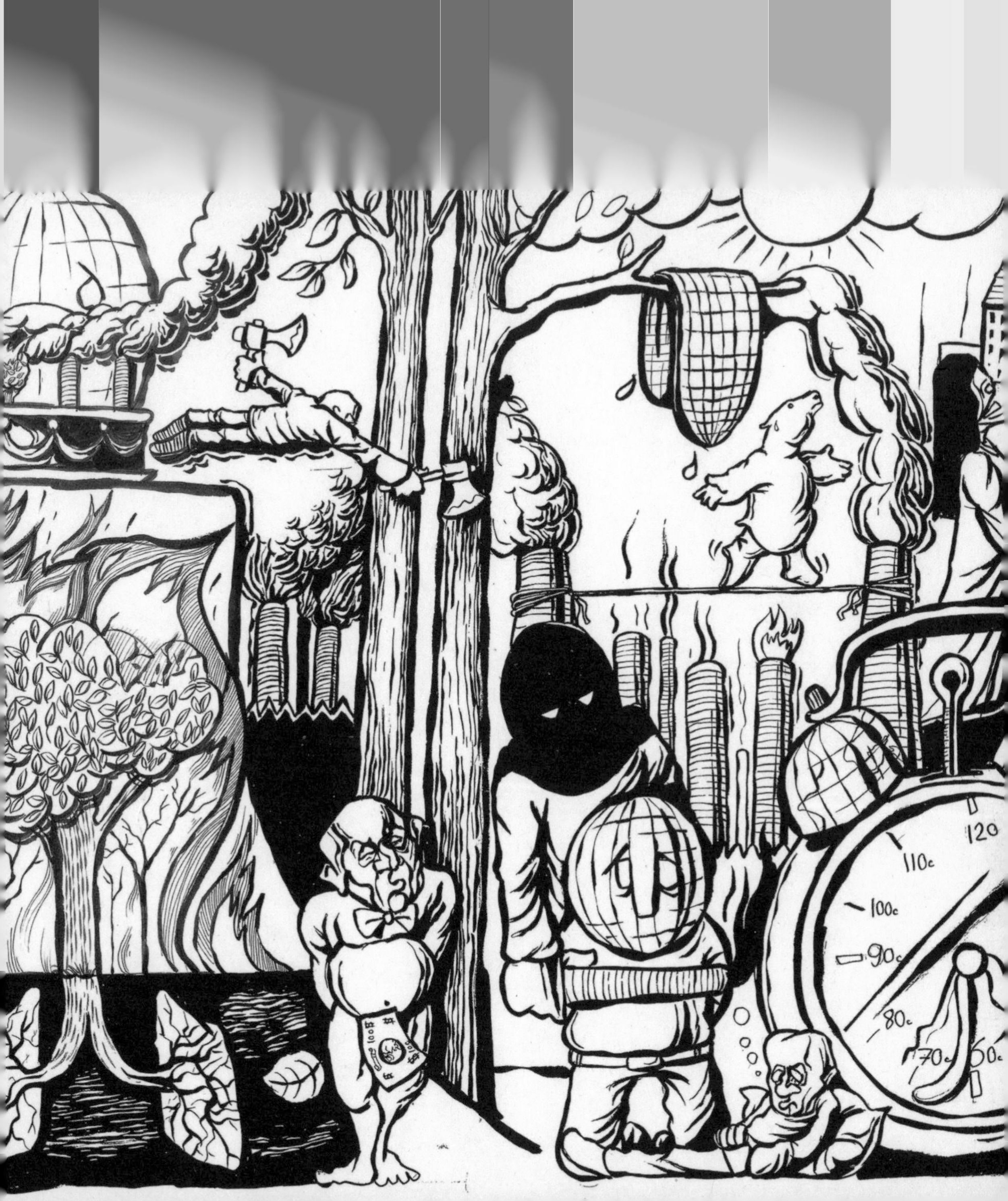
120
110c
100c
90c
80c
70c
60c

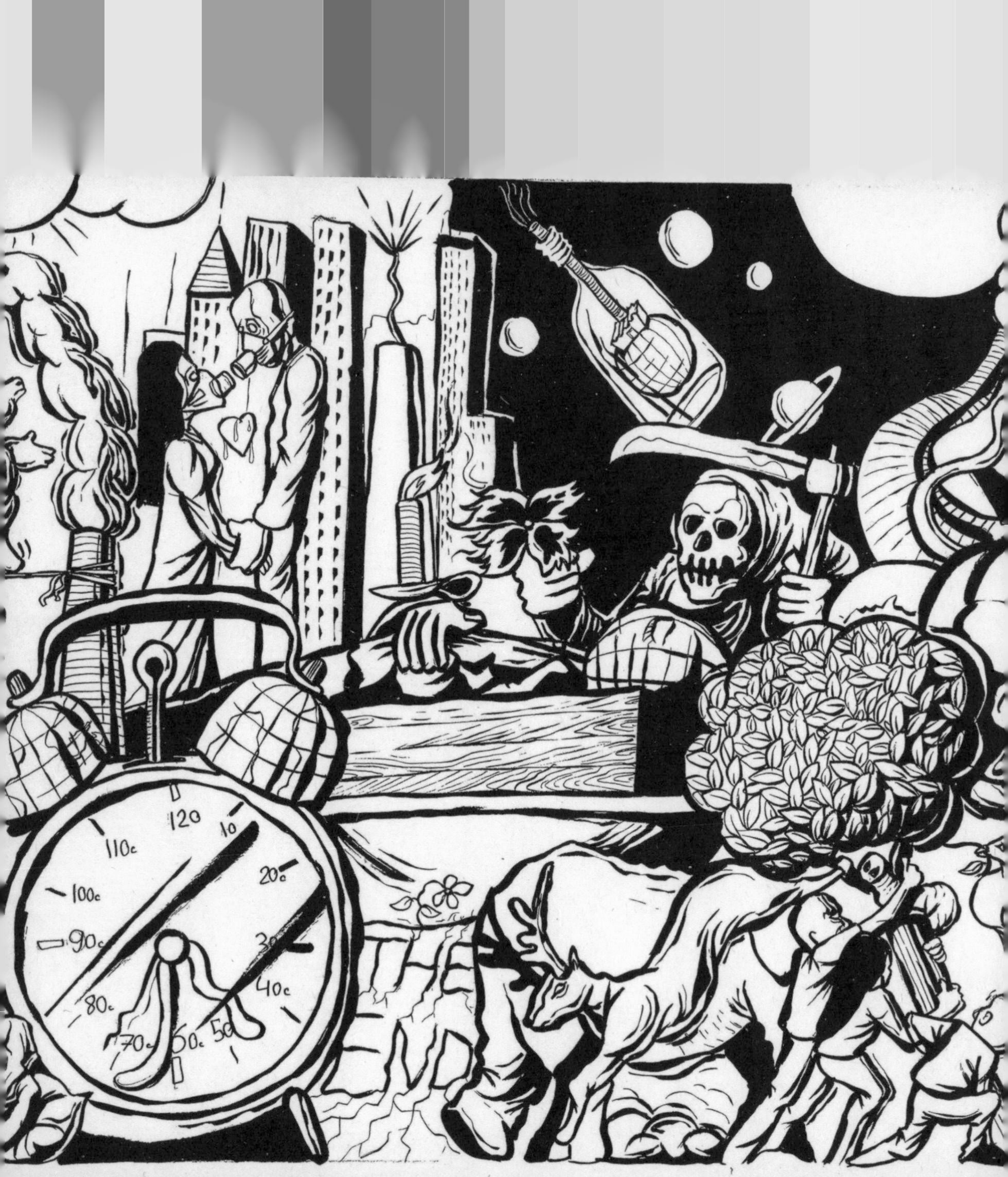
120
10
20c
30
40c
50
60c
70c
80c
90c
100c
110c

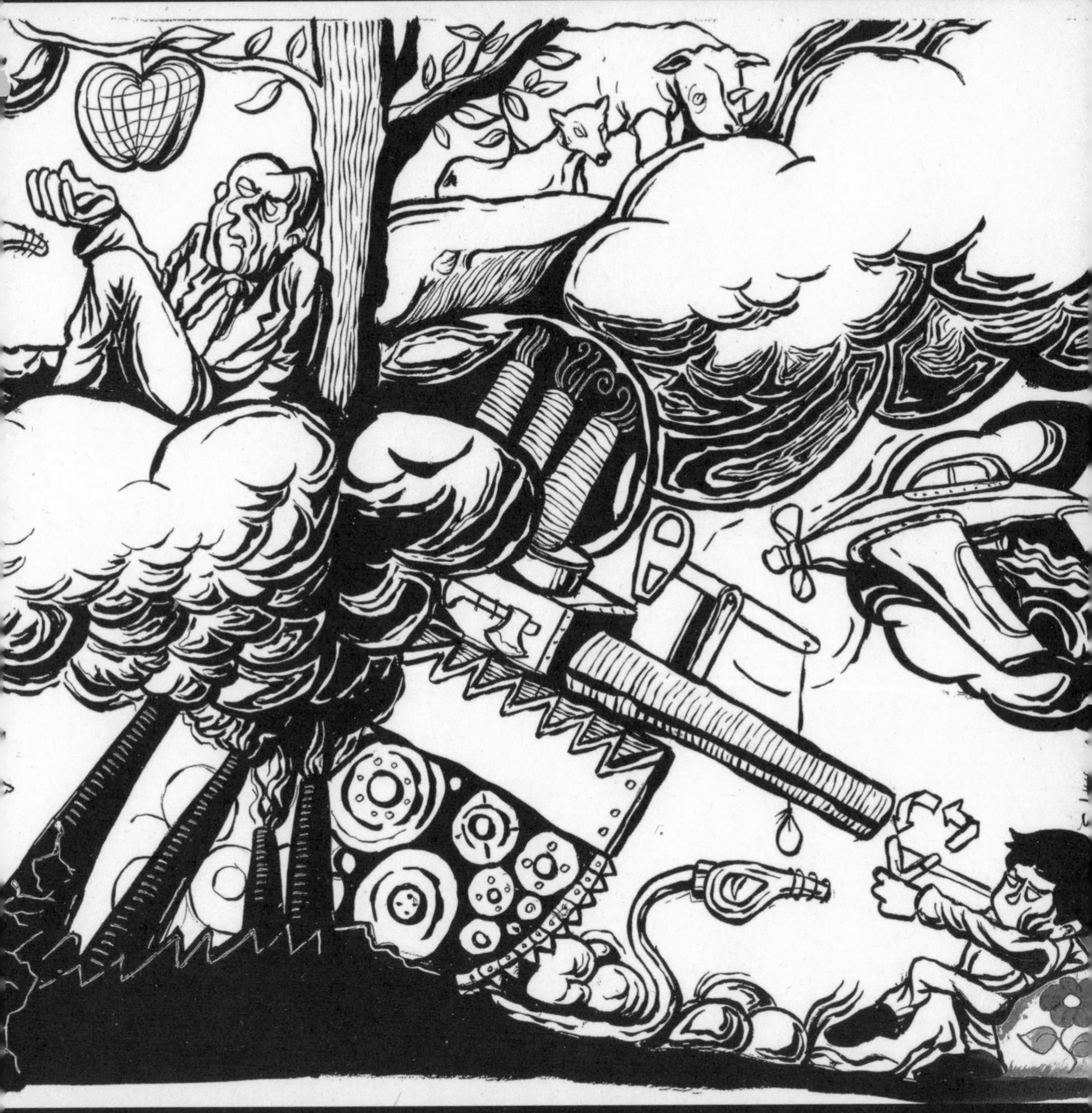

ANTARCTIC EXILE

Dreamed Dec. 2018
by Nere Kapiteni
Artwork by Rebecca Migdal

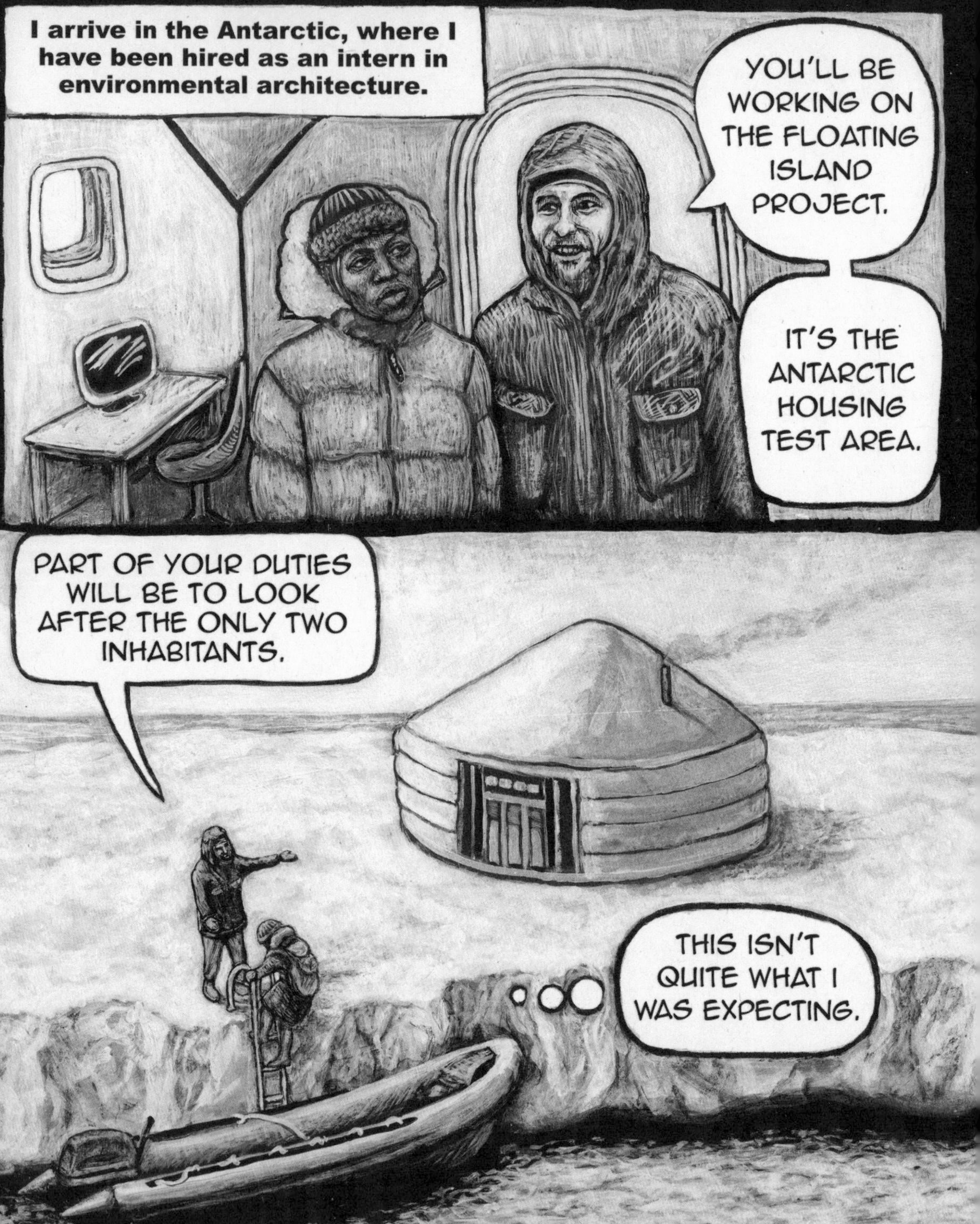

I arrive in the Antarctic, where I have been hired as an intern in environmental architecture.
YOU'LL BE WORKING ON THE FLOATING ISLAND PROJECT.
IT'S THE ANTARCTIC HOUSING TEST AREA.
PART OF YOUR DUTIES WILL BE TO LOOK AFTER THE ONLY TWO INHABITANTS.
THIS ISN'T QUITE WHAT I WAS EXPECTING.

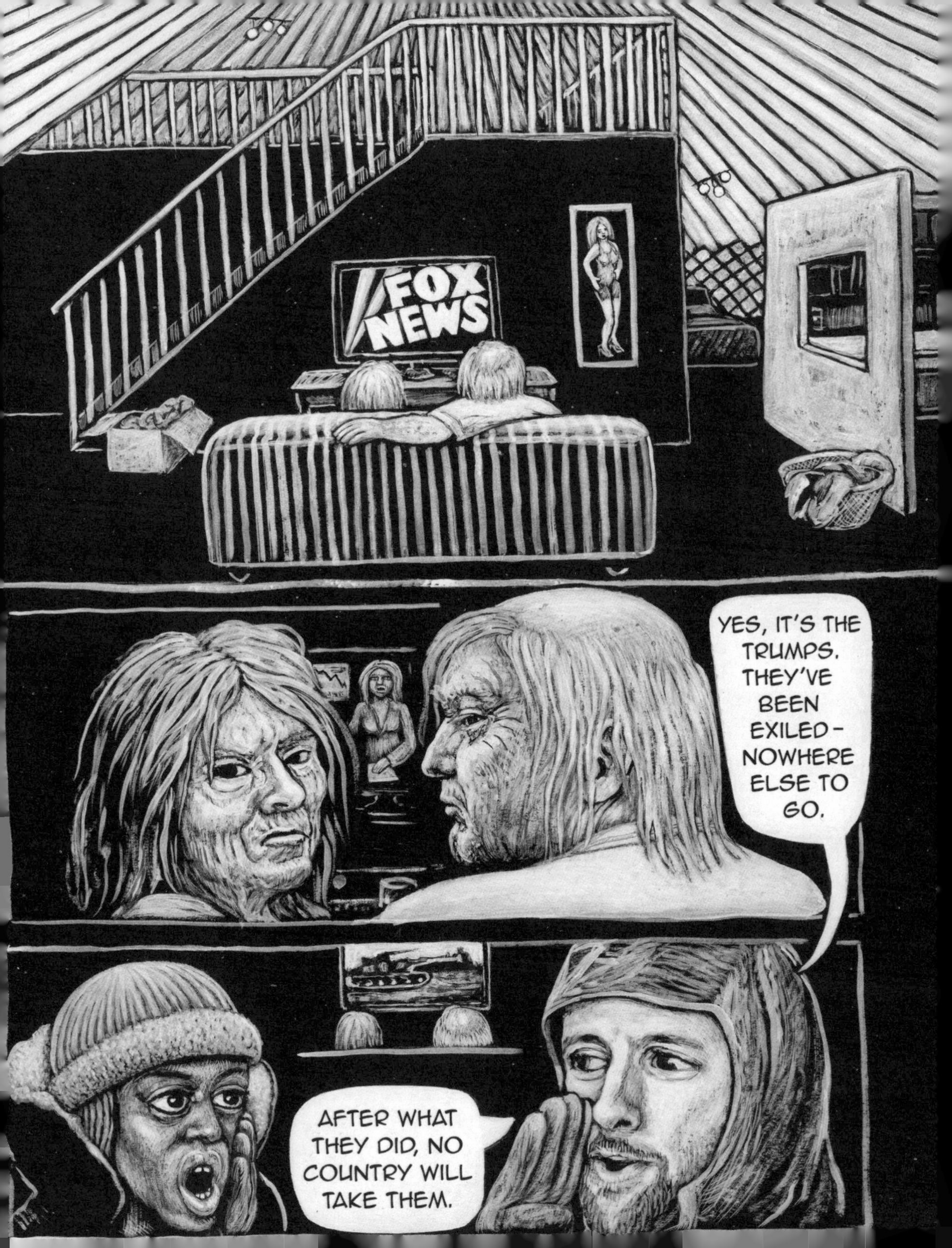
FOX NEWS
YES, IT'S THE TRUMPS. THEY'VE BEEN EXILED– NOWHERE ELSE TO GO.
AFTER WHAT THEY DID, NO COUNTRY WILL TAKE THEM.

EPIPHANY

Dreamed on January 6, 2020 by RLM
Art by Rebecca Migdal

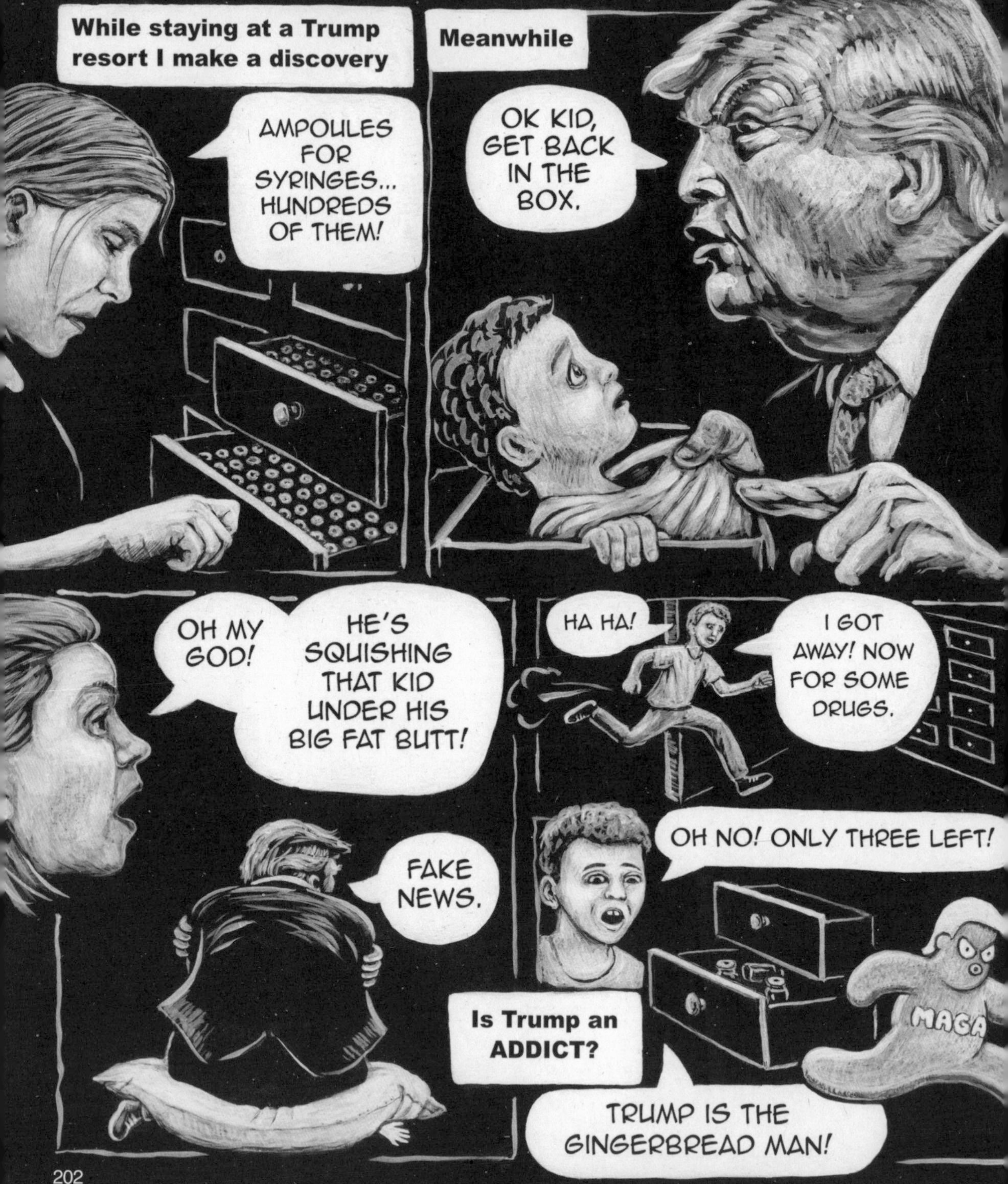
While staying at a Trump resort I make a discovery
AMPOULES FOR SYRINGES... HUNDREDS OF THEM!
Meanwhile
OK KID, GET BACK IN THE BOX.
OH MY GOD!
HE'S SQUISHING THAT KID UNDER HIS BIG FAT BUTT!
FAKE NEWS.
HA HA!
I GOT AWAY! NOW FOR SOME DRUGS.
OH NO! ONLY THREE LEFT!
Is Trump an ADDICT?
MAGA
TRUMP IS THE GINGERBREAD MAN!

SILVESTRE INTRODUCE HIMSELF FROM HIS SELF-ISOLATION IN Da Cave

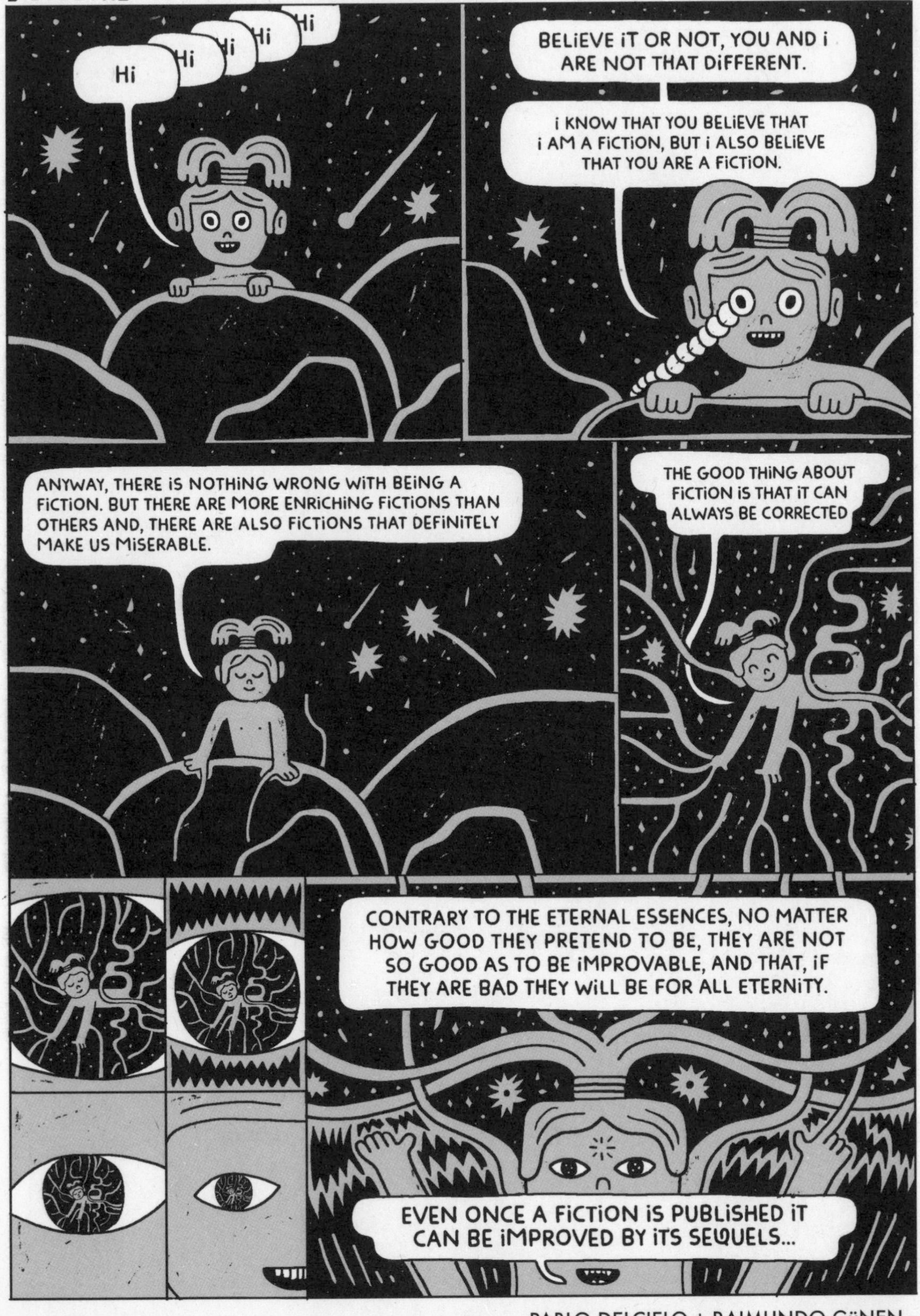
Hi
Hi
Hi
Hi
Hi
BELIEVE IT OR NOT, YOU AND I ARE NOT THAT DIFFERENT.
I KNOW THAT YOU BELIEVE THAT I AM A FICTION, BUT I ALSO BELIEVE THAT YOU ARE A FICTION.
ANYWAY, THERE IS NOTHING WRONG WITH BEING A FICTION. BUT THERE ARE MORE ENRICHING FICTIONS THAN OTHERS AND, THERE ARE ALSO FICTIONS THAT DEFINITELY MAKE US MISERABLE.
THE GOOD THING ABOUT FICTION IS THAT IT CAN ALWAYS BE CORRECTED
CONTRARY TO THE ETERNAL ESSENCES, NO MATTER HOW GOOD THEY PRETEND TO BE, THEY ARE NOT SO GOOD AS TO BE IMPROVABLE, AND THAT, IF THEY ARE BAD THEY WILL BE FOR ALL ETERNITY.
EVEN ONCE A FICTION IS PUBLISHED IT CAN BE IMPROVED BY ITS SEQUELS...

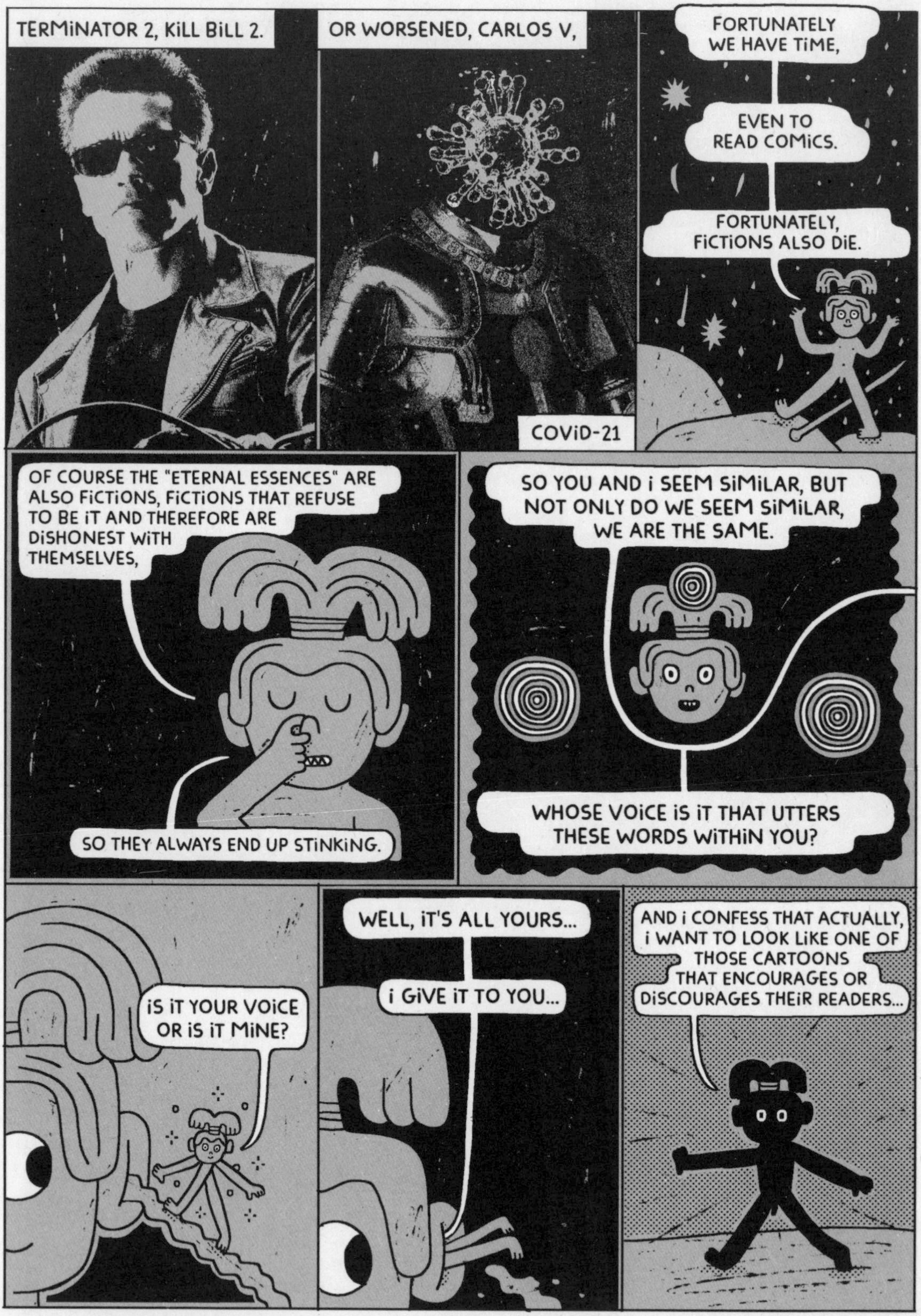
TERMiNATOR 2, KiLL BiLL 2.
OR WORSENED, CARLOS V,
COViD-21
FORTUNATELY WE HAVE TiME,
EVEN TO READ COMiCS.
FORTUNATELY, FiCTiONS ALSO DiE.
OF COURSE THE "ETERNAL ESSENCES" ARE ALSO FiCTiONS, FiCTiONS THAT REFUSE TO BE iT AND THEREFORE ARE DiSHONEST WiTH THEMSELVES,
SO THEY ALWAYS END UP STiNKiNG.
SO YOU AND i SEEM SiMiLAR, BUT NOT ONLY DO WE SEEM SiMiLAR, WE ARE THE SAME.
WHOSE VOiCE iS iT THAT UTTERS THESE WORDS WiTHiN YOU?
iS iT YOUR VOiCE OR iS iT MiNE?
WELL, iT'S ALL YOURS...
i GiVE iT TO YOU...
AND i CONFESS THAT ACTUALLY, i WANT TO LOOK LiKE ONE OF THOSE CARTOONS THAT ENCOURAGES OR DiSCOURAGES THEIR READERS...

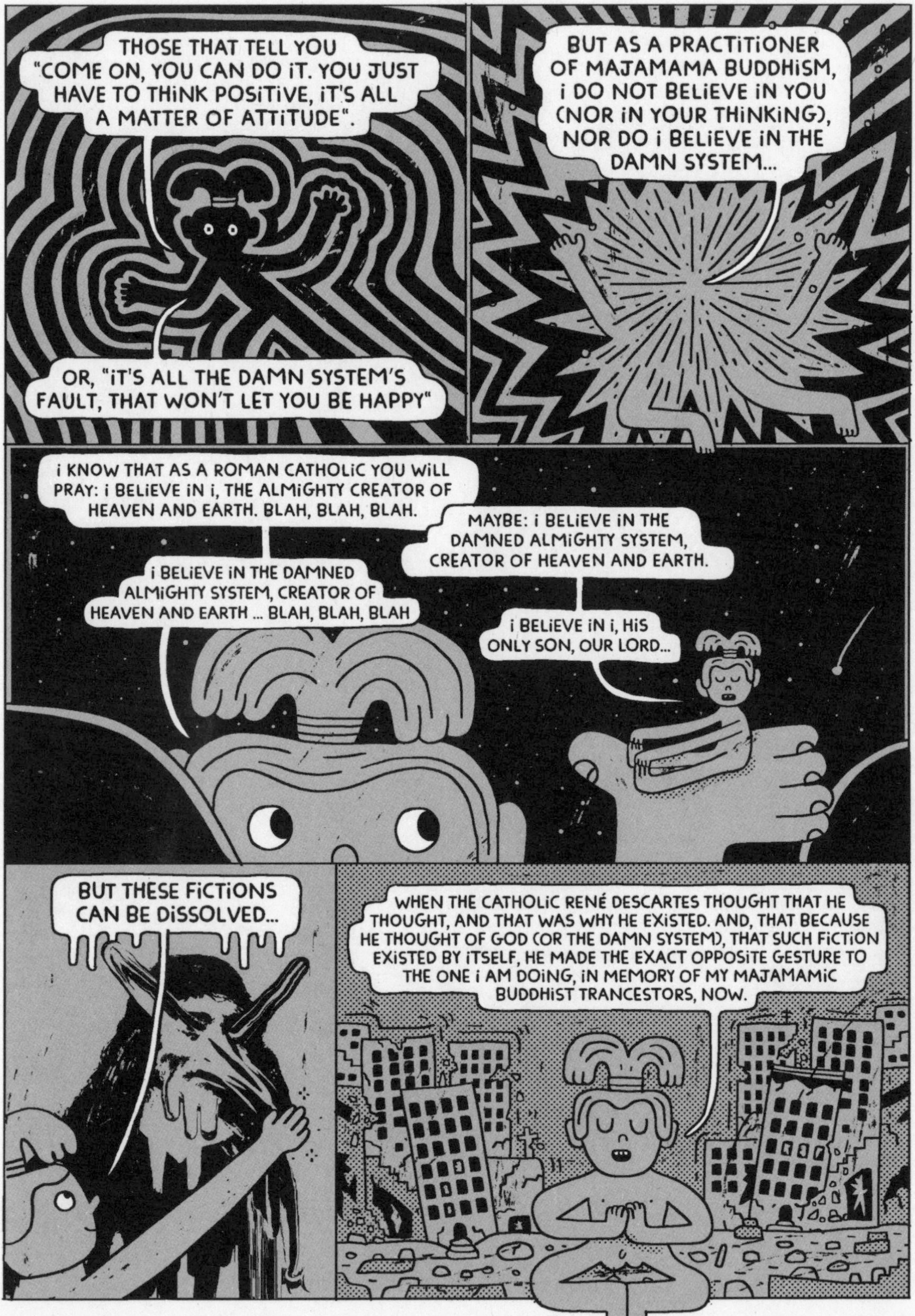
THOSE THAT TELL YOU "COME ON, YOU CAN DO iT. YOU JUST HAVE TO THiNK POSiTiVE, iT'S ALL A MATTER OF ATTiTUDE".
OR, "iT'S ALL THE DAMN SYSTEM'S FAULT, THAT WON'T LET YOU BE HAPPY"
BUT AS A PRACTiTiONER OF MAJAMAMA BUDDHiSM, i DO NOT BELiEVE iN YOU (NOR iN YOUR THiNKiNG), NOR DO i BELiEVE iN THE DAMN SYSTEM...
i KNOW THAT AS A ROMAN CATHOLiC YOU WiLL PRAY: i BELiEVE iN i, THE ALMiGHTY CREATOR OF HEAVEN AND EARTH. BLAH, BLAH, BLAH.
i BELiEVE iN THE DAMNED ALMiGHTY SYSTEM, CREATOR OF HEAVEN AND EARTH ... BLAH, BLAH, BLAH
MAYBE: i BELiEVE iN THE DAMNED ALMiGHTY SYSTEM, CREATOR OF HEAVEN AND EARTH.
i BELiEVE iN i, HiS ONLY SON, OUR LORD...
BUT THESE FiCTiONS CAN BE DiSSOLVED...
WHEN THE CATHOLiC RENÉ DESCARTES THOUGHT THAT HE THOUGHT, AND THAT WAS WHY HE EXiSTED. AND, THAT BECAUSE HE THOUGHT OF GOD (OR THE DAMN SYSTEM), THAT SUCH FiCTiON EXiSTED BY iTSELF, HE MADE THE EXACT OPPOSiTE GESTURE TO THE ONE i AM DOiNG, iN MEMORY OF MY MAJAMAMiC BUDDHiST TRANCESTORS, NOW.

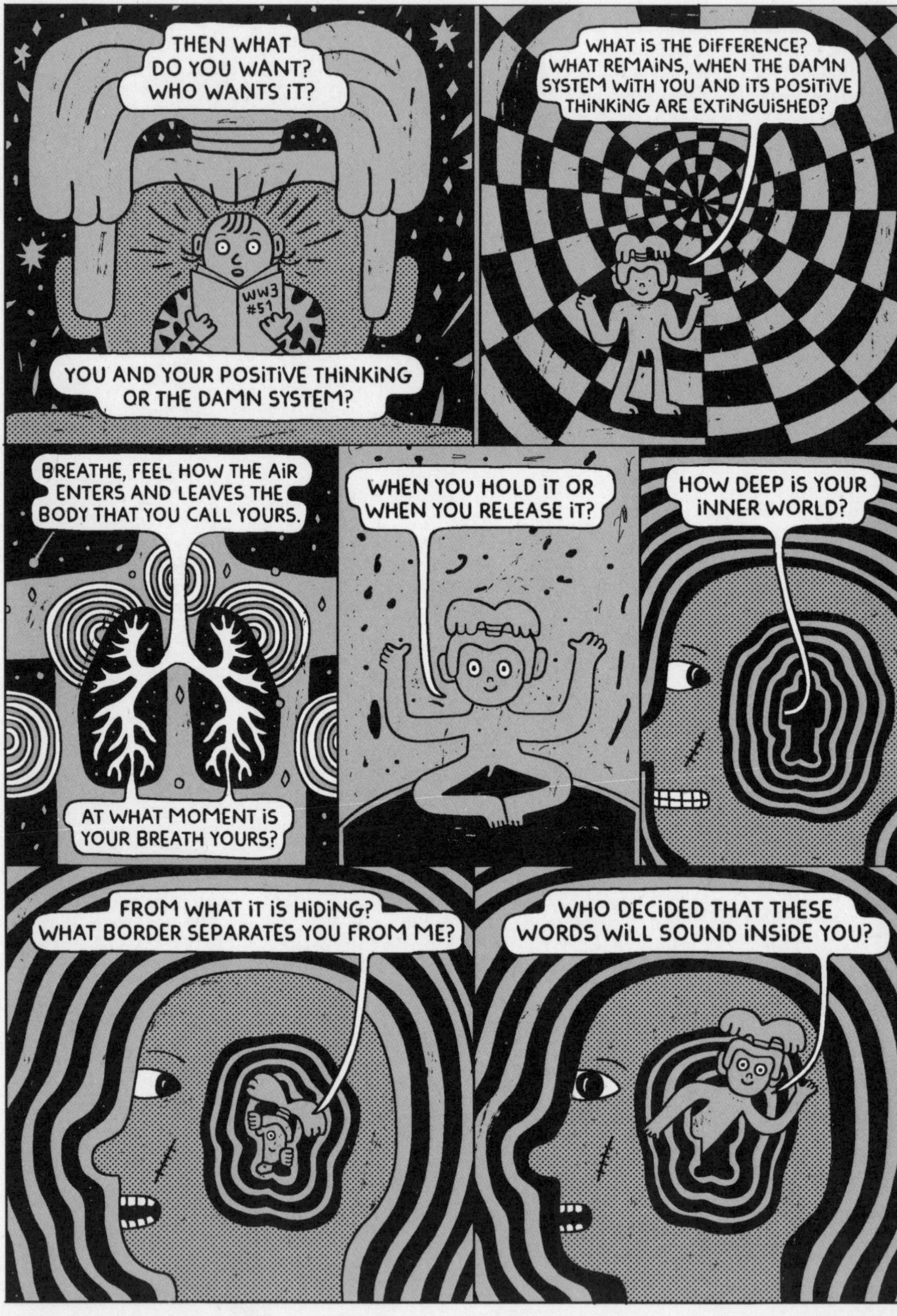
THEN WHAT DO YOU WANT? WHO WANTS iT?
WW3 #51
YOU AND YOUR POSiTiVE THiNKiNG OR THE DAMN SYSTEM?
WHAT iS THE DiFFERENCE? WHAT REMAiNS, WHEN THE DAMN SYSTEM WiTH YOU AND iTS POSiTiVE THiNKiNG ARE EXTiNGUiSHED?
BREATHE, FEEL HOW THE AiR ENTERS AND LEAVES THE BODY THAT YOU CALL YOURS.
AT WHAT MOMENT iS YOUR BREATH YOURS?
WHEN YOU HOLD iT OR WHEN YOU RELEASE iT?
HOW DEEP iS YOUR iNNER WORLD?
FROM WHAT iT iS HiDiNG? WHAT BORDER SEPARATES YOU FROM ME?
WHO DECiDED THAT THESE WORDS WiLL SOUND iNSiDE YOU?

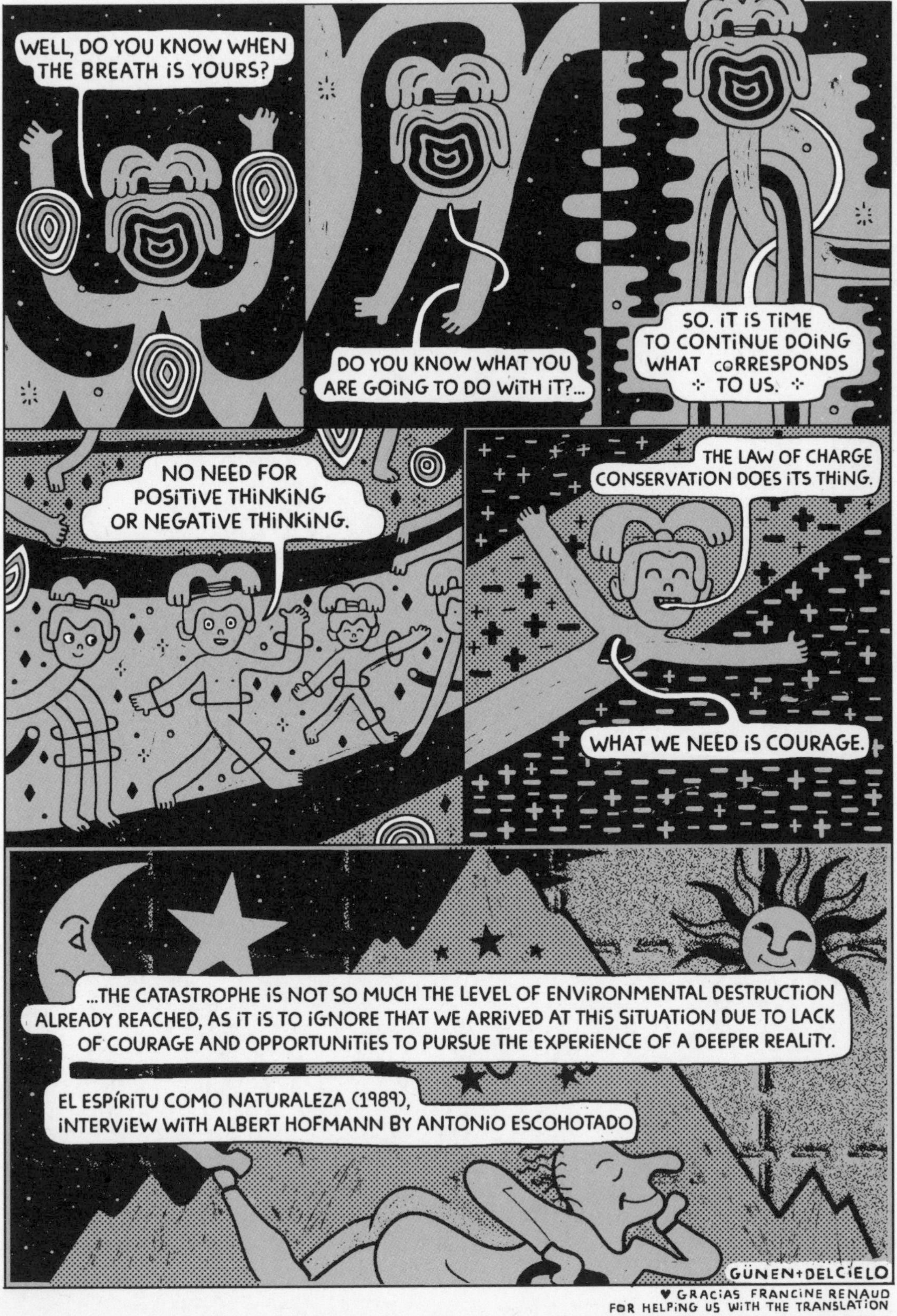
WELL, DO YOU KNOW WHEN THE BREATH IS YOURS?
DO YOU KNOW WHAT YOU ARE GOING TO DO WITH IT?...
SO. IT IS TIME TO CONTINUE DOING WHAT CORRESPONDS TO US.
NO NEED FOR POSITIVE THINKING OR NEGATIVE THINKING.
THE LAW OF CHARGE CONSERVATION DOES ITS THING.
WHAT WE NEED IS COURAGE.
...THE CATASTROPHE IS NOT SO MUCH THE LEVEL OF ENVIRONMENTAL DESTRUCTION ALREADY REACHED, AS IT IS TO IGNORE THAT WE ARRIVED AT THIS SITUATION DUE TO LACK OF COURAGE AND OPPORTUNITIES TO PURSUE THE EXPERIENCE OF A DEEPER REALITY.
EL ESPÍRITU COMO NATURALEZA (1989), INTERVIEW WITH ALBERT HOFMANN BY ANTONIO ESCOHOTADO
GÜNEN+DELCIELO

♥ GRACIAS FRANCINE RENAUD FOR HELPING US WITH THE TRANSLATION

WHAT WILL REMAIN

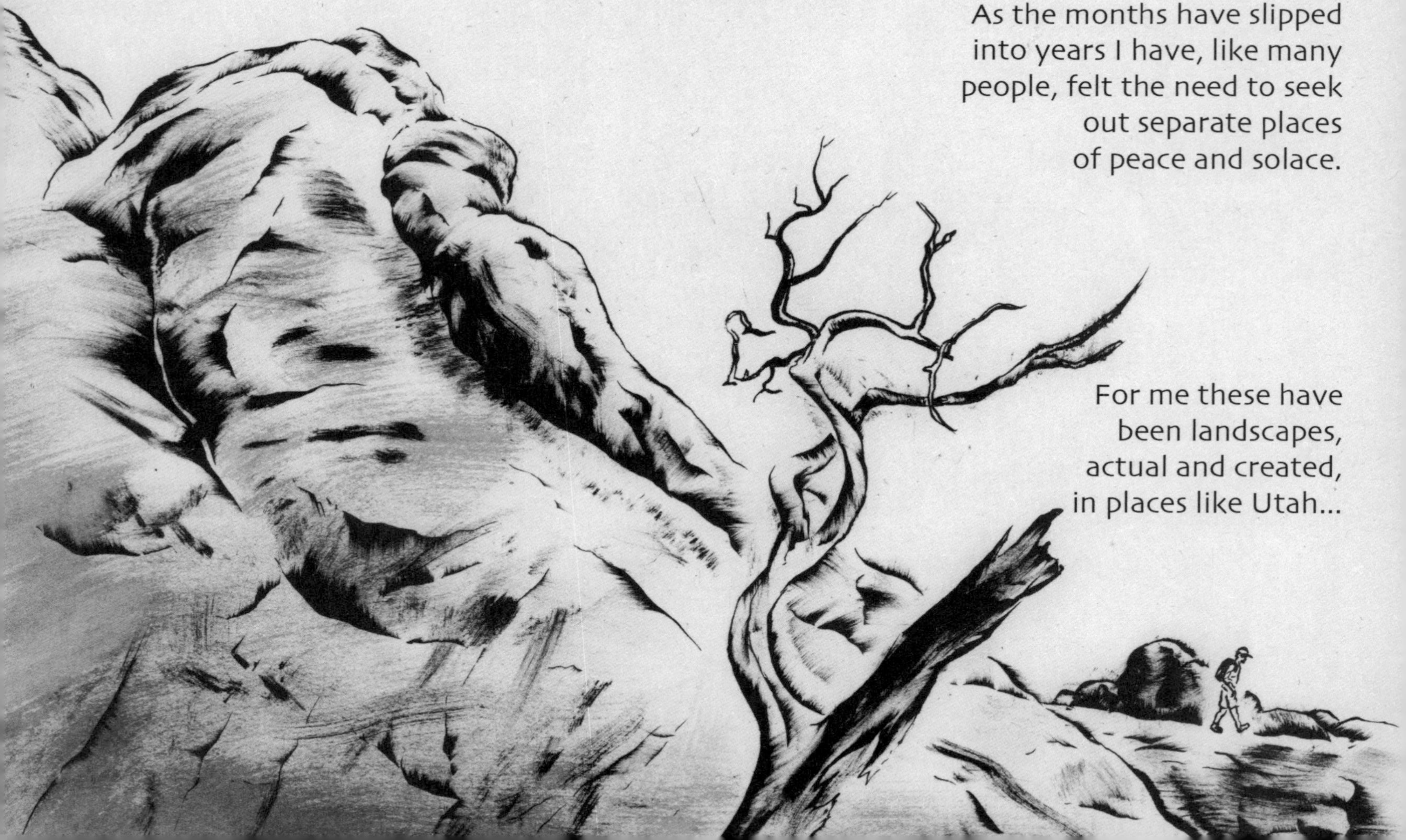

As the months have slipped into years I have, like many people, felt the need to seek out separate places of peace and solace.

For me these have been landscapes, actual and created, in places like Utah...

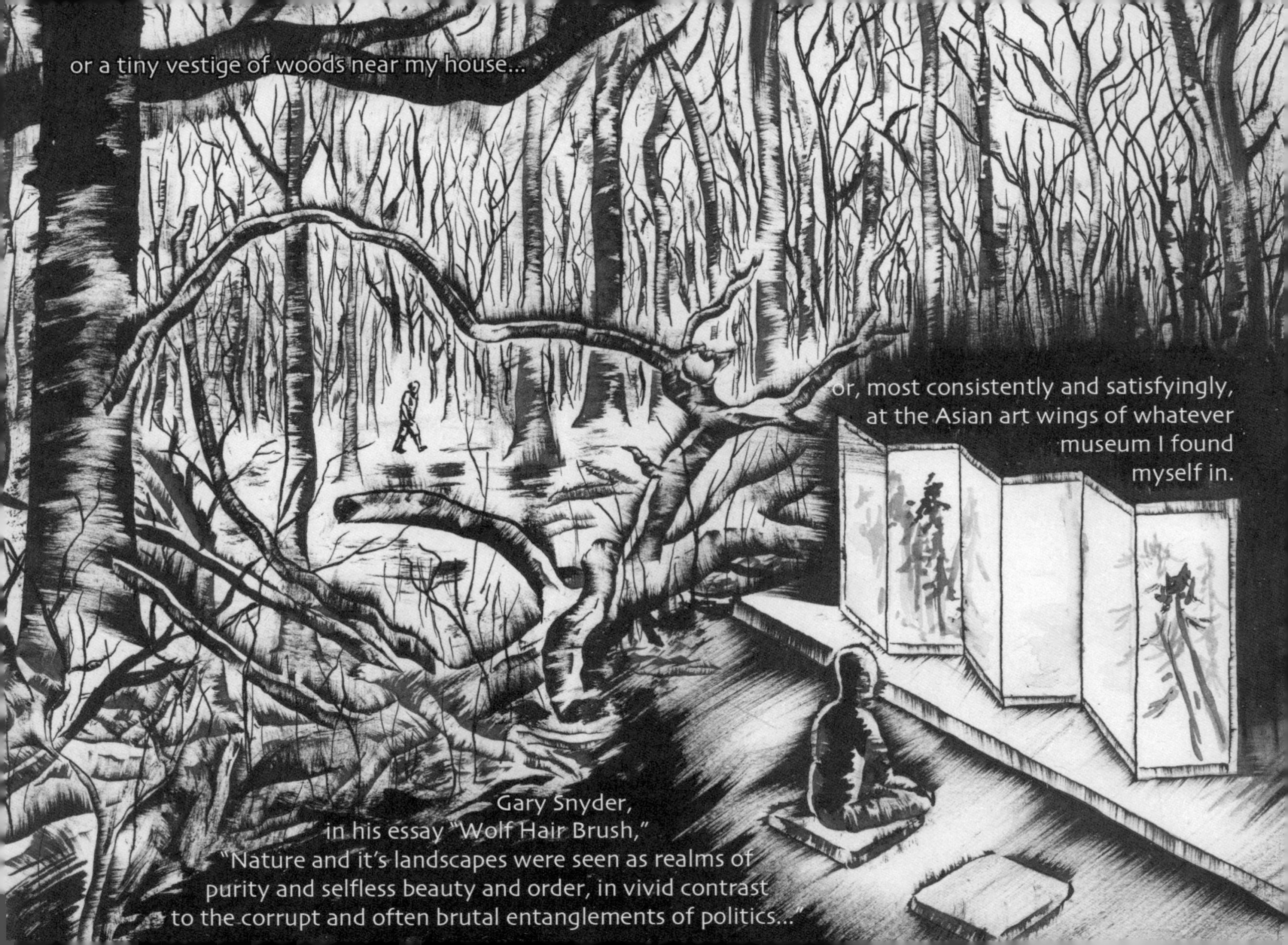
or a tiny vestige of woods near my house...
or, most consistently and satisfyingly,
at the Asian art wings of whatever
museum I found
myself in.
Gary Snyder,
in his essay "Wolf Hair Brush,"
"Nature and it's landscapes were seen as realms of
purity and selfless beauty and order, in vivid contrast
to the corrupt and often brutal entanglements of politics..."

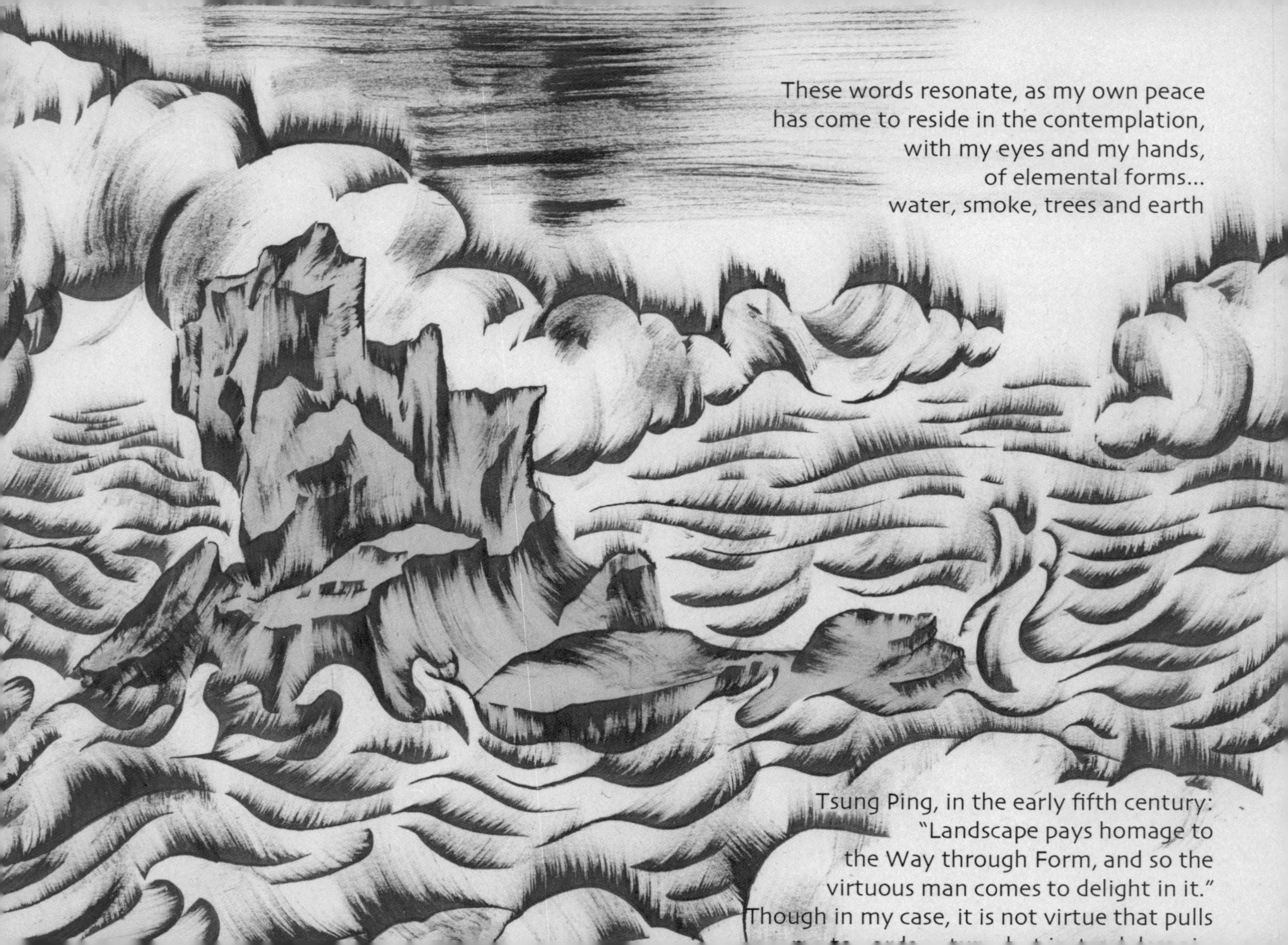

These words resonate, as my own peace
has come to reside in the contemplation,
with my eyes and my hands,
of elemental forms...
water, smoke, trees and earth

Tsung Ping, in the early fifth century:
"Landscape pays homage to
the Way through Form, and so the
virtuous man comes to delight in it."
Though in my case, it is not virtue that pulls

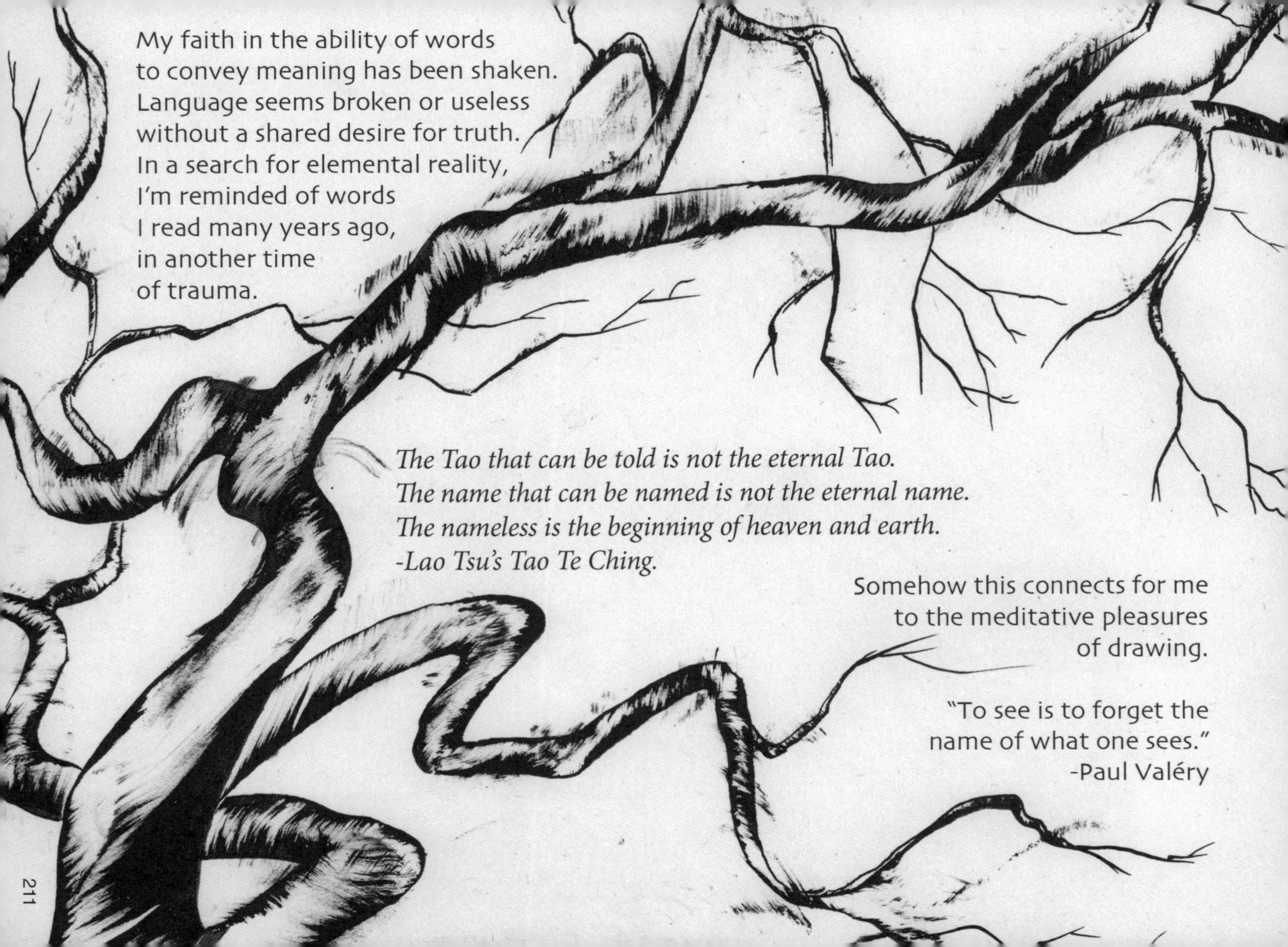

My faith in the ability of words
to convey meaning has been shaken.
Language seems broken or useless
without a shared desire for truth.
In a search for elemental reality,
I'm reminded of words
I read many years ago,
in another time
of trauma.

The Tao that can be told is not the eternal Tao.
The name that can be named is not the eternal name.
The nameless is the beginning of heaven and earth.
-Lao Tsu's Tao Te Ching.

Somehow this connects for me
to the meditative pleasures
of drawing.

"To see is to forget the
name of what one sees."
-Paul Valéry

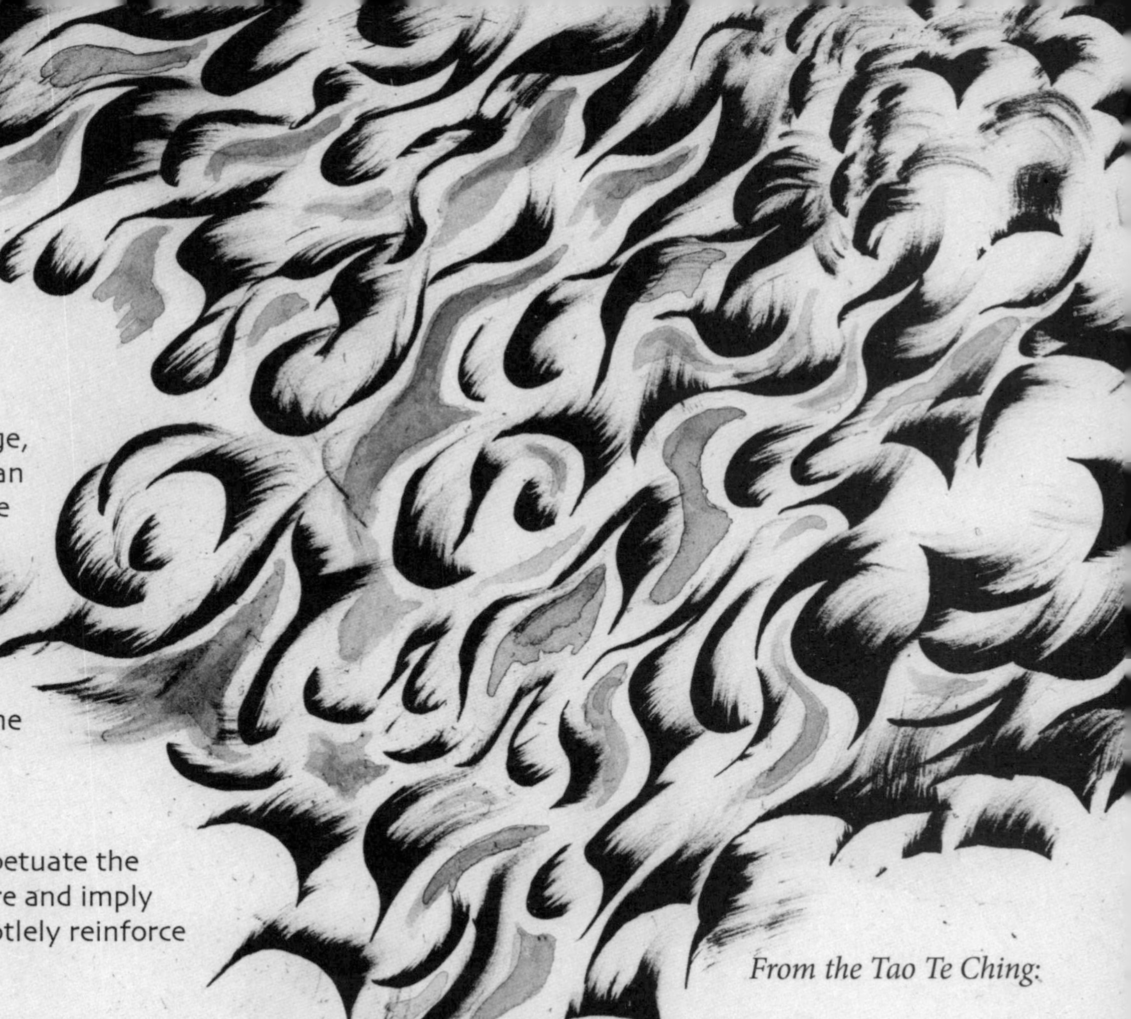

But we can't escape language.
It is human nature to name things.
It provides insight but also complicates.

Our new landscape needs a new name.

Anthropocene: the current geological age, viewed as the period during which human activity has been the dominant influence on climate and the environment.

Anthro: Human

With it's embrace of the monumental - the naming of an epoch, the word has the effect of both raising the stakes and clearly naming who's to blame.

But in centering humankind does it perpetuate the dynamic of man's dominance over nature and imply to be human is to exploit?–And thus subtlely reinforce a perceived inevitability.

Another name has been invented, the Capitalocene: the current geological age, viewed as the period during which capitalist activity has been the dominant influence on climate and the environment.
Does this name open the possibility that man could resist exploitation of the earth?

From the Tao Te Ching:

Conquering the world and changing it,
I do not think it can succeed.
The world is a sacred vessel
that cannot be changed.
He who changes it will destroy it.
He who seizes it will lose it.

Yet another possible contender to describe our current time is the Necrocene. An epoch defined by death.

“From the standpoint of the Necrocene, capital appears as a species, an opportunistic detritus feeder producing mass extinction...”
- Justin McBrien, Accumulating Extinction

Like a virus.

Theologian Thomas Berry places humanity at a crossroads between the Ecozoic era, characterized by a harmony with the planet’s eco-systems or a Techozoic era, where humanity completely dominates and exploits nature through technical mastery.

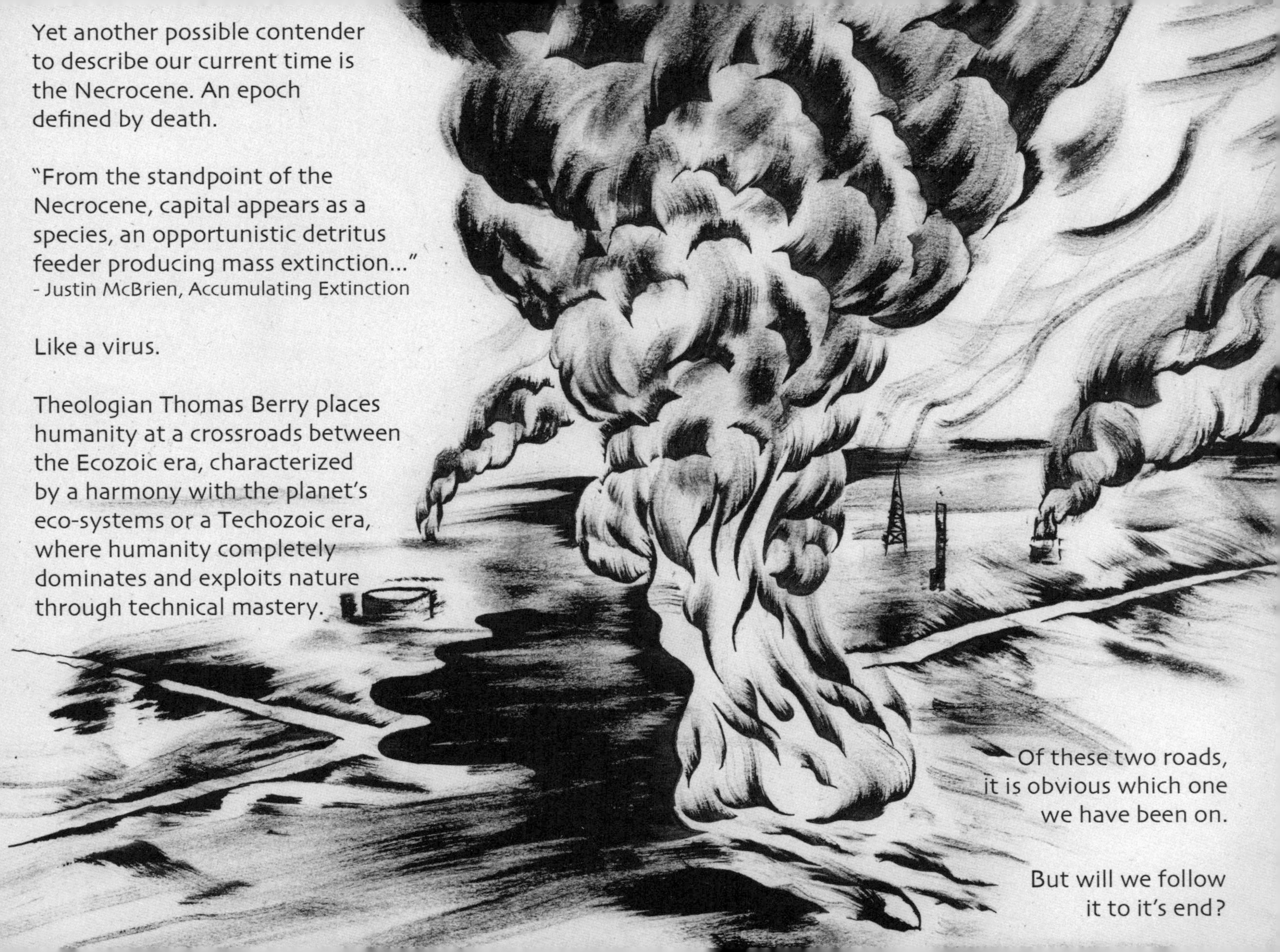

Of these two roads, it is obvious which one we have been on.

But will we follow it to it’s end?

The deepest expression of the Tao, or the Way, is in the interplay of absence and presence, the process of becoming and disappearing.
It is also the philosophical underpinning of the Chinese landscape tradition.

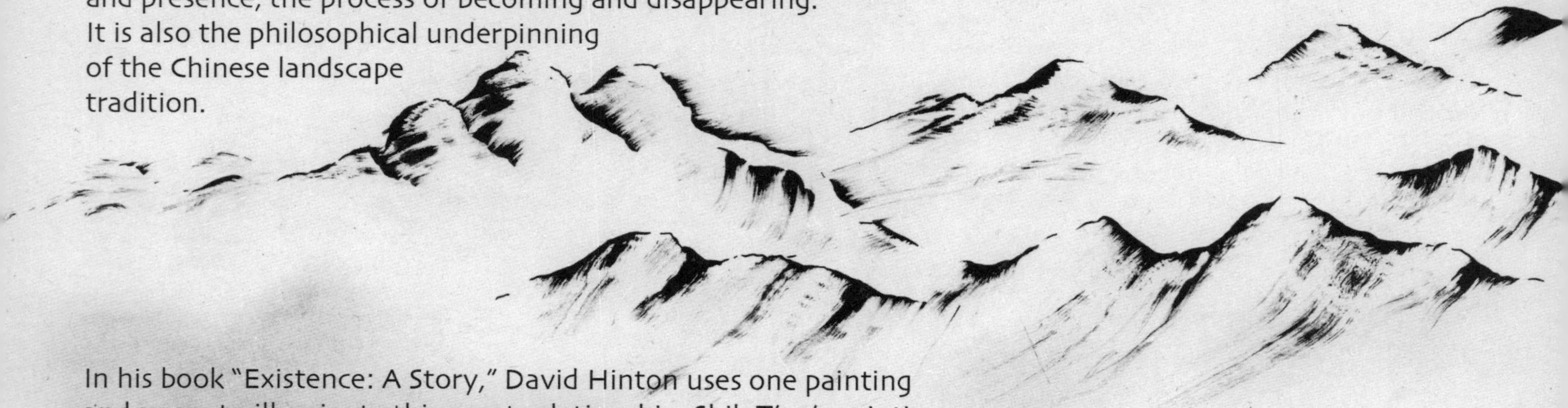

In his book "Existence: A Story," David Hinton uses one painting and poem to illuminate this exact relationship. Shih T'ao's painting "Broad-Distance Pavillion," depicts an artist-intellectual and his attendant overlooking a void shrouded in mist. That which is shrouded is revealed only in the text:

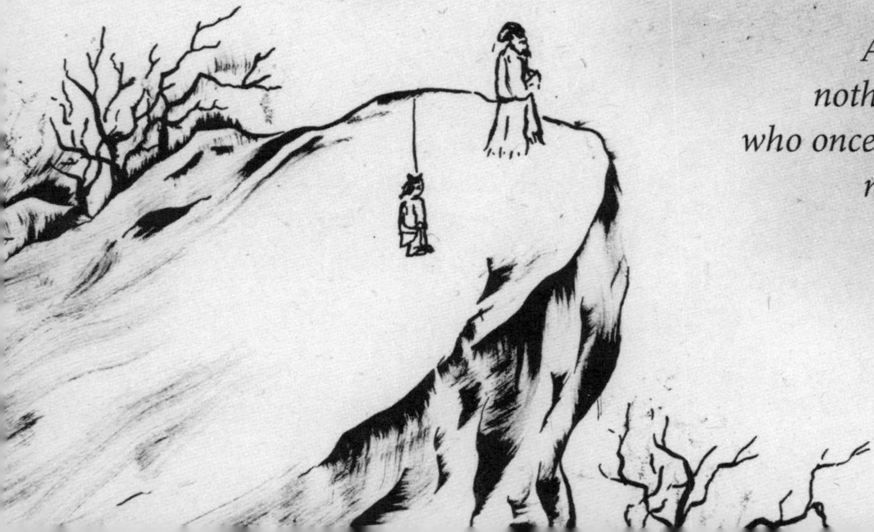

Abandoned houses, city-wall gates,
nothing left unbroken but a crimson wall:
who once tended these family orchards and gardens
now tangled in emerald wildgrass?

The image and the poem capture the act of "encountering an absence" as the writer Robert MacFarlane phrases it.
It can't help but also conjure a possible future- a world without us.

But Taoists don't separate the phenomenon of absence and presence into opposing realities but unite them into a single generative reality- Qi or Ch'i

This Ch'i is made visible in landscape painting.
It resides in the emptiness of the mist,
where forms blur.
In the writhing energy
of the mountainous
waves of stone.

So, if we destroy it all,
all the animal life,
all the plant life, as if it was
separate and disconnected from
us, we will ultimately
destroy ourselves.

If we push it all into
the absence, into a silence
beyond language,
then the mountains,
vessels of the unnamable
and eternal, are what
will remain.

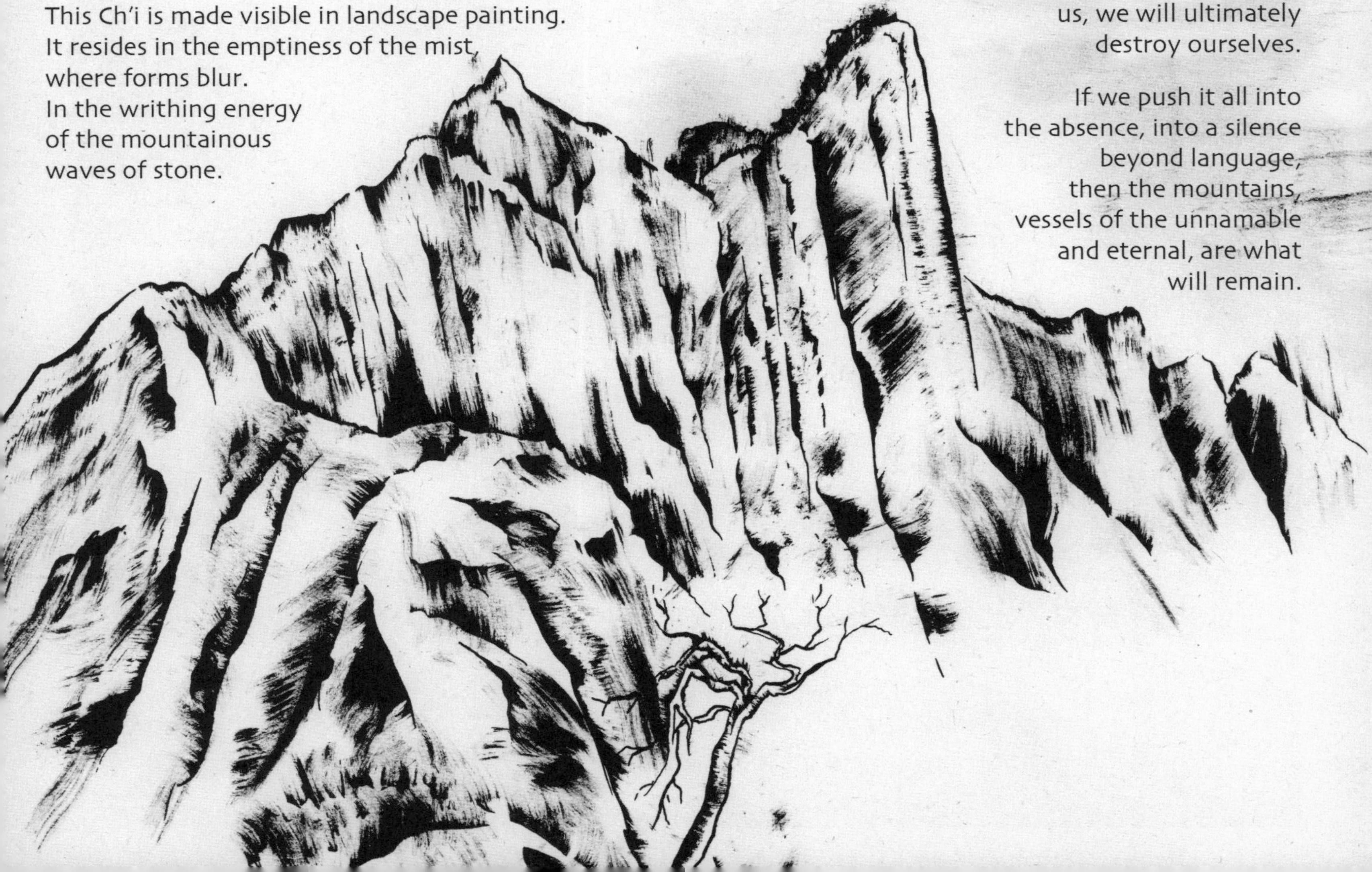

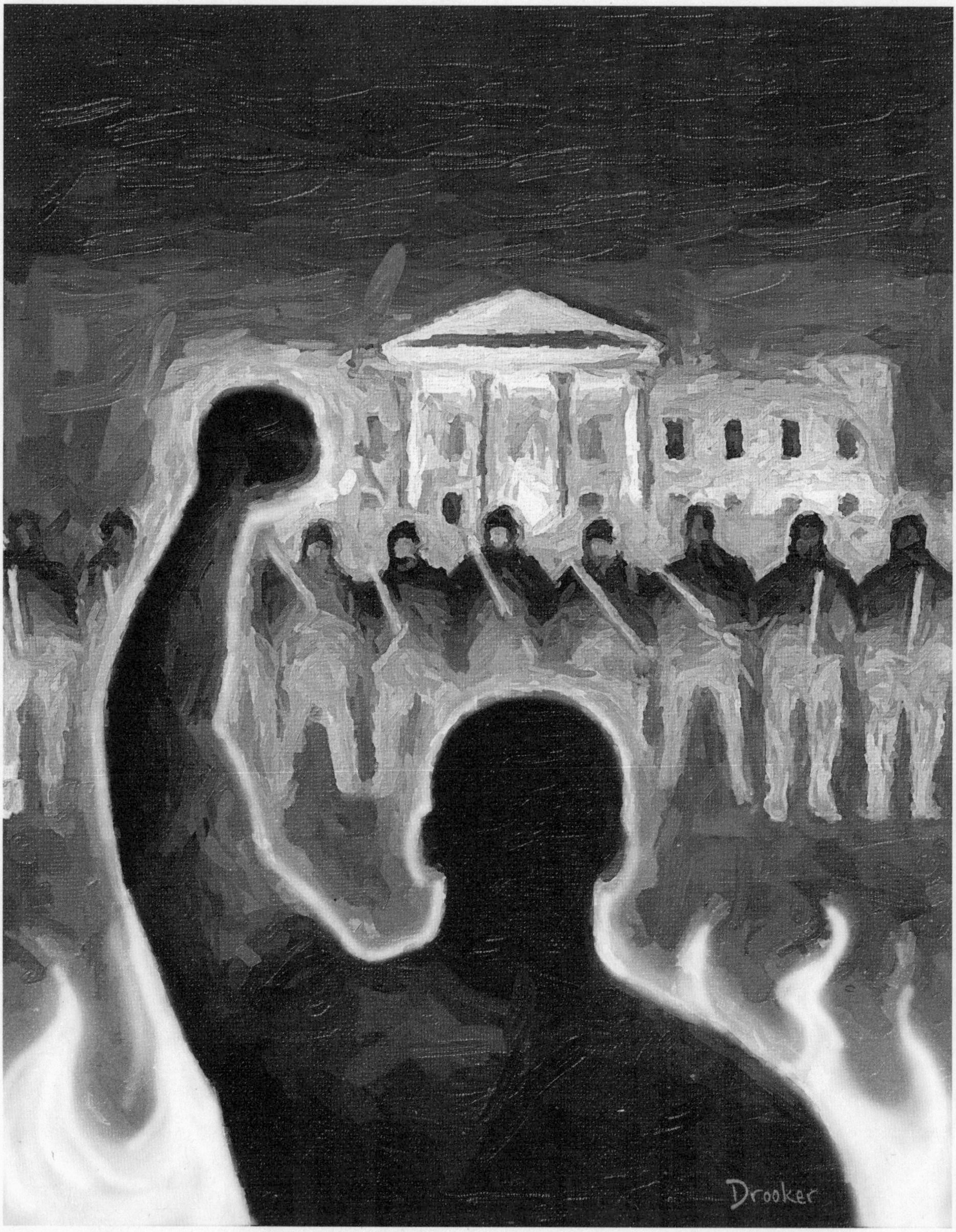
Drooker

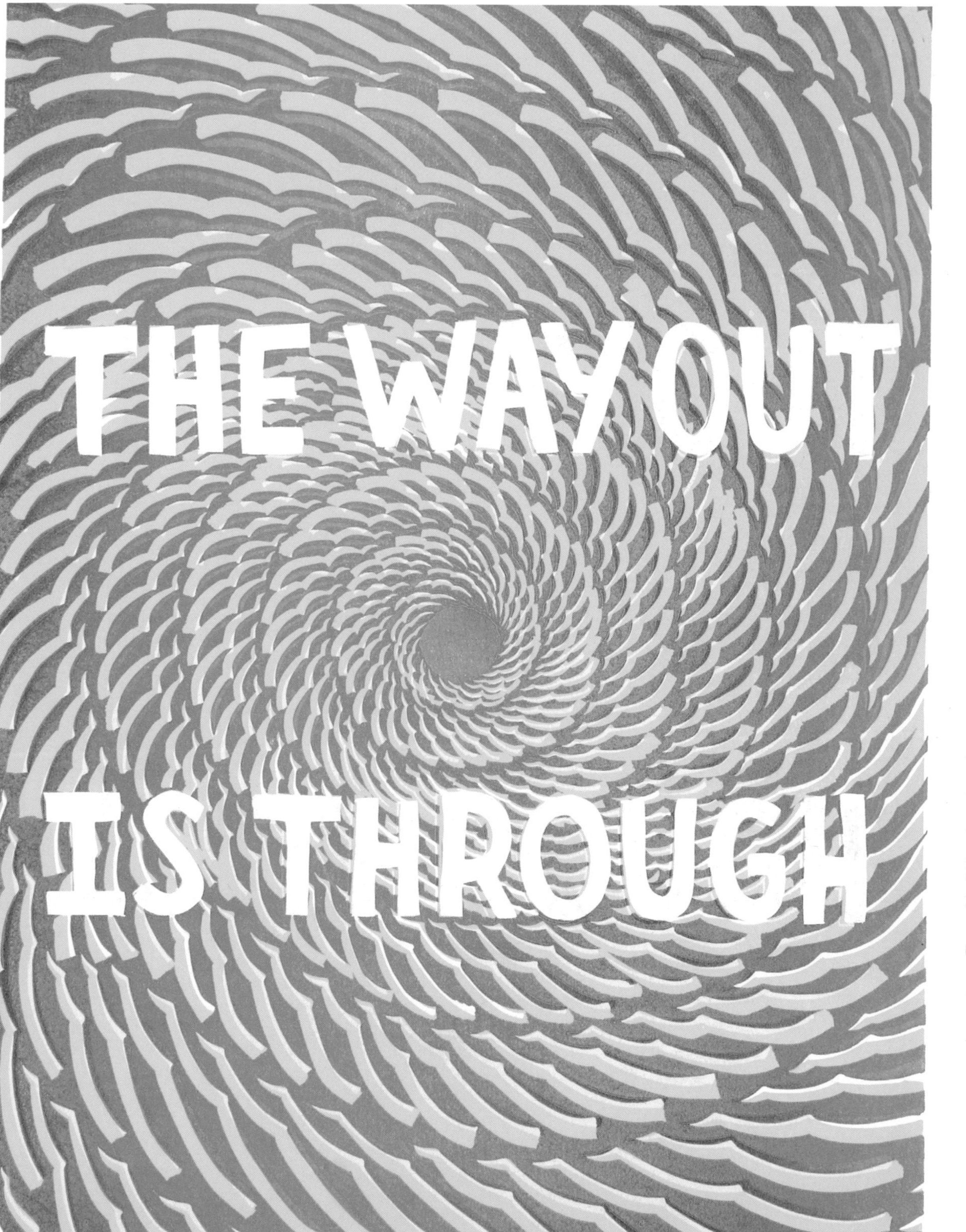
THE WAY OUT
IS THROUGH

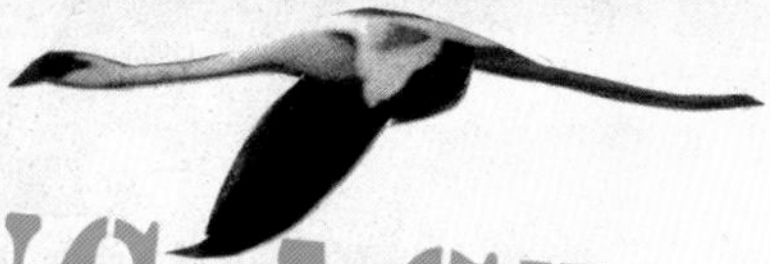

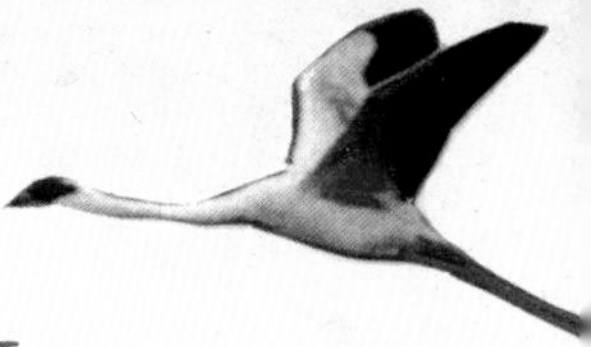

VANISHING ACT

by
Peter Kuper

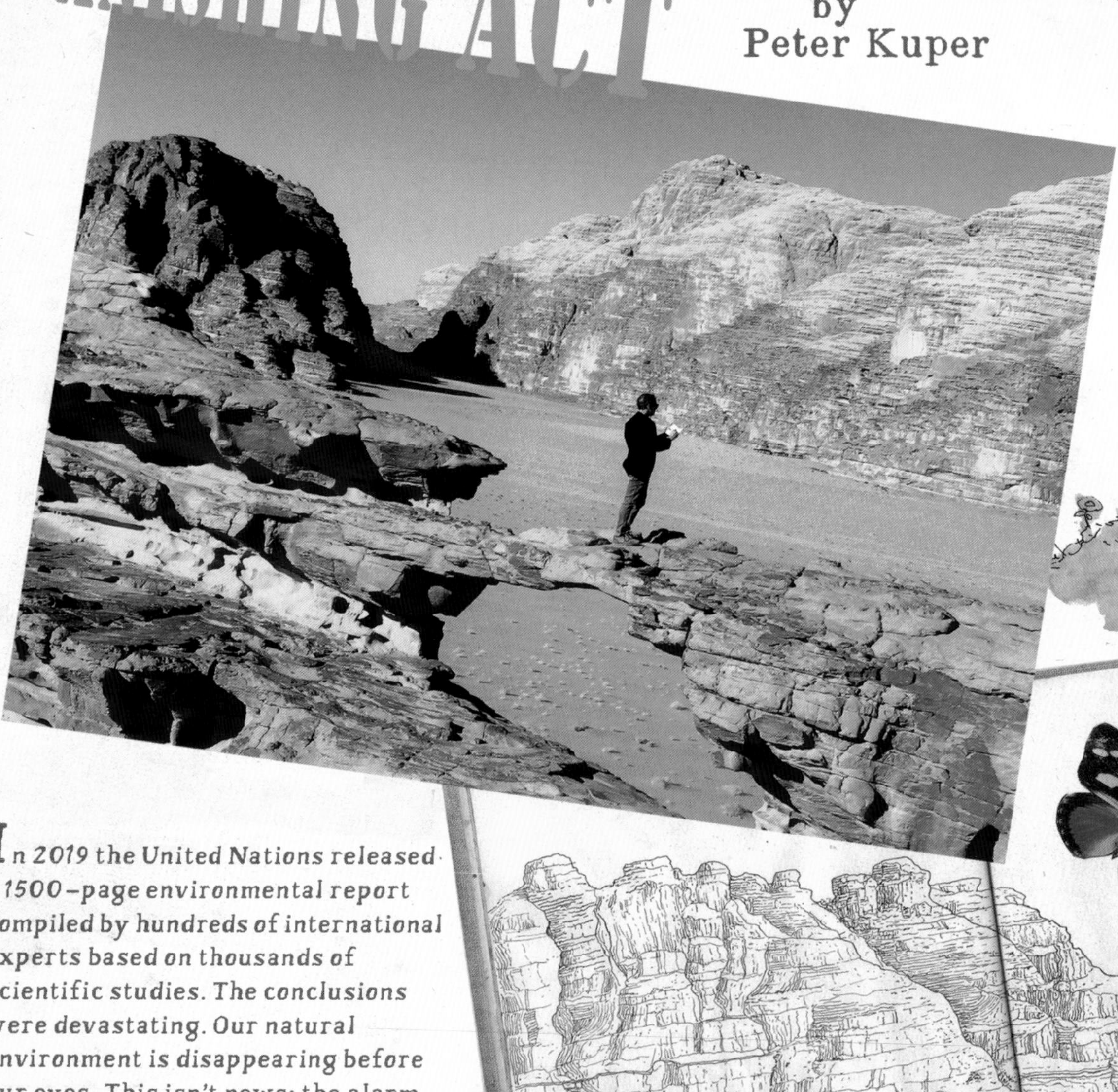

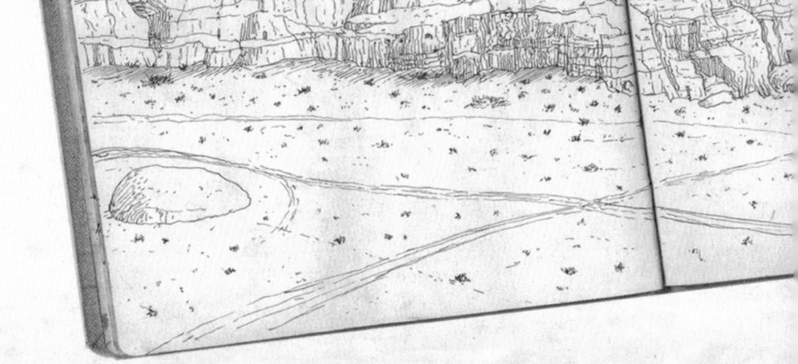

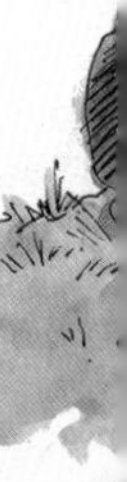

In 2019 the United Nations released a 1500-page environmental report compiled by hundreds of international experts based on thousands of scientific studies. The conclusions were devastating. Our natural environment is disappearing before our eyes. This isn't news; the alarm bells have been sounding for decades. Pondering the statistics, I found myself mentally traveling back to places I've recorded in my sketch-book—from Africa and South East Asia to South America and the Middle East, from dense rainforests to remote islands.*

*I'm aware that I've left a huge carbon foot-print getting to these places. My biggest trips came before I'd heard that term, but mea culpa.

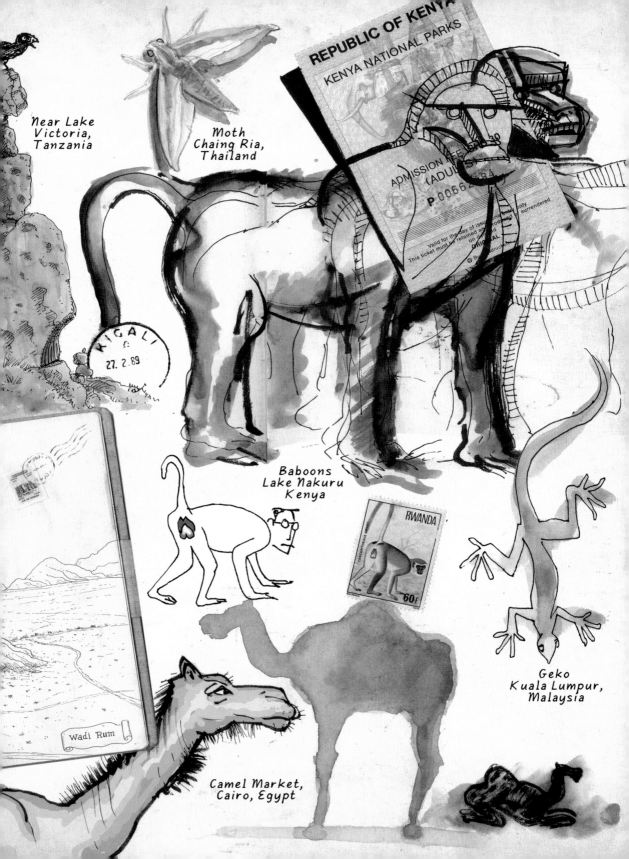

Near Lake
Victoria,
Tanzania

Moth
Chaing Ria,
Thailand

REPUBLIC OF KENYA

KENYA NATIONAL PARKS

ADMISSION FEE
(ADULTS)

P 00662

Valid for the day of issue and only
This ticket must be retained and produced
on demand
ORIGINAL

KIGALI
27. 2. 89

Baboons
Lake Nakuru
Kenya

RWANDA

60f

Geko
Kuala Lumpur,
Malaysia

Wadi Rum

Camel Market,
Cairo, Egypt

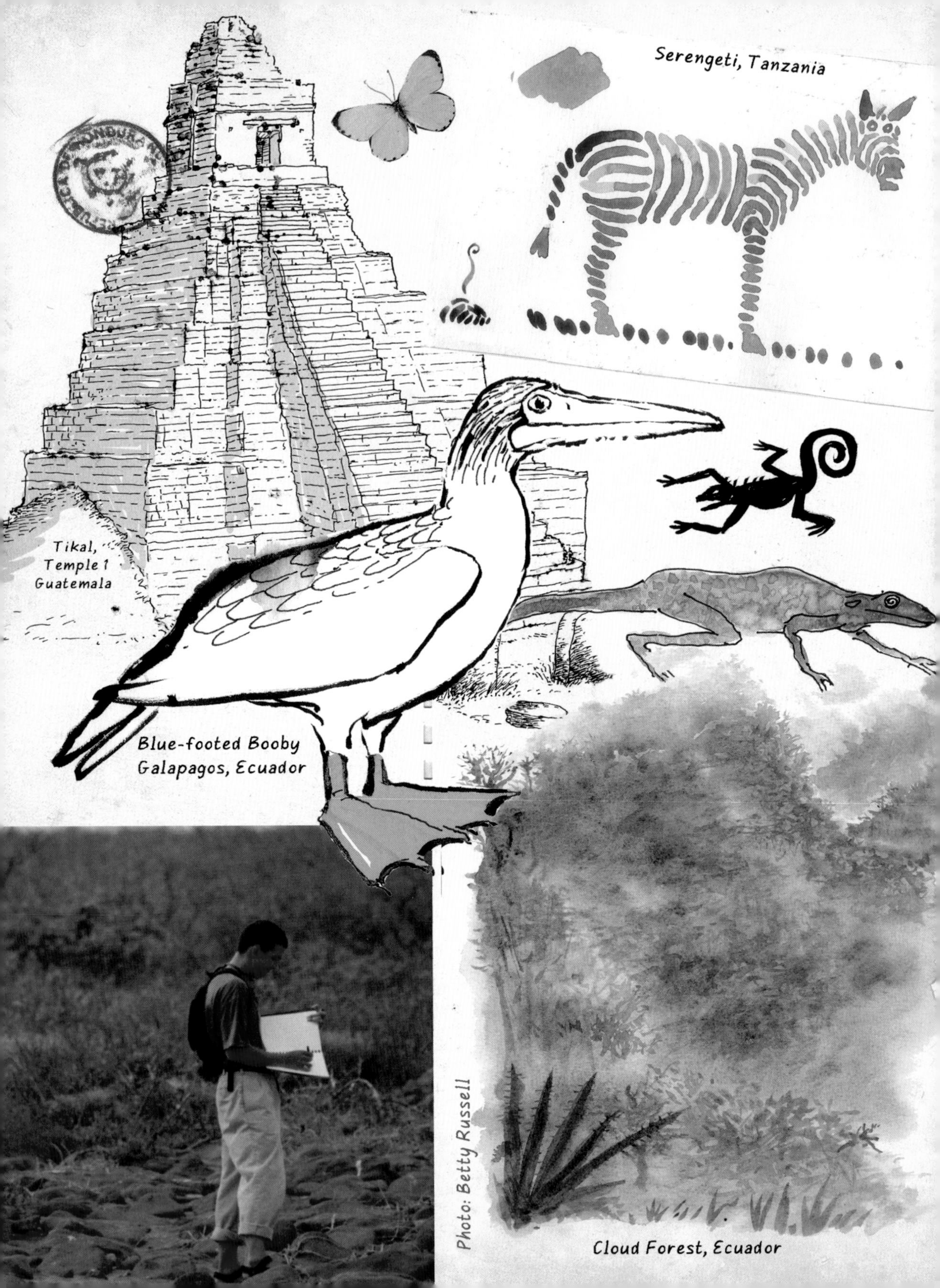
Serengeti, Tanzania
Tikal,
Temple 1
Guatemala
Blue-footed Booby
Galapagos, Ecuador
Photo: Betty Russell
Cloud Forest, Ecuador

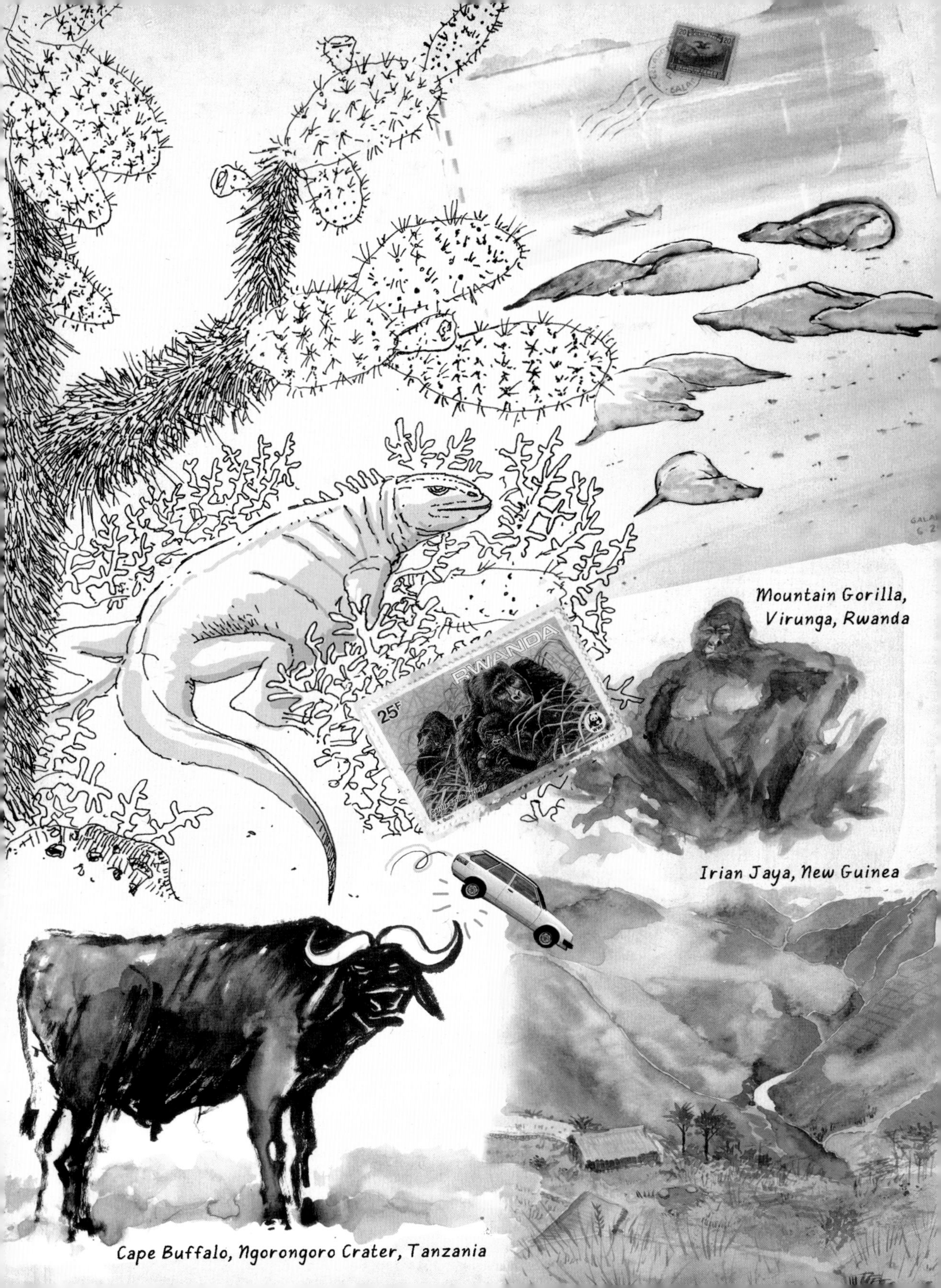
Mountain Gorilla,
Virunga, Rwanda
RWANDA
25F
Irian Jaya, New Guinea
Cape Buffalo, Ngorongoro Crater, Tanzania

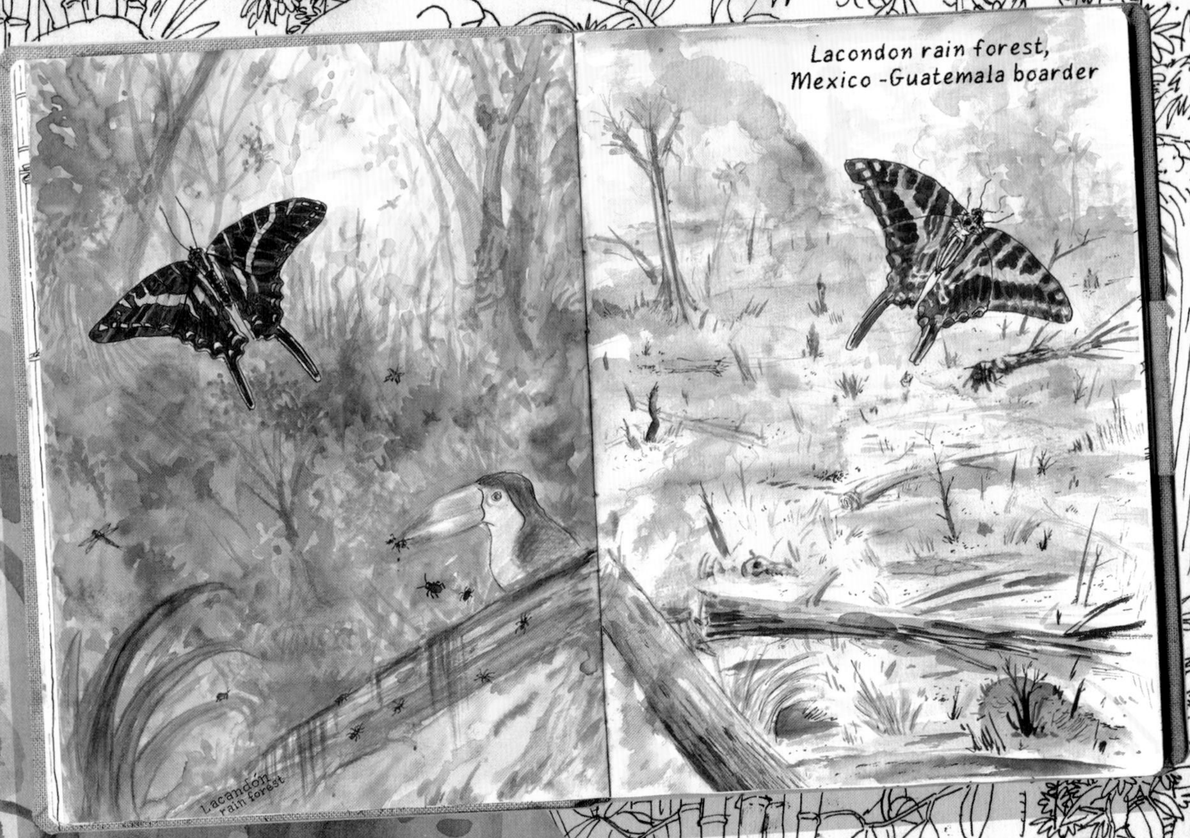
Lacondon rain forest,
Mexico -Guatemala boarder
Lacandón
rain forest

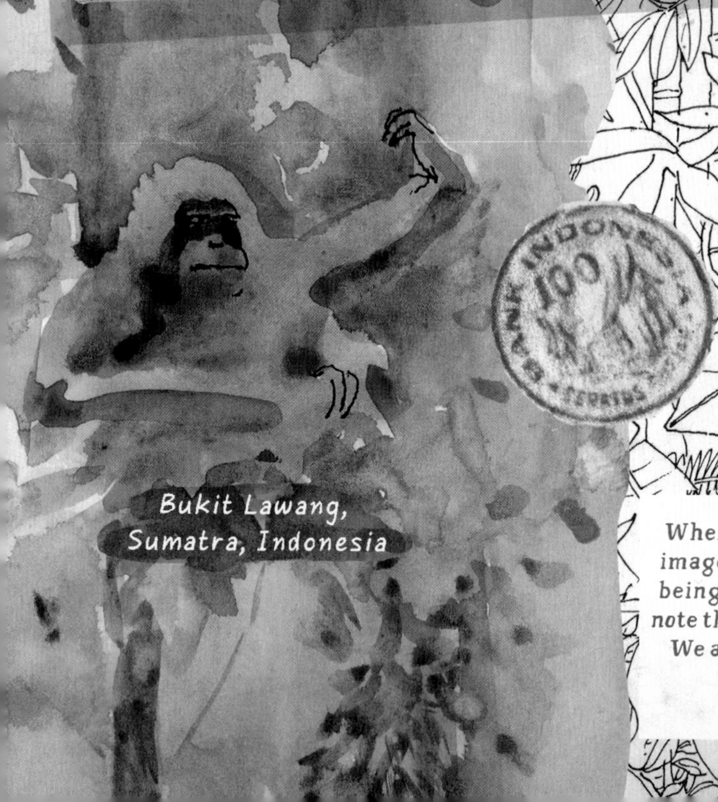
Bukit Lawang,
Sumatra, Indonesia
BANK INDONESIA
100
SERATUS

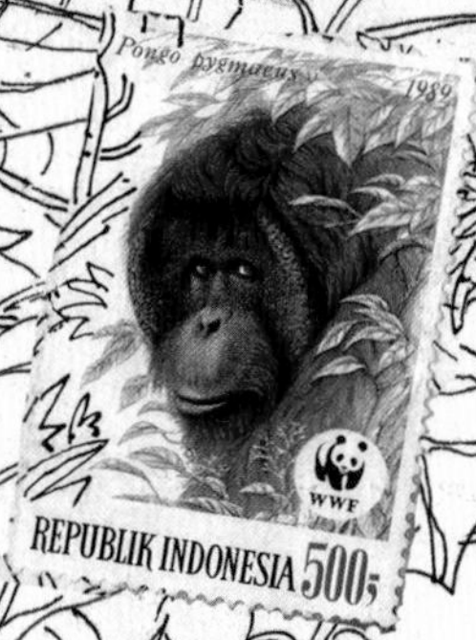
Pongo pygmaeus
1989
WWF
REPUBLIK INDONESIA 500

When I hear the word 'extinction' my first image is of dinosaurs. But that reference is being replaced every day by headlines that note the disappearance of species and cultures. We are now bearing witness to a planetary cataclysm that last occurred 66 million years ago.

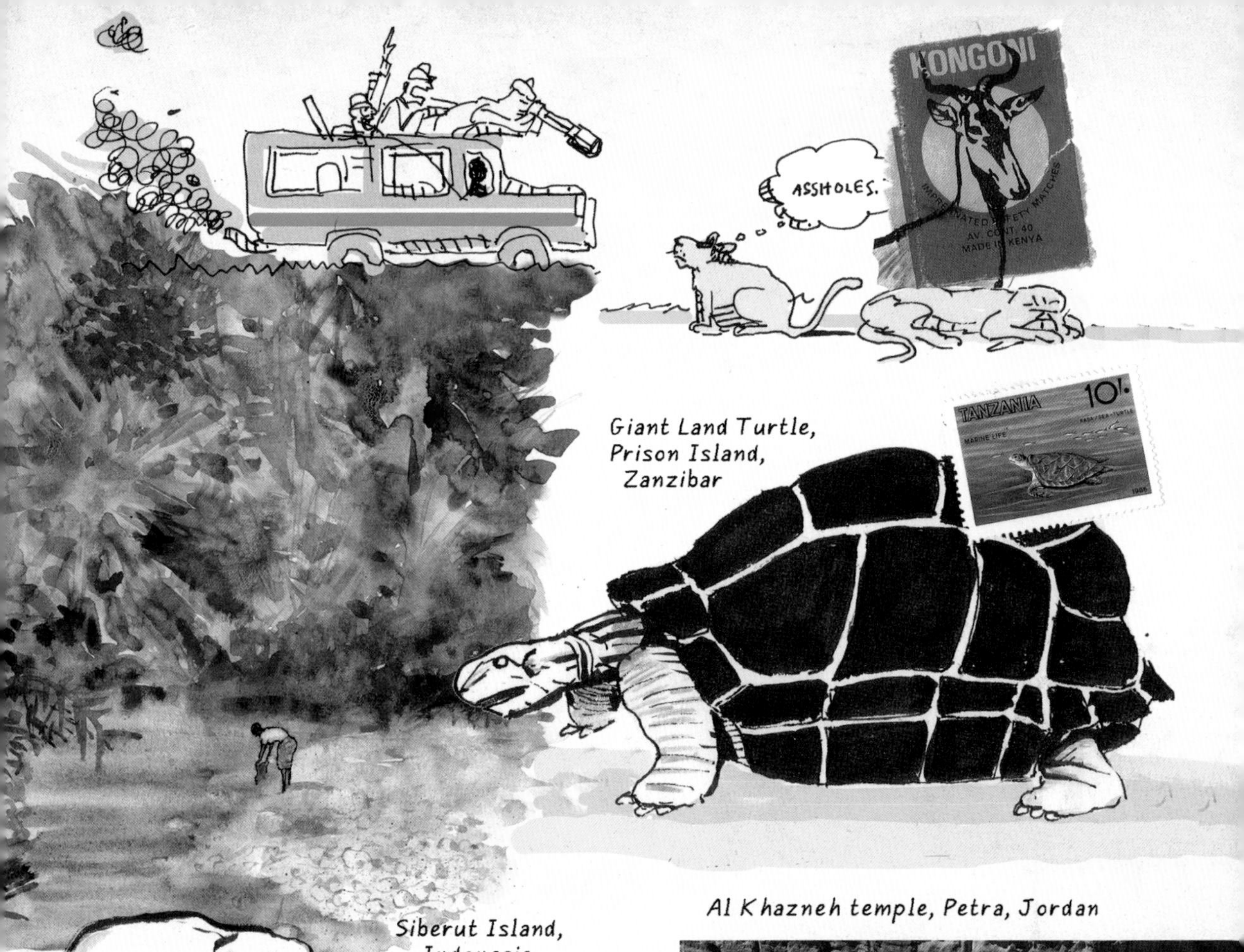
ASSHOLES.
KONGONI
AV. CONT. 40
MADE IN KENYA
TANZANIA
10/-
MARINE LIFE

Giant Land Turtle,
Prison Island,
Zanzibar

Siberut Island,
Indonesia

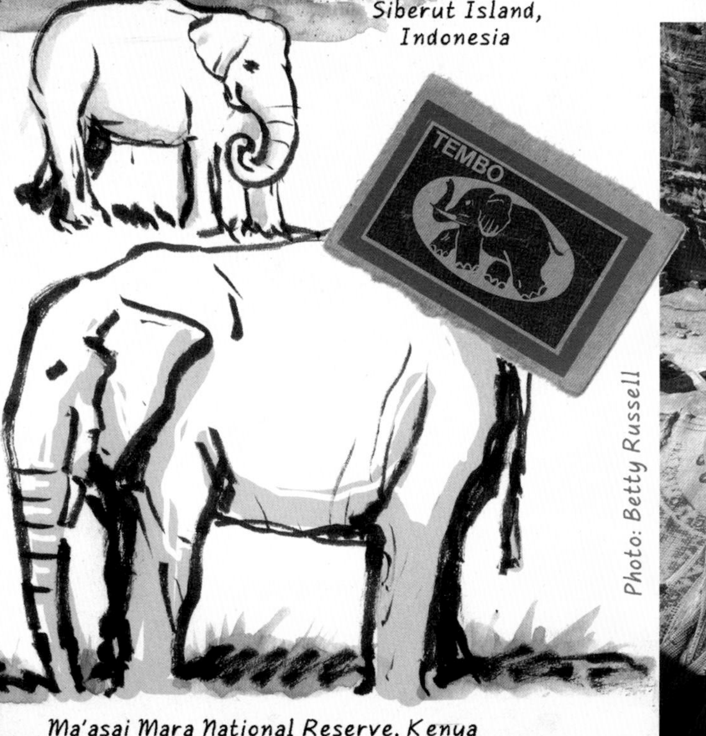
TEMBO

Ma'asai Mara National Reserve, Kenya

Al Khazneh temple, Petra, Jordan

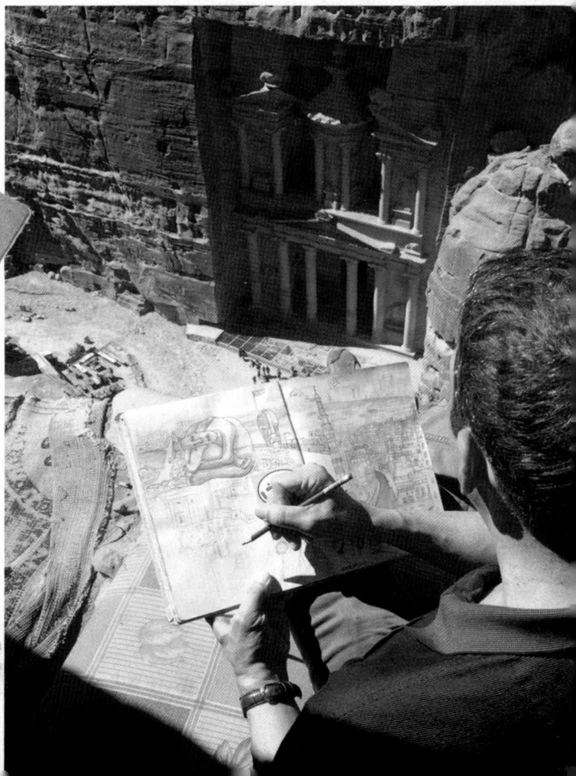

Photo: Betty Russell

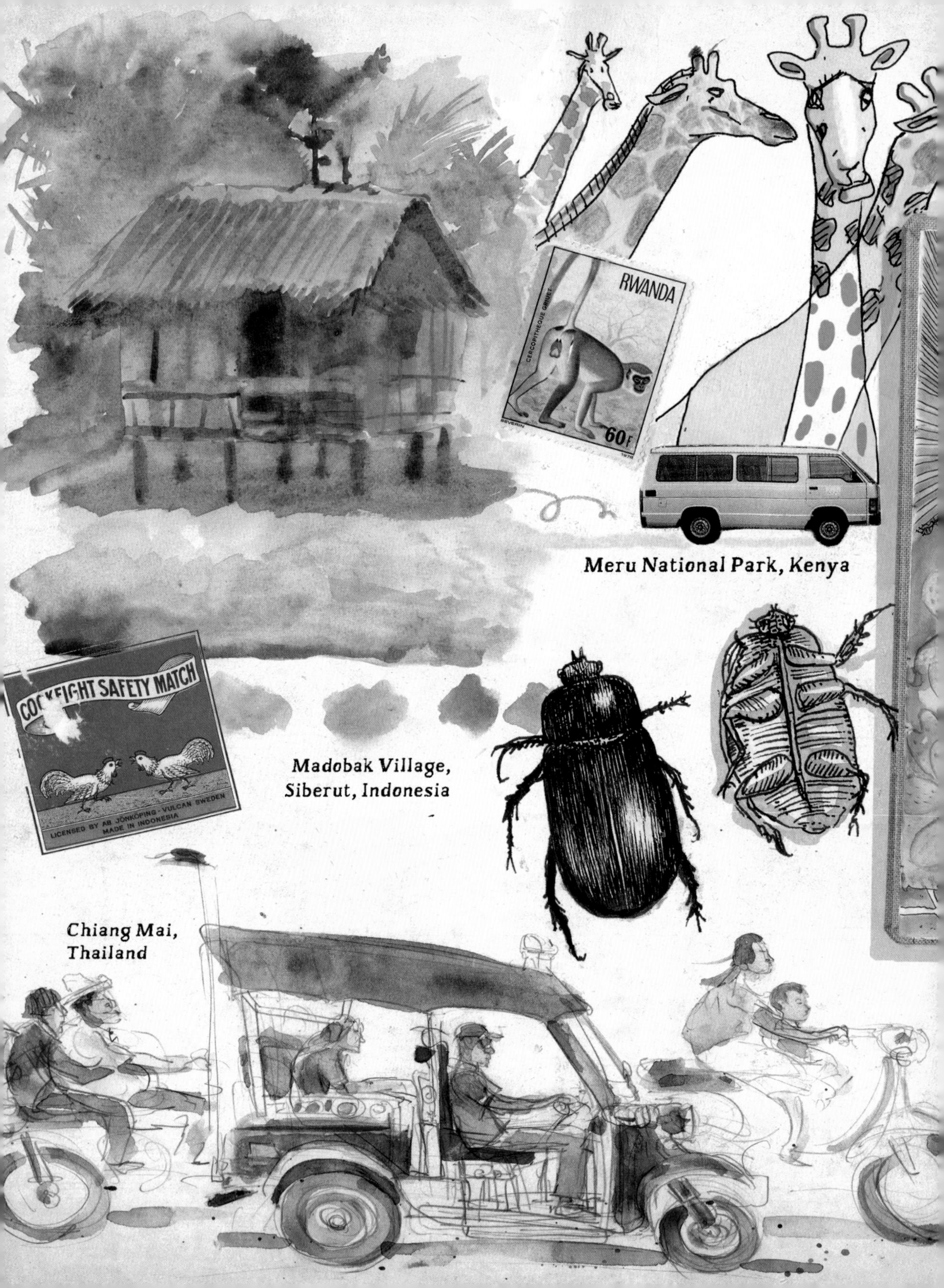
RWANDA
60F
Meru National Park, Kenya
COCKFIGHT SAFETY MATCH
LICENSED BY AB JÖNKÖPING - VULCAN SWEDEN
MADE IN INDONESIA
Madobak Village,
Siberut, Indonesia
Chiang Mai,
Thailand